<>

TERMS OF LABOR:
SLAVERY, SERFDOM, AND FREE LABOR

THE MAKING OF MODERN FREEDOM

General Editor: R. W. Davis
Center for the History of Freedom
Washington University in St. Louis

TERMS OF LABOR

SLAVERY, SERFDOM, AND FREE LABOR

≺ ≻

Edited by Stanley L. Engerman

STANFORD UNIVERSITY PRESS
STANFORD, CALIFORNIA
1999

Stanford University Press
Stanford, California
© 1999 by the Board of Trustees of the
Leland Stanford Junior University
Printed in the United States of America

CIP data appear at the end of the book

<>

Series Foreword

THE STARTLING AND moving events that swept from China to Eastern Europe to Latin America and South Africa at the end of the 1980s, followed closely by similar events and the subsequent dissolution of what used to be the Soviet Union, formed one of those great historic occasions when calls for freedom, rights, and democracy echoed through political upheaval. A clear-eyed look at any of those conjunctions—in 1776 and 1789, in 1848 and 1918, as well as in 1989—reminds us that freedom, liberty, rights, and democracy are words into which many different and conflicting hopes have been read. The language of freedom—or liberty, which is interchangeable with freedom most of the time—is inherently difficult. It carried vastly different meanings in the classical world and in medieval Europe from those of modern understanding, though thinkers in later ages sometimes eagerly assimilated the older meanings to their own circumstances and purposes.

A new kind of freedom, which we have here called modern, gradually disentangles itself from old contexts in Europe, beginning first in England in the early seventeenth century and then, with many confusions, denials, reversals, and cross-purposes, elsewhere in Europe and the world. A large-scale history of this modern, conceptually distinct, idea of freedom is now beyond the ambition of any one scholar, however learned. This collaborative enterprise, tentative though it must be, is an effort to fill the gap.

We could not take into account all the varied meanings that freedom and liberty have carried in the modern world. We have, for example, ruled out extended attention to what some political philosophers have called "positive freedom," in the sense of self-realization of the individual; nor could we, even in a series as large as this, cope with the enormous implications of the four freedoms invoked by Franklin D. Roosevelt in 1941. Freedom of speech and freedom of the press will have their place in the narrative that follows, certainly, but not the boundless calls for freedom from want and freedom from fear.

We use freedom in the traditional and restricted sense of civil and political liberty—freedom of religion, freedom of speech and assembly, freedom of the individual from arbitrary and capricious authority over persons or property, freedom to produce and to exchange goods and services, and the freedom to take part in the political process that shapes people's destiny. In no major part of the world over the past few years have aspirations for those freedoms not been at least powerfully expressed; and in most places where they did not exist, strong measures have been taken—not always successfully—to attain them.

The history we trace was not a steady march toward the present or the fulfillment of some cosmic necessity. Modern freedom had its roots in specific circumstances in early modern Europe, despite the unpromising and even hostile characteristics of the larger society and culture. From these narrow and often selfishly motivated beginnings, modern freedom came to be realized in later times, constrained by old traditions and institutions hard to move, and driven by ambition as well as idealism: everywhere the growth of freedom has been *sui generis*. But to understand these unique developments fully, we must first try to see them against the making of modern freedom as a whole.

The Making of Modern Freedom grows out of a continuing series of conferences held at the Center for the History of Freedom at Washington University in St. Louis. Professor J. H. Hexter was the founder and, for three years, the resident gadfly of the Center. His contribution is gratefully recalled by all his colleagues.

                                                            R.W.D.

≺ ≻

Contents

CONTRIBUTORS

David Brody
*University of California, Davis
(Emeritus)*

Seymour Drescher
University of Pittsburgh

David Eltis
Queen's University

Stanley L. Engerman
University of Rochester

Leon Fink
University of North Carolina

Peter Kolchin
University of Delaware

Clayne Pope
Brigham Young University

David Roediger
University of Minnesota

Amy Dru Stanley
University of Chicago

Robert J. Steinfeld
State University of New York at Buffalo

<><

TERMS OF LABOR:
SLAVERY, SERFDOM,
AND FREE LABOR

≺ ≻

Introduction

STANLEY L. ENGERMAN

T HROUGHOUT RECORDED HISTORY labor to produce goods and
services for consumption has been a central concern of society,
accounting for at least one-half of the waking hours of most of the
population.[1] For this reason alone the questions of the terms of labor—the arrangements under which labor is made to produce and
to split its product with others—is of great significance for understanding the past and the emergence of the modern world. For long
periods much of the world's labor could be considered under the
coercive control of systems of slavery or of serfdom, with relatively
few workers regarded as laboring under terms of freedom, however
defined.[2] Slavery and serfdom were systems that controlled not
only the terms of labor, but also the more general issues of political
freedom.[3] The chapters in this volume deal with the general issues
of the causes and consequences of the emergence of so-called free
labor in Europe, the United States, and the Caribbean over the past
four or five centuries, and point to the many complications and
paradoxical aspects of this change.

Although free labor, working for oneself or for others, existed in
most societies, free labor (for some, but not all) became the dominant form of labor arrangement in only some parts of the world,
and its impact remained limited in its geographic spread at any
time. As with slavery and serfdom, the shift to the importance of
free labor in the economic sphere also had implications for the consideration of political and other freedoms. Free labor often brought
with it, at once or after some time, a different set of political rights
and economic liberties than did slavery and serfdom; and in general, but not always, the freeing of labor has given rise to the development of a broader range of freedoms in the modern world.
Whether the rise of such general freedom is best seen as a sharp

break from the past or as another point along a continuum of freedom (or freedoms) is one of the central issues discussed in this volume, as are the various complexities of contracted arrangements—
formal and informal—and the nature of the controls introduced in
regard to the specific terms and durations of employment. To define freedom and to determine its relative changes over time is not
a simple task, as perhaps suggested by the fact that the same basic
set of labor arrangements has been described both as "free labor"
and as "wage slavery."[4] Nor, as we shall see, are the definitions of
"free labor" and of the "free labor ideology" always clear. Free labor initially was considered non-slave labor, yet it has been argued
that not all non-slave labor should be considered really free, given
the legal and economic constraints that exist in many societies.
The free labor ideology has been described as the belief in the relative superiority of free labor in comparison with non-free labor, at
times a progressive belief, but at other times considered a belief,
whether true or not, that has led to the obscuring of the limited
freedoms in society.

≺ I ≻

What Is Freedom?

As earlier volumes in this series demonstrate, the problem of defining and interpreting freedom is not an easy one. Similar problems
also arise in attempting to define free labor. Clearly, by contrast
with the economic, political, and personal controls of slavery and
serfdom, the growing importance of free labor in Western Europe
and its settlements overseas over the last four or five centuries
marked a significant change in the rights allowed to laborers. This
is the basis of the problem discussed by David Eltis, who describes
the beliefs which meant that Europeans would no longer enslave
other Europeans, but would, in the settlement of the Americas, be
quite willing and able to purchase and enslave Africans. This willingness to enslave Africans, and the willingness of Africans to become suppliers of slaves in the transatlantic and other slave trades,
led to a situation of an extensive black presence in the New World.
Down to 1760 about two-thirds of all immigrants coming to the
New World arrived as slaves from Africa, and there continued to be

differences in the legal rights of white workers and black slave workers. With the apparent moral and economic success of the free labor economies, these western nations generated ideas and programs generally based, according to Eltis, on the rights of individuals, which were used to attack, regulate, and then destroy serfdom and slavery. The antiserfdom and antislavery movements were, at the least, effective in legally ending serfdom in much of Europe in the late eighteenth and the nineteenth centuries, and slavery in the Americas, Africa, and Asia in the nineteenth and twentieth centuries.[5] Thus by the middle of the twentieth century the Western ideals of free labor and freedom had spread throughout much of the world.[6]

While the West originated the ideas that ultimately ended slavery, it should also be remembered that it was the West's series of technological and institutional innovations that had earlier led to an enhanced value of unskilled labor, permitting slavery to be profitable.[7] This led to the freedoms of some laborers being limited accordingly, while at the same time the freedoms of other individuals increased. While not, strictly, a zero-sum game, since these innovations often increased labor productivity, they also led, in the age of European expansion and after, to frequent variations in economic and political fortunes both within and between societies. Thus, these changes in production led, at the same time, to an expansion westward across the Atlantic Ocean of slavery and a movement eastward within Europe of serfdom.

Freedom has political as well as economic dimensions, and they need not always change in the same direction.[8] Politically, considerations of importance include the right to vote, the avoidance of autocratic command and dictatorial state political controls, and the ability to maintain private property rights against the state, as well as against others. The linking of command and control in the economic sphere with individual political rights is not always clear. Rights providing for free labor in the economy may exist in the absence of political freedoms, as appears to be the case for China today. It has long been argued that slavery meant only control of labor, and not control of the person and body of the enslaved.[9] And, quite clearly, political democracy and free labor for some members of society could exist and their presence argued on the basis of the unfree labor and lack of political freedoms of other individuals and groups.[10]

Slavery and serfdom have generally been permanent conditions, with the rulers having the right and ability to exploit labor and to control not only the serf or slave, but also their offspring. There are possibilities, such as manumission, to make slavery limited in duration. There are also some important examples of what may be regarded as temporary unfree labor, with employers having the legal rights to control labor for limited times, but with full rights restored to the individual at the end of some defined time period. Cases of temporary unfree labor include convict labor, indenture, military service, debt peonage, and apprenticeship, as well as the systems used to enforce types of agricultural and mining labor in various parts of the world. These include the encomienda and repartimiento in Spanish America and the cultivation system in Java. Because the reasons that workers accept, or were forced into, these terms vary by type of labor arrangement, controversies as to their legal treatment persist in the historical literature, as well as in legal disputes even today. Free labor, if defined as working for others, may also be a temporary status, because opportunities to become self-employed were possible.

There is generally a belief that free labor, defined in terms of its legal status, would receive more favorable rewards than would unfree labor. There is, of course, a significant sense in which low incomes, whatever their cause, limit the abilities of individuals and families to live autonomous and creative lives, so that low rewards and a set of political rules limiting freedom and the permitting of slavery may be seen as equally indicative of enslavement.[11] This concept of coercion raises questions about the importance of specific legal and contractual terms and also about the determination of who may obtain the surplus, if there is any, exploited from the laborer's production—clearly a key political as well as economic concern, and one influenced by the social and legal status of the laborer.

Free labor is not necessarily associated with a laissez-faire society, particularly if the latter is strictly interpreted. While small groups of individuals involved in transactions have generally been able to act on the basis of informal, but agreed upon, arrangements, nation-states require legal provisions to handle the many issues that arise when groups with different interests are involved. To introduce free labor will generally require some governmental measures, in the absence of which certain labor freedoms, including the right not to be enslaved by others, cannot be ensured. Reliance on government is, however, not a contradiction of the spirit of classical economic liberalism. Rather it is its necessary starting point, as seen in Adam Smith's discussion of the appropriate role of the state.[12]

It can be argued that one essential definition of the requirement for individual freedom is that there be no need to work, in particular to work for others, to obtain desired consumption goods. Without a need to labor, the worker would have a greater ability to avoid being controlled, whether by the bounty of nature or by the power of others. If this was not possible, how much labor would be required would depend upon the magnitude of consumption demands, the productivity of labor, and the ownership of land, labor, and capital. These magnitudes and controls are all potentially within the power of individuals and society to establish. Dramatic differences in working requirements could exist, in different places and at different times, with these differences reflecting variations in human tastes, desires, and abilities. While perhaps "true freedom" might mean the right not to work or to do only fulfilling work, and still to survive, neither is a prospect that could be easily accomplished either in the past or at present.

Slavery, serfdom, and other coercive techniques of labor control have existed throughout the world during the entire period of recorded history, and coerced labor has not been a discovery by, or unique to, the West. The West had been unique, less in its enslavement of others than in its giving rise to a prolonged ideological and political attack on slavery and in presenting the case for free labor, with "liberty and justice for all." All societies have had some individuals with some freedoms, often at the expense of others who generally were a greater share of the population and had only limited freedoms. Production by labor provided consumption goods for individual workers and their families as well as for employers or, more frequently, for the slaveowners or feudal lords who wanted to have more power, higher incomes, and more food provided.[13] The sharing of output between owners or lords and laborers was based on the amount of output produced or on the amount of time worked; or possibly the lord obtained all the surplus output after the subsistence needs of the worker and his family were met.

Some argue that not all exploitation should be regarded as the result of the behavior of others; individuals can, as some have it, even "exploit themselves."[14] This latter concept presumably refers to individuals forcing themselves to work harder to achieve goals that are considered (by the observer) undesirable. Such exploitation remains different in its essential aspects, such as the distribution of production, from the exploitation resulting from coercion by others.

There have been long scholarly debates on the ideological linking of slavery and freedom. In studying patterns of thought and belief in ancient Greece and in Rome, for example, Orlando Patterson has argued recently that it was the prior existence of slavery that helped to define the meaning of freedom—freedom being understood as the absence of slavery.[15] Alternatively, a focus on the importance of Enlightenment ideas in defining progress and human rights, and in the shaping of the arguments against slavery and serfdom, would suggest that it was the emerging ideal of individual freedom that helped to define the evils of slavery and made it possible to extend the idea of freedom to a broader set of different groups than had been previously the case.[16]

≺ II ≻

Freedom for Whom?

One of the striking characteristics concerning the terms of labor in the past and present has been the very different sets of arrangements permissible for different groups. It is well accepted that slavery (on this dimension serfdom is quite different) has generally been applied only to those considered outsiders by the members of the ruling society.[17] While correct, it is important to note that over time the specific nature of those who were to be considered outsiders varied, frequently changing from a rather broad conception of outsiders to one more narrowly defined, the insider group becoming larger and more inclusive. National group, religion, ethnicity, and race have been among the defining characteristics that have been used as the basis of determining who could be enslaved in the past. This issue of differences in terms is seen quite clearly in the settlement of the Americas, where the demand for labor did not lead to any enslavement of Europeans although indentured servitude was frequent. There was only a brief and limited enslavement of the resident native Americans, and slavery was limited to black persons imported originally from Africa (although there were to be, in all areas, some free blacks with limited rights).[18]

In some sense the antislavery argument has an exceptionally long history, since statements about the inefficiency of slave labor and the immorality of slavery date at least as far back as Greek and Roman slavery.[19] The basis of widening the antislavery argument and adding it to the political agenda was not mainly one of devising new arguments, but, rather, in redefining who were regarded as outsiders and who were (or could become) insiders and thus not subject to enslavement. Those free labor societies that have abolished slavery may be said to have resolved the outsider problem, since no one could be enslaved, property rights in other persons now being prohibited. Yet societies often maintain, by legal or nonlegal measures, varying controls over different groups and individuals. They may use a variety of categories (often similar to those used to define those who could be enslaved), including religion, nationality, gender, class, race, ethnicity, and age, as well as the extent of physical and mental abilities. Changing societal perceptions have meant that over time the nature and number of outsiders have changed, as have the acceptable manners in which outsiders and insiders could be treated. Similarly, in the past there have been variations in the range of permissible punishments and in the applicable legal constraints that could be applied to various groups, as well as different restrictions on the nature of the work that could be performed.

The range of controls over labor appears to be less dramatic in free labor societies than under slavery or serfdom, although the nature of controls introduced to benefit certain groups in the population may have become more sharply defined. For example, over time male members of the labor force may have wished to restrict, for a number of different reasons, the employment of women or, at other times, to either allow or coerce them to work.[20] Indeed, a basic part of the definition of freedom for ex-slave males in the post–Civil War South meant granting them extended controls over their wives and children, controls not as defined under slavery, but resembling those of free whites in the antebellum period. United

States residents have often regarded it as important to their employment and income position that further immigrants be excluded, whether permanently or temporarily. This exclusion meant forcing those who would have come from foreign lands to remain at home, presumably in economically less desirable circumstances. Here, as in other cases, the coercive impact of immigration legislation, of land policy, and of legal attitudes affecting labor unions influences the terms of labor in a manner less overtly coercive than did slavery and serfdom, but with significant economic effects.

≺ III ≻

The Rise of Free Labor Ideology and Changes over Time

It is generally argued that a free labor ideology emerged in the United States and Britain in the eighteenth and nineteenth centuries. This ideology had significant political impacts on laborers and played an important role in the ending of slavery in the Americas and of serfdom in Europe. This is the central theme of Seymour Drescher's chapter on British abolitionism and the impact of emancipation in the British West Indies. Following Adam Smith nonslave (free) labor apparently was widely believed to be more productive than slave labor, or this contention at least was seen as an argument central to the attempt to draw more people into the antislavery orbit. After examining the pre-emancipation development of the free labor argument, Drescher studies the various explanations provided by the abolitionists to deal with the apparently unexpected declines in plantation labor and output once slavery ended. The attempt to reconcile the universal gains expected from freedom with the reduced output levels achieved by freed labor in certain parts of the world remained a problem for political economists of the nineteenth century and later. The abolition of the forms of coerced labor was influenced by the contrast then made between relative production in free and in coerced labor systems. It was argued that the rapid economic growth in these modernizing areas, where a free labor ideology had developed, demonstrated the benefits to be expected from free labor. Slavery and serfdom provided an important counterpoint to the free labor arguments and these free labor ideals, in turn, became the basis for the attack on slavery and serfdom.

These arguments relating free labor and future economic expansion were not limited to Western Europe and North America, as Peter Kolchin describes when relating the ending of Russian serfdom, an event that occurred simultaneously with the onset of the American Civil War that was to end slavery there. In his discussion of the process of abolition of slavery, the legislation which implemented it, and the labor system that replaced it, Kolchin draws quite interesting comparisons with similar problems in other nations. As does Drescher for the British West Indies, Kolchin points to the disappointments with the outcome of the ending of legally coerced labor forms, in regard both to economic performance and to the nature of the freedom granted workers.

There are, however, several different sets of ideas that have come to be described as the free labor ideology.[21] The entrepreneurs and the laborers advocated the importance of free, not owned, labor, but with quite different expectations. Moreover, within the West there was a dramatic shift in emphasis regarding the meaning of free labor after the middle of the nineteenth century. To employers of labor who believed that slaves and servants had been too well taken care of, and who claimed that the plantations had been unprofitable due both to excessive labor costs and to the lack of proper incentives because rewards to labor did not depend on their production, free labor would provide a superior incentive scheme. Hunger and the threat of starvation served as a more effective means of coercing labor time and effort. Labor was considered free, because without a guaranteed alternative for the workers, they found it necessary to work for others. Some entrepreneurs did point to a more positive incentive than hunger: a stimulus to more work and better performance, they argued, was people wanting more consumption goods.

The free labor ideology of workers initially pointed to rather different aspects of the market for labor. The most comprehensive conception of the free labor ideology included self-ownership and autonomy; property ownership (to provide income as well as alternatives to working for others); control over working days and conditions (if working for another); consumer-oriented incentives and behavioral reinforcements (which would provide better living conditions and possibly some degree of upward mobility); and a belief in the "dignity of labor." Consistent with its origin among artisans, this free labor ideology pointed to the importance of working for oneself and not for others, a quite different sense of free labor than the entrepreneurial variant, but one that also had seventeenth- and eighteenth-century antecedents.

Over the course of the nineteenth century the emphasis of the worker's free labor ideology, while it maintained certain components, became more focused on the worker's freedom to voluntarily contract with employers and to try to obtain the best bargain possible in employment. Self-employment had become a more difficult goal to achieve, and as a consequence labor focused on limiting employer-introduced constraints on contracting. The free labor ideology had several different concerns, each with its primary benefits accruing to a different group. There was, however, enough in common, based on the contrast of free labor with slavery and serfdom, that the differing nature of its benefits have merged into one central theme and been used to define an historical era.

The definition and nature of free labor as seen by workers in the northern United States in the nineteenth century is the major concern of the chapter by Leon Fink. To these workers the attack on unfree labor became a critique of wage labor, which meant working for others, since free labor meant an independence from working for others. With the ending of chattel slavery, wage slavery was to become the most relevant evil. As Fink's discussion points out, in the specific political context the concept of free labor lost its simplicity and clarity, particularly once slavery and serfdom disappeared. The meaning it had for people differed, both over time and depending on the individual's status and position.

It is these changing legal and economic concepts of free labor that are of concern in Robert Steinfeld's chapter. By studying United States court cases, from colonial times until as late as 1987, Steinfeld sees that what might seem a clear distinction between free and unfree labor is anything but that. In several nations of Europe there were, throughout the nineteenth century, penal sanctions imposed by law on workers for breach of contract. Contractual voluntary servitude had a long history in the United States and other parts of the world. Court decisions in regard to specific performance of contracts limited individual freedom. Debt peonage, reflecting the inability to fulfill contractual terms of repayment, was frequently litigated against. As Steinfeld points out, the presence of free labor rests importantly on the meaning given to the concept of voluntariness, never very easy to define.

< IV >

Restricting Freedom in Free Labor Regimes

A central aspect of current debates on the meaning of free labor is the argument that factors often regarded as central to the definition of freedom contain inherent contradictions that reduce the promise of freedom. There are two important, related, considerations that present this problem most clearly. First is the distinction between liberty of person and liberty of contract. It is argued that the freedom to make contracts can lead individuals to enter into agreements that, either temporarily or permanently, restrict their freedom of action. Certain types of contracts have long been precluded in many societies—for example contracts voluntarily accepting enslavement and contracts regarding suicide.[22] More generally the acceptance, voluntarily, of contracts that include some loss of freedoms for a period, such as indentured servitude in exchange for transportation, are considered to be coercive because of the harshness of their terms. Similarly, as mentioned by Max Weber in his discussion of Babylonian law, and recently rediscovered by labor historians and philosophers, any worker might be regarded as in temporary slavery for the period of contracted work, because he or she must follow orders from his or her employer.[23] Free labor, if it means the loss of control when working for others, has thus been considered to be not free, because for periods of time and under certain conditions domination of one person by another is legally accepted.

Also important to understanding the meaning of free labor is the interpretation of the role of markets and the market economy. While the successful operation of markets requires a belief in the freedom of contract, the market may have coercive and constraining aspects, whether due to constraints imposed by nature or to coercion resulting from human control. The constraints and coercive measures imply limits to the range of alternatives open to the parties to the contracts, whether these contracts are formal or informal. If, for example, when next best alternatives are regarded by some parties, whether the individual or the historical observer, as very unpleasant factors, it has been argued that the value of legal freedom is weakened by the presence of these limited alternatives.[24] How unpleasant must this alternative be before it is to be regarded as coercive, even in the presence of full legal and political rights, is, of course, not always easy for different parties to agree upon. There is a tension that can arise between the value of freedom of choice and the ability to achieve adequate incomes. What the appropriate alternative policy by the state or by individuals to reduce the impact of constraint should be, is not obvious, and could possibly include state subsidies to individuals, centralized food distribution, and encouragements to out migration.

In examining the implications of all contractual arrangements, not just those regarding labor, it is often argued that the essential element is that the agreement between parties be voluntary and not coerced (except, perhaps, if the coercion were considered to be the result of natural forces). To others, however, attention must be given to the acceptability of the behavior and the outcome under the terms of the contract. All societies have certain imposed limits on freedom of choice. Self-enslavement is not an enforceable contractual agreement, nor are contracts which relate to an individual's suicide. The complexity in dealing with harsh outcomes of voluntary agreements is that it is never clear at what stage states or individuals should be able to opt out of agreements without disruption to the social and economic order. This problem emerged under systems of indentured labor, with the quite different migration schemes of the eighteenth and nineteenth centuries.

Several of the chapters in this volume discuss the argument that labor markets, even with apparent political and economic freedoms, are to be regarded as coercive. They argue that coercion via the market is indeed rather pernicious, as it may not be as apparent as the more direct coercion seen under slavery and serfdom. The apparent neutrality of the legal system and the outcome of market interactions provide a framework which many individuals are willing to accept because they set apparent limits on the power of most parties. What is regarded as coercive market behavior could be based on the outcome of legislation and other political and legal actions by a ruling elite, or else it could be due to the compulsions of nature, which does not provide the abundance necessary for all to avoid working for others. This distinction between human compulsion and the compulsion of natural forces, or of one's self, was clearly spelled out in the 1760s by the mercantilist Sir James Steuart.[25] Concerned with designing measures to increase national output, Steuart argued that people would be "slaves to others" (particularly for large-scale, unskilled, agricultural work) or, lacking that control, people would have to be "slaves to their wants," since a desire to increase consumption beyond subsistence would lead to a need to work more to produce and earn more.

Why people might want to consume more is, of course, a complex issue, including elements of indirect measures by others (for example advertising, creating false consciousness) as well as self-generated behavior. To be able to consume required working to obtain goods, either directly by producing them, or via transactions based on selling one's own production in the market or receiving payments in cash or in kind for working for others. Certain amounts of goods were required for subsistence, but because people often desire to consume more than that basic amount, they must do more work for this purpose.[26] If rulers have sufficient power, however, they may obtain goods for themselves by forcing others to do the work, obtaining by exploitation as much of workers' production over the subsistence needs as they desire. Perhaps, however, the rulers might wish to encourage a larger population, for military or other reasons, in which case they could transfer parts of the exploitable surplus to those whose incomes are low or below subsistence.[27]

Increased consumer demand might be the result of changes in tastes for leisure or for goods, of higher incomes, or of lower prices for these goods, due to technological or institutional changes. To the extent that lower consumer prices reflect changes in returns to labor or the spread of less favorable working conditions, a basic dilemma of economic growth is seen—are cheaper goods for large numbers of people worth the lower labor incomes and poorer working conditions?[28] Is an economic structure that generates more equality in consumption consistent with more inequality once allowance is made for non-pecuniary disutilities for those involved in production? And are the gains from the costs imposed on workers received by other workers in their role as consumers or are they gained only by the members of the ruling elite and the owners of the means of production?

Because the chapters in this volume generally focus on modern western Europe and America, they frequently focus on the indirect coercion attributed to law and to markets in what are generally regarded as free labor societies. Slavery and serfdom have historically been much more direct (and arguably less costly) methods of restricting individual behavior, employed by certain powerful individuals or cartels, in contrast with the use of the market system in extracting labor. In addition to the use of power to achieve economic goals, as in slavery and serfdom, coercion has also led to losses of freedom with the exercise of political power or religious power, even in states with only limited markets.

Different types of societies may have variations in the nature and form of restrictions imposed on the population. Even within the category of free labor societies different overall ends, as well as different means to achieve similar ends, may have developed, as a result of the nature of political power and bargaining. These can lead to alternative mechanisms of control to achieve given ends within a basically similar political and economic framework. While some relative equality of outcome might be regarded as one desired outcome from free labor, from the view of political freedom some degree of participation by the population in key policy decisions would also seem to be necessary.

Participation in decisions, or at least appearing to have the political power to influence them, is critically important in free labor societies. The government is instrumental in determining those economic constraints which influence incomes and living conditions, as well as the general political rules followed by society. In most nations the central government is responsible for laws and policies regarding contracts, monetary standards, immigration policy, land policy, educational policy, control of capital markets, aid to transportation development, none of which may directly influence the legal status of labor. These actions do, however, influence the laborer's economic returns and subsequent political power, and thus the alternatives available to laborers when making decisions in the market.

The argument for the benefits of free labor describes the political and economic conditions that would give the workers the ability to avoid restrictions and constraints. Indeed, the creation of a free labor force has been seen as the outcome of the successive removal of a series of restraints on labor and the acceptability by individuals of their ending within society's broader rules.[29] The initial opening of opportunities subsequently became the basis of the demands made by labor organizations and by broader groups of individuals. The policies and opportunities to limit coercion included various forms of mobility, such as geographic (hence the importance of land policy in influencing the ability to move to new locations), as well as changes in status, income, and wealth; education; property rights; self-improvement; temperance; the freeing of the market from ruling class controls; and the ability to cooperate in the formation of labor organizations. Limits on any of these could reduce the worker's economic or political power, or both, whatever might have been their implications for the legal status of labor.

The nature of the restrictions imposed on free labor varied with political and economic circumstances and reflected the possibilities open within the social framework. Thus, for example, temporary controls over the unemployed or those with low income in society can include variants such as the payment of poor relief or welfare to maintain and attract labor, the use of vagrancy laws to force work from those able bodied, or the enforcement of resident requirements to deny payments or to return individuals to their places of origin. Longer-term problems have been handled with a variety of measures, including legislation regarding immigration and emigration, changes in criminal law and the handling of convicts, the use of state labor for public works, and the expansion or contraction of the military via conscription. Threats of overpopulation in past times have led to a number of different measures regarding children: enslavement, infanticide, abandonment, the use of wet-nurses (then basically nearly tantamount to infanticide), and various forms of apprenticeship, each of which shifts costs of rearing away from the parents.

Most of the cases of slavery in the modern world might be best described as involuntary slavery. There is, however, a long history of voluntary slavery in many societies, voluntary to the family if not to the particular children or others involved in the transaction.

Individuals have sold themselves or, frequently, their children, measures resorted to when incomes are otherwise inadequate for survival. This practice was less frequent in the early modern West, which solved its overpopulation problems with the practices of infanticide and child abandonment rather than voluntary enslavement. Even the legal system can provide a range of permissible threats and punishments, including exile (deportation), imprisonment, enforcement of specific performance, and death. Thus even if the legal system is held to be a coercive influence upon society, questions arise about why specific restrictions and constraints were utilized at any particular time.

≺ V ≻

Paradoxes of Freedom

The conception of freedom is neither straightforward nor unidimensional. There are numerous aspects to economic freedom (free labor), political freedom, and social and cultural considerations, and it is not to be expected that all will necessarily point to the same conclusion. There are trade-offs confronted in interpreting freedom, trade-offs that individuals and groups must deal with in their decision-making. Current debates about the connections among economic freedom, political freedom, and economic growth mirror numerous earlier arguments about these relations. How do we evaluate the relative economic benefits that free labor achieved, despite their being given limited voting rights? What is the impact of limits on the rights to become a citizen of a nation, whatever the legal status of foreign labor? Clearly the pattern in the West has been for free labor terms to precede, often by centuries, political rights granted to the propertyless and those otherwise disenfranchised.

There are several major questions regarding the trade-offs in interpreting the meaning of economic freedom. First, does economic freedom necessarily provide the most favorable material conditions for the population? It is possible that increased economic freedom can lead to lower material output (although a higher overall level of utility for the members of society), while a loss of freedom has led, in the short- or the long-term or both, to greater material output, better physical health, and longer life expectation for laborers. The right to choose among economic alternatives may not only lead to less material consumption in the short run but, by yielding lower incomes, also limit the possibilities for upward mobility in the future. Choices regarding work, leisure, and working conditions influence the laborer's inter-temporal as well as intra-temporal trade-offs, with the choices made based on the tastes of individuals in conjunction with the economic circumstances available to them.

Second, what is the definition of the relevant group whose freedom and welfare is being examined? How far can the metaphor of slavery, with all its negative connotations, be applied? David Roediger's study of the antebellum American use of the slavery metaphor points to forms of division that existed among workers, limiting the power of the free labor coalition. To ex-slaves such as Frederick Douglass wage slavery of northern white laborers was a rather distinct form of slavery (if it could even be considered that) relative to the chattel slavery of the southern blacks. The abolitionists were, however, willing to accept the concept of "sex slavery" as used by the women's rights movement. The usefulness of slavery as a metaphor to cover many different cases remains a question even today, given its still frequent usage.

Within the West, until very recently the individual (in contrast with the family) was not generally regarded as the central welfare-maximizing unit; but rather it was the basic nuclear family, including wife and children, and often the more extended family, including parents and siblings, and kin groups. Outside the West the principal unit seems to be based on extended kin and lineage groups. Moreover, as in the West, there could be extensions made to include the overall nation-state (as underlies mercantilist thought) or even the entire world. The choice of relevant group poses problems because the improvement of conditions for, say, the household head may entail some restrictions for other family members. Thus Amy Dru Stanley points out the importance of female dependent labor in providing for the freedom of the males. The attitude regarding dependent labor in the household characterized both North and South, as well as many other parts of the world, and its claims were quite clearly argued in regard to policy towards ex-slaves in the postbellum South. The household labors of wives and children were considered to be the property of the male head of household. This period also saw increased attention to another form of dependency, vagrancy, raising issues about which individuals could be compelled to work. These attempts at distinguishing between free persons and dependents led to differential legislation among groups, often with some unexpected consequences. Women, children, disabled, and aged, among others, have long been given differential legal treatment, even before the emergence of a free labor ideology, and accorded different amounts of state intervention, however uncertain the legal definitions of children and disabled, and whatever the professed reasons for the distinctions made.

There is also an intergenerational element to family issues, given the importance of inheritance, whether through legal or other channels. The nature of family and kin has played an important role in many societies in the West as well as elsewhere, in part because these groups had often been responsible for aiding the destitute before the subsequent shifts of this function, first to the church and then to the state. What this suggests is that although we generally follow the tradition of focusing on individuals and individualism in the West, relations with family and kin have been central to individual behavior and need to be considered when interpreting patterns of historical change.

Third, even when the importance of family as a collective agency is accepted, have there been other collective agencies which have been considered essential for political, economic, and legal action? The dilemma between individual actions in contrast with group actions to benefit individual laborers is the subject of David Brody's chapter. Was free labor compromised by group activity, or was it socially acceptable for groups to bargain to obtain rights for individuals without being considered illegal collective organizations? The attitudes of United States courts have changed dramatically over the past centuries, becoming more accepting of collective actions in the workplace. That trade unions had to reconcile conflicting member interests, and that the members of the in-group often achieved their ends at some cost to non-members, have long been the basis of legal controversy. The many legal cases about the rights of workers to join together into labor unions to bargain with employers provides one example of this problem. The desire of unions to have legal approval for dealing with the specific contractual terms with business firms did not necessarily imply a more directed state role in the collective bargaining process. Rather, the belief was that once unionization was legally acceptable, bargaining would resemble a laissez-faire arrangement, with unions (representing laboring individuals) and firms negotiating without any further state intervention.

At issue, also, for unions which may be regarded as bargaining not only for wages, employment, and working conditions, but also in the interests of expanding the freedoms of individual workers, was the question of freedom of association and freedom of contracting if some workers wished to avoid union membership and its costs, even when receiving whatever benefits were obtained. That such collective agencies are necessary to equalize economic power with businesses or other groups in society has been a rationale for accepting their legality, another example of the trade-offs among freedoms that reality seems to require.

Perhaps the clearest example of the probable trade-off between economic freedom and economic growth arose in the nineteenth-century debates that provided the background to the end of slavery and of serfdom in Europe and many of its overseas offshoots. Arguments about free labor and, more generally, freedom (though not often with voting rights), were central, and these drew some extended responses from the advocates of slavery and of serfdom. The two major arguments made against these forms of coerced labor were first, their immorality and the sinful nature of their treatment of the enslaved and enserfed; and second, particularly important to examining the free labor ideology, the relative efficiency of free labor in contrast to slave and serf labor. The debate on the relative efficiency of labor generally centered on questions of labor incentives, so that the antislavery and antiserfdom arguments were somewhat similar.[30]

The achievement of slave and serf emancipations took a variety of different forms, reflecting differences in political and economic conditions, and the relative numbers and power of the owners. In some cases emancipation was immediate, in others gradual, for new-borns and those already slaves; in some cases it freed no slaves immediately, only the new-born, and then only after a protracted time period. In some cases emancipation was with compensation, in cash or bonds, paid to the slave owners or serfholders by governments or by the previously coerced workers; in others no such compensation was granted to landowners, who lost their labor even while being able to maintain their land. In some cases the ex-slaves underwent a period called apprenticeship, presumably to educate them in the system of free labor; in others this procedure was not introduced and ex-slaves were free to choose their new employment at once.[31]

As befits the Enlightenment ideals, it was claimed that the most moral actions would also be the most materially rewarding— and that all the good things would go together. It was argued that following the dictates of morality would increase the income and welfare of those formerly enslaved, and that the anticipated increases in output and productivity would lead to higher incomes for all, including the land-and-slave-owners and the consumers of the slave-grown commodities. While many abolitionists may have believed this argument, it no doubt also became an important aspect of the successful selling of the antislavery movement. This, of course, became a source of some embarrassment and a problem to be explained away when examining the aftermath of emancipation throughout the Americas. In relatively few cases, and those were generally areas with high ratios of labor to land and little land available for labor mobility, did the transition to free labor work out as advocates of the free labor ideology had expected (or hoped). This meant that to achieve the economic goals, the introduction of controls over either land or labor was required.[32]

Governments introduced controls in an attempt to get ex-slaves to labor for others. These involved limitations on land available for settlement, either via high prices or outright prohibition on the sale of land. Other policies were intended to lower the incomes of labor, via the imposition of taxes that would preclude avoiding plantation work in the interests of subsistence; and yet others involved treating non-plantation workers as vagrants, and thus being legally able to compel plantation work. Some policies intended to achieve the same outcome by less severe measures, such as providing laborers with small plots of land that would be insufficient by themselves to provide subsistence, requiring smallholder labor on the landowner's plantation. Alternatively, governments could seek to encourage higher levels of consumption by ex-slaves, leading them to increase plantation labor voluntarily. In addition, the import of indentured labor was meant to have direct effects on the quantity of labor as well as indirect effects on the local labor via its impact on wage rates.

These possibilities, all consistent with legally free labor as often understood, resemble the ranges of policies often introduced earlier within Western Europe and the Americas. To encourage labor, landowners pushed for a differential between the desired level of consumption and the level of earnings possible under existing arrangements, whether this was achieved by raising the desired income or by lowering the incomes that could be earned without plantation work. Control over land distribution was also essential, as the free workers of Britain and the United States had long argued. Thaddeus Stevens, in looking at the serf emancipation in Russia, regarded it as a great success and a model for the United States to follow, since the former serfs were enabled to acquire land at, what Stevens (but not Kolchin) claimed, were relatively low prices.[33]

Interpretations that emancipation was an economic failure were partly based on economic outputs, but there were social and demographic considerations as well. With freedom came some reductions in output, if not also labor input; affected were consumption levels and patterns, expenditures on health and education, the extent of life expectation, the ability to avoid or limit debt, and the opportunities to earn enough surplus incomes to purchase land for one's own productive use. Determining whether these low incomes reflected the impact of ruling class restrictions or the preferences of ex-slaves as to labor inputs of men, women, and children would point to one or a different interpretation of the outcomes. It would also help determine if the undesired outcomes were attributable to the introduction of free labor or to its continued absence. In either case, however, there was widespread disappointment about the achievements of emancipation and with the transition to free labor. Given the many disenchantments with major reforms affecting free labor, as well as other social reforms, perhaps such disappointments in the transitions from slavery and serfdom were to be expected.

Clayne Pope's chapter provides a link between the arguments concerning the free labor ideology and the actual outcomes for laborers in the United States in the nineteenth century. Rather than asking what people believed and how it influenced their behavior, Pope asks about the observed rates of social and wealth mobility, looking at both absolute and relative changes. Clearly, he argues, the ideology was based on some reality, since there had been considerable growth in income and wealth, improvements in health, and gains in occupational positions. His findings are consistent with the findings of most other studies of social mobility in this period. Yet these improvements also led to a sense of disappointment for those who had not yet been able to achieve what they now felt that they could hope for. Nevertheless, to look only at this sense of disappointment without understanding the empirical basis for rising expectations would be to miss important parts of the historical record.

≺ VI ≻

Conclusions

The problems of the post-emancipation societies pose significant questions about what freedom was, and what and whom it cost. Emancipation was reflected in the measures of declining outputs, and led to political debates about whether there were costs only at the time of the initial transition to freedom or if costs might persist for a longer time and even be permanent in the absence of subsequent policy changes. The use of schemes of apprenticeship to accompany emancipation was intended to ensure that the labor discipline necessary to provide for economic growth could be learned within a relatively short period. The empirical argument for free labor had been based upon the rapid post-1750 economic growth of the West, in comparison not so much with the actual economic conditions in slave and serf societies, as with expectations as to their future conditions.[34] The "free labor ideology" did not generally allow for the possibility of changes in the output-mix in free and coerced labor societies, and of different tastes of different groups of potential workers. To do so would have placed some apparent geographic bounds on the applicability of the "free labor ideology" and turned attention to the importance of distinctions based upon race, ethnicity, and climate.

Nevertheless, the ultimate triumph of this belief in free labor, with all its caveats and complexities, represented a crucial step forward to the modern world. It seldom accomplished all its early advocates had hoped for, in part because all the necessary conditions were not fully achieved and legacies of the previous systems remained, in part because the many different aspects of freedom led to some undesired or unexpected outcomes. Perhaps the best indication that, whatever its difficulties, the "free labor ideology" maintains its broad appeal is that it is no longer possible to seriously entertain questions about the renewal of serfdom and slavery, and if any aspect of legal slavery is still present in some nations it is universally regarded as a moral evil in today's world.

Slavery and Freedom in the Early Modern World

DAVID ELTIS

WHY IN THE LAST FOUR CENTURIES has the Western world developed the most extreme forms of both freedom and unfreedom, and what has this development to do with transatlantic migration, coerced and free? Assertions about the emerging uniqueness of the Western world's experience—or at least the part that had to do with freedom—were common in popular eighteenth-century literature, and as late as the mid-nineteenth century Southern United States newspapers could argue that slavery is "the natural and normal. condition of the laboring man, white or black," and that free labor was an unfortunate "little experiment . . . in a corner of western Europe," that had "failed dismally."[1] Advocates of free labor agreed with all but the "failed dismally" part of this statement. Adam Smith, Arthur Young, and others had pointed out that all Africans, all Asians, and most of those in the Americas were, if not under slavery, at least unfree in the Western sense, and that free labor was a term that could be applied to only a small percentage of the world's population—almost all of it living in northwestern Europe and related settlements.

Western exceptionalism was not of recent origin, nor was it shared equally by all of western Europe. The observations of Smith and others would have had almost the same validity if made three centuries earlier—at the time of the Columbian contact. There were certainly more slaves in southern Europe in 1492 than in 1772— slaves made up ten percent of the population of Lisbon in the 1460s. However, north and northwest Europe had been free of chattel slavery since the Middle Ages. Indeed the incidence of chattel slavery everywhere in western Europe had declined irregularly since Roman times, but the pace of the decline had been greater in northern than in southern Europe. More generally, free labor in the modern sense scarcely existed anywhere before the nineteenth century, but by 1800 the coercive element imposed on those who worked for others had been in decline for a better part of a millennium. From the Neolithic Revolution to the Middle Ages, every society had had some slaves. Suddenly there was a culture, and the larger part of a subcontinent, that did not. Perhaps we should regard abolition as originating before 1500, not after 1750.

Why did this trend fail to continue when Europeans established transoceanic societies? Social structures and the ideologies that sustain them have proved to be the most malleable of the cultural traits that migrants carry with them.[2] But Europeans not only reaccepted slavery in the face of New World realities, they gave it dimensions that had not previously existed. All the *major* slave societies in human history have been either European or under European control—Greek, Roman, Brazilian, Caribbean, and United States South. Three of these emerged in the Americas in the aftermath of European overseas expansion, and the slavery they imposed involved exploitation more intense than had ever existed before. It is inconceivable that any societies in history—at least before 1800—could have matched the output per slave of seventeenth-century Barbados or the nineteenth-century United States. European exceptionalism thus extended beyond the slave-free dichotomy noted by Young and Smith in that the slavery European migrants imposed had a large economic element that made it totally different from what existed in non-European societies—at any time. But if there were no slave plantations in the pre-contact Americas and Africa, neither was there a counterpart in the European Americas to the open systems of slavery that existed in Africa, the indigenous Americas, and the Middle East. Peoples of African descent—the only peoples brought across the Atlantic as slaves—had small chance of non-slave status, and smaller again of full membership in European settlement societies.

In Europe itself, on the other hand, the entrenchment of certain individual freedoms was such that there were frequently doubts about the legal status of those few enslaved peoples brought to Europe from the slave Americas. The slavery that evolved in the Americas in the three centuries between Columbus and Arthur Young was imposed by the very countries that occupied the "free" enclave to which the latter drew attention. It evolved during the Renaissance, Reformation, and Enlightenment—shifts in European thought that helped the rights of the individual to evolve into recognizably modern form.[3] In summary, at the end of the fifteenth century slavery did not exist in most of western Europe. At the end of the eighteenth century, it still did not exist in western Europe, but it had greatly intensified and expanded in those parts of the non-European world that Europeans had come to dominate. Europe was exceptional in the individual rights that it accorded its citizens, *and* in the intensity of its slavery, which, of course, was reserved for non-citizens.

≺ I ≻

Free and Coerced Migration

In the early years after Columbian contact it was by no means clear that a paradox of the scale and type suggested above would develop. Tables 1 and 2 chart the divergence of Europeans in Europe and of Europeans overseas. In table 1 the African arrivals in column 1 and the European departures in column 3 provide a rough sum of migration into each national jurisdiction in the Americas, whereas the sum of columns 2 and 3 gives the numbers carried on board the ships of each major national carrier.[4] Table 2 reduces some of the raw estimates in table 1—specifically the number of slaves carried—to percentages. Europeans took African slaves to the Americas and enslaved the Amerindians that they found there from the beginning. But initially, northwestern Europeans were little involved in transoceanic migration, and the proportion of Spanish- and Portuguese-controlled migration comprising slaves before 1530 was little different from the proportion of the Iberian population that was enslaved. Moreover, the institution of indentured labor—seen by many scholars as temporary slavery, and under which most English made their transatlantic passage between 1650 and 1780—was virtually unknown to Spanish and Portuguese migrants of the early modern period. Elaborate systems of dependency bound the majority of Iberian migrants to their social superiors, but these ties were not well suited to extracting intensive labor in mines and on plantations and were never used as such. After 1540 the transatlantic slave trade increased markedly with the result that between 1492 and 1580—covered by panel 1 of table 1—almost one quarter of the migrants to the New World were African slaves.

TABLE I

European-Directed Transatlantic Migration, 1500–1760 by European Nation and Continent of Origin (in thousands)

	Africans arriving in American regions claimed by each nation	Africans leaving Africa on ships of each nation	Europeans leaving each nation for Americas (net)	Africans and Europeans leaving for Americas (col 2 + col 3)
(a) Before 1580				
Spain	45	10	139	149
Portugal	13	63	93	156
Britain	0	1	0	1
TOTAL	58	74	232	306
(b) 1580–1640				
Spain[a]	289	100	188	288
Portugal[a]	181	488	110	598
France	2	1	4	5
Netherlands	8	9	2	11
Britain	4	4	126	130
TOTAL	484	602	430	1032
(c) 1640–1700				
Spain	141	10	158	168
Portugal	225	325	50	375
France	75	47	45	92
Netherlands	49	160	13	173
Britain	277	371	248	619
TOTAL	767	913	514	1427
(d) 1700–1760				
Spain	271	0	193	193
Portugal	768	903	270	1173
France	414	487	51	538
Netherlands	123	244	5	249
Britain[c]	1013	1342	372	1714
TOTAL	2589	2976	891	3867
(e) 1500–1760				
Spain[a]	746	120	678	798
Portugal[a]	1187	1779	523	2302
France	491	535	100	635
Netherlands[b]	180	413	20	433
Britain[c]	1294	1717	746	2463
TOTAL	3898	4564	2067	6631

SOURCES (number refers to row, letter refers to column):

1A, 2A, Philip D. Curtin, *The Atlantic Slave Trade: A Census* (Madison, WI, 1969), 116; 5A, ibid., for 1581–94; Enriqueta Vila Vilar, *Hispanoamerica y el Comercio de Esclavos* (Seville, 1977), 206–9 for 1595–1640; 6A, 10A, Curtin, *Census*, 116, 119 for 1581–1600; David Eltis, "The Volume and American Distribution of the Seventeenth Century Transatlantic Slave Trade" (unpub. paper, 1995) for 1600–40; 7A, Curtin, *Census*, 119; 8A, Johannes Menne Postma, *The Dutch in the Atlantic Slave Trade, 1600–1815* (Cambridge, 1990), 21; 9A, 15A, David Eltis, "The British

Transatlantic Slave Trade Before 1714: Annual Estimates of Volume and Direction," in Robert L. Paquette and Stanley L. Engerman, eds., *The Lesser Antilles in the Age of European Expansion* (Gainesville, FL, 1996), 182–205; 12A, 13A; Eltis, "The Volume and American Distribution," 13; 14A, Postma, *Dutch Slave Trade*, 21, 300; 17A, Curtin, *Census*, 25, 216; 18A, 18B less 15% for voyage mortality (it should be noted that Curtin's estimate of arrivals in Brazil for this period [959.0 thousand] is 18% greater than this figure); 19A, David Richardson, "Slave Exports from West and West-Central Africa, 1700–1810: New Estimates of Volume and Distribution," *Journal of African History* 30 (1989): 1–22; 20A, Postma, *Dutch Slave Trade*, 186, 191, 195, 212, 218, 220–21, 225; 21A, Richardson, "Slave Exports," less 150.0 thousand to Spanish Americas (Colin Palmer, *Human Cargoes: The British Slave Trade to Spanish America* [Urbana, IL, 1981], 110–11 adjusted, for 15% voyage mortality); 1B, 2B, Curtin, *Census*, 116 plus 20% voyage mortality (Spain/Portugal breakdown is a guess); 3B, Hawkins's voyages in Richard Hakluyt, *The Principal Navigations, Voyages, Traffiques & Discoveries of the English Nation*, 10 vols. (London, 1927–28), 10:7–66; 5B, 6B, 5A+6A plus 20% voyage mortality (Spain/Portugal breakdown is a guess); 7B, Hakluyt, *Principal Navigations* 7:95–96 indicates some early French slaving activity in Africa, but the French Americas contained few slaves and no record of French slave trading to the Iberian Americas has surfaced; 8B, Postma, *Dutch Slave Trade*, 21; 9B, 9A plus 20% voyage mortality; 11B, Spanish were reported buying slaves in Cacheo, 1678–83 (T70/10,1; T70/16, 50), though this may have been for Spanish markets. No records of Spanish ships selling in the Americas at this time have survived. An allowance of 150 a year is assigned to allow for such activity; 12B, 12A plus 15% voyage mortality plus Portuguese imports to Spanish America (9A less Dutch, English, and Spanish arrivals) plus 20% voyage mortality on these imports; 13B, 13A plus 20% voyage mortality, divided by two (half of all slaves taken to French Americas assumed in French ships); 14B, 15B, Volume appendix, table 1 plus 20% mortality; 18B, Jose C. Curto, "A Quantitative Reassessment of the Legal Portuguese Slave Trade from Luanda, Angola, 1710–1830," *African Economic History* 20 (1992): 1–25 for Angola; Patrick Manning, "The Slave Trade in the Bight of Benin, 1640–1890," in Henry A. Gemery and Jan S. Hogendorn, eds., *The Uncommon Market: Essays in the Economic History of the Transatlantic Slave Trade* (New York, 1979), 117 for Bahia; plus guess of 5 thousand for Upper Guinea-Brazil; 19B, Richardson, "Slave Exports," table 2; 20B, Postma, *Dutch Slave Trade*, 295; 21B, Richardson, "Slave Exports," table 1; 1C, 5C, Magnus Morner, "Spanish Migration to the New World prior to 1810: A report on the State of Research," in Fredi Chiapelli et al., eds., *First Images of America: The Impact of the New World on the Old* (Berkeley, 1976), 771 less 20% for returns; 2C, 6C, 12C, Vitorino Magalhaes-Godinho, "L'émigration portuguaise du XVe siècle à nos jours: Histoire d'une constante structurale," in *Conjoncture économique—structures sociales: Hommage à Ernest Labrousse* (Paris, 1974), 254–55 estimates gross emigration. This is divided by three to allow for movements to Atlantic Islands, Goa and returns; 7C, 13C, 19C, Leslie Choquette, *Frenchmen into Peasants: Modernity and Tradition in the Peopling of French Canada* (Cambridge, MA, 1997), 20–22, 162, multiplied by 5 (G. Debien, "Les engages pour les Antilles (1634–1715)," *Revue d'histoire des colonies* 38 (1951): 9–13, 141–42 found a ratio of 4:1 for the Caribbean and Canada); 8C, 14C, 20C, Jan Lucassen, *Dutch Long Distance Migration 1600–1900* (Amsterdam, 1991), 22–23 less 20% returns; 9C, Gemery, "Emigration from the British Isles," multiplied by 2 to allow for pre–1630 emigration; 11C, 5C multiplied by ratio of America's silver production, 1640–1700/1580–1640. For the latter see Arthur Attman, *American Bullion in the European World Trade, 1600–1800* (Goteborg, 1986), 20; 15C, Gemery, "Emigration from the British Isles," for 1640–50, plus David Galenson, *White Servitude in Colonial America: an Economic Analysis* (Cambridge, 1981), 216–18 plus 5% voyage mortality for 1650–1700; 17C, 5C multiplied by ratio of America's silver production, 1700–1760/1580–1640. For latter see Attman, *American Bullion*, 20; 18C, Magalhaes-Godinho, "L'emigration portuguaise," 255 estimates gross emigration. These divided by two to allow for movements to Atlantic Islands, Goa and returns; 21C, Galenson, *White Servitude*, 216–18 plus 5% voyage mortality.

NOTES:

[a] Spain and Portugal are treated as separate countries despite the Crowns of the two countries being united between 1580 and 1640.

[b] Includes Dutch Brazil.

[c] Includes migrants from Germany.

TABLE 2

Slaves Carried to the Americas as Percentage of
Total Migrants and as Percentage of Migrants on
Board Major National Carriers, 1500–1760

	Slaves as % of all migrants
(A) All Carriers Combined	
Before 1580	24.2
1580–1640	58.3
1640–1700	64.0
1700–1760	77.0
(B) Major National Carriers 1500–1760	
Spain	52.0
Portugal	69.0
Britain	63.0
France	83.0
Netherlands	90.0

SOURCE: Calculated from table 1

Panels 2 to 4 of table 1 show that after 1580, as more of the Americas came under European control and as the control of transatlantic migration passed steadily from southern to northwestern European hands, the coercive element in the migrant flow increased. Table 2 shows that the slave component increased from less than one quarter between 1492 and 1580 to nearly three quarters between 1700 and 1780. With few exceptions it would seem that within three generations of Columbian contact Europeans imposed or at least accepted slavery wherever they settled outside Europe. At the same time the trend toward less coercion within Europe continued unabated. Of the 23 percent of transatlantic migrants that were not slaves in the 1700–80 period, most crossed the ocean under indenture, or carrying a "labor debt." Indentured servitude grew out of the annual master-servant contract in English agriculture.[5] However, the length of the term and the master's power that evolved in the Americas would not have been tolerated within Britain itself. The position of the servant was not only inconsistent with modern conceptions of free labor, it was at odds with concepts of full membership of the community that held in early modern Britain.

The trend toward a large African component in transatlantic migration continued after 1780. By 1820, just prior to a transatlantic shift from Europe that saw over 50 million Europeans relocate in the Americas in less than a century, 90 percent of those coming across the Atlantic were African, not European. The peak years of the transatlantic slave trade, say 1680 to 1830, were sandwiched between early Iberian, then English emigration on the one side, and the later mass migration emanating from first northern and then southern Europe on the other. The forced, African component was much larger than the European component before the nineteenth century and occurred in part because of the voluntary nature of the latter. And much of the later European migration occurred because abolition denied employers in the Americas access to slaves.

The shift north in the control of migration was very pronounced. Before 1580 the Iberian nations accounted for almost all transatlantic movements of peoples. By 1700 to 1760 on the other hand, Britain, France, and the Netherlands were carrying twice as many people across the Atlantic as were the Iberians, with the British alone carrying nearly half of everyone shipped. Except for the Spanish, all European nations carried more Africans than Europeans to the Americas in the first three centuries after Columbian contact, but it was the nations of northwestern Europe that carried the most Africans and the most bound Europeans. Despite the size and high scholarly profile of British migration, the British actually carried three Africans to the New World for every European down to the beginning of the nineteenth century, and almost nine out of every ten people on British ships before 1800 were there under some obligation to labor for others upon their arrival in the Americas. It was the northwestern Europeans in particular who were likely to impose slavery or employ indentured labor whenever they found themselves in transoceanic lands. Yet over the preceding three centuries, it was these very nations that had developed concepts of the modern liberal state (and notions of personal freedom) that have become central parts of the western cultural domination of the late twentieth-century world.

Both the predominant labor regime and the nationality of the leading carrier were heavily influenced by exports from the Americas. Coerced and non-coerced migrant streams alike gravitated toward export-producing regions. Plunder and trade may have dominated the early decades of European expansion, but the main focus quickly became production, and between 1500 and 1760 the peak decades for migration within each national group coincided broadly with peak years of exports produced by coerced and free migrants and their descendants. Despite much scholarly attention, trade with indigenous peoples in the Americas was trivial. And in Africa, while African-produced gold predominated before 1700, the raison d'etre of the slave trade, which after 1700 became many times more valuable than gold, was the production of commodities in the European-dominated Americas. Long-distance migration in the pre-contact Americas and within Africa, or indeed Asia too, had never been as closely associated with commerce and production and the intensive forced involvement of other peoples. The terms of the charter for the Virginia Company of 1612 and the Royal African Company 60 years later are similar in the sense that the companies expected to profit from the production of goods on the other side of the Atlantic.[6] If transatlantic migration was an extension of migration within Europe, then productive enterprises located across the Atlantic, whether they used slave or non-slave labor, were initially very much replicas of Old World organizations. They drew upon the same pools of capital, management expertise, and in the non-slave sector, markets for European labor.

Thus it is not difficult to see why slaves formed an increasing proportion of transatlantic migration down to the nineteenth century, and but for abolition, might have done so down to the twentieth. From the standpoint of New World users of labor, slavery was an institutional arrangement particularly well suited to both trans-oceanic transportation and the kinds of tasks necessary to produce most New World exports. The best data concern British-directed migration. After an early period without a dominant crop, during which English settlement hung in the balance, tobacco and sugar exports correlated well with the movement of both Europeans and Africans to the English Americas. Similarly, the early Portuguese slave trade was tied to bullion exports from Spanish America and Brazilian sugar production. The Dutch were the only exceptions, in that (leaving aside the temporary Dutch occupation of northeastern Brazil) production in the Dutch Americas was trivial until the development of Surinam in the last quarter of the seventeenth century. Yet, as with the Portuguese, prior to the English Navigation Acts and Colbert's reforms of the 1660s, the Dutch organized, fetched, and carried for other nations.

The advantages of slave labor over free were not confined to relative productivity in the plantation Americas. Potentially, at least, slave labor was cheap to obtain in the Old World, and cheap to transport relative to free. Societies in all parts of the world have always generated criminals and prisoners of war, the conversion of whom into full chattel slaves could have occurred with few costs beyond those normally involved in keeping order and waging war. In addition, as millions of Africans found out, the preferences of involuntary migrants could be ignored during the transatlantic voyage. The crowding, feeding, selection and organization of people into barracoons and ships that followed from the voicelessness of slaves translated into large savings in migrants per ton. On the American side, because a buyer of a slave obtained the balance of a life of labor instead of a fixed term of years (and would be prepared to pay more for the former), transatlantic slave merchants could afford to organize longer and more costly voyages and thus draw on a wider range of provenance zones. It is thus not slavery that is difficult to understand, but rather the ethnicity of the slaves. In no case were Europeans brought as slaves and, apart from occasional members of an African elite on a business, diplomatic, or educational visit to Europe, Africans were never carried over as anything other than slaves. The switch from European to African migration thus also implied a switch from non-slave to slave labor in the dominant export sector. If the traffic in people from Africa to the Americas had been restricted to shorter terms *and* voluntary recruitment, it would have no doubt started later than the slave trade (if at all) and carried fewer people.

But why use Africans instead of Europeans? And, to pose a very much related question, why do so without any self-questioning—given the long absence of slavery from northwestern Europe? The divergence of slave and non-slave regimes within the European world via the revival of slavery and its imposition on the Americas is extraordinary. On the continent of Europe, Bartolomé de las Casas and, later, Jean Baptiste du Tertre encouraged reflection, and in the former case real change in the way aboriginal peoples were treated, but both accepted the idea that some peoples—specifically Africans—were natural slaves. Samuel Johnson's question, why "drivers of Negroes" should make "the loudest yelps for liberty," was not even posed more than a century earlier as the English

Commonwealth, fresh from overcoming the tyranny of the Crown, vigorously laid out the foundations of a Caribbean slave empire. Some English Levellers were prepared to countenance slavery as a punishment for Englishmen, though unlike African slavery in the Americas this never became a reality.[7] In the early- and mid-seventeenth century it was the remnants of villeinage in England rather than the emergence of chattel slavery in the Americas that preoccupied English observers.[8] More than a century later, as their slave empire approached its zenith, the British could still sing "Rule Britannia" including the line "Britons never, never, never shall be slaves" with no sense of irony.

<   II   >

Gender in Europe and Africa

A parallel situation existed with respect to European gender roles in that the scope for individual action that evolved in northwestern Europe in the early modern period was much more fully developed for males than for females. Women may have had slightly better occupational opportunities than they were to have during and after the Industrial Revolution, but they were hugely underrepresented in all skilled occupations and professions in seventeenth-century England and the Netherlands.[9] Likewise their legal rights were better than they were to become under the nineteenth century marriage property acts, but again primogeniture practices throughout the West—to take just one example—denied them anything approaching a legal status that matched that of males. Women were clearly not slaves in the sense that non-Europeans were to become. In addition, women in northwest Europe had significant reproductive rights compared to non-European women, particularly with respect to whether to marry and the choice of mate if they elected marriage. Yet the fact remains that the substance as well as the discourse on marriage that emerged in the pre-nineteenth century West demonstrated an unawareness of gender inequality. As with the slavery issue, even radical groups shared mainstream attitudes.

Just as European conceptions of ethnicity ensured that most transatlantic migrants before 1800 would be of African origin, so gender attitudes ensured that the European migration that did occur was overwhelmingly male. Because European women were systemically prevented from acquiring non-domestic skills and were regarded as unfit for field labor on plantations, they formed only a tiny fraction of the indentured servants that left Europe. In sharp contrast to African women, European females traveled across the Atlantic primarily as family members—in other words in their reproductive role—rather than as providers of labor. More important for the argument advanced here, contemporaries, while fully aware of the facts, considered gender imbalances unworthy of comment, much less debate. The relationship between ethnicity and gender—more specifically the contribution of attitudes toward gender to the decision that Africans would be used as slaves on New World plantations—is examined elsewhere, but it is immediately clear that, as with enslaved Africans, females in the early modern Atlantic world were not perceived as having the potential for full membership in the community.[10]

<< III >>

Western and Non-Western Conceptions of Freedom

Such blindness to differences in the way ethnic and gender groupings were treated is of central importance in understanding the slave-free dichotomy in the Western world and forms the main foundation of the assessment of the relationship between slavery and freedom offered here. The slavery that Europeans revived and refined was for non-Europeans, and it was for non-Europeans of both sexes. Indeed the absolute line of ethnicity would have been hard to enforce in a waged labor market. Even under apartheid, or in the post-reconstruction United States South, occupation and ethnic divisions never coincided with the exactness that existed in slave regimes in the Americas. Productivity of slaves was probably much higher in the nineteenth century than earlier; and as slave values increased, the capacity of slaves to resist, the treatment of slaves, and the "space" allowed them all likely improved.[11] Yet the African exclusivity of the institution remained absolute, as did the sharing of some occupations between male and female slaves. The power of the owner remained overwhelming through nearly four centuries. But it was this very ethnic divide that provided Europe-

ans with the blinkers necessary to come to terms with an institution that was so different from the labor regimes which they saw as
appropriate for each other.

The African exclusivity of slavery in the Americas is the first
key point in reassessing the slave-free paradox; the second is the
increasing reliance of Europeans and their descendants in the early
modern era on the odd institution (in global terms) of waged labor.
It is widely recognized that there were no equivalents to full plan-
tation-based chattel slavery among Amerindian or African cultures
at the time of the Columbian contact.[12] But what receives less attention is that there were few counterparts in the non-European
world to free labor and its associated market either, much less to
the modern labor force where employer and employed were equal
before the law. All European and early American societies contained vestiges of the medieval concept of labor as a common
community resource subject to community allocation and pre-
scription. The master's authority over the servant was in part a jurisdiction defined and delegated by society and in part a proprietal
right over persons exercised temporarily during servitude.[13] There
are interesting parallels between the relationship of an individual
to society that this potent mix of freedom and authority implies,
and its counterpart in the kin-group-based societies of African and
Amerindian peoples. But a global perspective suggests that European wage and free labor systems and the social structures that
supported them shared far more with each other than either did
with labor regimes that lay outside the European orbit.

Both waged and slave systems appear to have provided the basis
for a rate of economic growth in Europe that greatly exceeded that
in the non-European areas of the world. Slave societies around the
Atlantic may not have experienced industrialization directly, but
they probably at the least kept pace with their non-slave counterparts in output per capita, or output per acre or per unit of capital.
The nineteenth century evidence suggests that the productivity
advantage lay with the coerced rather than the free labor regions of
the Atlantic.[14] The evidence for the seventeenth century is less systematic, but the important point here is that in the post-
Columbian Atlantic world, Europeans and their descendants
owned and used slaves for the same reason that masters hired servants in the non-slave sector, which was to produce goods for sale

to others. Indeed, in the Atlantic world as a whole, the share of slave labor involved in such activities, especially goods destined for export, was no doubt greater than the share of non-slave labor similarly employed. A corollary of this also holds: the proportion of non-slave labor providing personal services and involved in "non-productive" activities was greater than its slave counterpart.[15] Just as important, masters in both labor sectors obtained the labor they needed from well-organized markets in which buyers and sellers responded to price changes. In short, setting aside the process of enslavement, employers of both free and slave labor bought their labor and set it to work to produce goods and services. The focus on production, particularly on production for sale in transoceanic markets, as well as the reliance on markets to obtain the necessary labor separated European- from non-European dominated slavery, and European from non-European non-slave regimes.

Despite parallels between the communal ties of pre-Columbian European societies and counterparts in Africa and the Americas, the balance between individual and group rights had, in relative global terms, shifted toward the former in Europe before the era of European expansion and well before the emergence of possessive individualism in the seventeenth century. Europe was characterized by the absence of a single dominating structure of government for the sub-continent as a whole. And within the European state, the curbs on the arbitrary acts of government were such as to give powers to individuals against surplus-extracting elites that did not exist in the non-European world. In the economic sphere, capital and labor could move within and beyond the sub-continent with considerable ease relative to any other part of the world in 1500. It was an environment particularly well suited to the "technological drift," in Eric Jones's words, that provided Europeans with the means to establish transoceanic trading and imperial links. Traditional ties still bound workers to master in early modern Europe. Free labor in the modern sense did not exist even in England and the early American Republic. A master-servant relationship gave masters a proprietal right so that non-performance by the servant was theft, with prison as the outcome. Yet choice of masters was increasingly possible even if the option of avoiding labor markets and working for oneself was less viable over time.[16]

Nor, from a global perspective, was the ability to choose between masters in northwest Europe regularly circumscribed by the threat of starvation after 1650. The last life-threatening food shortage in England occurred in 1623, later than in Holland and perhaps a century earlier than in France; but famines on an African or Asiatic scale had disappeared centuries before, if indeed they had ever occurred. For most social historians it is the harshness of the English Poor Laws and their counterparts in other European countries as well as their place in securing the position of elite classes that calls for analysis. Yet however miserable the support provided, there appear to have been few systems of poor relief in the non-European world of four centuries ago that attempted to offset deprivation as inclusively as say English parish relief, and none at all that left the realm of individual action so uncircumscribed. Relief in England by the early modern period was based on place of residence of the individual rather than membership of a group such as kin or family, and was not conditional on the surrender of long-term "rights in people," including labor.[17] Relative to Africans, Asians, and pre-contact aboriginal Americans, early modern Europeans were nutritionally secure, and less subject to natural or man-made catastrophe. Life expectancy in western Europe in 1500 was much lower than it was to become, but it was higher than anywhere else on the globe.

The key distinction is not that individuals in sixteenth-century Europe had more rights in relation to society than those in Africa and the pre-contact Americas, though this was probably true and certainly came to be the case. Rather it is that property rights in particular, especially those in human labor, one's own and others, were vested in the individual in Europe rather than the group.[18] Generally, status and rights in Africa and the pre-Columbian Americas derived not from autonomy and independence, but from full membership of a kin-group or some other corporate body.[19] Such a group would make collective decisions and hold, again collectively, at least some of the property rights in persons which in the European Atlantic world would be held by individuals. Europeans might purchase property rights in others (slaves) outright, or they might enter the labor market themselves and temporarily trade some of their own rights in persons in return for wages, but in either case there was an individual owner of the rights in persons and a market transaction.

To be a full member of the community in much of the non-European world meant having more social bonds and less autonomy than would a marginal person without kinship ties. Freedom meant a belonging, not a separateness.[20] By contrast, in Europe and the European Americas full membership of the community meant freedom from such bonds, full ownership of property rights in oneself, and, before the eighteenth century at least, the ability to avoid hiring out these rights to others in return for wages. It was not just intensive slavery that came out of the West. More fundamentally, it was the concept of rights, including rights to the labor of oneself and others, being vested in the individual rather than a group. The idea of full membership in society and, ultimately, freedom as independence from others deserves the title "the peculiar institution" to a much greater degree than did slavery.[21] European contact may or may not have gradually transformed African and Amerindian slavery, but from present-day perspectives it was the new concept of "freedom" or more precisely, the new relationship between the individual and society, rather than the new concept of slavery that had, and is having, by far the larger impact on the non-European world.

Western systems of slavery and free labor thus had the same roots—the relative latitude allowed for individual action in Europe in the era of expansion. It is likely that the very capacity of Europeans to sail beyond oceans and establish and maintain trading systems and empires hinged on a relationship between the citizen and the state, between elite and non-elite, and between employer and employed that was without precedent in non-Western societies in the scope it allowed for the individual. European overseas expansion could not have occurred without such scope, which implied freedom to enslave others. If neither Africa nor the Americas expanded overseas, it was, perhaps, because of their social structures rather than any shortfalls in wealth and technology. A corollary of this is that the impact of European values and social relationships on the non-European world seems far more important than the impact of European wealth and technology.

≺ IV ≻

Interactions between Slavery and Freedom

But if the two concepts, slavery and free labor, had the same roots, why in the very long run did one survive and the other wither; and to ask a related question—one perhaps that has to be asked first—how did the concepts and the practices of slavery and freedom interact and sustain each other in the European-dominated Atlantic world? As the European waged labor and slave systems diverged, they nevertheless continued to reinforce each other. The two were tied together by markets for products and factors of production. Although the Atlantic slave economy was never more than a relatively small appendage to the European economy, it provided a market for European goods and services, and at the same time was able to thrive because of the buoyant European market for tropical produce, and access to the largest capital markets in the world—Amsterdam and, later, London. While slave and waged labor systems drew on each other, it seems likely that the dependence of the former on the latter was rather greater than the reverse. There are major debates on the contribution of the slave systems to industrialization. Would the British have found it possible to fund government war-induced debt, or build canals or textile mills, or feed a rapidly growing population in the absence of Africa and the Americas? Probably. Would there have been a slave trade and plantations in the Americas without the credit and mortgage financing that flowed out from the European metropolitan centers?[22] Certainly not. As Adam Smith noted, the prosperity of the English sugar colonies was based "in great measure" on "the great riches of England, of which a part has overflowed . . . upon these colonies."

But among the strongest (and most ironic) ties between the slave and non-slave systems of the European Atlantic are those suggested by a closer look at the evolution of the waged labor force—especially in England where "modernization" proceeded fastest. Early English transatlantic migration was in fact intimately connected with this process. If "modernization" means anything today, it is the creation of a modern labor force—a phenomenon increasingly viewed by labor and economic historians as cultural rather than economic.[23] Seventeenth-century England may not have had slavery, but it did give masters large powers to enforce contracts. Those who would not enter such contracts, and who did not own sufficient land to support themselves, faced severe laws against vagrancy and idleness, the aim of which was the extraction of labor from those unwilling to volunteer it for wages. Migration—perhaps within England, but increasingly overseas—may be viewed as an attempt to avoid this status and achieve the pre-modern ideal of a piece of land and independence from the labor market. Thus, indentured servitude was something to be entered into voluntarily and endured temporarily by young people as an escape route from waged labor in much the same way as Eric Foner has posited for the Republican workers of the mid-nineteenth century urban United States.[24]

At some time in the centuries touched on here, however, worker aspirations in, first, England, and then the rest of Europe, shifted. Perhaps the essential meaning of modernization is worker acceptance of waged labor and a stress on consumption of goods and services—for which pecuniary income is necessary—over non-pecuniary rewards in the form of leisure or independence. As James Steuart said on the eve of industrialization, people must be slaves to others or slaves to want. The direct result of this was an increase in the supply of labor in the waged sector and, less directly, a stronger conviction in the advantages of waged as opposed to slave labor within domestic European economies. In the English case, the pamphlet literature circulating among the elite moved away from stressing low wages and draconian social legislation, and toward the advantages of high wages in creating enhanced worker productivity and a market for goods.[25] Among the goods European workers wanted were of course sugar, alcohol, tobacco, and eventually cotton goods, all of which meant slavery.

It is hard to avoid the conclusion that it was not just the European and African slave merchants that helped ensure Africans would become slaves in the Americas; it was also the aspirations of the European worker. The demand for cheap plantation produce was part of a gradual, secular rise in well-being that set in after 1650 in the English case, and later elsewhere in Europe. This was accentuated by changing values on the part of the worker as plantation produce formed a part (albeit miniscule) of the goods that the "modernized" worker now began to demand, as well as by the associated willingness to respond to higher wages on the part of more English and later European workers. Given the European taboo against European slaves, modernization of the English work force thus meant more slavery in the Americas for Africans. A similar process—termed a "first consumer revolution"—has been observed among indigenous populations as they came into initial

contact with European goods. But the additional work effort required for Amerindians and Africans to obtain such consumer
items went into the acquisition of commodities (or in the African
case, slaves) for trade rather than a formal labor market. No more
than Europeans would Africans and Amerindians work voluntarily
in mines and sugar plantations in gang labor conditions, though
unlike Europeans many of them were not given the choice.[26]

But shifts in worker attitudes toward consumption had further
and ultimately quite different impacts on the free-slave dichotomy
pursued here. In the very long run the shifts served to make slave
and wage systems incompatible and helped destroy the former. By
the late eighteenth century waged workers worked longer and
harder in order to consume. Higher productivity and the emergence
of an industrial sector were associated with the emergence of a free
labor force in the modern sense where employers no longer held
property rights in the employed and where the two groups were
considered legal (as opposed to material) equals. If possessive individualism and the market system seemed equally compatible with
waged and slave labor before say 1750, they appeared ideologically
much closer to the former than to the latter by the nineteenth century.[27] Shifts in worker attitudes in the waged sector of the European Atlantic world thus encouraged the rise of antislavery; after
its success the European world attempted to impose only one labor
system—the waged—on the non-European world, instead of two.[28]

To summarize, early modern Europeans shifted property rights
in labor toward the individual and away from the community. As
noted above, such a situation was consistent with either free or
slave labor. With respect to Europeans it led eventually to the former. As applied to non-Europeans (at least in the eyes of Europeans) it led to the latter. The European route to free labor for themselves ensured African subjection to the other (and polar) implication of the evolution of property rights in labor in Europe—full
chattel slavery. Europeans who had initially worked in the plantation fields as non-slaves in Brazil and then the Caribbean gradually
withdrew from such activities in the seventeenth century, though
in the absence of Africans and Amerindians (and after the attendant rise in wages) some would no doubt have continued to work
under such conditions. The geographic pattern of African slave use
in Europe in the sixteenth century (mainly southern) was some-

what similar to what it was to become in the Americas in the
sense that regions closest to Africa were most likely to use slave
labor.[29] If Europeans had enslaved their own, there would have been
far more slaves in the early modern Americas. The fact that African slavery in the Americas took longer to evolve than any European counterpart would have done—at least in North America—is
accounted for by the greater costs of moving people from Africa as
opposed to Europe; and if Africans had been allowed European migrant shipping conditions, higher shipping costs would have slowed
the evolution of the African slave trade (and the trade in plantation
produce) even further.[30]

The slave-free dialectic and the associated paradoxes are undoubtedly starkest in early modern northwestern Europe, and particularly England. The Europeans with the most advanced capitalist culture, the Dutch and the English, had by 1700 moved domestically furthest toward the modern conception of the labor force
and away from subjecting their own citizens to forms of forced labor.[31] These were the countries with the harshest and most closed
systems of exploiting enslaved non-Europeans. They were also the
countries that came to dominate Europe's relations with the non-
European world: the Dutch specializing to a greater degree than the
English in Asia, and the English in the Americas. The English and
Dutch conception of the role of the individual in metropolitan society was closer to the modern Western ideal than was that of
other European states. It made it impossible for their own subjects
to be chattel slaves or even convicts for life. For some scholars the
enslavement of Africans made possible the fuller development of
individual rights in England and the Netherlands. But the thrust of
the present analysis is that the English and Dutch view of themselves may have ensured the accelerated development of African
chattel slavery in the Americas (and Asian slavery in the East Indies).

≺ V ≻

The Slave-Free Paradox

The emphasis here on what is ultimately a non-economic argument allows a re-evaluation of the work of other scholars who have

addressed the slave-free dichotomy. The tensions posed by slavery
in the Americas came to be recognized in the late eighteenth and
nineteenth centuries. Given the not coincidental growth of abolitionism, the initial result of this recognition was the demonization
of slaveowners and slave traders. Slavery was now seen as aberrant
and certainly temporary. The conception of slavery as a "peculiar
institution" was born in the abolitionist era. The view that some
peoples were slaves by nature to which Las Casas subscribed came
to be tempered by the idea that slavery was one stage through
which all "uncivilized" peoples progressed toward a measure of
freedom.[32] But in this form, as the influence of Ulrich Bonnell Phillips suggests, it remained widely held into the twentieth century. If
slavery was a temporary condition and all peoples were potentially
equal, then it might be assumed that the paradox of the extremes
of slavery and freedom appearing in the Western world would be a
temporary phenomenon.

From the mid-twentieth century the literature lurched toward
explanations in terms of the economic self-interest of Europeans.
For world systems scholars, slavery is associated with an early
phase of European capitalism called "mercantile" or "merchant" as
opposed to a later version termed "industrial" capital. Slavery and
the slave trade have a central role in the growth of the former and
therefore flourish with merchant capitalism, but they are incompatible with the latter and go into decline when industrial capitalism becomes dominant. But even when the former is in the ascen-
dant, slavery is profitable only in the Americas, or "periphery." In
the metropolitan center of the European world system, it is always
more profitable to use free labor. The pattern of slave-free use is
thus explained by the self-interest of European capitalists.

The absoluteness of the barrier that prevented Europeans from
becoming slaves suggests that the world systems model, in which
European capitalists organized coerced labor on the periphery and
free labor in the core economies, is at least incomplete. We should
have expected at least some Europeans—the prisoners of war, felons, and displaced Irish who were forced to the colonies—to have
been slaves. Yet Portuguese degradados in Angola, Brazil, and Goa,
French convicts sent to Canada, their Spanish counterparts who
built the massive Havana fortifications, and the thousands of
Cromwellian prisoners were never chattels and were always sub-

ject to "Christian usage."[33] More fundamentally, the ethnic barriers, like the gender barriers that barred European women from skilled manual occupations, lead us to question all explanations of European expansion that hinge on unrestrained mercantile and mercantilist capitalism. If, as seems likely, European slaves would have been available more cheaply than Africans (as providing women with skills would have reduced the cost of skilled labor), then European merchants could not have been both profit maximizers and prejudiced (or outright racist and sexist) at the same time. If sexual and ethnic chauvinism did prevail over profit—which is likely—then between 1500 and 1700 Europeans operated within cultural constraints. At least the image of naked predatory capitalism that dominates the current historiography of early European expansion requires some modification. Indeed, a more pecuniary or profit-maximizing or "capitalist" attitude would have meant less African slavery (and greater equality for females) in the Americas.

An alternative method of dealing with the parallel evolution of more extreme forms of freedom and coercion—which also relies on the self-interest of European capitalists—rests on the argument that there was little substantive difference between waged workers and slaves. If the freedom of the waged labor market was at root a freedom to starve, freedom was therefore largely illusory. Slavery in the colonies and wage labor at home appear as two different methods of coercing workers and, as some English radicals argued in the early nineteenth century, the difference between the two was small. Abolition of slavery, when it eventually occurred, simply imposed a new form of coercion on the ex-slaves, and both the rise of slavery and its abolition thereby become less in need of an explanation. Much recent work on the post-emancipation Caribbean is consistent with this approach. From such a perspective, the economic elite, especially in northwestern Europe, used different methods to reduce the economic independence of non-elites in Europe on the one hand and in the Americas on the other. By the nineteenth century it had become necessary to rely on wage labor, effectively if indirectly controlled, in all parts of the Atlantic world. Once more, the tension between Western freedom and Western slavery is reduced—once we understand the true interests of European capitalists and the strategies they adopted. Variants of this draw on Gramsci, for whom slavery, or perhaps the abolition of slavery as espoused by the elite, becomes a way of legitimizing the ruling classes and making the conditions of European workers seem acceptable by comparison with those of slaves.[34]

Yet the self-interest of capitalists or indeed economic motivations in general seem, by themselves, to provide an unpromising route to understanding or setting aside the paradox. Slavery was certainly an economic system offering costs well below those possible using waged labor. But if the system was so effective, why was it confined so absolutely to non-Europeans? As for the contrast (or rather lack of) between free and slave labor—free laborers and slaves themselves had no doubts on the distinction between labor regimes, and slaves had no hesitation in attempting to achieve non-slave status, however defined and hedged, at least in the European dominated world. Having experienced slavery, Frederick Douglass was particularly sensitive to the differences between slave and non-slave labor. To underline the peculiar awfulness of the former, he several times informed crowds he was addressing that a job vacancy had been created by his escape from slavery, and that free laborers could offer their services as slaves to fill it.[35]

The various attempts to deal with the paradox—best embodied perhaps in the work of David Brion Davis, Seymour Drescher, Edmund S. Morgan, and Orlando Patterson—have tended to explore the paradox rather than attempted to resolve it in terms of class or economic interests. The cultural evolution and economic growth of the West that has shaped the modern world embodies a tension between coercion and freedom of choice which may be elaborated or understood, but not reduced, dismissed, or readily explained. For Patterson the tension long predates European overseas expansion. Freedom as a social value could not exist without slavery in the sense that in all societies what is marginal defines what is central. The conception of freedom as autonomy from personal and social obligations was perhaps possible only if an antithetical slave status defined as total dependence on another existed. Sparta, with helots rather than pure chattel slaves, had narrower concepts of individual freedom than Athens, where slavery was extensive and closed, and where the rightlessness of slaves was frequently set against the rights of adult male citizens. Both here and in Rome, the appearance of full chattel slavery was associated with the disappearance of any status intermediate to the slave-free polarity—a situation with some analogies to the early modern European Atlantic world.[36]

In seventeenth-century England, the term "slavery" was applied to many situations of perceived injustice, and it already represented something devalued. The implication, clearly, was that Englishmen should be free of such restraints. Historians of North America have developed variants of this relationship to explain social cohesiveness and the ability of slaveholders to espouse an ideology in which the right of peoples to be free from oppression had a central place— "peoples" and "social order" being for those of European descent.[37] On the other hand, historians also see a dramatic reversal in this mutually sustaining relationship helping to overthrow the slave system from the end of the eighteenth century. In the era since slavery disappeared from the Americas, Western concepts of freedom have tended instead to draw on and define themselves in terms of what is perceived as a lack of freedom in non-Western societies.[38]

Yet before the eighteenth century, these associations seem, if not invalid, somewhat overdrawn. Personal freedom in the seventeenth-century Netherlands appears much more rooted in the social structure, religion, and immigration trends of the Low countries than in the coercive activities of a few thousand Dutchmen in Asia. The Dutch did not even enter the Atlantic slave trade until the 1630s, and compared to the Portuguese and the English they remained of marginal importance until well after 1660. Likewise it would be difficult to attempt to link any of the political or religious upheavals of England in the 1640s and 1650s to a nascent slave system on one small island over 4,000 miles away, involving at most 30,000 people in 1650—less than half of whom were slaves. Even at the time of the English Revolution, the English slave system in the Americas was of trivial importance compared to the domestic economy and society. It did not occupy a large part of the domestic consciousness.[39] In no sense did the English or Dutch live with slaves as did their counterparts in ancient Greece and Rome. In the English case, the Irish would seem more promising territory for this type of analysis, but while the Irish were conquered, expropriated, and absorbed into the English economy as thoroughly as any Mediterranean peoples into say the Roman Empire, they were neither enslaved nor reduced to serfdom as were the victims of those earlier Western slave societies, ancient Greece and Rome.

After 1700 the slave empires of the Americas were of larger significance to Europe in all senses, but the rise of movements to abolish slavery in the 1780s makes it hard, initially, to track the effects of slavery on freedom and vice versa. Abolition may have helped validate waged labor systems in Europe and reinforce the position of political and economic elites, but the fact remains that the slave systems themselves were abolished in the process. Moreover, in ideological terms, surely the employers of labor in England would have found it more useful to have slavery in the colonies continue rather than come to an end. Slavery would have acted as a continuing reminder to free laborers of how much worse their predicament might be and indeed, as the mining serfs in seventeenth-century Scotland discovered, might become. In any event, in the post-1700 world, it seems that Europeans, especially the English, rather quickly outgrew any need for slavery to define concepts of freedom for themselves even supposing that they had once felt such a need. In short, whatever the powerful validating influences of American slave systems on concepts of freedom, and more specifically waged labor systems, of the North Atlantic, the influence of free over slave systems of the early modern world was greater rather than vice versa. There is no suggestion in any European country of a "bargain" between workers and elite to reserve slavery for Africans and Amerindians, and to guarantee at the same time wider freedoms for non-elite Europeans.[40]

The possibility of enslaving other Europeans lay beyond the serious intent of any European class or nation even before the onset of the early modern period. Slavery in the Americas was created by the freedom that Europeans had in Africa and the Americas, a freedom that was unrestricted by social structures and values that held in the non-European world—the same factors that underlay the rise of waged labor systems. In stark contrast to classical times, however, this freedom of the individual against the group did not include the right to enslave other Europeans. European conceptions of the "other" ensured that only non-Europeans could be slaves. Given the transportation and production cost advantages of slave labor there can be little doubt that if European slavery could have been enforced, slavery in the Americas (white slavery) would have been very extensive in the sixteenth century. The flow of specie and plantation products from the Americas to Europe would have been greatly accelerated, because it was simply much cheaper to take slaves from Europe than Africa.

The work of Drescher, Patterson, Davis, and Morgan has moved beyond explanations rooted in the self-interest of a European elite, but with the exception of Drescher, each of these scholars, in very different ways, makes freedom in the Western world dependent to some degree on the slave systems that western Europe also developed. To these might be added the work of Robert Steinfeld on the demise of indentured servitude and the emergence of modern conceptions of free labor. For Steinfeld, the indenture contract could not survive a nineteenth-century world that had known slavery, at least in the United States.[41]

In contrast, what I have tried to argue here is the reverse of these positions—that freedom as it developed in Europe meant in part the freedom to exploit others. Freedom thus made possible the slavery of the Americas. The present argument focuses on the links between freedom in Europe and slavery in the Americas. Specifically, the conditions—mainly environmental—that made Europe different from the rest of the world also created a social structure where the extremes of slavery and freedom were possible. It also stresses the significance of slavery being confined to those of African descent and downplays the European awareness of the slave-free paradox (as opposed to a consciousness of their own liberty, at least in the English case) prior to the late eighteenth century. Slavery was associated with very high land-labor ratios of the early modern Americas, but the slaves themselves were normally drawn from outside the community or kin group. Europeans, indigenous Americans, and Africans alike enslaved only outsiders. Of course, while European conceptions of freedom made slavery possible, they also in the end ensured its demise. To return to where this chapter began, abolition—the idea that no one should be a slave—was as quintessentially and uniquely Western a concept as was slave labor in the Caribbean.

Free Labor vs. Slave Labor:
The British and Caribbean Cases

SEYMOUR DRESCHER

"FREE LABOR" MADE its first significant appearance as a legal and cultural construct in the Anglo-American world of the eighteenth century. In one sense labor became free wherever employers lost the legal right to invoke criminal penalties for premature departure or non-performance. The defining characteristic of free laborers was that their violations of voluntary labor agreements were not punishable by imprisonment or physical coercion. "Free labor," however, was also used in another sense. In certain contexts the term applied to all labor performed by "freemen," that is anyone who was not legally and permanently bound to labor for others. In this second sense the fundamental distinction was between freemen on one hand, and villeins, serfs, and slaves on the other. In Great Britain a freeman might well be penally liable for breaches of contract late into the nineteenth century.[1]

This second distinction, between the labor of freemen and that of slaves, underlay one of the great social transformations of the eighteenth and nineteenth centuries. The relative merits of each form of labor became crucial to a small number of articulate groups: abolitionist elites; the slave interest; pro- and anti-abolitionist pamphleteers; Members of Parliament; and political economists. Their arguments, however limited in scope, potentially affected the lives and well-being of millions who were generally indifferent to the particulars of the comparison. In turn, the political and economic outcome of the broader struggle over the fate of slavery affected the agendas and rhetorical strategies of the debaters. The origin, development, and results of the long debate are the subject of this chapter.

⋖ I ⋗

Before Abolitionism

On the eve of the American Revolutionary War the British domin-
ions encompassed the largest slave system in the Americas. Of the
two and a half million human chattels in the New World, more
than one third were the property of the subjects of George III. Less
than a century later the final segment of that original Anglo-American slave system was brought to an end in the American Civil
War. In the interim the British themselves had abolished the portion of the slave system under their own control and assumed the
diplomatic, naval, and popular world leadership in ending the
transatlantic slave trade.[2] The Anglo-American Atlantic system
was terminated despite the fact that in the century before Lincoln's
Emancipation Proclamation the slave population of the Americas
more than doubled and more Africans were landed in the Americas
than during the previous three centuries of the Atlantic slave trade.
Liberation depended upon a complex political process in which
hundred of thousands of individuals, agitating for abolition on both
sides of the Atlantic, were pitted against hundreds of thousands of
defenders of the system. Between the 1760s and the 1860s slavery
was established, expanded, or resurrected in some areas while it
was being curtailed, gradually abolished, or violently destroyed in
others.

The dismantling process was accompanied by a major cultural
struggle to devalue the slave trade, slavery, and the products derived from slavery. At the end of the Seven Years War the overwhelming majority of articulate individuals in Britain counted Caribbean slaves as among the most valuable work force per capita in
the world. By the time of British slave emancipation in 1833 the
overwhelming majority of British condemned slave labor as incompatible with their religion, their civilization, their traditions,
and their honor. Some also undertook to demonstrate, in what the
British called their "great experiment," that their newly freed ex-
slaves were also more productive than their still enslaved counterparts in other regions.[3] The entire slaveholding world was to see
that emancipation was compatible both with the maintenance of
the political order and with continuity of production, profitability,
and prosperity for both planters and workers. The great experiment

would confirm the providential order governing the world—that "right never comes wrong."[4]

In many ways, this robust linkage between freedom and labor was unprecedented. For most of human history the expression free labor was an oxymoron. Freedom and labor were conceptually assigned to separate spheres of human existence. In the ancient classical view a human activity so intimately linked to the provision of life-sustaining needs was inherently servile. It was the natural activity of those, like slaves and animals, who were the means of freeing citizens for participation in virtuous activity and thought. Correspondingly the "free man" was one who "neither lived under the constraint of, nor was employed for the benefit of, another."[5] Even when labor was not confined to slaves or foreigners, it was considered best to restrict citizenship to non-manual laborers or to regard the latter as incomplete members of the community.

The inherent servility of labor perpetuated itself long after slavery had ceased to be characteristic of or even legally acceptable in early modern Europe. However, the attributes of civil freedom and citizenship could be expanded to include all of the natives of a society without severing the connection between labor and servility in the perspective of the elite. By the late sixteenth century the absence of slavery on the soil of a commonwealth might be extolled as characteristic of one's nation, while labor's inferiority and the fitness of laborers "onlie to be ruled" were simultaneously affirmed. Jean Bodin, notably hostile to slavery, proud of its disappearance from France, and concerned to have the most servile subjects acknowledged as members of the community, still wanted those engaged in mechanical operations or hired for wages excluded from the exercise of government. Even when the distinction between voluntary and involuntary, or time-bound and indefinite, labor obligations began to become significant in legal and popular culture, labor itself remained understood as service—an alienation or limitation of one's property in one's own working capacity for the duration of a contract.[6]

While the division between autonomous personal status outside the work situation and service within it emerged in northwestern Europe, a rigorously constraining form of slavery was simultaneously expanding overseas. By the eighteenth century it was impossible to imagine the Atlantic system without slavery and the slave

trade.[7] Coerced labor and indentured servitude, widely institutionalized in the New World before the massive importation of Africans, had been the original means of producing overseas commercial exports. By 1700 African slavery was the labor system of
choice in the tropical Caribbean basin. Africa, Europe, and the
Americas contributed varying elements of labor, capital, technology, and commodities into a highly coordinated system of exchange and production. Inhabitants of all four Atlantic continents,
as well as of Asia, dynamically expanded their involvement in the
Atlantic economy. The antislavery initiatives against European-
sponsored slave systems after 1780 were undertaken in the teeth of
powerful economic incentives offered to the systems' beneficiaries.[8]

Throughout the Atlantic basin and the Americas from Canada
to the Rio de la Plata and from Iberia to the Cape Colony, all societies legalized chattel slavery. Even Atlantic European communities
without slaves or slaveholding colonies in the Americas attempted
to participate in the slave trade. In northwestern European societies, however, chattel slavery was, from the beginning, anomalous
to their internal legal and social orders.[9] Contrasting extremes of
freedom and slavery in the Atlantic system were to be found in
northwestern Europe and in their sugar island colonies in the West
Indies. By 1700 the same northwestern European societies that
were so reluctant to enslave their own members took coerced African labor in the plantation Americas for granted.

Arguments varied, but the combination of abundant, fertile, and
unhealthy land rewarded a division of labor that maximized African and slave labor. Slavery was rationalized, even racially, as essential to tropical labor.[10] Whether residually, as in Montesquieu's
formulation, or empirically, as in the surveys of Arthur Young and
the French *Encyclopédie*, the tropics was considered the zone *par
excellence* of unfree labor. Thus, even when labor itself was imagined as integral to an individual's autonomy and rights, the notion
was initially considered irrelevant to the extra-European environment. The extensive early modern European literature on freedom
bore little relevance to behavior and institutions in the transatlantic system or to the non-European inhabitants of the continents
"beyond the line." In early modern Europe "beyond the line" consisted of that vast zone, west of the Azores and south of the Tropic

of Cancer, where relations between Europeans were not governed by diplomatic norms within Europe.[11]

Economic- rather than political-rights discussions reshaped Europe's vision of freedom's potential impact upon labor relations. Everywhere until the mid-eighteenth century (and in some areas well into the nineteenth) slavery was reckoned merely a different, not an inferior or incompatible, form of organizing labor in the enormously varied environments of the European world system. In economically oriented thought, the motivations of laborers were now linked to the maximization of wealth. Laborers could be creative as well as "mechanical" factors of production. Thus James Steuart, in the 1760s, distinguished between what he called *industry* and *labor*. Labor remained relegated to servile unfreedom. Industry invoked voluntary, self-motivated work. Under slavery, the master could dictate the very motions of the worker; under liberty "every head is at work, and every hand is improving in dexterity." Did this mean that "industry" was superior to "labor"? On the contrary, what mattered was the nature of the work. If some were slaves to others, free laborers were slaves to their wants. The free worker was assigned a mind but not an economic edge: where hands were needed slaves were preferable, where heads were appropriate the advantage lay with liberty. Large-scale manufacturing as well as agriculture could take advantage of the "simplicity of slavery." The most obvious example of slave labor's superiority was drawn from the West Indies: "Could the sugar islands be cultivated to any advantage, by hired labor?"

For Steuart, what really limited access to the benefits of using slavery everywhere was not the superior *industry* of free men, but the political "spirit of the times." In the islands the mode of reproduction reinforced the Caribbean slaveholders' advantage. The ability to purchase slave labor from Africa gave the planters a still wider range of choices and, "were not the expenses of rearing children supposed to be great," asked Steuart rhetorically, "would slaves ever be imported? Certainly not." As long as Africa remained what he termed the "warren" of New World labor, the planter could shift some of the costs of reproduction and child mortality away from the Caribbean plantations. In Europe massive recourse to slavery was not a political or moral option. Elsewhere, it was maintained for *non*-Europeans without wounding the metropolitan "spirit of the times." Therefore, New World bondage had been "very *luckily*, if not *politically*" established to promote the economic well-being of the metropolis. Slavery was deployed in simple and laborious agricultural operations where hands, not heads, were wanted. Indeed, because slavery discouraged invention and industry, were any colony to rival the industry of the mother country, one needed only to allow the unrestricted introduction of slaves, whose "natural effect" would undercut competitive economic development.[12] Where both forms were permitted, the nature of production and reproduction determined the choice between slavish and industrial labor.

For James Steuart the geographic separation between liberty and slavery remained clear and unproblematic. By the last third of the eighteenth century, however, the two zones began to impinge upon each other. An increasing stream of black slaves from the periphery to Europe generated continuous friction over the metropolitan status of colonists' claims to their property in persons. European legal systems faced a choice. Some, like those of England and Scotland in the 1770s, nullified slave law within their jurisdictions. Others, like those of France and the Netherlands, were brought around to temporarily allowing properly registered slaves to be warehoused in Europe for re-export abroad within a given time period.[13]

Equally significant was the development of colonies of predominantly European settlers in British North America, facilitating the New World extension of Europe's commercial and free labor societies. This development generated discussions of the effects of free and slave labor along the borderlands between predominantly free and servile labor forces. In the two decades before the American Revolution Virginia planters attempted to restrict the slave trade to their colony. They aimed to preserve the colony's racial balance. Some also wanted to capture more of the European movement of arts and skills from their rapidly improving neighbors to the north.[14] From his own perspective slightly to the north, Benjamin Franklin identified the psychological and demographic depletion wrought by slavery in the British Caribbean: "The Negroes brought into the English Sugar Islands have greatly diminished the Whites there; the Poor are by this means deprived of Employment, while a few Families acquire vast Estates . . . The Slaves being worked too hard, and ill fed . . . the Deaths among them are more than the Births; so that a continual Supply is needed from Africa. The Northern Colonies having few Slaves increase in Whites. Slaves also pejorate the Families that use them; the white Children become proud, disgusted with Labour, and being educated in Idleness, are rendered unfit to get a Living by Industry."[15] Franklin, like James Steuart, projected vastly different social results from slaves and free laborers, but discovered a very different object lesson for his fellow North Americans.

Metropolitans were also beginning to use slavery as a way of distinguishing themselves from both their European predecessors and their non-European contemporaries. European "moderns" embraced the notion that their societies were dedicated to expanding their collective wealth through trade and industry, and to legitimizing the material aspirations of ordinary people. As in Franklin's moral economy, idleness was linked to apathy, to enfeeblement, and to sterility. Industry promoted productivity and reproductivity. Both the Classical and the Caribbean worlds, distinguished by dependence upon slavery, had been marked by demographic, technological, and intellectual stagnation.[16]

The most distinguished metropolitan exponent of this new world view was Adam Smith. *An Inquiry into the Nature and Causes of the Wealth of Nations*, published in 1776, supplied a distinctive economic argument to the British abolitionist movement when it emerged a decade later. For Smith, wealth and liberty ("opulence and freedom") were the two greatest blessings one could possess. The modern world was a world of commerce, creating a network of interdependence and resting upon the joint voluntary labor of a great multitude of workmen.[17] The opening theme of the *Wealth of Nations* was labor. In its productivity, its division, and its maintenance lay the chief source of societal improvement. The optimum source of labor itself was the free action of the laborer. Ample rewards for free labor increased the activity, the diligence, and the expeditiousness of the very population whose satisfaction and freedom, as both workers and consumers, was the true aim of an "opulent and free" society.

In such a world slavery was not only morally objectionable but economically defective. Freedom for laborers was as beneficial for the masters as for the workers. Smith encapsulated the argument: "The experience of all ages and nations, I believe, demonstrates that the work done by slaves, though it appears to cost only their maintenance, is in the end, the dearest of any. A person who can acquire no property, can have no other interest but to eat as much and to labour as little as possible. Whatever work he does beyond what is sufficient to purchase his own maintenance can be squeezed out of him by violence only, and not by any interest of his own." The costs (the "wear and tear") entailed in maintaining and reproducing labor were at the expense of employers of both freemen and slaves. Free workers cost their masters less because the poor were generally more frugal and efficient in maintaining themselves than were slaveholders in maintaining their slaves.[18] Smith's formulation became a general article of abolitionist faith, ordaining the ultimate triumph of voluntary labor.

No subsequent formulation proved to be so straightforward or so compelling to antislavery advocates during the next three generations of political struggle against the Atlantic slave trade and Caribbean slavery. The whole world of historical experience was scoured to bear further witness that slave labor was "in the end the dearest of any." Smith's own demonstration was historical. The *Wealth of Nations* envisioned a succession of dominant modes of production in western Europe, corresponding to a series of economic stages from hunting and gathering, through ancient slavery, to modern voluntary wage labor. In this schema, of course, the New World presented a major problem.

If the western European sequence argued in favor of the superiority of wage labor, the reverse seemed to have been the case across the ocean, above all in the West Indies, where slavery had superseded indentured servitude. Before writing the *Wealth of Nations*, Smith himself had noted that bound labor was the prevailing form on the planet. Moreover, he anticipated that slavery was unlikely to disappear from the world for ages to come, if ever.[19] He offered two reasons for this contrast between the optimality of free labor and the ubiquity of bound labor. The first was a general noneconomic human trait, love of dominating. This motive, of course, was not particularly helpful in explaining why the same western Europeans used one form of labor in Europe and another in the West Indies. The second reason was both economic and relevant to the paradox. It related to Smith's view of the generality of West Indian planters as agricultural profit-seekers, not feudal lords or rentier gentry.[20] The planters' choice of labor in the Caribbean was based more on profit than on pride or prejudice. Sugar was so valuable a product in Europe that the planter could afford the service of slaves. Indeed, the crop's profitability, with slavery, was greater than any other in the Atlantic world. In a book replete with policy assessments, the *Wealth of Nations* did not suggest that planters in the West Indies could increase their profits still further by emancipating their labor force.

If one read the *Wealth of Nations* less selectively than abolitionists were inclined to do, one could discover other serious qualifications to his general axiom of free labor superiority. But two relevant omissions from the *Wealth of Nations* were as great a boon to future abolitionists as its formulation of free labor superiority. In discussions of slavery in the Americas Smith spoke of only two types of laborers—freemen and slaves. Aside from apprentices and miners in Britain itself, Smith seemed uninterested, to the point of total silence, in the existence and history of convict or indentured labor in America, especially the seventeenth-century displacement of British indentured servants by slaves in the sugar islands.[21] The process would receive short shrift in the debates over the British slave system before emancipation. During the age of abolition European freemen and Caribbean slaves would be juxtaposed in a stark dichotomy.

Smith's second omission was even more significant. It concerned his major hypothesis about the relative costs of "wear and tear," that is the reproduction of "the race of journeymen and servants."[22] He rarely turned to the New World for evidence of slave labors' dearness. When he did, Smith seemed interested in using evidence drawn from the urban clusters of North America, not from the plantations of the West Indies, where the reproduction costs of the "race" of servants were borne by the warren of Africa. Left to themselves over the course of two centuries, the choice of all New World sugar planters of all nations had been to replace all other forms of labor by African chattel slaves.[23]

≺ II ≻

From Abolitionism to British Emancipation 1787–1833

To abolitionists who cited Smith, the differences between the labor systems of the slave colonies and the labor system of Britain were starker than anywhere else in the world. James Ramsay, the first major polemicist against Caribbean slavery in the 1780s, casually appealed to the principle of free labor superiority. Humanity, he asserted, could anticipate emancipation without any qualms, because "he who can procure a freeman to work for him, will never employ a slave." By a reckoning that was to be commonplace during the age of abolition, a free laborer doubled the output of a slave. Moreover, when the freeman died, his place was supplied by "natural" generation, not at "enormous expense" from the slave market. Thomas Clarkson, the abolitionist movement's first national canvasser, went still further in asserting free labor superiority. He boasted that sugar was already being raised by free men in Cochin China at one-seventh the cost of the British Caribbean product.[24]

Faith in the superior efficacy of free labor (as exemplified in eighteenth-century Britain) did not depend solely on a reading of Adam Smith. The "fruitlessness of compulsory labour" was proved "every day in every workhouse in the kingdom. There is in proof too, the felons in the hulks, who produce not a fourth part of the ballast which is raised by the adjoining barges, where men are working on their own account." The problem was always whether this experience could be transferred overseas. For generations to come such calculations elicited the rejoinder that the amount of labor extracted from the exploited and insecure freeman must therefore be far greater than what was being extracted from slaves. In this respect, West Indian slaves must be better off than free English manufacturers and peasants. Ramsay's reply anticipated the general abolitionist response. Whether or not a European peasant reaped more of the necessities of life from his labor than a Caribbean slave, the free laborer's reward came from the "charms of liberty itself." Freedom softened his toil while it doubled his exertions. After work it secured him his own time, his family, his immunity from arbitrary cruelty. The putative attraction to employers of lower costs of reproduction and security against discontent became articles of abolitionist faith.[25]

A major objection of the slave interest to major alterations of the British slave system was the universally acknowledged observation that freed slaves in the West Indies never remained in the cane fields. During the very early phase of the antislavery attack, when only the slave trade was being targeted, abolitionists suggested hiring free blacks as domestics and returning slave domestics to the field as substitutes for foregone Africans.[26] Over the longer run, however, the abolitionists deployed the modernist's attack on slave labor's inherent servility and brutishness. West Indian free blacks did not work in the fields, and frequently remained idle, because planters demeaned labor. Slavery degraded labor, not the reverse. In a slave-tainted environment, what free persons would "subject themselves to the driver's lash, who are not absolutely forced to submit to such a degradation"? The West Indian system's peculiar defect was "it's (sic) utter forgetfulness of *mind*" and motive in reducing humans to "the vilest of brute species."[27] If slavery polluted labor, every step toward freedom would restore the innate pride, intelligence, and energy of labor.

From their first mass campaign against the African slave trade in 1788 to their agitation against colonial "apprenticeship" fifty years later, abolitionists committed themselves to creating one world of labor relations. As William Wilberforce emphasized on the eve of the abolition of the British slave trade in 1807: *"the principles of justice are immutable in their nature and universal in their application; the duty at once, and the interest, of nations, no less than of individuals."*[28] The supreme object and obligation of abolitionism was to dissolve the applicability of different norms "beyond the line."

However, the abolitionist elite were far from comfortable about using the generic assertion of free labor's universal superiority as a guide to policy making beyond the line. For decades, while theoretically armed with the good news of free labor superiority, most parliamentary abolitionists opposed the immediate application of this immutable principle. Until well after the Napoleonic wars, and despite their creed of the unity of religion, justice, and policy, abolitionists virtually ignored what historians have termed the "free labor ideology" in its *economic* sense.[29] The principle of slave labor inefficiency was usually tucked modestly into the back pages of antislavery polemics.[30]

The abolitionist elite were even more circumspect in their direct appeals for popular action than in their tracts. Their major *Abstract of Evidence* on the slave trade in 1791 simply avoided the free labor argument. The popular petitions reiterated this reticence. Fewer than one in twenty of the great mass petitions in 1792 referred to the inferiority of slave labor.[31] One rationale for this rhetorical reticence seemed to derive from the policy priorities of the abolitionist leaders between 1787 and their first major victory twenty years later. The abolitionists' first target was the African slave trade. In the West Indies slaves represented upwards of fifty to one hundred million pounds of sunken British capital. Direct attacks on the Caribbean system would also evoke plausible counterarguments that parliamentary emancipation was unconstitutional. The planters could then claim full monetary compensation for the confiscation of their legally sanctioned property. Finally, attacking slavery itself raised the spectre of overseas slave rebellion in response to public agitation for their emancipation.[32]

Nevertheless, in arguing that an inevitable improvement would result from giving the "blessings of freedom" to the West Indian slaves, abolitionists continually exposed themselves to the charge of hypocrisy in postponing emancipation. In response, abolitionist leaders declared that "insanity alone could dictate" immediate emancipation.[33] In 1807 they demonstrated this conviction. As the slave trade abolition bill reached its final stage in Parliament, a young MP moved for the emancipation of all infants henceforth born in the colonies. Wilberforce immediately opposed this motion as unsafe and ruinous.[34]

The abolitionist rationale for delay was straightforward: too high a proportion of Caribbean slaves were African "savages," debased by both superstition and enslavement. Slaves as a group required a long transition to absorb proper work habits, religion, and civilization. Free labor would be superior only when, through gradual "amelioration," the slow-growing plant of "true liberty" overcame the slave's indolence and licentiousness. In his first writings on the subject, Henry Brougham, later a parliamentary pillar of antislavery, could not even imagine testing the principle of free labor among uncivilized Africans, the "common enemy of civilized society."[35] What the *Wealth of Nations* seemed to affirm as a universal effect of free agency in labor was deemed disastrous as an immedi-

ate policy in the West Indian situation of 1807. The singular situation created by the effects of the slave trade therefore left the free
labor ideology technically intact, because free labor superiority
could be tested only by "truly" free men.

Historians have tended to accept this formulation of abolitionist belief in free labor superiority as modified by the peculiar situation imposed upon the victims of the slave trade. The British elite
as a whole has been widely characterized as adhering to the principle of free labor superiority until emancipation and beyond.[36] Was
it just a peculiarity of the peculiar institution that rendered Caribbean slave laborers unfit to compete as free laborers, or did abolitionists themselves harbor deep doubts about the ability of even
free-born free laborers to compete with the contemporary slave system?

James Stephen, the most knowledgeable member of the abolitionist elite, actually rejected the hypothesis of free labor superiority in the sugar islands. The abolitionists, of course, knew from the
beginning that the least controversial way to end both the slave
trade and the slave system of production was to supply free labor
sugar at "a *cheaper rate.*"[37] In the early 1790s they turned hopefully
from one potential "free labor" competitor to another, to the British East India Company, to North American maple sugar extrac-
tors, to the new African colony of Sierra Leone.[38] By the time abolitionists finally succeeded in prohibiting the British slave trade, in
1806–7, all of these original potential free labor alternatives had
failed to displace slave labor. New World slaves supplied more than
95 percent of the North Atlantic's sugar.[39]

The strategy before the 1820s of postponing political agitation
for emancipation to a distant future also muted the "consumerist"
aspects of the free labor argument. In focusing upon the acquisitive
potential of self-motivated free laborers, the "modernist" political
economists had emphasized the "positive" incentives for increasing consumption as well as production. Indeed, the mass consumption of slave-grown products (tobacco, sugar, coffee, and cotton)
presumably indicated the willingness of British laborers to work
more assiduously for erstwhile luxuries and amenities. Voluntary
labor increased not only the supply of worldly goods but the range
and value of metropolitan demand.[40]

Yet, as applied to the West Indies, neither abolitionist argu-

ments nor their policies tended to have a consumptionist orientation. In focusing upon the slave trade abolitionists initially emphasized the vast potential of Africa, not the Caribbean. Eliminating
the internecine warfare inspired by slaving would rapidly transform
"one-third of the inhabitable globe" into a vast emporium for British commerce. In the Caribbean, on the other hand, abolitionists
could offer only a gradual increase in colonial purchases of British
exports, contingent upon the slow improvement of the still-en-
slaved bulk of the population.[41] Moreover, another aspect of abolitionist behavior tended to depress, rather than to expand, the British consumption of West Indian produce. Beginning in 1791, an
abolitionist consumer's mobilization launched a mass boycott
against slave-grown sugar. The boycott's effect upon West Indian
sugar producers was negligible, but it sometimes raised the cost of
sugar to those consumers who purchased only "free" East Indian
sugar offered for sale in Britain.[42]

   In 1806 when the prospect of slave trade abolition was imminent, Joseph Barham, one of its few West Indian parliamentary
sympathizers, felt that the time was ripe to challenge slavery economically. Barham suggested using Britain's recently acquired, and
undeveloped, colony of Trinidad as an ideal laboratory for demon-
strating the superiority of free labor. He wanted the British government to sponsor the migration of free Chinese laborers, famed
for their good labor discipline. Wilberforce was initially inclined to
support a project so favorably framed in favor of free labor. But
James Stephen, the main author and strategist of the Foreign Abolition Bill of 1806, warned Wilberforce against supporting Barham's
project. As the acknowledged abolitionist expert on the West Indies, Stephen predicted nothing but disaster in such an experiment.

   Stephen had already anonymously registered his opinion that
slave labor had a decisive advantage over both free and other forms
of involuntary labor in the sugar islands. He argued primarily from
his knowledge of the results of slave emancipation in the French
colonies of St. Domingue and Guadeloupe during the 1790s. Stephen convinced Wilberforce that the experiment's failure would
discredit all who sponsored it, including abolitionists. In print he
again (anonymously) denounced the Trinidad free labor project as
preposterous. The case of Trinidad throws crucial light on early
abolitionist assumptions. In 1802, when Trinidad's development as

a slave colony with an unimpeded African slave trade still seemed likely, Stephen urged the exclusive importation of "free negroes." Even as he pleaded for this policy, Stephen conceded that slave labor was the most profitable form of labor. In the sugar colonies, free (and even indentured) labor had to be permanently protected against slave labor. From the beginning, Stephen could not even imagine a competitive situation.[43]

In Parliament, Stephen himself successfully opposed another petition for a free labor experiment, in 1811. Now he could invoke the failure of the earlier Trinidad experiment as proof, that "while slavery existed in the West Indies it was impossible that free labor could succeed in competition with it."[44] When Stephen openly offered this conclusion, not a single abolitionist rose in Parliament to oppose or even soften this categorical dismissal of free labor superiority. Nor did any parliamentary abolitionist of the next generation ever suggest another pilot experiment.

Following peace with France in 1814 and the revival of the French Atlantic slave trade, Stephen added a detailed codicil to his firm evaluation of relative labor competitiveness. British slavery, now dependent exclusively upon natural reproduction, would henceforth, Stephen predicted, be undercut by the foreign "buying" systems. Painful as he found it to confess this to a prime minister who had always opposed abolition of the slave trade, Stephen candidly parted company with his abolitionist colleagues' principle that "breeding" was cheaper than "buying." The British slave interest was unable to benefit politically from this private confession by their most knowledgeable and effective opponent.[45]

The abolitionist leadership launched a second major offensive against the British overseas slave system in 1823. They directly attacked British Caribbean slavery itself and requested Parliament to sponsor gradual legal emancipation. In attacking slavery, abolitionists felt impelled to resurrect their long-muted free labor ideology. Adam Smith was resuscitated and a search was undertaken to cull further support from economists. In view of the burgeoning authority of political economy the results were meager. Few British political economists had bothered to reiterate, much less to elaborate, Smith's brief passages on slave and free labor. In the half century between the *Wealth of Nations* and the first campaign for gradual abolition there were probably fewer passages published comparing slavery and free labor by any major British political economist than had already appeared in the body of Smith's own work.

One of Smith's most renowned successors was, in fact, a source of anxiety and embarrassment to British abolitionists. France's J.-B. Say, in his famous *Treatise on Political Economy* (1803/1814), offered calculations which explicitly contradicted the *Wealth of Nations* on the productivity of colonial slavery. Like Smith, Say argued that West Indian slave labor was profitable and productive, but he also argued that slave labor, in cost-benefit terms, was *at least* as efficient as that of free labor in France.[46] These calculations were so disturbing to his English translator that he took sharp issue with Say in a series of footnotes to the *Treatise*. Another British abolitionist felt it necessary to extract a letter from Say acknowledging at least that slavery was incompatible with modern economic development. Say's distinction was not unlike James Steuart's contrast between "industry" and slavery.[47]

Given a golden opportunity to demonstrate the utility of their science in favor of a massively popular public policy, the political economists demurred. In 1828, the economist R. J. Wilmot-Horton was as explicit in Parliament as James Stephen had been seventeen years before: "free labor would not be found as effectual as the labor of slaves in the production of sugar." At the very peak of mass antislavery petitioning and parliamentary debates on immediate emancipation in 1833, Montifort Longfield gave an inaugural lecture in the Chair of Political Economy at Trinity College, Dublin. He solemnly announced that the question of emancipation was too complicated and too agitated "to be fit for a Professor's chair." Longfield would say only that "when it is said that free labor is cheaper than that of slaves, or the contrary, the proposition must be considered false if taken universally."[48] The Chair was the legacy of Adam Smith but the voice was the voice of James Steuart.

In the presence of academic equivocation, abolitionists reworked Adam Smith on their own, emphasizing his "wear and tear" argument. They reinforced him by comparing British Caribbean population statistics with Malthusian population principles. Malthus posited the general propensity of human populations to procreate to the limit of available natural resources. The British Caribbean after 1807 offered the anomaly of a generally declining slave population.[49] Despite the advantages that this strategy offered

to defenders of slavery in America, the abolitionists had no com-
punctions about comparing the West Indian slave population decrease to the high natural growth rate of slaves in the United States
South. West Indian planters countered by declaring that their declining slave populations were a temporary effect of British slave
trade abolition. Their arguments were often statistically more sophisticated than those of the abolitionists. Yet they always carried
the rhetorical burden of having to explain away the clear and simple fact of declining numbers within an Anglo-American world of
otherwise rapidly expanding populations.

In appealing to their countrymen for political steps toward
emancipation, abolitionists now more insistently invoked the positive motives to labor as portrayed by the optimistic economics of
the eighteenth century. Industry in a labor force implied a willing
effort on the part of the worker. A worker, like all others, sought to
"better his condition." He became bonded to an ever receding
threshold of amenities. Freed slaves would be doing more than ex-
changing hunger for the lash. They would be making the same
"voluntary sacrifices of time and ease . . . which influence other
classes of mankind." Abolitionists presented case after case of free
men, from Java to Mexico, who were productively employed in the
cultivation of tropical goods. These cases validated the hypothesis
that the urge toward self-improvement offered more than sufficient
security for the maintenance and even enhancement of West Indian sugar production after emancipation.[50]

No other element of antislavery propaganda infuriated the West
India interest as much as these sweeping assurances of improved labor
performance after the ending of slavery. As far as the planters were
concerned, abolitionists were propounding a general argument in defiance of transatlantic realities. The axiom of universal free labor superiority was extrapolated from a purely local experience. England
was the country in Europe where the desires for greater varieties of
products yielded "the greatest improvement of which human nature
is susceptible." However, insisted the defenders of Caribbean slavery,
political economists were well aware of how few laborers yet possessed the incentives requisite to this "positive" motivation for labor.
West Indians insisted that, even in the very heartland of industrial
England, free men still alternated between working when destitute,
and, if well paid, refusing to work for more than minimum comforts.[51]

For these workers, accumulating leisure was a better way of "bettering one's condition" than was maximizing one's income. Verification of this limited-aspirations hypothesis was found in the "short week" favored by many free industrial workers in Britain, and in the aversion to plantation labor by all free blacks in the Caribbean. As a substitute for subsistence satisfaction, the creation of unlimited wants remained more of an imagined future than a global reality. West Indians challenged "the whole world to produce a single satisfactory precedent, where a similar ratio exists between population, capital and space, of slaves, in any numbers, who have been made free, executing the necessary duties of tropical sugar labour for wages [or any equivalent income] consistent with the maintenance of the . . . necessary and average profits of plantations." They denied even *the probability of such a result.*[52] Planters' demands for compensation stemmed from that argument.

The condition of Haiti was of great interest to those who debated the merits of slavery and the merits of gradual abolition between the end of the Napoleonic Wars and the final mobilizations for immediate emancipation after 1830. For abolitionists, Haiti's reproductive performance was its principal asset. Although the numbers were hotly contested, Haiti's official figure, indicating a virtual doubling of the population from the outbreak of the slave revolution in 1791 to the 1820s, stood in sharp contrast to the declining slave population of Britain's sugar colonies. Haiti appeared to conform to Malthus's principle of high natural increase in regions of low population density.

On the other hand, Haiti's economic performance was a boon to West Indian propagandists who wished to demonstrate the inefficiency of free labor in the Caribbean. There was no disputing the fact that when slave St. Domingue became free Haiti, its position as the world's premier producer of tropical exports had long since vanished. By the 1820s, Haiti had been virtually eliminated as a sugar producer for the North Atlantic sugar market. Appeals to the Haitian case were rendered still more complicated by disputes about the place of its population on the spectrum from free to coerced labor. Slavery had disappeared, but Haiti's rural code allowed for deep infringements on personal liberties in the name of labor continuity. Was it the level of coercion that caused Haiti's low productivity and competitive failure, or had coercion preserved whatever was left of Haiti's productive and competitive capacity? When the British colonial secretary introduced the motion for immediate emancipation in 1833, he simply claimed that the San Domingo case was inconclusive and irrelevant. Many abolitionists and antiabolitionists agreed with him.[53]

Neither the arguments of Smith and Malthus nor the relative performances of Haiti and the sugar colonies convinced the British government to accelerate slave emancipation. Two major abolitionist mass mobilizations and the post–Reform Act election of 1832 reinforced the impact of the greatest slave uprising in the history of British colonization in Jamaica. Together they forced emancipation onto the political agenda of the first Reform Parliament in 1833. No contemporary suggested that the desire for more efficient free labor was a significant motive among Jamaican slave rebels or among the 1.3 million men and women who gathered to sign petitions for immediate emancipation in Britain.

Those responsible for the government of the colonies had to be more concerned about the anticipated motivations and performance of slaves on the verge of freedom. At the Colonial Office, James Stephen's son James feared the effects of the choices that would become available to the majority of laborers in the British Caribbean. Drawing upon the experience of Britain's other developing overseas colonies, he and others concluded that as long as labor had the option of access to cheap land the cost of labor would remain high, probably too high for the full maintenance of the plantation system. Henry Taylor, the head of the Colonial Office's West India division, was dismissively skeptical about the doctrine that slave labor was dear in the Caribbean. Taylor, Stephen, and Viscount Henry Howick, a convinced supporter both of emancipation and of laissez-faire in political economy, mulled over various combinations of legal constraints on prospective freedmen. Without exception all were designed to maximize the continuity of plantation labor.

Empirically, Colonial Office social planners and the slave interest were not far apart. In parliamentary hearings before emancipation, West Indian planters overwhelmingly testified that freed slaves never returned to the cane fields. Slaveholders inferred that freed slaves probably would not work at the prices offered to the owners of rented slave gangs during slavery. There was clearly a market for *non*-gang labor, which could be roughly reckoned at the prices of those slaves who were allowed to hire themselves out in various other occupations. As for the field slaves themselves, there is no evidence that they had any interest whatever in their potential cost-effectiveness as free laborers for planters. No parliamentary committee requested their testimony. Some leaders of the Jamaica slave uprising of 1831 seemed to have envisioned freedom in terms of working for wages. Others imagined remaining growers of sugar. Neither of these imagined futures (nor the destruction of crops and infrastructure occurring in so many uprisings) bespeaks a profit-and-production-oriented activity within the plantation complex.

Some historians assume the general dominance of a universalized "free labor ideology" in Britain in 1833. However, the distinction between constraints upon labor in high and in low density conditions was clearly assumed by all advocates of emancipation in the Colonial Office and in the Cabinet. They muted their public emphasis on the significance of the distinction for two reasons. Slaveholders were offering analogous arguments and would use them to argue for a delay in emancipation. Even after the House of Commons supported the government's general motion for immediate emancipation, such arguments could be used to maximize the coercive components in the detailed system of freed labor regulation. Abolitionists feared that West Indian planters would use any institutional opening to recreate an approximation of the old constraints. In Parliament, most abolitionists spoke in favor of reducing non-market constraints on ex-slaves to the absolute minimum that the majority would accept.

Outside Parliament, abolitionist propaganda stuck to the idea of an exclusive choice between *Wages or the Whip*, backed by the Smithian generic pronouncement on slave labor inferiority. There was no middle ground left between slave labor and free labor.[54] Emancipation, insisted the abolitionists, would now vindicate the superiority of free labor, even for the capitalists. But what, as the slave interest protested, if it did not? We have only fleeting glimpses about how the rank and file of those who attended abolitionist rallies and signed antislavery petitions reacted to the pessimistic prognosis. Responding to West Indian predictions of falling production, George Thompson, Britain's most popular antislavery lecturer, resolved the issue of post-emancipation production in a cascade of contempt. So what if Haitian exports were already down by two-thirds, and so what if the West Indian consumption of British exports was also to decrease? Would Ireland be worse off if she too exported less, keeping her produce "for home consumption"? The only reported response was "*Loud Cheers.*" Even Haiti and Ireland, contemporary bywords for economic failure, could not deter cheering antislavery gatherings.[55]

≺ III ≻

From British Emancipation to United States
Emancipation, 1834–1865

Between them, the great mass campaigns of 1831–33 and the Jamaica slave uprising of 1831 convinced Parliament and the government that there was no longer any middle ground between slavery and immediate legal emancipation. Members of the government and of Parliament, however, were not so sanguine about the potential outcome as were abolitionist crowds. The administration was deeply worried about the continuity of labor under a regime of wages. The colonial secretary, introducing the Emancipation Bill of 1833, called it a "mighty experiment." The notion stuck, and for a generation thereafter emancipation was referred to as "the great experiment." Radicals like Daniel O'Connell were prepared to express total confidence in the success of an immediate transition to wage labor, without either transitional limitations or monetary compensation to former owners. The abolitionist leadership, which had emphasized the need for special transitional measures in the Caribbean for 40 years, also reversed itself. Responding to demands and priorities from out-of-doors, they moved successive amendments to minimize the delay in arriving at complete freedom of contract.

However, for the majority of the political nation, the government, the colonial bureaucracy, the overwhelming majority in Parliament, and the West Indian commercial interests, continuity of sugar production was of vital importance. The final act reflected the deep uncertainty that free labor plantations would sustain, much less increase their previous level of production and thereby undercut slave labor competitors.[56] It provided for a huge compensation package of twenty million pounds. Masters were allotted up to six years of mostly unfree labor ("apprenticeship") from their ex-slaves. Above all, protective duties were continued in favor of British colonial sugar. In one sense, the maintenance of protection was a remarkable commentary upon antislavery propaganda. For a decade, abolitionists had taunted the West India interest for clinging to protective duties in favor of its own slave-grown sugar. This showed that "monopoly" alone shielded "a forced cultivation" from competition with free (that is, East Indian) sugar. If West Indian slave labor in the colonies was more productive than free labor, how did it happen "that in the case of the West Indies all the recognized principles of political economy should be thus strangely reversed"? What could better demonstrate that free labor competition would eliminate slavery? Yet at their moment of triumph, the abolitionists fell strangely silent about the possibility of realigning the West Indies with "all the recognized principles of political economy" and about convincing slave Cuba and slave Brazil of the inefficiency of slave-based "forced cultivation." Freely opposing the government both on the length of apprenticeship and on the terms of compensation, abolitionists silently consented to the continuity of protection.[57]

British legislators thus anticipated, although they underestimated, the "wear and tear" on the labor supply and discipline that would result from the transition. A "cushion" of West Indian surplus sugar for British domestic consumption had characterized British colonial production since the beginning of the nineteenth century. During the apprenticeship period (1834–38) the quantity of sugar exported from the British West Indies to the United Kingdom fell by 10 percent, while the London sugar price rose 40 percent.[58] Another wave of popular pressure forced the early termination of apprenticeship in 1838. West Indian production fell again. It now met less than two-thirds of British consumption.

The government erratically responded to pressures and counterpressures from West Indian proprietors, freedmen, consumers, abolitionists, and an increasingly powerful free trade movement. For the first time since 1807 British governments cautiously began to open the ex-slave colonies to transoceanic migrant workers: to voluntary and unencumbered labor from the Americas and Europe and to indentured contract labor from Africa and Asia. The flow of free labor from the Americas and Europe proved to be both insufficient in numbers and ineffective in performance. The flow of indentured labor from Africa and Asia was also initially hampered by the still-powerful abolitionist lobby, which denounced indentured labor as a new system of slavery.[59] The government also attempted to encourage the expansion of free labor sugar plantations in Africa and Asia. Its major African venture—the Niger expedition of 1840–41—was a complete disaster. Further east, the effort was more successful, but mostly in areas where one or another form of coerced labor system was introduced, indentured Indian labor in British Mauritius and the "Cultivation System" in Dutch Java.[60]

In terms of commercial pressures, the shortfall in Caribbean production combined with high metropolitan consumer prices to put both British colonial sugar producers and abolitionists on a collision course with the rising British free trade movement. A potential conflict had existed from the beginning of the abolitionist movement, when Dean Tucker had cautioned Ramsay that the Atlantic slave system would never really be undermined until sugar could be produced more cheaply by free men than by slaves. Tucker was totally wrong in one respect. During the 50 years after his warning British antislavery moved from victory to victory while sugar produced by non-slaves made little headway against slave-produced sugar. Before emancipation all metropolitan attempts, like those of the abolitionist merchant James Cropper, to form an economic coalition of East Indians, British industrialists, free traders, and abolitionists against the plantation slave system monopoly fell far short of abolitionist hopes or expectations.[61] The economic reason was clear. As political abolitionism got under way, British colonial sugar almost ceased to be effectively priced above world market levels. From the 1790s until slave emancipation "it was the world price which largely determined the remuneration which West Indian producers received. Had Foreign sugar been admitted at the same rate of duty it would not have affected the consumers by more than a few percentage points."[62]

If emancipation brought a sharp reduction in the exports of sugar and coffee to the metropolis from the British Caribbean, the first results seemed far more satisfactory from the perspective of the ex-slaves. Exports of sugar from the West Indies to Great Britain fell by nearly 30 percent in the decade after the end of apprenticeship, but exports of clothing from Britain to the West Indies rose by more than 50 percent between the years immediately before emancipation (1832–34) and the years following the abolition of apprenticeship (1839–44). Even more impressive was the sharp rise in West Indian wheat consumption. Wheat flour had never been more than an occasional luxury for most slaves, handed out to gangs assigned to hard labor, or as part of special Christmas rations. Given that basic tropical foods grew in abundance, imported flour and flour products were obvious post-emancipation indulgences. Imports of wheat flour to the British West Indies more than doubled from just before emancipation to just after apprenticeship.[63]

As emancipation loomed, West Indian planters had attempted to make the most of the earlier abolitionist concession that slaves did not yet have enough of civilized laborers' "artificial wants." In this sense the slaveowners' fears proved to be completely unfounded. Ex-slaves used their new wages and independent earnings to purchase riding horses, gigs, and conspicuously fine clothes. One of the major missionary champions of emancipation in the colonies happily testified to members of Parliament that freedmen in the islands "were decidedly better off than English workmen." A British Guiana magistrate asserted that "the peasantry, as a body . . . can boldly challenge comparison with the happiest and best paid laborers of the most fertile districts in England." The consumerist aspects of freedom, which had remained marginal to the abolitionist case before emancipation, now featured centrally in abolitionist discourse. References to the 30–40 percent decrease in British West Indies sugar could be countered by noting the sharp rise in the ex-slaves' standard of living and the stimulus this gave to British manufacturers. Wages were high, new villages were founded, and educational opportunities for ex-slaves expanded. At the end of apprenticeship even West Indian vagrancy and contract laws had to be made more lenient than they were in England. This legislation was rolled back in the 1840s, but only to the extent that it was made identical with British metropolitan labor statutes.[64]

The cost of these results, however, elicited a rising crescendo of hostile propaganda from consumer and free trade advocates in Britain. Emancipation dragged the question of free trade into the center of the debate over colonial sugar. The termination of colonial apprenticeship coincided with the re-emergence of free trade as an urgent public issue. Two protected interests were quickly fused in political discourse: West Indian sugar and English corn. The limits of the free labor ideology in abolitionist circles was again demonstrated at the second World Anti-Slavery Convention, in 1843. A free trade group attempted to alter the slave-grown sugar exclusion plank of the first convention in 1840. They argued for revision on the basis of free labor superiority, which the previous convention had also unanimously upheld. Refusing to accept free labor superiority as grounds for approving a change of policy, the chairman convinced the meeting to move the previous question.

The campaign for ending protection of free labor sugar came to a climax in 1846. Abolition of the domestic British Corn Laws was swiftly followed by the progressive reduction of protective duties favoring British colonial sugar. The debate leading up to this change had disoriented the abolitionist rank and file, sharply reducing their leadership's former ability to mobilize the larger public. Some abolitionists believed that the demise of plantation sugar would result in the expansion of smallholding and the "peasant option," or at least a combination of wages and subsistence farming satisfactory to the ex-slaves. Others feared that stagnant sugar production would be followed by a declining standard of living among free labor within the colonies and a negative assessment of the great experiment by other slaveholding societies. The latter tended to realign themselves with British West Indian planters in favor of continued protection. Free trade sympathizers countered that heavily protected sugar was already useless as evidence of free labor's superiority. The split fragmented the unified abolitionist movement in the mid-1840s.[65]

Within Parliament, even members who most strongly regarded the well-being of the ex-slaves as the "great experiment's" principal criterion of success could not ignore the government's general criteria of political and economic success. A dwindling number of die-hard abolitionists were reduced to fighting rear-guard actions in favor of differential duties on sugar grown by "free labor." As the victory of world free trade over protected imperial free labor became imminent, its most ideologically interesting effect in Parliament was the unanticipated revival of James Stephen's overt argument against free labor superiority. In 1833, no one could have

imagined that William Wilberforce's own son would announce in
Parliament, just thirteen years after emancipation, that West Indian free labor could not compete with slaves. Samuel Wilberforce
was as unequivocal in his pronouncement as the elder Stephen had
been 35 years earlier: slave labor in the Caribbean was "absolutely
cheaper" than free labor in raising sugar.[66]

British sugar production stabilized and slowly revived after the
crisis of trade liberalization. However, the revival came at the price
of a shift in the terms of labor, the expansion of the market in East
Asian indentured servants. What abolitionists in Parliament and in
the Colonial Office had once denounced as a "new system of slavery" was institutionalized as voluntary indentured migration to the
British colonies. During the 1850s the magnitude of this new
source of labor surpassed the transatlantic flow of African slaves,
now reduced by aggressive British diplomatic and naval action. In
contrast to the first four decades of the nineteenth century, the
British colonies now recaptured the major share of labor flowing to
the plantation Americas. While densely populated Barbados could
expand production without recourse to the new bondsmen, the recovery of sugar in sparsely populated Trinidad and Guyana depended heavily upon them. Jamaica, with lower fertility and less
recourse to migrant labor than Trinidad, and a far lower population
density than Barbados, stagnated.[67]

Planters "beyond the line" were uniformly unimpressed with
the great experiment. Even in relatively undynamic slave colonies,
whose imperial governments were vaguely committed to eventual
emancipation, slaveholders preferred the coercive discipline of
their slave plantations to the results they observed in the British
free labor colonies. Where planters could still acquire fresh slaves
for use on fresh land, they bought; where they were asked to participate in planning for emancipation, they balked. In Britain the
debate over the merits of free and slave labor now shifted from
sugar to cotton. As the United States' sectional crisis deepened, the
British metropolitan cotton interest requested government encour-
agement for further experiments in free labor for producing a product, almost 90 percent of which remained dependent upon slave labor. Former free trade industrialists of Manchester found themselves in the embarrassing position of pleading for political help in
developing alternatives to American agriculture. During the Amer-

ican Civil War they were concerned about enhancing the level of production in the cotton-growing systems of India, Egypt, Algeria, or Brazil, asking few questions about their levels of labor coercion.

≺ IV ≻

The Impact of the Debate in Britain

What were some of the long term implications of the discussion of free vs. slave labor carried out in the British press, lecture halls, and Parliament for nearly a century? The first was the novelty of the emergence of slavery's very existence as a major public issue. Before 1750, the question of slavery's comparative cost and efficiency was not a matter of political debate anywhere in the world. In the New World tropics, it was generally assumed that *some* form of bound labor was necessary to establish and expand commercially viable agriculture, especially in those activities requiring the organization of labor on a large scale. Before the rise of political abolitionism, no economist, including Adam Smith, maintained that slavery was less valuable or more expensive than free labor in the Caribbean sugar islands. When political abolitionists raised the possibility of substituting free for slave labor, they assumed a process requiring considerable time. Most of the early rulers of post-emancipation St. Domingue/Haiti likewise imagined that they could not dispense with coerced labor.

Abolitionist propaganda abstractly valorized free labor. Yet the superiority of free labor, endlessly restated, never became the centerpiece of the abolitionist argument—or even one of its high rhetorical priorities. The coincidence between coerced labor and New World sugar production, right down to British emancipation, was simply too close to overcome the doubts of planters and governments. Abolitionist leaders were themselves divided over the ability of free labor to sustain sugar cultivation competitively in the West Indies. Therefore British abolitionists tended to argue piecemeal and not always consistently from one measure to the next. Until the abolition of slave trade in 1807, they argued that "breeding" would prove to be more profitable than "buying." Between abolition and emancipation in 1833 they argued that wages were more effective than whips. The main point was always to limit the slaveholders' options: prohibiting transatlantic imports and constricting inter-colonial imports (1788–1834); constraining planters' abuse of laborers (1823–38); limiting apprenticeship and legal coercion (1834–38); maximizing the constraints on importing indentured labor (after 1838). During the 1830s and early 1840s abolitionists, at the height of their political influence, continued to narrow planter options, to denounce vagrancy laws and other modes of employer discipline, and to counteract planter manipulation of the new order. Some fought to maintain the briefly rising standard of living of the freedmen and to protect their bargaining position as workers against both metropolitan free traders and employers of indentured labor.[68] Over the long term, however, they could not persist in securing more protection for Caribbean free laborers than those available to metropolitans.

Insofar as abolitionists intensified the scrutiny of the conditions of slave labor in the sugar islands, they also stimulated scrutiny of free labor conditions at home. In the pre-abolitionist era the status of metropolitan laborers as "freemen" seems to have been an unexamined assumption. Aside from those affected by legally designated exceptions (Scottish miners, convicts, and apprentices) all laborers in Britain and all Europeans in the Americas fell under the rubric of freemen. For Adam Smith "the principal attributes of villanage and slavery being thus taken away from them they now, at least, became really free in our present sense of the word Freedom."[69] In the *Wealth of Nations*, waged workmen were invariably designated as freemen and always as the opposite of slaves, or serfs.

Ironically, the abolitionists' politicization of the free/slave dichotomy stimulated a political culture that consistently engendered negative images of metropolitan free labor. In other words, contrary to a hypothesis that antislavery rendered the ills of metropolitan labor less visible, abolitionism forced some members of an otherwise united elite, out of sheer self-defense, to expose the social costs of British free labor. If abolitionist petitions were often disproportionately supported by urban workers, antiabolitionists generated polemical critiques of metropolitan conditions. They did their best to publicize every sore of the British poor, those employed and those unemployed, those imprisoned in parish poverty and those displaced by clearances. As soon as abolitionists won their first major legislative victories, metropolitan radicals quickly adopted the iconography and imagery of abolitionism to compare the sympathy offered to African slaves with the unheeded complaints of "slaves at home."

With the abolitionist shift of focus to gradual emancipation in the 1820s, both West Indians and spokesmen for British labor compared the conditions of labor and workers' standards of living on both sides of the Atlantic. Abolitionists themselves emphasized the elements of slave treatment in the sugar islands, above all else the whip and sexual domination, that set slave labor apart from metropolitan labor. They avoided emphasizing hours of labor or material conditions of living, where differences were less obviously, if at all, in favor of metropolitan laborers.

Most significantly, each mass abolitionist mobilization escalated metaphors of enslavement in Britain among political radicals: in agitation against child factory labor, in protests against the hardening of the Poor Law, in arguments against the exploitation of women and the exclusion of the poor from the suffrage. Militant reformers found it advantageous to denounce waged labor as a variant of bondage "wage slavery." Occasionally the analogy was embarrassing enough to stimulate abolitionists into publicly aligning themselves with a particular metropolitan reform (e.g. child labor protection). The decades immediately before and after emancipation (c. 1820–40) were peak years for negative comparisons of British with Caribbean labor. The slavery metaphor was also effectively incorporated into the campaign against penal transportation in the 1830s and 1840s: "After 1834, to denounce any British institution as a form of slavery was to damn it." This propensity was reinforced during the late 1830s and early 1840s by the temporary coincidence of rising living standards among the ex-slaves and the onset of the hungry forties in Britain. The stage had been set for inflammatory racial polemics like those of Thomas Carlyle, comparing affluent idle blacks in the islands with impoverished and overworked British laborers at home.[70]

Invoking slavery and freedom as the two mutually exclusive forms of labor therefore had important cultural repercussions. Before the rise of abolitionism, slavery performed a variety of ideological functions. It served to differentiate freeborn Britons from an external world dominated by arbitrary power and abject servility. It also served to dramatize internal "assaults" upon metropolitan freedom. Recasting the binary opposition of freedom and slavery in terms of specific relations of production in Britain and the West Indies paradoxically increased slavery's potential ideological functions. The contrast was used both to reinforce the distinctiveness of British liberty and to illustrate its decline or subversion. Moreover, the same groups often responded to both themes. At one moment large numbers of Britons (including workers) were mobilized to sign petitions condemning overseas enslavement as unworthy of their free-born heritage. At another moment large numbers of people from the same groups were mobilized to condemn the decline of their own freedom or living conditions. The more detailed the criticism and the more popular the attack on colonial slavery, the more salient became the repertoire of antislavery rhetoric for deployment at home.[71]

Nevertheless, it is equally significant that the debate over colonial slavery did not lead to a concerted ideological attack against the elaborate provisions in English law to prevent servants, especially in agriculture, from leaving their masters before the terms of their service had expired. Even the slave interest's long litany of metropolitan ills failed to highlight the penal sanctions available to employers against laborers in Britain. The tactical reason for their omission seems clear. Had slaveholders concentrated on those sanctions, abolitionists would have pounced upon the differences between those sanctions and the array of uncontracted powers used by planters against their chattels. Abolitionists would have challenged West Indian planters to contract their power to match metropolitan legal standards. On the other hand, abolitionists seeking to stress the chasm between overseas slaves and domestic freemen rarely wanted to call attention to the very ancient fact that some British workers were still answerable with their bodies for breaching their labor agreements.

On only one occasion did abolitionists call attention to the penal constraints upon free metropolitan workers. In 1827, West Indian propagandists made much of the coercive provisions in Haiti's new Rural Code. Abolitionists quickly responded by referring to the sanctions listed in Blackstone's *Commentaries* against vagabondage and breaches of contract in England. Presumably, some forms of labor coercion were neither incompatible with civic freedom nor confined to the Caribbean. Nevertheless, abolitionists

were obviously uncomfortable about discussing coerced labor at
home. They self-protectively added: "We are not bound, neither are
we disposed, to bestow any laudatory epithets either on [these laws
of England] or on the corresponding clauses of the Haytian Code,"
or on their "humanity."[72]

Some historians of slavery have hypothesized that British antislavery campaigns effectively displaced public awareness of the
emerging labor conditions of the Industrial Revolution.[73] However,
those metropolitan ills were persistently targeted in response to
abolitionist campaigns. First West Indians and later political radicals protested the increasing number of English women and children pushed into mines, mills, factories, and workhouses. Nor did
the large numbers of men, women, and children pushed from their
homes and fields in Scotland go unnoticed. If the debate over slavery overlooked any aspect of metropolitan labor relations, it was
the laws for enforcing labor contracts of free-born English agricultural laborers.[74] The most "traditional" of labor coercions in Britain
was the least directly targeted abuse in the long debate over slavery.

For 50 years the abolitionist leadership did successfully con-
strain the geographic terms of imperial labor relations. There was
relatively little discussion of slavery in the British East Indies before the Emancipation Act. The magnitude of slavery and other
forms of coerced labor in India and Ceylon was not seriously considered until the termination of "Negro Apprenticeship" in 1838.
Only then was India prominently placed on the British abolitionist
agenda. In 1840 it was on the agenda of the first World Anti-Slavery
Convention, held in London. The number of "slaves" in India was
quickly discerned to be far greater than those who had already been
liberated by the Act of 1833. Equally significant was the recognition of Eastern diversity. Bondage in India seemed to lack the sharp
"capitalistic" features of slavery in the New World. This belated
recognition of the variations and complexities of "free" laborers in
India was to become a defining characteristic of the post-emancipation generations.[75]

As the line between Eastern and Western slavery blurred it became clear that a century of debate over the relative merits of free
vs. slave labor had been both initiated and constrained by a mass
movement to eradicate the differences between conditions of labor

in Britain and in her slave colonies. The superiority of free labor, "demonstrated" universally by political economy and exemplified in the history of western Europe, was projected "beyond the line" in order to extend the benefits of freedom throughout the British empire and the entire world. After three generations of intense debate the discussion began to break out of the dualistic frame of reference in which both the abolitionists and their targets had conducted it.

As the political stakes were reduced by full legal emancipation, Herman Merivale offered a comprehensive retrospective of the process of abolition. His *Lectures on Colonization and the Colonies*, delivered at Oxford in the immediate aftermath of colonial apprenticeship (1839–41), were reprinted, with additional comments, on the eve of the American Civil War. Merivale, Professor of Political Economy at Oxford, and Undersecretary for the Colonies, was now prepared to consider slavery as eminently fit for a professor's chair, but the discussion acknowledged the impact of the abolitionist crusade. Merivale expressed his anxiety about presenting a "mere economical consideration" on matters "so deeply interesting to every social and moral feeling of our nature."

Merivale registered the impact of another historical process on the discussion of slavery. Surging British migration to the temperate zones of the planet encouraged a further globalization of the discussion of overseas labor. He sought to integrate Caribbean labor into the general phenomenon of the terms of free labor in societies with low densities of population. In this frame of reference, Australian convict labor, not Caribbean slave labor, was the "dearest labor of all."[76] Merivale now boldly brought Smith's unheralded reservations about the optimality of free labor to the foreground. He accepted the axiom of the dearness of slave labor with an italicized caveat: *"wherever abundance of free labour can be procured."* "Beyond the line" was back in action. In Merivale's reading, New World slavery reemerged as an eminently rational response to conditions in the Americas and the tropical Atlantic system. Within this frame of reference both Smith and Say could be recruited to support the unequivocal conclusion that it was more profitable to cultivate the virgin soil of the Americas by the "dear labor" of slaves than to cultivate the depleted soil of Europe by the "cheap labor" of freemen.[77]

Nor was slavery an anachronistic residue from an earlier stage of history. It was an integral part of the capitalist present. Not only could slave labor produce more agricultural value in Cuba than could free labor in France or in Germany, but it could continue to do so for the foreseeable future. Merivale made his economic prognosis unequivocal: "no economical cause can be assigned on which we may rely for the extinction of slavery." Abolitionists who hoped for a gradual redefinition of capitalist interests were delusional, at least until the forests of the Americas had been cleared and cultivated from the Atlantic to the Pacific. The gap in Smith's explicit analysis of the special nature of the Atlantic slave system allowed Merivale to imagine a hypothetically unending stream of slaves across the Atlantic economy unless checked by countervailing political power.

In this perspective, the abolition of the British slave trade in 1807 was "the real death-blow" to British West Indian prosperity. The good news, at least for fellow economists, was that the coming of free trade in sugar had not caused, and might even have averted (through economic shock therapy), the complete downfall of the British West Indian sugar interest. The upshot of Merivale's analysis was that large-scale production of exportable tropical staples would probably continue to be organized by compulsory labor, whatever the results of the "experiments then in progress."

The Caribbean labor force would also continue to be non-European, partly the result of the high mortality rate of Europeans in the tropics. What had been conventional wisdom in the mid-eighteenth century was a global statistical conclusion a century later. Empirically, mounting evidence showed that the "wear and tear" of Europeans was greater in the West Indies than in the temperate areas of the Americas or the South Pacific to which they were overwhelmingly choosing to migrate. In 1860, as in 1760, non-European compulsory labor was still the labor of choice for rational capitalists who chose to cultivate the vast undeveloped parts of the tropics. The robustness of Merivale's prediction was amply demonstrated during the century after British slave emancipation. The twenty millions who left India, mostly as indentured servants, between the 1830s and the 1910s amounted to twice the number of Africans forcibly landed in the Americas during the four centuries of the Atlantic slave trade.[78]

The phenomenon of indentured servitude, ignored by Adam Smith, forced itself back into the economists' field of vision. Merivale did not even bother to disguise the fact that the new stream of indentured servants flowing into the West Indies was not "free" labor, even if it was not the old slavery. For Merivale, indentured servitude rather evoked the analogue of military recruitment, both in the benefits (reliability) and the drawbacks (inefficiency) brought by such recruits to the plantations. In the canefields, all of the potential dexterity, ingenuity, frugality, and efficiency of free laborers was not a sufficient substitute for the continuous presence, reliability, and pliability of indentured servants, answerable with their bodies for breaches of contract.

Unlike their mid-eighteenth century predecessors, political economists of the mid-nineteenth century had no need to invoke extra-economic motivations, such as the urge to domineer, in order to explain the establishment and maintenance of slavery. The choice of slavery overseas could be entirely accounted for in terms of the peculiar but widespread combination of soil fertility, population densities, and tropical commodities. J. E. Cairnes would offer the same combination of economically active ingredients to explain the character, career, and aims of *The Slave Power* (1862) in the United States of America at the time of Southern secession. Neither Merivale nor Cairnes took issue with Smith's emphasis on the superior efficiency of free labor *qua* labor. They did take firm issue with the universality of that superiority. From the perspective of both capitalists in the tropics and economists in Britain, free labor simply had not been, nor was it now, "superior" to slavery. Absent abolitionism, slavery was simply a way of organizing scarce or reluctant labor, a condition which has recurred throughout human history rather than occurring only at its beginning.[79]

Despite all these concessions to the rationality and profitability of slavery in their own and perhaps future generations, mid-nineteenth century British political economists had more access to evidence in favor of the superiority of freedom than their eighteenth-century predecessors had possessed. Comparisons confined to British metropolitan and colonial labor systems had produced not-always-reassuring conclusions about the relative condition of European peasants and proletarians. However, the rapid development of nineteenth-century overseas zones of free labor also constituted a broadening evidentiary base in favor of freedom. Merivale's invocation of Alexis de Tocqueville's contrast between dynamic Ohio and sluggish Kentucky was only one striking example.[80] By 1860, industrial New England and the mid-Atlantic states and agricultural Australia and North America implied that freedom within social relationships, in general rather than in particular labor relationships, assured the long-run superiority of the free society tortoise over the slave society hare. Political economy could not predict the distant moment when compulsory labor would finally succumb, but it forecast the ever more rapid expansion of prosperous free labor in the frontier of the temperate zone.

≺ V ≻

Conclusion

What, then, of the "great experiment" in the British West Indies? The results were mixed, and especially disappointing to those who had held out the brightest hopes for simultaneous increases in commercial productivity and in the ex-slaves' standard of living. One great target audience of the experiment, the planters and governments of other slave societies, seemed particularly unimpressed. Although British Caribbean laborers in 1860 still seemed remarkably orderly in comparison with their European counterparts, very few ex-slave colonies had demonstrated an ability to expand or even sustain production without the further aid of compulsory labor. Exemplary successes, like Barbados, were not frontier societies like the United States, Cuba, and Brazil. Compared to the "triumphant progress" of free labor communities in North America or in the southern Pacific; or to the "scarcely less brilliant, though sinister and insecure prosperity of Cuba and Louisiana," the British Caribbean colonies in 1860 seemed "stationary at best, subsisting but not accumulating."[81] They matched neither their American free labor brethren in their standard of living, nor their Cuban slave labor brethren in productivity. They were already assuming the status of less-developed societies that would be theirs over the following century.[82]

For British consumers, the results were of diminishing significance. A decreasing proportion of their sugar came from the British

West Indies. By 1860, the literature comparing free labor in Britain and in the British Caribbean was also diminishing in quantity and intensity. In general, the British Caribbean was a place "where no marked improvement strikes the eye, even where there are no signs of absolute decay."[83] "Race" subtly gained credence as an explanatory device. Merivale vigorously defended black workers against "the common" representation of them as destitute of the ordinary capacity of workers. In densely populated Barbados they were "as regular in their daily labour as the operatives of the old communities of Europe." Even there, however, their numbers made the planters less anxious to innovate. No ex-slave colony received an evaluation as clearly progressive.[84]

The imaginary line between free and slave labor that ran between northwestern Europe and most of the rest of the world when Adam Smith wrote the *Wealth of Nations* had shifted a century later. Political action had ended or provided for the gradual ending of slavery throughout the zones of expanding European settlement. However, penally coerced labor continued to be the dominant form of labor in the production of commercial crops in the tropics. With the repositioning of the line between free and unfree labor, race loomed larger than ever as a dividing line in determining the migratory flow of labor.

The great debate over the relative merits of free and slave labor ended with the return of the excluded middle. In this sense the battle between advocates of slave labor and those of free labor in the Atlantic system was a dramatic interlude between periods of more nuanced assessments of the performance of labor under various regimes of constraint and choice. During the age of British abolitionism, political economists were probably more wary of offering deflationary assessments of free labor superiority than either before or after. Even at the height of abolitionist influence, however, there never seems to have been a moment when faith in free labor superiority reigned uncontested in Britain, including among the abolitionist leadership.[85] The idea of such superiority was also vigorously challenged in Europe, Africa, and America.

In cultural terms, the true measure of the abolitionist achievement lay less in a national conversion to the superiority of free labor, than in the psychological "wear and tear" wrought by abolitionist political agitation against doubters always on the moral defensive. The overwhelming asymmetry of mass opinion that slavery had to come to an end may have caused a very brief suspension of disbelief in the high risk of commercial failure. Colonial slavery did not, however, come under massive and sustained attack in Britain because it was incompatible with capitalism. Still less was it brought to an end because it was a defective form of capitalist labor. Antislavery mobilized against those non-economic characteristics of colonial slavery that most distinguished it from contemporary legal and social relations in western Europe. Viewed from Britain, New World slavery rested upon an extraordinary, and extraordinarily brutal, exercise of power. It was institutionally, if not always empirically, indifferent to the dignity, the bodies, and the relationships of the enslaved. Masters could claim nearly absolute property rights in the persons they bought or inherited. Such claims extended well beyond the demand for "ordinary labor service," as the most dependent laborer in England understood that service. Masters routinely escaped public punishment for acts that would have cost them their liberty or their lives in the metropolis. In this sense, the supreme achievement of the abolitionists was to have shifted the terms of debate over the terms of colonial labor by eliminating chattel property from the range of options available to employers. In a process drawn out over three generations, the attack upon slavery also set in motion a series of changes that altered the terms of labor in other parts of the globe as well.[86]

After Serfdom: Russian Emancipation in Comparative Perspective

PETER KOLCHIN

THROUGHOUT THE WESTERN WORLD, "freedom" was the watchword of the nineteenth century. In a remarkably short period of time, slavery, serfdom, and forced labor in general—for centuries accepted as legitimate and compatible with human progress—came to seem backward, inefficient, and immoral, while "free labor" acquired the status of God-given norm, decreed by both economic and natural law. Beginning with the northern states in the aftermath of the American Revolution and ending with Brazil a little more than a century later, systems of coerced labor fell throughout Europe and the Americas, replaced by a confusing medley of social relations that differed in many ways but were all based on relationships defined as "free." In terms of numbers of people involved, by far the largest of these social transformations occurred in Russia, where in 1861 an imperial decree initiated the emancipation of approximately twenty-three million privately held serfs.[1]

Contemporary observers recognized the importance of the Russian case, first as a symbol of reaction and oppression in an increasingly liberal world, and then as a confirmation of their faith in the triumph of free labor. Western travelers routinely linked Russian to American bondage as remnants of an earlier era, and described the stifling impact of serfdom on Russia—"farms are untilled, enterprise deadened, invention crippled, education neglected . . . labor is the badge of servility"—much as they did that of slavery on the American South.[2] Once Russian emancipation was under way, Western abolitionists seized upon it as a heaven-sent lesson for the southern United States, heaping exaggerated praise on the "tsar-liberator" Alexander II and suggesting that if autocratic Russia could so enthusiastically embrace liberty, surely democratic America could do the same. Arguing for land distribution to the ex-slaves, Pennsylvania's Radical Republican Congressman Thaddeus Stevens termed the tsar a "wise man" for providing the ex-serfs with land; "the experiment," he proclaimed, "has been a perfect success." Even more enthusiastic was English missionary J. Lang, who praised the Russian government for its enlightened behavior at a time when "American slavery . . . is still a fearful blot" and suggested that "the influence and example of these emancipated serfs will operate on the world, and will show that, while so bene-ficial a revolution has taken place successfully in Russia, other countries may learn to 'go and do likewise.'"[3]

What, in fact, was the reality of Russian emancipation, and how did it compare with emancipation elsewhere? I would like to pres-ent an overview of this question, focusing on four broad topics. First, I will give a brief summary of the process of emancipation in Russia, outlining the general terms of the emancipation settle-ment. Second, I will examine agricultural labor relations, looking at what replaced the coerced labor that had been at the center of serfdom. Third, I will address the question of change versus conti-nuity: to what extent did emancipation produce significant changes in Russia, both in the lives of the peasants and in society at large? Finally, I will discuss the responses to emancipation and the struggle among different groups of Russians over the meaning of freedom. In treating these topics, I would like to keep a broad comparative perspective, examining the Russian case in the con-text of developments elsewhere (especially the United States South), for I believe that those developments can help shed light on Russian emancipation at the same time that an examination of what happened in Russia raises questions of fundamental interest to students of the Americas.

≺ I ≻

The Process of Emancipation

Emancipation came to Russia, as it did almost everywhere else, from above—albeit with considerable prompting from below. (The one great exception occurred in the French colony of Saint Dom-ingue, where slaves took advantage of divisions created by the

French Revolution to wage their own revolution, culminating in the creation of the Republic of Haiti in 1804.)[4] Slaves and serfs were hardly passive recipients of freedom: depending on local circumstances, they took advantage of specific conditions (such as the American Civil War) to strike blows for freedom and undermine the old order;[5] in many countries, either rebellion or the fear of rebellion helped persuade authorities of the need for change.[6] In Russia, however, as in Brazil, Jamaica, Martinique, Prussia, and the United States South, it was a central or metropolitan government that made the final decision for emancipation, over the widespread opposition of slaveholders and serfholders.

Despite their unhappiness, however, the Russian masters, like those almost everywhere else—the one great exception *here* was the United States South—acquiesced in the emancipation decision, once that decision was made. They groused and grumbled, but lacking the locally-based independence and political power of planters in the United States South, they did not offer armed resistance to abolition.[7] Their subservience, ironically, strengthened their position in post-emancipation society. From the point of view of the central government, southern slaveholders were traitors who had abdicated their right to help shape the new dispensation; Russia's noble landowners (*pomeshchiki*), by contrast, remained the bulwark of the autocracy and were given an important role in implementing the new order. Equally important, their interests received substantial consideration.

The emancipation manifesto of 1861 was hardly the result of a hasty decision. Historians continue to disagree over the precise motivation of Alexander II and his advisers in opting for abolition. Some stress their fear of peasant unrest, while others emphasize their perception of serfdom as an impediment to economic development or military efficiency, a perception reinforced by Russia's disastrous showing in the Crimean war of 1854–56. Although the coming of abolition is beyond the scope of this chapter, suffice it to say here that the final decision to proceed with emancipation was based on a consensus reached over several decades at the highest governmental levels that serfdom was an anachronism—in social, political, economic, and moral terms—that must, somehow, at some time, be abolished. This consensus was already well established before Alexander II's accession to the throne in 1855; his predecessor Nicholas I, who reigned from 1825 to 1855, established no fewer than ten secret governmental commissions that grappled unsuccessfully with what was euphemistically termed the "peasant question." Preparation of the emancipation legislation under Alexander followed the same tortuous route: over a four-year period it was discussed and debated by one ad hoc committee after another, at both the central and the provincial levels, before finally being promulgated by the tsar on February 19, 1861.[8]

Almost as significant as the consensus over the desirability of emancipation was a second consensus, reached only gradually and over intense opposition from many noble landowners and their spokesmen, that together with their freedom, peasants should receive—and pay for—land. Instrumental in this decision was the desire to "keep the peasants peasants," that is, to avoid the emergence of a large landless proletariat that would threaten social stability and introduce the kind of social tensions and antagonisms that conservative Russians widely associated with Western Europe. (High-ranking officials were familiar with previous landed emancipations undertaken in Prussia and Austria, but the men who debated the terms of the coming Russian emancipation typically accentuated the uniqueness of the Russian social order and insisted—in the words of one prominent nobleman—that "in setting about to change our peasants' way of life . . . we must not imitate, but create something new and distinctive." More on the minds of Russian policy-makers than the positive example of previous landed emancipations was the negative example provided by the peasantry's supposedly abysmal plight in Russia's three Baltic provinces, where some 800,000 serfs had been the beneficiaries of a landless emancipation between 1816 and 1819. Although opponents of reform continued to stress the inviolability of noble property rights and to argue that a landowning peasantry would be disastrous because "without supervision and incentive, the majority of peasants . . . are so lazy that to sustain themselves they prefer beggarliness to work," the government architects of emancipation—and Tsar Alexander himself—agreed that emancipated peasants must have their own land.[9]

The Russian emancipation decree not only was the product of far more careful preparation than its American equivalent; it also set in motion a far more complicated operation. The thirteenth amendment to the United States Constitution consisted of 43 words barring slavery and involuntary servitude, "except as a punishment for crime," and giving Congress power to enforce the amendment with "appropriate legislation." The legislation accompanying Alexander II's emancipation manifesto contained hundreds of pages of densely-written text, divided into numerous separate acts, rules, appendices, and decrees. But the length of the legislation pales into insignificance compared to its complexity. The manifesto was read in church services and on public squares, and copies of the legislation were distributed by special couriers not only to government officials but also to noblemen and peasant representatives on estates throughout the empire. As one historian noted, however, the act was "so verbose, so full of variables, so loaded down with qualifications and exceptions, and in general so astonishingly involved and complicated, that it is difficult to understand how any serf could ever by any possibility have known what rights might be hidden in this legislative haystack." One is tempted to replace the word "serf" with the word "historian."[10]

Let me try to summarize the terms of emancipation, providing a drastic simplification of its extraordinarily complex and confusing provisions.[11] The new legislation created an elaborate governmental machinery to oversee the transition to freedom. At the local level, a new group of officials known as "peace mediators" were to supervise peasant affairs and peasant-landlord relations. Appointed by provincial governors, all the peace mediators were noblemen and most were serfowners themselves. The number of mediators— initially 1,714, or typically 30 to 50 per province—was reduced in 1865, and the institution was finally abolished in 1874. Supervising the peace mediators (and rural life in general) was a vast array of new administrative agencies: at the district (*uezd*) level, the District Conference of Peace Mediators (and, later, the District Office for Peasant Affairs); above it, the Provincial Office for Peasant Affairs; and at the top the Main Committee for the Organization of Village Condition. All the members of these agencies—as well as other officials who interacted with them, including the district police chief (*ispravnik*), the district marshal of nobility, and the provincial marshal of nobility—were noblemen.[12] And below them, the former serfs remained subject to still another administrative level composed of peasant officials.[13]

The February 19 manifesto and legislation initiated a gradual rather than an immediate emancipation. Serfs received their "personal freedom" at once—they could no longer be sold or arbitrarily subjected to punishment, and they now had the right to marry at will, participate in judicial proceedings, and own personal and real property—but they remained under the "estate police and guardianship" of their former owners. Equally important, as "temporarily-obligated" peasants they continued for the time being to owe those owners essentially the same labor (*barshchina*) and quitrent (*obrok*) obligations they had as serfs, although the obligation to provide their owners with payments in kind (such as butter, eggs, milk, and chickens) ceased "immediately and everywhere."[14]

Under the watchful eyes of the peace mediators, landlords (or their representatives) were within one year to draw up "statutory charters" specifying the obligations and land allotments of their temporarily-obligated peasants, following detailed guidelines that varied according to local conditions. The statute that covered Great Russia, New Russia, and Belorussia established three geographic zones (nonblack-earth, black-earth, and steppe), which in turn were subdivided into nine, eight, and twelve "localities." For each locality, a guideline was set for the maximum and minimum size of peasant landholdings, calculated collectively for an entire estate, with the minimum equalling one-third the maximum (except in the steppe zone, where rather than a minimum-maximum range there was a prescribed allotment that varied according to local conditions). *Barshchina* would henceforth be limited to 40 days per year for men and 30 days for women; in the place of most compulsory labor, the temporarily-obligated peasants would owe their former owners an annual *obrok* in cash, ranging from 8 to 12 rubles per male "soul" for peasants holding the maximum allotment, and proportionately less for those with smaller holdings.[15]

Once drafted, a charter was to be presented to the peace mediator for verification, with the help of the owner or his agent, six peasant representatives, and "three conscientious outside witnesses" (usually neighboring peasants); if a landowner failed to compose a charter on time, the peace mediator was to draft it himself. The verified charter would then be read to all the peasants, in a communal gathering, and signed by representatives of all parties; if the peasants did not approve a charter, they would instead indi-

cate the reasons for their opposition. The peasants' approval, however, had little bearing on the ultimate implementation of a charter: in the absence of their consent, the peace mediator was obliged
to attach a detailed explanation of their objections (and, under certain circumstances, to get the approval of the Provincial Office for
Peasant Affairs) but he was not obliged to pay any heed to those
objections. Indeed, a majority of charters were implemented without receiving peasant endorsements.[16]

All charters were to be in force by February 19, 1863, two years
after the issuance of the emancipation manifesto. At the end of
this two-year transition period, house servants received full freedom—but no land. All other serfs remained "temporarily obli-
gated," however, until—through a complex process known as "redemption"—they began paying for their land allotments and became "peasant proprietors."

Redemption of the peasants' "farmsteads" (usad'by)—the small
plots of land attached to their houses—was mandatory immediately upon implementation of the statutory charters, but redemption
of their much more extensive field land was a long, drawn-out af-
fair that could occur either through a voluntary agreement between
temporarily-obligated peasants and their landlord or through that
landlord's unilateral decision. The peasants' redemption bill was
determined by capitalizing their annual obrok at 6 percent; that is,
a six-ruble obrok would yield a redemption price of 100 rubles. An
alternate option was for peasants to accept small allotments—
equal to one-quarter the maximum size—with no redemption payments; fewer than 10 percent of the serfs—although the number
was much higher in some areas—opted for these so-called "gratuitous" holdings.

The redemption of the remaining allotments was handled in a
complex three-sided arrangement involving government, landlords,
and peasants. The government advanced pomeshchiki most of the
redemption money that they were to receive from their peasants—
80 percent if the peasants received maximum-size holdings, 75 percent otherwise—partly in 5 percent government bonds and partly
in certificates that would gradually be converted into such bonds.
Those landlords who had imposed redemption on their serfs received only this 75 to 80 percent, but those who had come to voluntary agreements with their serfs received the additional 20 to 25

percent of the redemption fee directly from the peasants, under
terms mutually agreed upon, usually involving payment in money
over several years but sometimes involving payment in labor as
well. Far more onerous to the peasants was their obligation to re-
pay the government—with interest—the money it had advanced on
their behalf; this repayment was to be spread out over 49 years,
with each annual installment amounting to 6 percent of their redemption loan (and thus the equivalent of their old *obrok*). The
peasants' total redemption payment, stretched out over 49 years,
would equal 2.94 times the value of their redemption loan (.06 x
49).[17]

The pace of peasant redemptions—which in most cases had to
be undertaken collectively, by commune, not by individual peasants—was initially slow; at the beginning of 1864, fewer than one-
tenth of all former serfs had left temporarily-obligated status. The
rate of redemptions picked up, however, in the second half of the
1860s, before slowing once again in the 1870s; by early 1870 about
two-thirds of the former serfs were peasant proprietors, and by 1881
more than four-fifths were. (Of these, slightly under half had come
to voluntary agreements with their landlords; the majority had redemption imposed on them.) Two imperial decrees of 1881 transferred all remaining temporarily-obligated peasants to redemption
status as of 1883, and slightly reduced the payments that both they
and existing peasant proprietors would henceforth owe. Still, the
peasants continued to struggle with their redemption payments for
another two and one-half decades until, under mounting revolutionary pressure, an imperial manifesto of 1905 cut those payments
in half for 1906 and canceled them entirely beginning in 1907.[18]

How should one characterize this emancipation process, aside
from pointing to its complexity? A number of comparative observations seem pertinent. Russian emancipation was gradual, like that
in many other places—such as Prussia, Brazil, and the British colonies—but unlike that in the United States South. Russian masters
found their interests well looked after through financial compensation undertaken by a sympathetic government, like slaveowners in
the British West Indies and noble landowners in Prussia and Austria but, again, unlike masters in the southern United States. The
Russian peasants received land, but they were forced to pay for it—
at an inflated price, with interest.[19]

One may also judge emancipation in terms of continuing societal interest in the well-being of those freed. Here, I think, Russia followed something of a middle course. The former serfs did not suffer the kind of neglect experienced by freedpeople in post-emancipation Brazil, where after abolition the government paid little attention to the plight of the ex-slaves; indeed, the "peasant question" continued to be at the heart of Russian thought and a central concern of government policy. In this respect, Russia may be said to have experienced a post-emancipation "reconstruction" period—one of general reform activity followed by reaction—in much the way the United States did, and the peace mediators may be thought of as a rough Russian equivalent to Freedmen's Bureau officials in the United States.[20] And, like emancipation in the southern United States, that in Russia generated an enormous amount of paperwork, much to the delight of subsequent historians.[21]

But in contrast to the situation in the United States, where the Civil War left a Federal government more concerned with the rights of the freedpeople than with the interests of their masters, in Russia the machinery in charge of supervising emancipation remained in the hands of those with a vested interest in limiting the scope of change. The conservative orientation of the Russian emancipation program is clearly reflected in the drafting of the statutory charters, for asking landlords to draw up charters outlining the new relations with their peasants smacks of nothing so much as asking the foxes to guard the chickens. Given the complexity and class bias of the emancipation legislation of 1861, as well as the enormity of the undertaking, it is in many ways hard to imagine a less promising formula for the transition to freedom than that prescribed for the Russian peasants.

≺ II ≻

Free Labor

Despite this unpromising framework, emancipation was part of—and an impetus to—a significant social transformation that touched diverse aspects of Russian life. This transformation by no means obliterated traditional relations, for much of the old persisted even under radically new conditions. This was especially true of peasant life, which changed substantially less, I think, than the life of southern blacks in the 1860s. Overall, however, emancipation nudged Russia away from the old order—a conservative, autocratic society dominated by a small landed elite—toward the new, in which hereditary privilege played a diminished (and diminishing) role.

Let us begin with the labor system, for that was at the heart of serfdom and central to the hopes and fears of virtually everyone touched by emancipation, from the peasants who worked the land and the noblemen who owned both them and the land to the bureaucrats who agonized over how to abolish bondage while preserving social stability. If the nature of the old system was clear, the essence of the new was remarkably murky. Determined to forestall the emergence of a large landless proletariat, the framers of the emancipation legislation had decided on a landed emancipation. But if the emancipated serfs were to receive land of their own, who would cultivate the fields of their former owners? And on what terms? What, in short, was "free labor" all about?

In approaching this question, it is useful to start by considering briefly the nature of the old order that was now being replaced. Russian serfdom was a complicated system that, originating in the sixteenth and seventeenth centuries with the binding of peasants to the land, had evolved by the second half of the eighteenth century into something close to chattel slavery. Juridically, the power of a *pomeshchik* over his serfs differed little from that of an American planter over his slaves. Serfs could be bought and sold, assigned as much work as an owner chose, and punished according to that owner's arbitrary whim. During the first half of the nineteenth century, the government passed a series of laws designed to prevent "mistreatment" of serfs, but similar laws concerning treatment of slaves were widespread in the southern United States (and elsewhere). In both Russia and the United States, it was against the law to kill or torture a bondsman or woman; in both, despite occasional interventions, the law provided only very tenuous protection to the bound population. Significantly, both defenders and opponents of serfdom frequently used the word "slavery" (*rabstvo*) in describing the condition of the Russian peasants—the same word they used to described the condition of black slaves in America.[22]

The juridical bondage provided by Russian serfdom shaped but did not entirely define the labor system that accompanied it. Russian historians have traditionally distinguished between "serf law" (*krepostnoe pravo*) and "serf economy" (*krepostnoe khoziaistvo*), and the distinction is a useful one. Although in theory, a noble serfholder owned everything on his estate—including land and peasants—most peasants were allotted land, collectively, which they came to regard as their own. Many *pomeshchiki* were absentee proprietors, but even when they were not they typically interacted little with their peasants (except for those who were house serfs), dealing with them primarily through intermediaries—managers, stewards, and elected representatives of the peasant commune. Badly outnumbered,[23] most noblemen felt uncomfortable in the presence of their peasants and practiced a considerable amount of "benign neglect" toward them, allowing them to organize their lives according to their own traditions, so long as they produced the requisite income. The peasants, meanwhile, came to accept as theirs by right what was theirs by custom: "we are yours," the peasant tells his owner in the popular proverb, "but the land is ours."

Under these circumstances, a dual economy characterized Russian serfdom, one in which peasants both supported their owners and engaged in their own economic activities.[24] Serfs owed their masters a variety of obligations, which could include labor, money, or goods, or a combination of these. At the same time, the serfs were required to support themselves: they fed themselves from produce that they grew on their allotted land, and depending on local conditions, they also engaged in various handicrafts, such as woodworking, and hired themselves out to engage in work that could range from barge hauling to factory labor. During the last century of the serf regime, Russia was increasingly marked by a regional division of labor: in the fertile "black-earth" region, noblemen typically sought to maximize their own agricultural production and therefore required extensive labor services from their serfs. (Legally, *pomeshchiki* could impose as much labor as they wanted on their serfs, but according to widely-accepted custom, the norm for adult workers was not "supposed" to exceed three days per week.) In the more northerly "nonblack-earth" region, noblemen were less interested in agricultural cultivation, and frequently imposed *obrok* rather than labor obligations on their serfs; such serfs had more time to engage in their "own" cultivation, as well as in "proto-industrial" employment. In the terminology of the American South, they were allowed to "hire their own time."

In short, the serfs worked both their owners' land and their "own" land (which legally belonged to their owners). This dual system continued to operate after emancipation as well, although not in precisely the same way. The removal of the element of coercion that was at the heart of serfdom required some immediate modifications, and additional changes occurred over the course of subsequent decades.

With respect to *land*, the essence of the emancipation settlement, as reflected in the provisions defining statutory charters and redemption, amounted to requiring the peasants to purchase the allotments that they had customarily used as serfs. The land that they received, however, was not always the same—either quantitatively or qualitatively—as what they had previously held; drafting and implementing the charters led to widespread readjustments of peasant landholdings. Peasants whose holdings exceeded their locality's maximum allotment, as prescribed by the emancipation legislation, suffered "cutoffs" (*otrezki*), while those with holdings smaller than the minimum gained "add-ons" (*prirezki*); other peasants chose the "gratuitous" allotments equal to one-quarter the maximum size but requiring no redemption payments. While some peasants gained and others lost land in this process—*pomeshchiki* were especially eager to encroach on peasant holdings where land was most valuable—the charters provided on average for a modest but significant reduction in the size of peasant landholdings. In addition, because *pomeshchiki* played the dominant role in drafting the charters, peasants often found that their new allotments were less desirable than their old in terms of location, fertility, or access to water, woods, and roads.[25]

With respect to peasant *obligations*, the essence of the emancipation settlement was to replace the labor and *obrok* that serfs had owed their masters with the redemption payments that they now paid for the purchase of their landed allotments. The size of these payments was based on the size of the *obrok* dues set in the statutory charters, which in turn were on average modestly lower than the old *obrok* that serfs had paid. Compared to peasants who had

been on *barshchina*, for whom the end of obligatory labor constituted an enormous immediate benefit, those who had previously
been on *obrok* experienced substantially less material change. As
before, these peasants were allotted land; as before, they made annual payments (previously *obrok*, now redemption). But because
the charters typically provided for larger reductions in the size of
allotments than of *obrok*, the annual redemption payments owed
by post-emancipation peasants were slightly higher—calculated per
desiatina of allotment land—than their *obrok* payments had been
under serfdom.[26]

After emancipation, peasants continued to cultivate both their
own land and that of their former owners. Widespread fears on the
part of *pomeshchiki* that without compulsion there would be no
one to work their land proved to be greatly exaggerated. In the immediate aftermath of emancipation, there were some reports of a
decline in the quantity and quality of work that peasants performed on noble lands. Reporting from Kaluga province in the
spring of 1861, for example, the Emperor's personal envoy, Major
General N. G. Kaznakov, noted that cultivation of seigneurial land
was significantly reduced, although he considered "exaggerated"
the estimates of local *pomeshchiki* that one-quarter of the normal
spring crop remained unsown; "of course," he added in a comment
more typical of provincial noblemen than high government officials, the labor of temporarily-obligated peasants "cannot be as
successful as serf labor, under the fear of personal and speedy punishment by the owner."[27] But other reports suggested that agricultural work was proceeding normally, and in general emancipation
in Russia caused substantially less disruption of routine agricultural cultivation than it did in the southern United States, let alone
much of the Caribbean. In most areas, peasant allotments were too
small to provide full support for their proprietors; as a consequence
peasants often had to supplement the meager income they could
eke from their land with outside work that included work for
neighboring *pomeshchiki*.[28]

Former serfs worked for noble landowners under a variety of arrangements. Upon occasion, eager to cultivate good relations with
powerful neighbors, peasants performed small tasks for noblemen
"out of respect," without payment. The free labor system that replaced serfdom, however, was predicated on compensation for

work. Some peasants hired on as wage laborers for nearby *pomesh-chiki*, either on an annual basis or for occasional odd jobs. Others worked under a version of sharecropping known as *otrabotka*, whereby in exchange for cultivating a *pomeshchik*'s land (usually with their own implements), they received additional land from that *pomeshchik* for their *own* cultivation. Still others became migrant laborers who every year left their villages in the spring and traveled south and east to the steppes, where they were recruited at "hiring fairs" to work on huge, grain-producing estates for periods ranging from one to six months.[29]

Despite continuing peasant cultivation of noble lands, emancipation initiated a gradual, long-term shift from noble- to peasant-dominated agriculture. Many noblemen—who under serfdom had already shown strong absenteeist tendencies—balked at the prospect of directing the labor of free peasants, and numerous reports circulated during the 1860s, 1870s, and 1880s of landowners forsaking agriculture for less stressful occupations. "The gentry let their estates go after Emancipation, neglected the fields and meadows, and ran off into [government] service," complained nobleman A. N. Engelgardt in 1872, soon after arriving at his ancestral estate in Smolensk province for the first time in fifteen years. "The gentry do not farm, they have abandoned the land, they don't live on their estates." In fact, despite regional variations—the decline in noble landholding was greatest in the nonblack-earth provinces; by contrast, in the most fertile regions, including especially the steppe land of the southeast, large-scale commercial farming by noblemen continued to prevail—such laments accurately depicted the overall trend, as noblemen continued to sell and rent land to peasants eager to expand their insufficient allotment holdings. Between 1861 and 1905, the amount of land owned by nobles decreased by about 40 percent; by the latter date, nobles owned only 22.1 percent of Russia's agricultural land, whereas peasants owned 67.9 percent. (The remaining 10 percent was owned by merchants and members of other intermediate classes.) Even these figures substantially understate the decline of noble agriculture, however, since some noble-owned land was *rented* to peasants. Unlike the American South, where former slaves gained only a tiny fraction of the land and planter-dominated agriculture continued to characterize the economy, post-emancipation Russia saw the relentless "peasant-ization" of agriculture.[30]

Evaluating emancipation's impact on the broad contours of land and labor relations is a tricky undertaking, the outcome of which depends in part on one's perspective. In one sense, not much changed. Serfs held landed allotments and owed their masters obligations that were paid in cash, kind, labor, or a combination of these; ex-serfs held landed allotments, owed redemption payments, and sometimes worked for noble landowners or paid them cash in exchange for land to augment their existing holdings. Not only did the redemption price that noblemen received exceed the existing value of the land, but peasants owed interest on their redemption loans that over the decades almost equalled the principal debt. Meanwhile, as the peasant population grew, the size of their holdings—measured per soul or per household—decreased, so that peasant holdings in 1905 were smaller than they had been under serfdom. No wonder most peasants—and many Soviet historians—judged emancipation to be a "predatory, serfholder's reform," one that led more to impoverishment and suffering than to fulfilling aspirations for true freedom.[31]

Despite these harsh realities, however, emancipation produced a fundamental realignment in the relationship of labor to land and peasant to nobleman. Under serfdom, noblemen had owned virtually all of Russia's private land (that is, land not held by the state or court), as well as the peasants who lived on that land. The emancipation settlement freed those peasants, ended their compulsory labor obligations, and—in exchange for payments that were usually slightly smaller than those that serfs on *obrok* had owed to their masters—gave them legal title to more than half the land that had previously been noble-owned. Although the redemption price of that land exceeded its 1861 value, a sharp rise in the price of land during the remainder of the nineteenth century meant that in terms of *current* value, the peasants' land was soon worth substantially more than they paid for it. Meanwhile, during the half-century after 1861, noble landowners disposed of an additional 40 percent of the land remaining in their hands immediately upon emancipation, mostly in sales to peasants. In short, a serfholding economy based on coerced labor had been transformed into a peasant economy in which noblemen owned less than one-quarter of the land and engaged in substantially less than one-quarter—perhaps as little as one-tenth—of the agricultural production. The continuity that marked many areas of day-to-day life masked a major transformation in the social and economic order.[32]

≺ III ≻

Change and Continuity

This theme of fundamental transformation masked by very real continuity is evident in many areas of life in post-emancipation Russia. Let us begin with the economy. Despite the grandiose predictions of Russian free labor advocates, who, like those in the United States and Britain, assumed that abolition would usher in a golden era of progress and prosperity, post-emancipation Russia remained backward. Indeed, in terms of such basic indices as per capita income and infant mortality it actually fell further behind the economically advanced nations of Western Europe and the United States during the half-century after emancipation. The period did see significant industrial development, however, as well as accelerated urbanization, increased agricultural output, and an economy that grew at an overall rate of some 2 percent annually between 1860 and 1880 and somewhat faster thereafter. In short, although most Russians remained abysmally poor, the post-emancipation years saw significant economic modernization.[33]

It is worth noting that in this respect the Russian story differed sharply from that of some other post-emancipation societies—especially those in the Caribbean—and resembled that of the United States South. In much of the British West Indies, emancipation dealt a sustained blow to the commercial economy, as ex-slaves withdrew in massive numbers from plantations and sought to set themselves up as independent proprietors; Jamaica did not regain its pre-emancipation level of per capita income until 1932. Events were similar in Haiti, where blacks fell into a condition of impoverished autarky with the almost total collapse of sugar production; by the twentieth century, the land that was once the pride of France's American empire had become the poorest country in the New World. In the southern United States, by contrast, emancipation did not herald the collapse of the commercial economy; indeed, production of cotton for market expanded to include a significant number of upcountry whites who had been isolated from the market before the Civil War. Although the post-emancipation South remained substantially poorer than the North, it experienced rapid industrial development. The South, like Russia, experienced a prolonged agricultural depression during the late nineteenth century, a depression that produced severe hardship in both countries; neither, however, suffered the devastating economic dislocations that occurred in much of the West Indies after emancipation.[34]

Economic development in post-emancipation Russia was accompanied by a series of social reforms designed to bring the country into the nineteenth century. (In this respect, too, developments in Russia resembled those in the southern United States much more than those in the Caribbean or Brazil.) The emancipation settlement of 1861 applied only to serfs, who were privately held by noble landowners; similar reforms were extended to peasants held by the royal family in 1863 and to those held by the state in 1866. Reforms aimed at modernizing the army cut the normal term of military service to six years followed by nine more in the reserves (under Nicholas I it had been reduced from twenty-five to fifteen years), sharply curtailed use of corporal punishment, and introduced a more equitable system of conscription. Legislation in 1864 totally overhauled the archaic judicial system, simplifying the court structure and significantly reducing the arbitrary quality of Russian justice. A final important reform of 1864 was the introduction of local self-government in the form of provincial and district zemstvo assemblies which, although dominated by noblemen, included peasant representatives as well.[35]

The changing character of Russian society is particularly evident in the fate of the nobility. The conventional wisdom that the post-reform nobility suffered an economic crisis has been challenged—I think effectively—in recent years. What is clear, however, is that the nobility underwent a transformation. Before emancipation, it represented an entrenched elite, a hereditary caste with a host of legally defined privileges of which the most important was the exclusive right to own serfs. Although estate distinctions—and especially estate consciousness—persisted, the abolition of serfdom sharply reduced the significance of being a nobleman and initiated Russia's transition, in historian Seymour Becker's words, "from a society based on estate privilege to one based on the legal equality of individuals." "Nobility will end, in Russia

as in other countries, by being a mere honorary distinction," predicted Frenchman Anatole Leroy-Beaulieu in 1893.[36]

The declining salience of nobility is evident in a number of indices, but probably the most significant are those that reveal the nobility's separation from the land (see above, section II). This separation
should not be taken as a sign of noble poverty; land rose sharply in
value during these years, and *pomeshchiki* who sold their land received substantial compensation. It is a sign, however, of the nobility's transformation from a privileged landowning estate to a diverse
group of landowners, businessmen, and professionals; whereas in
1861 about four-fifths of all noblemen held land, by 1905 fewer than
two-fifths did. An even more dramatic drop occurred in the proportion
of government officials who were landowners, as government service
expanded at precisely the same time that noblemen were abandoning
the land: by 1902, only about 14 percent of civil servants were noble
landowners. It is this kind of change that has led one historian of the
Russian nobility to conclude that "by the end of the century the first
estate was no longer a meaningful social entity."[37]

And what of the peasants? Emancipation brought them a pleth-
ora of changes, big and small, obvious and obscure. Gone were the
days when they had to secure their master's permission to marry or
travel off the estate; gone were the days when they had to fear that
an owner's irascible temper would subject them to corporal punishment. "All right, Aleksandra Sergeevna, here's for you," cried a
peasant woman in Kaluga province upon learning that she no
longer had to provide free provisions for the noble table; "now I'm
free," she proclaimed as she "unceremoniously gave the finger (a
greasy finger) in the direction of the manor house." The most immediate change that peasants felt was an increase in freedom that
significantly reduced interference in their personal lives.[38]

Peasants used this increased freedom in a variety of ways. Like
the freed slaves in the southern United States, they associated education with their new status and enthusiastically sponsored the
formation of village schools, schools that were only later taken
over by the government.[39] They took advantage of their new geographic mobility (again, like the former slaves) to pursue economic
opportunities, as increasing numbers left their villages to seek employment elsewhere, often in a nearby city.[40] Within the villages
there was an increase in social stratification.[41]

Emancipation also affected family relations among peasants. As many men sought employment away from their home villages, women took on new roles and suffered new burdens. "In the villages there remain only the elderly, young children, and women," complained one observer from Kaluga province as early as 1863. "More and more, agriculture lies on the[ir] shoulders."[42] Meanwhile, the extended family came under increasing pressure. Serfdom had bolstered the authority of the *bol'shak*, the head of the peasant family who ruled with an iron fist over the three-generation household. But now, as one observer put it, "Along with the bond between master and serf, that between father and son—the family bond, has become slackened. They have tasted of freedom, and . . . in the same way that the serf is rid of the master's yoke, the son strives to rid himself of the yoke of paternal authority . . . Young couples want to be independent of the old people. They each want a house and lot of their own." As newly-married couples moved to set up on their own, the size of peasant households tumbled; in Voronezh province, for example, the average number of peasants per household fell from 9.49 in 1858 to 6.87 four decades later.[43]

These changes, most of which in a variety of ways increased peasant autonomy, were highly significant. Nevertheless, it is important to put them in proper perspective. Russian serfs generally suffered considerably less owner interference, and hence enjoyed considerably more independence, than did most American slaves.[44] The increased autonomy made possible by emancipation, therefore, represented a less dramatic break with the past for Russian peasants than it did for American blacks.

Indeed, many of the changes that occurred simply reinforced tendencies that already existed. When Russian noblemen abandoned the land, they were fulfilling the logical culmination of their longstanding absentee orientation; emancipation now enabled them to go one step further, and dispose of their landholdings entirely. Similarly, the increase in peasant stratification that followed emancipation represented not an entirely new phenomenon, but rather the accentuation of a longstanding pattern, for the relatively high degree of peasant autonomy had permitted considerable stratification even under serfdom.[45] In short, there was a basic cultural continuity that survived many of the new departures; to oversimplify, one might suggest that whereas in the American South emancipation made it possible for blacks to strike out in new ways, in Russia emancipation made it possible for peasants to develop more fully many of their traditional ways.[46]

Nowhere is this so evident as in the augmented authority of the *mir*, or village commune. Literally constituting the world of the peasants ("mir" means world and peace as well as commune), the *mir* was a pervasive peasant institution under serfdom, what one prominent historian has described as "the organizing basis of all village life." Through it peasants ordered their lives and handled day-to-day problems. Through its elected representatives, the commune settled minor disputes among peasants, maintained a reserve of grain and money to help the needy in time of crisis, and determined who should be drafted into the army to meet the village's quota of recruits. In most of Russia (but not in the Ukraine or Belorussia), the commune periodically reallocated peasant land allotments and obligations, to make sure that the burden was shared relatively evenly; everywhere, communal officials served, simultaneously, as the landowners' lowest level estate administrators and as the peasants' representatives in dealing with those landowners (and with the outside world in general). Noblemen—and the government as well—usually had little to do with individual peasants; instead, they dealt with them through the commune. Russian peasants lived, to a degree unknown by American slaves, highly communal lives.[47]

In two ways, emancipation accentuated the centrality of the commune. First, the emancipation legislation explicitly recognized the commune as an organ of local self-government and expanded its role by introducing a new administrative level, the township (*volost'*), which consisted in most cases of several communes. Second and more important, by sharply reducing the authority of landlords over peasants, emancipation left the commune's authority strengthened in relative terms; communes rather than noble lords, for example, now decided whether, and under what circumstances, peasants could leave their home villages. As historian Alfred J. Rieber has recently noted, "the state had virtually no effect on peasant culture . . . It was a kind of absentee government."[48]

It is not just the commune's formal authority, but also the continuing loyalty of peasants to traditional communal values, that remained central to rural life. Such loyalty is evident in their continued suspicion of almost all outsiders, including populists who came to preach revolution among them and teachers who came to uplift them. It is also evident in their widespread conviction—despite real enthusiasm for learning to read and write—that "too much" education, especially for girls, was dangerous because it would subvert traditional ways.[49] But it is perhaps most strikingly evident in the persistence of "samosud" or communal mob justice, whereby peasants meted out their own punishments to troublemakers rather than resort to formal court proceedings.

Such punishments, determined communally in the village assembly, often involved ritualized ceremonies similar to Western European charivaris, designed to shame (and hence control) perpetrators of minor offenses such as petty theft and adultery. Here, as one scholar has described it, "the typical . . . performance consisted of parading an offender through the street either on foot or in a cart, in some cases wearing a horse collar, while villagers followed along . . . beating upon oven doors . . . pots and pans, washtubs . . . and singing songs. Women were often stripped naked or had their skirts raised before being led around the village; men might first be stripped and then tarred and feathered." But peasant justice could also impose far more gruesome torture on those deemed true threats to the communal order. Horse thieves—widely detested as the basest of villains—"were castrated or beaten in the groin until they died, had stakes driven into their throat or chest, were branded with hot irons, and had their eyes put out." Those accused of witchcraft (usually old women) were sometimes drowned, burned, or beaten to death.[50]

In short, traditional values displayed remarkable persistence. Peasants continued to look upon the commune as their world, one that provided security in an age of change and confusion. The end of serfdom brought major changes to Russia, but rather than leading to the rationalization of village life that many reformers expected, emancipation, by augmenting the already considerable autonomy of the commune, actually reinforced the peasants' commitment to many of their traditional ways.

≺ IV ≻

Disillusionment

In order to understand this continued peasant commitment to traditional ways, and why it proved so disturbing to so many Russians
who were *not* peasants, it is necessary to come to grips with the
differing ways in which Russians understood—and responded to—
freedom and free labor. Concerned about the potential for disorder,
the government went to extraordinary lengths to explain the nature of the emancipation settlement and prevent the spread of
"misunderstandings." These efforts included a two-week initial delay in releasing the emancipation manifesto, to avoid risking peasant disorders during pre-Lenten Carnival Week; the widespread distribution to peasants, noblemen, and government officials of the
emancipation manifesto and legislation; directives to church officials on how to make sure that local priests would explain the legislation "according to the letter of the law" rather than "spread any
kind of false rumors"; and the dispatch to each province of a special high-ranking imperial emissary whose job was to ensure the
orderly initiation of the emancipation process. Nevertheless, confusion and misunderstanding quickly set in, as different social
groups reacted to emancipation with remarkably different hopes,
fears, and expectations. "I have the manifesto and legislation on
the peasants," wrote an estate steward from Nizhnii Novgorod
province, "but so far it is difficult for me to understand them
clearly." Confusion soon gave way to disappointment and disillusionment, and by the 1870s a widespread sense of failure existed
among almost all social groups, a feeling that somehow things had
gone terribly wrong.[51]

Disillusionment prevailed among the peasants almost from the
start. Long adhering to what Soviet historians termed "naive monarchism"—that is, the belief that the tsar was really on their side
but was prevented from carrying out his just will by the greedy noblemen and corrupt officials who surrounded him—peasants expected much of emancipation and inevitably received too little to
satisfy those expectations. They possessed a strong sense of their
rights, one of the most important of which was their right to the
land. Now, in February 1861, the day of deliverance seemed at
hand.[52]

What they heard when the emancipation provisions were explained to them, however, was another matter. The details were confusing enough; who knew what all this talk was of statutory charters and temporarily-obligated status, of peace mediators and gratuitous holdings, of redemption and capitalizing *obrok* payments at 6 percent? What was clear was that this was not the *real* freedom they had been promised, that someone was trying to put something over on them. Almost immediately, rumors expressing an intense sense of betrayal began circulating among the peasants, rumors that the "golden charter" the tsar intended to announce was being suppressed by nobles and officials, or that the emancipation edict needed to be "read properly" by people who knew how to interpret it, or that those peasants who withheld giving their approval to the statutory charters would receive real freedom on February 19, 1863, exactly two years after the initial manifesto. "We do not recognize the manifesto of February 19," villagers from Subulak, in Orenburg province, told a local official, "because the tsar promised us liberty, but now they force us to pay or work for land, and there can be no liberty without land."[53]

A surge of unrest swept the countryside during the spring of 1861, as peasants resisted imposition of what they were convinced was a fraudulent emancipation settlement. The period of most intense violence came to an end by the middle of the summer, with the opening of the new organs of rural administration, but a high level of tension continued to engulf the Russian countryside, tension that sporadically flared into confrontation. If specific grievances triggered specific acts of resistance, the more generalized backdrop for the unrest was the peasants' widespread dissatisfaction with the terms of the emancipation settlement, dissatisfaction that facilitated the spread of "false rumors" and the holding out for a *real* freedom that would give the former serfs the land they worked and end the obligations they owed to their former masters. Convinced that right—as well as the tsar—was on their side, peasants refused to work under conditions that smacked of serfdom, refused to sign statutory charters that seemed to perpetuate the old order, and continued to trust in the coming of a new dispensation that would usher in the real freedom they knew was coming. Time after time, peasants expressed their disbelief in the terms of the new order. Arriving at an estate in Voronezh province to verify a statutory charter, peace mediator Astaf'ev found "that the peasants of the village of Vsesviatskoe consider the statutory charter not only contrary to their expectations, but totally illegal and arbitrary"; when he read the charter to the assembled crowd of 150, almost all of them cried out, "We do not want it, this will not be! We will not allow this!" Only after the district police chief arrived with soldiers two weeks later did the unrest subside, but the official still considered it prudent to leave a military command in the village to prevent the recurrence of trouble.[54]

After early 1863, with completion of the statutory charters, the rural disorders gradually subsided. During the post-emancipation decades, however, peasants continued to harbor a deep feeling of betrayal, even as they also continued to have faith in the goodness of the tsar. One way that they expressed their resentment was by refusing to pay their redemption fees, or paying less—later—than they owed; by the 1870s, peasants almost everywhere had fallen into massive arrears on their redemption payments. And in the late 1870s and early 1880s, as the twentieth anniversary of emancipation neared, rumors once again circulated about the imminent arrival of the long-awaited "true" freedom, which would include distribution of noble lands. Pointing to the spread of "socialist propaganda" that included accusations that "the nobles want to murder the tsar" because he intended to confiscate their land, an alarmed landowner in Tambov province wrote to the head of the political police that peasants were talking of the need to "wring the landlords' necks" and "distribute property and land. The local police take no measures against this," he lamented, "and hardly even know about it."[55]

Other Russians found the course of events equally disillusioning. Liberal and radical intellectuals, who during the preparation for emancipation in the late 1850s had felt real excitement over the impending changes and had reveled in the new intellectual freedom of Russia's first era of *glasnost'*, quickly became embittered by the government's failure to fulfill their hopes for a democratic society. In 1858, exiled publicist Alexander Herzen, flush with anticipation of the coming emancipation, had shared Thaddeus Stevens's evaluation of Alexander II as a "tsar liberator"; "the name Alexander II henceforth belongs to history," he exulted. In 1861, after learning the details of the new settlement, Herzen's influential paper *Ko-*

lokol (*The Bell*) denounced the imposition of a "new serfdom"; proclaiming the people's need for "land, liberty, and education," it declared that "the land belongs to no one but the people."[56]

Noblemen, meanwhile, resented the loss of status that accompanied the freeing of their serfs, complained that under the new dispensation peasants were refusing to fulfill their obligations, and as we have seen increasingly manifested their displeasure with rural conditions by abandoning their landholdings. Others, especially in the 1880s and 1890s, sought to recapture the good old days by taking part in a "noble reaction" in which they preached conservative values, advocated a return to the land, and strove to preserve the purity and exclusivity of the nobility in the face of the rise of supposedly crude, money-grubbing capitalists. Before emancipation, ownership of serfs had been the chief common denominator— and privilege—of the nobility; with the loss of that privilege, noblemen also lost a sense of purpose and self-definition and experienced an inevitable sense of decline.[57]

To government officials, who ran the gamut from liberal reformers to steadfast reactionaries, everything seemed to be going wrong as well. Peasants and noblemen were both dissatisfied; former serfs were increasingly falling into arrears in their redemption payments; the countryside was still mired in poverty; and peasant villages were marked by ignorance, superstition, corruption, and inefficiency. A sense of spiralling crisis led to the appointment of commission after commission, whose members, beginning in the 1870s, vigorously debated what had gone wrong; once again, the peasant question—supposedly resolved by the reforms of the 1860s—was at the center of the debate. Although commission members approached this question from varying perspectives, they increasingly focused on that central peasant institution, the commune. Conviction that the commune sapped individual initiative and was a prime source of rural inertia and backwardness led eventually to the so-called Stolypin reforms of 1906, designed to enable peasants to acquire personal title to their communal land allotments and to consolidate widely separated strips of land into compact parcels.[58]

Recently, historians have begun to question whether conditions were really so bad in post-reform Russia. Some have denied that there was an agricultural crisis, arguing that production (and pro-

ductivity) expanded throughout the last third of the nineteenth
century. Others have challenged the prevalence of peasant poverty
and noble decline. These challenges have, in turn, provoked rebut-
tals from those convinced of the accuracy of the traditional picture.[59]

It is not my intention to get involved here in this complex debate, for I believe that the sense of failure and crisis that pervaded
so much of Russian society in the post-reform era stemmed less
from "objective conditions" than from the inner dynamic of emancipation and its aftermath. It is worth noting that perception of
tragedy, of failure, of things gone wrong was pervasive in numerous
other post-emancipation societies, from the Caribbean to Brazil.
Nowhere was the transition from coerced to free labor easy or pain-
less; everywhere, emancipation was followed by intense class
struggle marked by differing understandings of what freedom was
all about, and a general sense of disillusionment over what was to
have been the dawning of a bright new era.[60]

It was in the United States, however, that feelings of hardship,
disappointment, failure, and missed opportunities most closely ap-
proximated in intensity those in Russia. Blacks, adhering to their
own particular version of "naive monarchism," looked to the federal government to provide them with 40 acres and a mule; like
Russian peasants, many of them subscribed to what Frederick Law
Olmsted termed "the agrarian notion that the result of labour belongs of right to the labourer," and found it difficult to conceive of
freedom without possession of the land they had worked. Instead of
receiving such freedom, however, they suffered from racial discrimination and new forms of exploitative labor relations. Other
groups were hardly happy with developments. Southern whites
bemoaned their humiliation by the hated Yankee conquerors who
supposedly placed the "bottom rail" on the top; northern whites
who went south after the Civil War as teachers, missionaries, and
politicians were ostracized, reviled as "nigger lovers," and subjected to escalating physical violence. Northern Republicans, too,
suffered bitter disillusionment, either with the Reconstruction
process itself or with the failure of the government to sustain it. To
almost everyone, in short, it seemed as if things were going
wrong.[61]

I would suggest that such perceptions of failure—in Russia as in the United States South—were dictated less by the reality of harsh conditions (although conditions were harsh) than by the dynamics of emancipation itself. Emancipation accomplished a great deal; in both countries historians commonly associate it with a basic transformation—some use the term "revolution"—of society.[62] But revolutions often prove disappointing to supporters as well as opponents, for they typically raise expectations that are almost impossible to meet. This was certainly true of emancipation, which in both Russia and the United States generated enormous excitement associated with reform movements—Reconstruction and the Great Reforms—followed by sharp political and social reaction.

Thoughtful observers, whether foreign or Russian, sometimes recognized this process of dashed expectations. British journalist Sir Donald Mackenzie Wallace, for example, attributed the negative view of emancipation that he found among educated Russians in the 1870s to "shattered illusions. They had expected that the Emancipation would produce instantaneously a wonderful improvement in the life and character of the rural population, and that the peasant would at once become a sober, industrious, model agriculturalist," he continued. "These expectations were not realized." The same point was made by Frenchman Anatole Leroy-Beaulieu, who described emancipation as a "revolution" and "a great success" but noted that "to many of those who took part in the work, it proved disappointing." Asking how this "seeming anomaly" was to be explained, he drew a direct analogy with the French Revolution: "In the same way that, in France, the failure of 1789 and the bankruptcy of the Revolution have been proclaimed, the bankruptcy of the emancipation and the failure of the reforms have been denounced in Russia."[63]

An especially revealing—and two-sided—approach to this theme of dashed expectations came from the pen of Aleksandr Nikitenko, a highly unusual former serf who, after securing his freedom as a young man in 1824, became a university professor and government official and left a remarkable diary of his life as an official censor. On the one hand, as a Russian, Nikitenko expressed a typical disillusionment with the course of post-emancipation events. Noting that "in the early years of the present regime I was enthralled by its splendid and noble beginnings, which promised Russia a better order of things without upheavals and victims," he

observed that "it wasn't long before I became bitterly disillusioned
and convinced that it was our fate to begin fine deeds but not to
carry them to their conclusions." Increasingly conservative, he deplored the "shameless radical strivings of this generation" even as
he lamented the arbitrary rule of the autocracy, the small-minded
and self-serving character of the bureaucracy, the greed of the nobility, and the ignorant lethargy of a peasantry "not yet roused
from a thousand-year sleep." "How will it all end?" he inquired in
despair. But at the same time, as an observer of Russian society,
Nikitenko saw through the very disillusionment that he himself
expressed, and explained the social despair that gripped Russia in
terms of dashed hopes and subjective perceptions. Noble landowners "had expected to receive some new rights" in return for giving
up their serfs, but "their expectations were not fulfilled, and so
now they are dissatisfied." "The condition of the peasants"—
whom Nikitenko elsewhere labelled "practically perfect sav-
age[s]"—"has generally been improving since their emancipation,"
although "their mode of life is still very unsatisfactory almost everywhere in the empire." Meanwhile, gripped by unrealistic expectations, reformers had grown despondent. "They expected that the
most orderly existence . . . would logically follow [the reforms];
that our ways would immediately change for the better; that industry and agriculture would flourish; that wealth would flow through
the entire country like a river." But "all these golden dreams did
not come true. You can't change overnight what has taken centuries to ruin and distort."[64]

I would submit that the extraordinary expectations with which
so many Russians approached emancipation virtually guaranteed
that it eventually would be viewed as a failure. This was especially
so because despite widely shared hopes that emancipation would
usher in a glorious new era, participants differed sharply in precisely what they expected. Reformers, both in and out of government, typically saw emancipation as part of a revolution that
would produce a prosperous "free labor" society of hardworking,
industrious, and frugal citizens. Almost everywhere, however, the
bondsmen revealed that their conception of freedom differed from
that of either their former masters or their liberators. Their goal, as
they demonstrated in a variety of actions, was not increased efficiency, but rather increased autonomy and independence. In this

desire, they took part in the effort typical of freedpeople elsewhere as well to build their own "moral economy" rather than become the kind of "free" workers envisioned by the architects of the new social order. The continued adherence of Russian peasants to the "customary law" of the village commune was matched, for example, by a marked preference of blacks in much of the southern United States for sharecropping over wage labor, which to many of them did not seem so different from slavery, and by a widespread withdrawal of Jamaican blacks from the plantation economy. More than anything else, the freedpeople wanted to do things their own way.[65]

There is an irony here, for at the same time that former bondsmen decried the new dispensation as not sufficiently free, they demonstrated an unexpected attachment to many of the old ways. If "freedom" was a term that almost everyone found appealing, it was also a contested concept over which people continued to struggle. The freedpeople and their "benefactors" had very different ideas about the nature of the new order—about the meaning of freedom and of "free labor"—and were bound, at some point, not only to be disappointed but to be disappointed in each other. In Russia, that disappointment shaped much of the history of the post-emancipation era.

From Autonomy to Abundance:
Changing Beliefs About the Free Labor
System in Nineteenth-Century America

LEON FINK

THE MEANING OF FREEDOM when related to the workplace has long been both idealized and contested by Americans. Even in the early colonial period—when the greatest proportion of people were toiling in one or another unfree state—the facts of "free land" and scarcity of labor offered the potential of hitherto undreamed-of advantages for the laboring classes. The debates of the Revolutionary and Constitutional eras first considered the problems of wealth, poverty, and labor in a young republic. The nineteenth century, however, marked by conflicts over slavery on the one hand and industrial revolution on the other, offered more distinctively American responses to the age-old questions, who shall work? and for what terms? In this chapter I mean to concentrate on the changing perspectives which nineteenth-century Americans adopted toward the free labor system. In addition I want to emphasize the continuing uncertainty—built into our laws, our industrial relations, and our popular culture—over what restrictions if any the concept "free labor" imposes on the nature of work itself as well as on the worker's relationships to others beyond the workplace.

In 1970, the American economist Evsey D. Domar, with debts both to a turn-of-the-century Dutch scholar, Herman J. Nieboer, and to Adam Smith's *Wealth of Nations*, posited a "land/labor ratio thesis" as a barometer of the likelihood of a coercive (characterized by serfdom or slavery) versus free (or market-driven) labor system in a given society. Of the three relevant elements to Domar's thesis—free land, free peasants, and non-working landowners—"any two elements but never all three can exist simultaneously." Testing a model which seemed especially apt for the early-modern Russian countryside, Domar affirmed with only slight hesitation its workability for the American case. "The American South fits my hypothesis with such embarrassing simplicity as to question the need for it," he proclaimed. It was obvious, in short, why slaves were imported. With abundant economic alternatives, no free people could be harnessed to the tasks required by a landowning class. The only uncertainty for Domar was "the failure of the North to use [slaves] in large numbers . . . Besides social and political objections, there must have been economic reasons why Negro slaves had a comparative advantage in the South as contrasted with the North."[1]

Critics have tended to jump on the land/labor ratio thesis as an all too crude and narrow explanation of a complex social system like slavery.[2] For my purposes, however, the problem with the thesis is not only the rigid economism mandating labor regimes but also the utterly passive and residual meaning (*not* slave, *not* serf) attached to the concept of free labor. As we shall see, in the nineteenth century, when they were most self-consciously preoccupied with the subject, Americans decidedly did not agree among themselves on what they meant by the free labor system under which, at least by the end of Reconstruction, they all professed to live.

≺ I ≻

Free Labor in the Early Republic

In the earliest years of the American Republic, tension surrounding both the concept and lived experience of free labor lay just below the surface of a culture adjusting to political democracy. National leaders of the immediate pre- and post-Revolutionary period tended to subordinate—if they did not openly denigrate—democratic economic claims, favoring instead mercantilist or free-market models of national wealth creation and social stability. Among out-and-out defenders of class hierarchy, for example, Alexander Hamilton openly mistrusted popular government and backed a democracy limited to those with wealth and learning, while John Adams believed both in a "natural aristocracy" of talent and an inevitable quest for distinction and conspicuous luxury by those in the "upper ranks" who will always try to distance themselves from the lower classes.[3] But for others, less politically or culturally patronizing of the masses, it was the logic of the marketplace itself which imposed limits on what could be done to endow free labor with a measure of social protection. Benjamin Franklin, for example, the ex-printer who would long serve for some precisely as a symbol of opportunity for the free laborer, in his own writing relied on classical political economy and the law of supply and demand to deny that the rich oppress the poor or that any instrument beyond workers' own lazy habits was to blame for social inequalities.[4] And even the artisan-hero Tom Paine expressed a Smithian confidence that the wealth-creating machinery of the free market (aided perhaps by modest tax redistribution to benefit the poor via small yearly pensions) offered the surest guarantee of access to property for the laboring classes.[5] Among the Founding Fathers, perhaps only Thomas Jefferson, with his mordant fear of monopoly and his preoccupation with the republican virtue inhering in widespread property ownership, offered an ideological brace (albeit one never translated into public policy) against growing inequalities.[6] In short, in the formal thinking behind the American Revolution settlement, there was little to suggest, let alone promise, any kind of commitment to the quality of life (except perhaps the right to vote) for the free worker.

Indeed, it was not the traditional status of free labor but that of chattel slavery that temporarily appeared most threatened by the assault on British sovereignty. Preoccupation with "independence" and fears of dependency, subordination, and even enslavement on the part of Amerian colonials vis à vis imperial Britain inexorably led many to identify slavery itself as both a moral abomination and a miscarriage of reason. As David Brion Davis has noted, "a growing number of evangelicals and *philosophes*, of Quakers and revolutionaries . . . were coming to sense that American slavery might symbolize all the forces that threatened the true destiny of man."[7]

In practice, however, the impact of the American Revolution for both slave and free worker was less in the formal documents or leading thought of the period than in events and thoughts "on the ground." For African-American slaves the conscience-stricken moments among whites of the Revolutionary period proved a nonstarter. For white laborers, on the other hand, the residual effects— in terms of both expectations and fears—of the extraordinary liberty and economic opportunity which had already given parts of eight-

eenth-century America the reputation as the "best poor man's country in the world," possessed long coattails. As John Adams had
noted in 1761, "An idea of equality . . . seems generally to prevail,
and the inferior people pay but little external respect to those who
occupy superior stations."[8] Such independence and relative abundance, of course, escaped many: among the poorer artisan classes of
late eighteenth-century Philadelphia, for example, as historian Billy
Smith reminds us, life was "nasty, short, and brutish."[9] Yet the
revolutionary mobilization itself added to the ranks of those who
felt a direct stake not only in the infant nation's political freedoms
but also in the protection, if not extension, of control over one's own
property and one's own labor. For artisans as well as yeomen farmers, an economic independence created by happenstance became
something explicitly defended and worth fighting for.

After the Revolution, as Gordon S. Wood has perhaps best documented, Americans continued to exhibit an "extraordinary touchi-
ness" surrounding fears of dependency. The mechanics' associations
and Democratic-Republican societies of the 1790s expressed a "furi-
ous attack on aristocracy" including the concept of natural aristocracy shared by Adams and Jefferson. A pent-up egalitarian anger likewise inspired New York sailmaker George Warner's 1797 reference to
"judges, lawyers, generals, colonels and all other designing men" who
had once disdained the laboring orders and all because they had "not
snored through four years at Princeton."[10] In the same year Massachusetts farmer and self-styled "laborer" Willam Manning characteristically defined America as a society divided between the Many and the
Few "who live without labor" and "have always made out to destroy
free government soon or later."[11] Although Manning's own radical
nostrums for legislation, education, and taxation never found an audience, his reliance on a labor theory of value echoed widely among
contemporaries. In displays throughout the port cities of the new nation, artisan supporters of the young republic typically celebrated
their own identity with the new nation behind banners such as that
found among New York mechanics in 1815, "By Hammer and Hand
All Arts Do Stand." By 1809, Parson Weems, the country's leading
popular historiographer and hagiographer, had transformed the Founding Fathers into hard-working producers and mechanic heroes, presenting even the genteel Washington as a man "on horseback by the
time the sun was up."[12]

≺ II ≻

Manufacturing and the Problem of Free Labor

Soon, however, consensual agreement on the free labor ethic, which could incorporate a wealthy Washington or Franklin into the same social framework as a struggling apprentice or hired farmhand, broke down under the impact of the expanding division of labor in manufacture and the accompanying perception of deepening cleavages of income and power among the citizenry. That such issues developed simultaneously with abolitionist attacks on slavery and with spirited Southern defenses of the "peculiar institution" further complicated contemporary discussions of the labor question.

For many commentators and outside observers, free labor in antebellum America was a matter of celebration and near-utopian achievement. The idea of the "workingman's paradise"—an open and egalitarian society where manual labor, at least in the North, was honored and rewarded as nowhere else in the world—was widespread.[13] To be sure, the reality of a new, voluntary labor order was more complicated, as revealed in the subtle evolution of the code of master-servant relations embedded in the common law. As Robert J. Steinfeld has documented, proceedings in the antebellum decades all but eliminated direct coercion in the fulfillment of labor contracts. Possessing the legal and political rights of self-government, white male laborers could quit work with physical impunity; no one could physically compel one free citizen to serve another. While a worker could "freely" leave his contracted work, however, he could not expect to recover disputed wages. Moreover, so long as he remained in the employment relationship (legally "leasing" his labor to another), "the employer was legally entitled to command that labor as if it were his own."[14]

Effectively, therefore, the power of property ownership that predated the flowering of both American free labor and universal suffrage reappeared in the realm of private economic relationships. Though this new and more subtle form of class control would long haunt American worker movements, there is no reason, historically, to belittle the legal-institutional move toward voluntarism and formal, public equality under the law. Indeed, in the circumstances of a booming economy, massive population growth, and opportunities for geographic expansionism, most contemporaries were willing to accept the legitimacy of a capitalist social division of labor as an inevitable aspect of material progress.

Still, there were a few significant hitches. For one, there was general acknowledgment of a growing deterioration in the crafts accompanying manufacture—a marked loss, as historian Jonathan A. Glickstein has described it, in the "intellectual component" of work. For many of the more fortunate, to be sure, awareness of a permanent, unskilled manual working class posed no serious intellectual or political problem. That the most disagreeable manual labor should be both ill-rewarded and distributed among society's "most impoverished, uneducated, and powerless people" was practically a given in polite society.[15] Such stigmatization of manual labor had a long and widespread pedigree; as Glickstein notes, the mid-nineteenth century term "nigger work" carried transatlantic meaning.[16]

Yet even those inclined to accept as inevitable the bastardization of craft expressed reservations about its social implications. An accounting of the harmful effects of division of labor, for example, was already well developed in the eighteenth-century writings of economists Adam Ferguson and Adam Smith: "The man," wrote Smith, "whose whole life is spent in performing a few simple operations . . . has no occasion to exert his understanding . . . [He] generally becomes as stupid and ignorant as it is possible for a human creature to become."[17] Smith and other transatlantic liberals opted for mass education as an antidote to the deadening influence of the labor process. For Horace Mann, father of the American common school movement, for example, the virtues of free labor would depend directly upon the qualities of mind that the laborer developed (or was permitted to develop) *outside* the workplace.[18]

The visible tendency toward the degradation of manual wage labor also placed heightened focus on opportunities to escape permanent residency in such a state. In this respect the rise of northern antislavery thought reflected both a cultivated pride in a dynamic northern free labor culture and fear about possible social stagnation. The dignity of labor which became a constant theme of northern culture and politics represented not merely the Protestant ethic of pride in a "calling" (which might have existed in a static, steady-state society) but rather a commitment to the idea of social

mobility and economic growth.[19] A commitment to the "right to
rise" ultimately became the guiding light for the Free Soil, Free Labor movement and subsequently, the Republican Party. Westward
migration emerged as the answer to urban poverty and wage slavery for the Republicans; the extension of chattel slavery to the
valuable western lands as the chief threat to access to the American dream. "Free labor" for the cross-class alliance around the Republicans meant labor with economic choices, with the ultimate
opportunity to quit the wage-earning class. By this logic, as Eric
Foner emphasizes, "the man who remained all his life dependent
on wages for his livelihood appeared almost as unfree as the southern slave."[20] "It is not the fault of the system," Abraham Lincoln
explained, "if a man did not rise above the position of wage earner,
but because of either a dependent nature which prefers it, or im-
providence, folly, or singular misfortune."[21] Prepare each individual
for the great race ahead, remove all obstacles to the operation of
the free market, northern middle-class opinion suggested, and
democratic society would flourish.

There were two social groups, however antipathetic toward
each other, who took a much tougher line on the failings of the
free labor system. One group encompassed the slaveholders and
their political defenders. Faced with Republican and abolitionist
attacks on the slave South as a stagnant economy that discouraged
the free labor social ethic of hard work and frugality, southern
writers variously challenged both the theory and the practice of the
northern behemoth that would undo them. A few paternalists like
Virginia planter George Fitzhugh attacked the core assumptions of
possessive individualism upon which a capitalistic, free labor society was based. According to such critics, the responsibilities of
master to slave in a slave society (like the obligations of a feudal
lord to his vassals or of the paterfamilias to wife and children) offered a more secure and "organic" human community for protec-
tors and protected alike than did the competitive marketplace.[22] As
former labor radical-turned-pro-slavery conservative Orestes Brown-
son told a Maryland Catholic College in 1853, "The North, like the
South, consists of freemen and slaves, but you [in the South] call
your slaves by their proper names, and . . . relieve them from the
cares and burdens of freemen."[23] More commonly, however, slavery
defenders, like their antislavery counterparts, accepted the virtues

of free labor, but they suggested that the presence of a black race (or "mudsill class") fit for the drudge work of society better allowed deserving whites to live out the republican values that they so ardently preached.

In this idea of "Herrenvolk democracy," southern commentators could draw freely upon the deplorable conditions of northern industrializing centers while holding out the hope of a less-stratified path of development for white skilled labor, farmers, and merchants in the South. Attacking the hypocrisy of northern abolitionist rhetoric, slavery defender Peter Walker described "the men who talk of the 'dignity of labor'" as those who "unless the click-clack of the tongue can be accounted labor, willingly for themselves forego all its dignities and divine incarnations."[24]

A second group, composed of antebellum labor radicals, posited the most specific remedies for the gap between free labor ideals and class-stratified realites. The ideology of American labor protest and the subsequent organized labor movement derived (as Sean Wilentz has most notably documented) from the English radical Ricardians of the 1820s, who, drawing on the bedrock belief of classical economists in the labor theory of value, turned that belief to socially critical ends. Positing a split in market society between the "producing classes" (who deserved full return on their labor) and "non-producing" elements of parasitical landlords and speculating merchants, the English radicals (popularly represented in the United States by Robert Owen and his son Robert Dale Owen) quickly reached an understanding audience among American artisans on the eastern seaboard who, within an economy of explosive growth, boom-bust cycles, and spreading division of labor, were experiencing dimming hopes of self-employed status. The result was an outpouring of "utopian" critique on the one hand and hard political organizing on the other.

The utopian critique of wage labor drew simultaneously on moral and economic logic. For the New Jersey Quaker physician Cornelius Blatchly, the Philadelphia printer Langton Byllesby, and the New York mechanic Thomas Skidmore alike, private accumulations (especially via inheritance) of land and capital had rendered mute the Jeffersonian rights to "life, liberty, and the pursuit of happiness." Free labor, by this logic, required independence from the economic dependence on others; and all else was slavery. The ordinary hatter or shoemaker, wrote Byllesby, was trapped in a relationship that "takes from one man the products of two days' labour and gives him in compensation the product of only one day of another."[25]

Much critical discussion in the antebellum era focused on the division of labor which was intimately and conspicuously associated with the rise of manufacturing. The issue of "drudge work"—associated in the public mind with immigrant ragpickers, child chimney sweeps, as well as mill work more generally—highlighted the question of whether there were not some limits to what the marketplace might be allowed to impose on "free" laborers. On the radical end of ideological responses, American Fourierites (best known for their experimental Brook Farm Association) directly challenged the division of labor between manual and non-manual endeavors and proposed an equal division of repulsive tasks among community members.[26] On the most conservative end, meanwhile, were those who defended unregulated drudge work either on the basis of natural selection—in an echo of mudsill class theory, for example, some argued that the presence of Irish laborers "liberated" native American workers to higher occupations—or on a variety of practical grounds. Antebellum Massachusetts legislators thus turned back proposed ten-hours legislation on grounds (familiar to present-day ears) that to set selective limits to the conditions of free labor would lead to the closure of the state's factories.[27]

Those closest to the "degradation" of work, however, neither fully accepted nor categorically rejected the dawning realities of industrial capitalism. As it developed among the artisan classes, trade unionism identified the self-respect of the free laborer less with utter independence and absolute equality than with bargaining power over the mimimal conditions and rewards acceptable for a given job. In what Wilentz calls "classical republican trade unionism," New York's General Trades' Union "never questioned private property per se . . . But by claiming their labor as their _own_ property, by linking that definition to what they perceived as the new inequalities in the workshops, and by then asserting their exclusive rights, as wage earners, to regulate their wages, the organized journeymen turned the most fundamental of entrepreneurial ideas—the very notion of labor as a commodity—on its head and threw it back at their employers."[28]

Antebellum worries over the dignity of labor also allowed for two important social exclusions. As free workers puzzled over their own status in a market society, their proximity to chattel slaves raised an awkward problem. On the one hand, white workers sensed ever more keenly the "dangers of dependency and a strong suspicion of paternalism." On the other hand, as David Roediger has argued, racial separation from the slave "could reassure wage workers that they belonged to the ranks of 'free white labor.'" The latter impulse, in particular, would tend to separate rather than unite black and white workers, both before and after emancipation. Those who would readily organize to guard against "white slavery" and the curse of "nigger work" were as likely to bar the doors of their shops to black workers as to attack their employers.[29]

The very perception by antebellum artisans that their traditional autonomy and capacity for self-employment were under threat also led them, as Jeanne Boydston has documented, to define their social roles in more explicitly gendered terms. Cherishing a vision of the family secure from the vicissitudes of the marketplace, men began to link the concept of "free labor" with a family wage large enough to sustain an entire household. Contemporary notions of gender roles and gender identity effectively designated men as the only proper recruits for regular, paid labor while consigning women to the protected sphere of the home. New York General Trades' Union leader Ely Moore thus warned that employer avarice would create a class of "breadless and impotent" workers, and an 1836 report of the National Trades' Union "charged that because women's wages were so low, a woman's efforts to sustain herself and family are actually the same as tying a stone around the neck of her natural protector, Man, and destroying him with the weight she has brought to his assistance."[30] By continuing to regard female workers as a marginal class and economic aberration (effectively ignoring their centrality within the early industrial workplace) labor reformers put off a true reckoning with the contemporary marketplace. In such circumstances even champions of the value of women's labor like Catherine Beecher found it difficult to criticize truly exploitative conditions for women workers without implicitly validating the normative arguments for separate spheres, including the banishment of women from competitive fields with male laborers.[31]

◅ III ►

Gilded Age Crisis in Free Labor Ideology

Free labor ideology as a set of propositions which dominated public debate and discussion reached its apogee in the late nineteenth century. The end of the Civil War and the rise of a new, nationally-consolidated economic order briefly catapulted the terms of labor to the center of political struggles. Even as an emergent mass labor movement sought to use active citizenship to redefine the parameters of the marketplace, industrial employers burnished their authority with new constitutional interpretations of the "right of free labor," which drastically limited state or collective interference with private property. By the early twentieth century (and especially by the end of World War I), such basic value conflicts within the polity were less resolved than effectively transcended via appeal to new possibilities for material abundance and the spreading culture of consumption.

The post–Civil War debate about free labor began with the status of the ex-slaves. Slave emancipation starkly raised the question of the meaning of freedom. As a policy matter, Reconstruction focused on securing and protecting political rights of citizenship. But at the grassroots level, the freedpeople themselves interpreted the term in more expansive fashion. "Freedom meant more than simply receiving wages," Eric Foner summarizes. For emancipated blacks, just as for antebellum artisans, freedom implied economic autonomy (or at least the opportunity to attain such by honest effort) as well as a more general self-distancing from white control in matters of religion, community, and family life. "Gib us our own land [and] we take care ourselves," a Charleston black told a Northern correspondent, "but widout land, de ole masses can hire us or starve us, as dey please."[32] Although the logic of such righteous passion did not prevail, and property remained overwhelmingly in the former slaveholders' hands, blacks lived out their beliefs to the extent that they effectively refused to maintain gang labor under the supervision of an overseer, preferring tenancy or sharecropping—so long as they were "free."

Beyond the denial of land to ex-slaves, the official postbellum political settlement set new, and important, limits to free labor ideology. Ironically, an earlier, egalitarian interpretation of free labor, which linked economic independence to citizenship—and thus to a larger vision of a political community—gave way to a more individualistic emphasis on rights of property at the very moment when individual workers themselves became overwhelmingly dependent on powerful employers. The shift was most notable in the judiciary's narrowing definition of the legitimacy of marketplace regulation as well as in the self-justifying ideology of business leaders themselves.

As new productive relations associated with industrial capitalism substituted the worker's wage for direct ownership of productive property, legal discourse, as William E. Forbath has argued, reduced the definition of "the worker's freedom," to "liberty of contract" and "ownership of the capacity to labor."[33] Beginning with Justice Stephen Field's influential dissenting decision in the *Slaughter-House Cases* of 1873 and culminating in the *Lochner v. New York* decision of 1905, the United States Supreme Court enshrined a liberal, laissez-faire interpretation of republican ideology as the law of the land. Extending the due protection clause of the Fourteenth Amendment to corporations, the court effectively stigmatized both legislative regulation (such as limiting hours or requiring cash payment) and much union protest activity as infringements on employer property rights and the individual worker's "right of free labor."[34]

In elite circles the narrowing of free labor doctrine to individual property rights was paralleled by appeals to the common man to shift his traditional rights preoccupation altogether to a newer basis of social fulfillment. In an age of exploding wealth, abundance itself—and the ability of the ordinary worker to share in material prosperity—formed the linchpin of the cult of economic mobility. Disregarding earlier concerns among Americans about monopoly power and social inequality, steel baron Andrew Carnegie, for example, preferred to identify the aims of democracy with the material capacity of modern-day capitalism. The natural endowment of the country, the ethnic character of the people, and equal opportunity afforded by democratic suffrage and a free public school system allowed the country to "lead the civilized world" in "freedom from debt, in agriculture, and in manufactures."[35] And if prosperity alone did not suffice as a cultural ideal, the self-help literature which proliferated at the turn of the century commonly stressed the link between individual character and material success. As the Reverend Alexander Lewis put it: "There is always a way to rise, my boy/Always a way to advance;/Yet the road that leads to Mount Success/Does not pass by the way of Chance,/But goes through the stations of Work and Strive,/through the valley of Persevere;/And the man that succeeds while others fail,/Must be willing to pay most dear."[36]

Although a new order of triumphant industrial capitalism had little place for the ambiguities of free labor ideology, defenders of the older idealism did not go down without a fight. The emergence of the predominantly white, post–Civil War labor movement, in fact, carried the argument voiced among ex-slaves in Reconstruction over the property entitlement of free labor status to a different terrain. For self-conscious members of the "producing classes," the fact that by 1870 two-thirds of the American workforce were hirelings posed a stark ideological dilemma for a culture in which the lack of property and independence was associated with slavery or "wage slavery."[37] Revisionist assaults on liberal economic orthodoxy drew on an extended tradition of farmer and labor movement as well as anti-bank, anti-corporate pamphleteers.[38]

But Henry George's *Progress and Poverty* (1879), with its attack on land monopoly as the source of urban-industrial ills, likely offered the most powerful contemporary reiteration of rights in property as the basis of democratic citizenship. Citing a growing contemporary "contrast between the House of Have and the House of Want," George warned, "To base on a state of most glaring social inequality political institutions under which men are theoretically equal, is to stand a pyramid on its apex."[39] The connection of economic reform to an earlier fight against slavery was heralded by William Lloyd Garrison, Jr.'s own conversion to the single-tax cause: "How can we make men and women sober and self-respecting," asked Garrison, "who breed together in slums and swarming tenements because natural opportunity for work is denied them? With land rescued from speculation and easy of access to everyone who wishes to use it, who doubts that improved conditions would lessen depraved appetites and brutality?"[40] The People's Party of 1892 carried the producers' cause to its political high-water mark. Its platform ridiculed the "sham battles" of the dominant political parties and pointed to the positive role for a "free government built upon the love of the whole people for each other and for the nation."[41]

Within the Gilded Age labor movement, escape from the degradation of wage slavery followed two distinct strategic pathways. Beginning with the National Labor Union in the late 1860s and continuing through the Knights of Labor which grew to more than three-quarters of a million members in the mid-1880s, this was the heyday of experiments in producer and distributive cooperation, or as one advocate put it, "the organization of production without the intervention of the capitalist."[42] By the 1890s, the cooperative impulse, although never able in practical terms to compensate for the problem of capital investment, had spread to the greatest wave of experimentation in wholesale cooperative (or so-called utopian) communities since the 1840s. Indeed, in perhaps the most ambitious of such experiments, J. A. Wayland's Ruskin Colony attempted to blend modern technology and corporate efficiency with an egalitarian reward structure.[43]

Rather than avoid or dismantle the wage system altogether (as intended by cooperative and socialist alternatives), a more common approach was to limit its social damage. To be sure, regulation of the labor market came from diverse directions, with initiatives variously waged by the direct action of strikes and boycotts or through political campaigns for legislative relief. But the central ideological claim of much labor reform activity was articulated in the shorter-hour campaigns of the early 1870s, as analyzed by historian David Montgomery:

"Day labor," explained an Eight Hour League handbill issued in Philadelphia, "is the only important article of commerce which has no fixed standard, its length being determined by the necessities of the seller, or the generosity of the purchaser." But if the commodity offered for sale by the worker (his strength and knowledge) had no fixed limit, and if he could deliver that commodity to its purchaser (the employer) only by placing himself at the latter's disposal, the worker, had in effect, delivered himself into a day's bondage for a day's wages . . . The remedy proposed by labor reformers was to draw a clear delineation between that part of the workman's day which might be purchased for wages and that which remained inalienably his own.[44]

Capturing the spirit of Gilded Age labor revolt, the chorus line of what one historian has called the most popular labor song of the nineteenth century declared "Eight Hours for Work, Eight Hours

for Rest, Eight Hours for What We Will."[45] By this logic, the length
of the worker's freedom was measured by the *shortness* of his time
on the job. "Eight hours today, fewer tomorrow," American Federation of Labor chief Samuel Gompers defined the cause in the mid-
1880s. For Big Bill Haywood of the more revolutionary Industrial
Workers of the World a quarter of a century later, the point was
still the same: "The less work the better."[46]

≺ IV ≻

*Progressive Reform and the Shift from Free
Producer to American Consumer*

Although the labor-populist version of free labor ideology was generally turned back on both the industrial and the political fronts, it
left an important heritage for twentieth-century reformers. Indeed,
the core assumptions for a revived, "progressive" regulation of the
industrial marketplace were hatched in a late Gilded Age alliance
of labor activists with a new generation of economic thinkers.
When this alliance began to bear fruit some decades later, however,
some of the core assumptions of an older free labor political stance
had been traded in for a program that better accommodated itself to
the facts of capitalist enterprise.

Belying its pragmatic outcome, a combination of Christian socialism and German historicist thinking first inspired the "institutional economics" of Edmund James, Richard T. Ely, the Reverend
C. S. Walker, Henry Carter Adams, and Simon Nelson Patten, who
together helped to organize the American Economic Association in
1885.[47] Drawn to the cooperative ideals of the Knights of Labor and
committed to a "midway" position between laissez-faire capitalism and revolutionary socialism, these academic reformers strongly supported collective bargaining based on trade union rights.[48] Of
these thinkers, Adams and Patten effectively laid the bridge for the
last great departure in American free labor ideology, the shift from
producerism to consumerism.

Adams attempted to translate an equal rights doctrine inherited
from an age of individualism and entrepreneurship to an age of industry. The growing concentration of capital which accompanied
the rise of modern industry convinced Adams that the laboring

classes must unite or lose the meaning of free citizenship. But Adams went further in connecting unionization to "rights of proprietorship in the industry to which they gave their skill and time," thereby imposing both duties and restrictions on the owners of capital.[49] Anticipating later concepts of social pluralism or countervailing power, Adams envisioned a "crystallization of a common law" of labor rights leading to the establishment of an Industrial Federation. Stopping short of the state socialism of the German model, workers would receive "the benefits of industrial partnership without disturbing the nominal or legal ownership which existed."[50] In blending his historicist understandings of the pliability of economic institutions with a sensitivity for America's liberal individualist past, Adams adopted a substantial if still delimited role for the state that historian Mary Furner has defined as the essence of a "new liberalism" of the Progressive Era.[51]

Like Adams, Patten developed a theory of labor rights attuned to the transformation of a modern-day economy. Creation of a social surplus, at once the objective and product of industry, as Patten argued in *The Theory of Prosperity* (1902), made possible a new realm of "economic freedom" which must be shared with all working people. Among the "rights" of the age of affluence, Patten asserted, was a right to leisure and recreation, made all the more necessary by the deadening influences of the industrial division of labor. Besides general rights to a working life of at least minimal comfort and safety, Patten identified two special rights: a right to relief, for "the social surplus is more than sufficient to provide for all the exigencies that persons cannot control" and the right to independent incomes for women, regardless of their relationship to the labor market.[52] Over time, as Furner argues, the pioneering reconceptualizations of the rights of labor as articulated by an Adams or a Patten would "[broaden] from matters such as the right to organize and bargain collectively to include social insurance, the living wage, unemployment compensation, and other forms of income security, as well as the general principle that every citizen had a right to a job."[53]

The new labor-oriented rights talk issued not only from the male-dominated academy but also from a powerful circle of women reformers centered in settlement houses and voluntary organizations. Confronted with the legal roadblocks surrounding comprehensive statutes for shorter hours or minimum wages, Hull House activists like Florence Kelley turned to a gendered strategy of appealing to communal responsibility for the particular plight of women and children. Shorter hours legislation for women only (ultimately upheld by the courts in *Muller v. Oregon* [1908]) thus first served, according to Kathryn Kish Sklar, as "a surrogate for laws for all workers."[54]

Altogether, the new economic wisdom of the intellectuals—centering on labor's necessary participation in a growing social surplus—found a most ready counterpart in a labor movement itself desperate for a foothold in the industrializing economy. Indeed, it might be said that the movement's own "stewards" had framed similar arguments even before they assumed "scientific" authority from the academy. Thus, as early as the shorter hours movement of the 1870s, labor leaders had begun to turn an argument about exploitative work into one about material rewards. "The *idea* of eight hours," declared Ira Steward in 1865, "isn't eight hours, it is *less poverty*." Steward even added a convincing jingle to drive the point home: "Whether you work by the piece / Or work by the day / Decreasing the hours / Increases the pay."[55]

The practical goal of participation in, rather than defiance of, modern industrial structures dominated the union movement by the end of the 1880s. The new strategic logic was perhaps first summarized by George Gunton, a former labor leader and self-taught economist who published *The Economic and Social Importance of the Eight-Hour Movement* in 1889. Arguing that the "success of the employing class depended on the extent of the consuming class," Gunton offered a precociously proto-Keynesian logic on behalf of trade union rights, shorter hours, and higher wages that would anticipate the public posture of organized labor and its allies for decades to come.[56] Indeed, this same equation of *free labor* with *active consumption* was ultimately confirmed in the Preamble to the Wagner (or National Labor Relations) Act of 1935: "The inequality of bargaining power between employees who do not possess full freedom of association or actual liberty of contract, and employers who are organized in the corporate or other forms of ownership association substantially burdens and affects the flow of commerce, and tends to aggravate recurrent business depressions, by depressing wage rates and the purchasing power of wage earners in industry."[57]

Together, emissaries of the workers' movement and new-liberal politicians and social scientists thus helped to redefine the essence of nineteenth-century free labor claims. In principle, indeed, they set the stage for a modern-day reconciliation of democratic culture with an ever expanding private marketplace. At the academic end, for example, the optimistic Simon Nelson Patten heralded a day of universal fulfillment via what one scholar has summarized as a "business-generated abundance society . . . far more ethical than old-fashioned 'agrarian scarcity'."[58] And by 1963, when the United Steel Workers Union of America could produce a contract that "gave every employee with more than five years service a thirteen-week vacation, with pay, every five years," who could quarrel with the basic logic that tied modern-day freedom at once to purchasing power and freedom *from work*?[59] Indeed, even the most radical American labor representatives placed consumption near the heart of their conceptions of the good life. Big Bill Haywood described the "ideal society" to Paterson silk mill weavers in 1913:

It will be utopian. There will be a wonderful dining room where you will enjoy the best food that can be purchased; your digestion will be aided by sweet music which will be wafted to your ears by an unexcelled orchestra. There will be a gymnasium and a great swimming pool and private bathrooms of marble. One floor of this plant will be devoted to masterpieces of art and you will have a collection even superior to that displayed in the Metropolitan Museum of Art in New York . . . Your work chairs will be morris chairs, so that when you become fatigued you may relax in comfort.[60]

< V >

Conclusion: Free Labor and the Price of Ideological Progress

It is worth taking stock of this change over time, briefly identifying both the gains and costs of such ideological "progress." Pre-industrial conceptions of free labor centered on the autonomy of the workman, the (white male) producer as independent citizen. The appeal to autonomy initially provided a strong moral critique of the manufacturer's steady division of labor, a framework for an imaginative cooperative alternative to corporate capitalism, and a platform for resisting managerial tyranny at the workplace. It weakened, however, to the point of obsolescence both from the technological reality of machine production and the political reality of capitalist control of an ever-expanding demographically diverse industrial workforce. In its place by the end of the century stood a new doctrine of labor rights less explicitly oriented to the process and control of work itself than to the social distribution of work's economic rewards. On the one hand a neat adaptation to the shifting terrain of a material world over which working people had little direct control, the switch from "quality" of work status to "quantity" of work reward seemed to dull the concept of free labor itself. Indeed, if things had gone according to plan—at least the plans of liberal ideologists—the standard of living might have all but replaced the standards of work (or terms of labor) as the subject of twentieth-century social conflicts.

In practice, however, the path to consumerism from producerism was slowed on at least two counts. First, out of both market logic and ideological will, employers regularly resurrected "freedom" as a labor-management issue by opposing trade union recognition and arbitrarily imposing their own, elaborate work rules on the shop and office floor. The result, even without the articulation of a new free labor covenant (at least outside socialist calls for public ownership or syndicalist visions of worker-centered direction of industry), evoked appeals to powerful older chords. Studying skilled workers of the first third of the twentieth century, for example, David Montgomery measured periodic outbreaks of "control strikes" focused on "enforcement of work rules, union recognition, discharge of unpopular foremen or retention of popular ones, regulation of layoffs or dismissals, and actions of sympathy with other groups of workers."[61] Often bursting the bounds of organized labor discourse (in 1920, for example, 58 percent of those on strike were without union sanction), the control issue sprang from the irreducible needs of informal work groups and loomed even in nonunion industries "as a submerged, impenetrable obstacle to management's sovereignty." Striking steel mill laborers in 1920 reportedly showed "not the slightest interest in what [their work] means or how it affects the operations of the mill around them . . . Their favorite saying was, 'What the hell!'"[62] Similarly, women textile workers joined a strike at Elizabethton, Tennessee, in 1929 in rebellion against an arbitrary work regimen, which included company surveillance of the washroom. "If we went to the bathroom," reported one striker, "they'd follow us, 'fraid we'd stay a minute too long."[63]

A more formal appeal to a heritage of worker freedom, to be sure, echoed in the great campaigns for labor union organization and recognition. Congress of Industrial Organizations President John L. Lewis predicted in a 1937 nationwide radio address that a great struggle was coming to America, a struggle that would resolve "whether the working population of this country shall have a voice in determining their destiny or whether they shall serve as indentured servants for a financial and economic dictatorship which would shamelessly exploit our natural resources and debase the soul . . . and . . . pride of a free people. On such an issue there can be no compromise."[64] By combining demand for a higher living standard with the dignity of free citizenship, Lewis tapped a tradition with a rich history. For generations, unskilled immigrant laborers, in particular, had made the connection. For Slavic steelworkers in Homestead, Pennsylvania, in the 1880s, for example, as historian Paul Krause observed, the search for "modest material comfort and independence" (summarized in the Slovak expression *za chlebom* or "daily bread") was carried out at once in resistance to the regime of Andrew Carnegie and in July 4th celebrations of American freedom.[65] Indeed, some farseeing twentieth-century managers (sometimes with the explicit aim of avoiding unionization) have attempted to reincorporate the democratic-participatory thrust of the union message within company culture. "Quality control circles," popularly associated with Japanese industrial practices of the post–World War II era, thus offer at least a token of worker-centered decision-making on the job, a freedom otherwise absent from the factory floor.

If usually in less ringing tones, such messages about the need for worker "voice" or "dignity" have echoed in labor struggles to the present day. Even in comparatively conservative and virtually union-free southern industries, mundane issues of daily employment sometimes touch deep political and normative responses. In 1958, for example, Henderson, North Carolina, textile employees struck in vain for more than two years to try to salvage a grievance system that could save them from arbitrary dismissals.[66] In 1993 several hundred Guatemalan refugees—recruited to a Morganton, North Carolina, poultry factory as a cheap and docile labor force—

likewise provoked a strike when one of their number was permitted only 30 seconds for a bathroom break.[67] This latter episode hints at the truly monumental challenge of a twenty-first century workplace governed by global patterns of labor recruitment as well as capital migration. During the years of the Cold War, Western governments (and their trade union federations) resurrected the concept of "free labor" as the antithesis of control of the workplace by authoritarian communist regimes. Today, however, neither governments nor unions seem to be able to match the power of multinational corporations. As a result previous living standards as well as on-the-job rights and protections for workers appear in jeopardy. As long as such circumstances remain, the terms of labor and the terms of freedom will likely remain closely entwined.

Changing Legal Conceptions of Free Labor

ROBERT J. STEINFELD

FOR CENTURIES, LABOR HAS been conventionally divided into two opposite types, "free" and "coerced." And it has been widely assumed that no real difficulties were presented in saying which was which. The line separating the two types of labor is still understood to be drawn naturally and unproblematically at the point where "coercion" in labor relations begins or ends. What I mean to show in this chapter is that the process of drawing the line between "free" and "coerced" labor turns out to be much more problematic than conventional accounts take for granted. I begin this chapter by taking a closer look at what that task involves, because a better understanding of the vexed process of line drawing will make it easier to grasp how it was possible for the legal definition of "free" labor to change so much over time.

≪ I ≫

Free Labor and Involuntary Servitude in
Modern Federal Courts

In 1963, David Shackney was found guilty by a jury in Federal District Court in Connecticut of holding Luis Oros and members of his family in "peonage" and "involuntary servitude."[1] Shackney ran a chicken farm in Connecticut and being unable to find American farm laborers who were willing to work for him went to Mexico to recruit workers. There he met Luis Oros and induced him, his wife, and his eldest daughter to sign a two-year contract, written in Spanish, to work on Shackney's farm. The contract term was to begin on August 15, 1961. The Oroses were to

care for 20,000 laying hens . . . the hours of work were to be from 6:30 A.M. until the work was completed, with three breaks . . . "because of the fact that our work will be handling living things which must be carefully cared for, this work must be done every day, 7 days a week and 365 days a years with no exception," . . . they were to receive a furnished place to live, with heat, electricity and gas for cooking, and sufficient food; and . . . their combined salary should be $160 per month for the first year and $240 for the second, half of which was to be deposited in a joint bank account as security for their performing their obligations.[2]

Shackney incurred expenses for procuring visas and transporting the Oroses from Mexico, and had them sign twelve $100 notes in order to recover these expenses. Later, he had them sign six more $100 notes. The notes, at Shackney's insistence, were co-signed by a friend of the Oroses in Mexico who owned his own house. Shortly after they arrived at the farm, Shackney raised the combined salary for the family to $200 per month. But at the end of each month, "the Oroses received no cash since Shackney would get them to endorse the checks and would tear up two $100 notes."[3]

The thrust of the government's case against Shackney was that he was holding the Oroses in "peonage" and "involuntary servitude" by virtue of the threats he made against them to harm them if they left before fulfilling their contractual obligations.

Oros and Maria Elena testified they were always afraid. Of prime importance was the fear of deportation if they left . . . A further fear-engendering factor was a threat in February, 1962, that unless Oros paid the notes that Rosalio had co-signed, "somebody take my friend's house, and this thing I know when I sign the notes, and this is where I am scared to leave the farm."[4]

Shackney appealed his conviction to the United States Court of Appeals for the Second Circuit. Judge Friendly, writing for the three judge court, surveyed earlier judicial decisions and found that the prohibition on "involuntary servitude" in the Thirteenth Amendment was meant to

abolish all practices whereby subjection having some of the incidents of slavery was *legally* [emphasis added] enforced, either directly by a state's using its power to return the servant to the master . . . or indirectly, by subjecting persons who left the employer's service to criminal penalties. Rather plainly, however, the term goes farther.[5]

It also extends, Friendly said, to cases in which a private individual holds a person to labor by physical force or threats of physical force.[6] But it extends even farther. An earlier lower federal court decision had found "involuntary servitude" resulted where an employer threatened to prosecute a house servant and have her imprisoned if she left, even though the threat was completely empty, since no ground for criminal prosecution actually existed.[7] The issue which Friendly had to resolve was whether the term extended even farther, and if not, to develop criteria to draw a line between threats that gave rise to "involuntary servitude" and threats that did not. Friendly had no doubt that the threat to foreclose the friend's house did not give rise to "involuntary servitude" "as it is within the rights of a mortgagee to threaten to enforce the security which the contract gives him for nonperformance."[8] But the threat of deportation required a more extended analysis.

In the end, Friendly decided that because this threat offered the workers "a choice between continued service and freedom, even if the . . . choice [of freedom] entail[ed] consequences that are exceedingly bad," it did not give rise to "involuntary servitude." "While a credible threat of deportation," Friendly continued, "may come close to the line, it still leaves the employee with a choice [between continued service and freedom], and we do not see how we could fairly bring it within [the statute] without encompassing other types of threat, quite as devastating in the particular case as that of deportation may have been to the Oroses."[9] Friendly saw that bringing such a threat within the statute could have serious implications for the entire system of employment based on voluntary contract. "The most ardent believer in civil rights legislation," he wrote, "might not think that cause would be advanced by permitting the awful machinery of the criminal law to be brought into play whenever an employee asserts that his will to quit has been subdued by a threat which seriously affects his future welfare but as to which he still has a choice, however painful."[10]

Friendly concluded that the statute punishing the holding of persons in "peonage" or "involuntary servitude" "applies only to service compelled by law, by force, or by the threat of continued confinement of some sort."[11] According to Friendly's opinion, in other words, only when the choice presented to a worker is a choice between continued service and physical confinement, or continued service and physical violence, is the choice to continue service not considered a free choice, but instead "involuntary servitude." In other cases, where the choice presented to a worker is between continued service and other "consequences that are exceedingly bad" the choice of continued service amounts in law to a free choice and gives rise to "voluntary" employment, rather than to "involuntary servitude."

Interestingly, in a concurring opinion in the case, Judge Dimock disagreed with Friendly. He thought that other kinds of threats might also produce "involuntary servitude" if they "subjugated" the will of the worker. "To a drug addict," he wrote, "the threat of deprivation of his supply is certainly more overbearing than the threat of almost any kind of force, yet it is a means falling outside of the majority's guilt criterion."[12] The real test was whether a person's will had been overcome by a threat, not whether the threat was of a certain type.

But the test Judge Dimock was proposing had long been criticized by jurists. As early as 1918, Justice Holmes wrote that "[i]t always is for the interest of a party under duress to choose the lesser of two evils. But the fact that a choice was made according to interest [rather than the will being overborne] does not exclude duress. It is the characteristic of duress properly so called."[13] John Dawson, writing several decades later, put the paradox of voluntariness and duress in even more vivid terms. "[C]ourts ha[ve] been slow to realize that the instances of more extreme pressure were precisely those in which the consent expressed was more *real*; the more unpleasant the alternative, the more real the consent to a course which would avoid it."[14]

In 1987, the United States Supreme Court took up the task of trying to develop a satisfactory test to distinguish "involuntary servitude" from "free" labor. Ike and Margaret Kozminski were accused of holding two mentally retarded men in "involuntary servitude" on their dairy farm in Michigan.

The Kozminskis subjected the two men to physical and verbal abuse for failing to do their work and instructed herdsmen employed at the farm to do the same. The Kozminskis directed [the men] not to leave the farm, and on several occasions when the men did leave, the Kozminskis or their employees brought the men back and discouraged them from leaving again. On one occasion, John Kozminski threatened [one of the men] with institutionalization if he did not do as he was told.[15]

The Kozminskis were convicted in a federal district court, but on appeal the Supreme Court reversed the conviction, and remanded for a new trial under the test they then set forth. Justice O'Connor, writing for the majority, declared that "our precedents clearly define a Thirteenth Amendment prohibition of involuntary servitude [as labor] enforced by the use or threatened use of physical or legal coercion."[16] But then Justice O'Connor went on to give examples of "physical" and "legal" coercion which stretched those terms to include forms of coercion that normally would not be considered "physical" or "legal." Discussing the padrone system of the late nineteenth century, against which Congress had legislated under its power to implement the Thirteenth Amendment, O'Connor wrote:

[t]hese young children were literally stranded in large hostile cities in a foreign country. They were given no education or other assistance toward self-sufficiency. Without such assistance, without family, and without other sources of support, these children had no actual means of escaping the padrones' service; they had no choice but to work for their masters or risk physical harm.[17]

It certainly seems that the physical harms which confronted these children as an alternative to continued service included going hungry, going without shelter, in general, going without. But these would normally be considered "economic" threats.[18] What O'Connor has laid bare in an effort to bring the Padrone precedent within the scope of the term "physical coercion" is that "economic" threats actually do involve, at times, the "risk of physical harms." O'Connor also thought that "legal" coercion might be broader than Judge Friendly believed. Depending upon their special vulnerabilities, she wrote, "it is possible that threatening an incompetent with institutionalization or an immigrant with deportation could constitute the threat of legal coercion that induces involuntary servitude."[19]

Justice O'Connor seems to have been torn in opposite directions. On the one hand, citing Judge Friendly's concern that the entire system of voluntary employment might be compromised by an extension of the kinds of threats recognized as giving rise to "involuntary servitude,"[20] Justice O'Connor was determined to limit the kinds of coercion which can give rise to "involuntary servitude" to "physical" or "legal" coercion. On the other hand, not wanting unduly to restrict the kinds of circumstances that might be seen to give rise to "involuntary servitude," she offered a broad and flexible definition of what "physical and legal" coercion might involve.

In a concurring opinion in which Justice Marshall joined, Justice Brennan expressed deep dissatisfaction with the test the Court adopted. It suffered from the same problems that Judge Dimock thought Judge Friendly's test suffered from. It was simultaneously too broad and too narrow. On the one hand, certain types of "physical or legal" coercion may not actually be coercive enough to give rise to "involuntary servitude."[21] On the other hand, certain types of "economic, social, or psychological" coercion may.[22] But the problem, for Justice Brennan, was to draw a line that would include these other forms of coercion, and yet not bring within the scope of the test the kinds of threats made in the course of ordinary employment. Drawing on Holmes's insight, Brennan wrote: "[i]t is of course not easy to articulate when a person's actions are 'involuntary'."

In some minimalist sense the laborer always has a choice no matter what the threat: the laborer can choose to work, or take a beating; work, or go to jail. We can all agree that *these choices are so illegitimate* that any decision to work is 'involuntary'. But other coercive choices, even if physical or legal in nature, might present closer questions. Happily, our task is not to resolve the philosophical meaning of free will, but to determine what coercion Congress would have regarded *as sufficient to deem* any resulting *labor "involuntary servitude* [emphasis added]."[23]

A test which encompassed other forms of coercion, Justice Brennan worried, would force the courts repeatedly to make the difficult, and necessarily normative, judgment that a particular choice presented to a worker was *"so illegitimate"* that it was transformed in law from a voluntary choice to work in order to avoid a more disagreeable alternative, into its opposite, coercion "sufficient to *deem* the labor 'involuntary servitude'." "One can ... imagine," he wrote, "troublesome applications of that test, such as the employer who coerces an employee to remain at her job by threatening her with bad recommendations if she leaves."[24]

To circumvent the deeply problematic task of trying to distinguish disagreeable choices offered to workers which give rise to "involuntary servitude" from disagreeable choices offered to workers which give rise to "voluntary" labor, Justice Brennan suggested that the test be refocused. "The solution," he wrote, "lies not in ignoring those [other] forms of coercion that are perhaps less universal in their effect than physical or legal coercion, but in focusing on the 'slavelike' conditions of servitude Congress most clearly intended to eradicate."[25]

I thus conclude that whatever irresolvable ambiguity there may be in determining . . . the degree of coercion Congress would have regarded as sufficient to render any resulting labor "involuntary" . . . Congress clearly intended to encompass coercion *of any form* that actually succeeds in reducing the victim to a condition of servitude resembling that in which slaves were held before the Civil War. While no one factor is dispositive, complete domination over all aspects of the victim's life, oppressive working and living conditions, and lack of pay or personal freedom are the hallmarks of that slavelike condition of servitude.[26]

Justice O'Connor, however, expressed deep concern over Justice Brennan's proposed test. She feared that it would reach as "involuntary servitude" oppressive work conditions that were maintained only through "economic" coercion. "This formulation," she wrote of Justice Brennan's opinion,

would be useful if it were accompanied by a recognition that the use or threat of physical or legal coercion was a necessary incident of pre–Civil War slavery and thus of the "'slavelike' conditions of servitude Congress most clearly intended to eradicate." Instead finding no objective factor to be necessary to a "slavelike condition," Justice Brennan would delegate to prosecutors and juries the task of determining what working conditions are so oppressive as to amount to involuntary servitude . . . The ambiguity in the phrase "slavelike conditions" is not merely a question of degree, but instead concerns the very nature of the conditions prohibited. Although we can be sure that Congress intended to prohibit "'slavelike' conditions of servitude," we have no indication that Congress thought that conditions maintained by means other than by the use or threatened use of physical or legal coercion were "slavelike."[27]

In 1987, the Supreme Court was still wrestling with the problem of trying to separate labor into opposite kinds, voluntary and involuntary. All the proposed tests for doing so involved either political or moral judgments, or psychological ones. Justice O'Connor's test, even if we ignore the broad definition she gave to "physical" coercion, mandated that as a matter of constitutional law, only certain forms of "coercion" could give rise to "involuntary servitude"; other forms of "coercion" could only give rise to "voluntary" employment. Justice Brennan recognized that what the

majority view necessarily involved was a political or moral judgment that certain kinds of hard choices presented to workers to
elicit their labor were, in his words, "so illegitimate" that we
"deem" the labor "involuntary servitude." Of other hard choices
presented to workers, we simply say that the worker "voluntarily"
chose labor as the lesser evil, implicitly making a judgment that
such a hard choice was not "so illegitimate" that we should
"deem" the resulting labor "involuntary servitude." Needless to
say, as Justice O'Connor pointed out, Justice Brennan's test of
"slavelike conditions" necessarily involved its own set of political
or moral judgments.

The line drawn between voluntary and involuntary labor, free
and coerced labor, turns out not to be a natural or logical one, one
that merely marks where coercion begins or ends in labor relations;
it is a line drawn on the basis of difficult political and moral judgments. And as such, it is a line which has been drawn differently in
different places, at different times. Indeed, what the modern judges
all take for granted, that labor elicited as the result of threats of
imprisonment is involuntary servitude, is a judgment that became
universally accepted in the United States, and in many places in
Europe, only during this century.

<< II >>

Free Wage Labor During the Nineteenth Century

During a good part of the nineteenth century, free wage workers
were subject to imprisonment for breaches of their employment
agreements in England, Prussia, and a number of other European
states. In the twentieth century, the criminal enforcement of labor
contracts has come to be viewed as rendering labor given under
them "coerced" or "involuntary," but that was far from being the
view of many nineteenth-century Europeans.[28]

It is important to understand, moreover, that nineteenth-century European rules imposing penal sanctions for labor contract
breaches were part and parcel of the creation of free markets. As
one historian has recently observed,

it was not until the eighteenth century, in Western Europe, England, and
North America, that societies first appeared whose economic systems de-

pended on the expectation that most people, most of the time, were sufficiently conscience ridden (and certain of retribution) that they could be trusted to keep their promises . . . Only to the extent that [the] norm [of promise keeping] prevails can economic affairs be based on nothing more authoritative than the obligation arising out of promises.

Both the growing force of the norm of promise keeping and its synchronization with the spread of market relations are clearly inscribed in the history of the law of contract . . . For the first time the law strained to make promisors generally liable for whatever expectations their promises created. Never before had promises counted for so much in human affairs, and never before had the penalties for being short-willed and unreliable been so severe.[29]

Large scale free markets were not feasible without reliable contract enforcement.[30] And this was as true of free markets in labor as free markets in other commodities. But labor agreements, it was widely believed at the time, could not be reliably enforced against largely propertyless workers by means of money damages.[31] Penal sanctions were viewed, at this time, as nothing more than a normal contract remedy in situations in which money damages could not be counted upon, a necessary part of a regime of free contract in labor markets.

In 1845, Prussia implemented a policy of "freedom of trade" (Gewerbefreiheit).[32] As part of this liberal, free market reform, the relationship between masters and their journeymen in the artisanal sector, and factory workers and their employers in the expanding industrial sector was made a matter of free contract.[33] For breach of these freely negotiated contracts, factory workers, journeymen, and other wage workers were subject, under the 1845 reforms, to penal sanctions, including prison. The law declared that "Journeymen, helpers, and factory workers, who leave work without permission and without legal justification, or are guilty of shirking, or gross disobedience or insistent obstinacy, are to be punished with a fine up to twenty Thalers or prison up to fourteen days."[34] Penal sanctions for contract breaches by factory workers were eliminated by the Industrial Law (Gewerbeordnung) of 1869,[35] but continued to apply to a range of other kinds of workers until after World War I.

Prussia was far from being alone in nineteenth-century Europe in imposing criminal sanctions for contract breaches upon wage workers. In England, which possessed the most advanced laissez-faire economy of the period, much harsher penal sanctions for contract breaches by wage workers were in force. English workers could be imprisoned for up to three months for quitting before the expiration of their contracts, for leaving work without permission, or for disobedience at work.[36] The English laws had also been put into place during the period in which a highly regulated economy was giving way to free markets based on liberal ideas. Between 1720 and 1843, the English Parliament passed more than half a dozen statutes that mandated penal sanctions for breaches of contract.[37] Between 1857 and 1875 about 10,000 workers a year were criminally proceeded against in England for breaches of their labor contracts.[38]

Because the labor of skilled craft workers was especially valuable to employers it was mainly against these workers that penal sanctions were applied in England. Industrialization gave a tremendous boost to artisanal sectors of the economy.

Industrialization, even considered in the restrictive and potentially misleading sense as something that happened simply to manufacturing industry rather than to all sectors of the economy, was far from being a one-way procession into the factory. Mechanization of one sector or process in an industry, and its move into the factory, could well generate increased demand for handwork and outwork in other sectors. The classic example was in the cotton industry, where from the later eighteenth century the rise of the spinning mills had led to an enormous expansion in the number of handloom weavers, most of them outworkers (a minority were pseudo-factory workers, working in large weaving sheds for a single employer), and many of them rural workers with dual employments in farming.[39]

But skilled craft workers were by no means all or even primarily employed as outworkers. Much of the industrial output of the country was produced by skilled craft workers plying their traditional trades in establishments employing 25, 50, 200, or more craftsmen. Potters, tinplate workers, cutlers, glassmen, puddlers, furnacemen, and a range of other similar workers made up a large proportion of those proceeded against under the master and servant acts.[40]

Not very much has been written explaining the abolition of penal sanctions for breach of contract by factory workers in Germany in 1869, but the process in England has been described in great detail. Beginning in the early 1860s, organized labor mounted a long campaign to have penal sanctions repealed. In 1875, Parliament finally responded to the growing power of labor by repealing the legislation which had long mandated imprisonment for contract breaches. In England labor prevailed in this campaign not only because of its growing electoral influence,[41] but also because it succeeded in having its reinterpretation of penal sanctions widely accepted in English culture, including English legal culture. From ordinary contract remedy entirely consistent with the liberal principle of free contract, penal sanctions began to be recharacterized as a contract remedy that was inconsistent with the liberal principle of equal treatment under law (it was not equally available to workers when employers breached contracts),[42] and then over the ensuing 25 years, as a contract remedy which turned "contracts of service" into "contracts of slavery."[43] In this way criminal sanctions became a contract remedy that was inconsistent with the longstanding liberal tradition that prohibited contracts of slavery. It seems clear that many nineteenth-century Europeans drew the distinction between "free" and "coerced" labor differently than we do, but that they began to redraw this distinction by the end of the nineteenth century.

< III >

Involuntary Servitude in Nineteenth-Century
American Fundamental Law

The modern American constitutional definition of free labor, the one that all the judges simply took for granted in the cases with which we began this chapter, was similarly arrived at only after a long struggle over how the line should be drawn to separate the kinds of hard choices that would "coerce" the labor of workers who confronted them, from the kinds of hard choices that left workers "free" to choose labor as the lesser evil.

American fundamental law on the subject of "coerced" labor goes back to the language of the Northwest Ordinance, which was enacted by Congress in 1787. The Ordinance declared that "There shall be *neither Slavery nor involuntary Servitude* in the [Northwest] territory otherwise than in the punishment of crimes, whereof the Party shall have been duly convicted."[44] The Ordinance applied to an area which encompassed the present day states of Ohio, Michigan, Indiana, Illinois, and Wisconsin. But the lan-

guage of the Ordinance was later incorporated into the Thirteenth
Amendment to the United States Constitution, which abolished
"slavery" and "involuntary servitude" everywhere in the nation.

It is primarily to the interpretation of the term "involuntary
servitude," first in the Ordinance and later in the Thirteenth
Amendment, that we must turn for an understanding of the changing definition of "free" labor in American fundamental law. As we
examine these interpretations, however, we should keep at least
two things in mind. First, adult white indentured servants were
still being imported into the United States in 1787, and would continue to be imported in significant numbers, on and off, until 1820,
and in smaller numbers until at least 1830. It seems likely that the
framers of the Northwest Ordinance would have considered these
contractual arrangements to be "voluntary" rather than "involuntary." But second, these imported indentured servants were the
only adult white workers subject to penal sanctions (or specific performance) for labor contract breaches in the United States by the
early nineteenth century.[45] The reasons for this state of affairs are a
bit of mystery. We do know that before the middle of the eighteenth century, statutes in a number of American colonies subjected "hired" workers to penal sanctions for contract breaches.[46] But
over the course of that century these statutes began to disappear
from the colonial codes.

It was a struggle over the legality of indentured servitude under
the provisions of the Northwest Ordinance that produced the first
judicial interpretations of the term "involuntary servitude." The
Northwest Territory shared its southern border with two slave
states, Virginia and Kentucky. When settlers began to arrive in the
Northwest Territory from these states, many brought slaves with
them, and still others argued that it would benefit the new territory if more slaves could be imported. One expedient used to hold
slaves in the Territory in the face of the prohibitions contained in
the Ordinance was to have them sign indentures committing them
to 20, 40, or more years of service, either before they were brought
into the Territory or after they arrived.

When the question of the legality of black indentured servitude
was brought before them, the courts of two states that had been
carved out of the Territory during the early decades of the nineteenth century produced two very different interpretations of pre-

cisely what practices were prohibited by the prohibition on "involuntary servitude." In deciding the case of *Phoebe v. Jay* in 1828,[47] the Illinois high court framed the issue in terms of whether a laboring agreement had been *entered* into "voluntarily." If it had, then legal enforcement of the resulting agreement through specific performance or penal sanctions did not change the labor from voluntary to involuntary. The labor was "voluntary" because the worker had "voluntarily" agreed to perform it. All that was involved was the enforcement of a contract freely entered into.[48] Given the long history of indentured servitude in this country, and the common practice of penal sanctions to enforce labor contracts in Europe, the Illinois court's view of "involuntary servitude" was probably quite widely shared at the time. The Illinois rule did leave unresolved the question of how harsh the terms of a "voluntary" labor agreement would have to be before the agreement would be considered a contract of slavery and impliedly prohibited by the flat prohibition against slavery contained in the Ordinance. But under the Illinois rule, any state of servitude short of outright slavery could apparently be entered into in conformity to the Ordinance so long as it had been done "voluntarily."

Under the Illinois rule the court did have to face the question of precisely what circumstances rendered a decision to sign an indenture "voluntary" or "involuntary" in the first place. In *Phoebe v. Jay*,[49] a black woman had signed an indenture to serve for 40 years pursuant to a process established by a state statute. The statute authorized masters to bring slaves into the territory, so long as they presented the slave to a clerk of the court of common pleas within 30 days, "and in the presence of said clerk . . . agree[d] to and with his or her negro or mulatto upon the term of years which the said negro or mulatto will and shall serve his or her said owner or possessor."[50] If a black person refused to sign such an indenture, the master was empowered under the statute to return the person to the state in which he or she had been previously held in slavery. The Illinois court entertained no doubt that the decision to sign an indenture made by a black person confronted with this set of hard choices must represent a "coerced" decision rather than the "free" choice of a lesser evil. "I conceive that it would be an insult to common sense," Justice Lockwood wrote for the court, "to contend that the negro, under the circumstances in which [s]he was placed,

150 Robert J. Steinfeld

had any free agency. The only choice given [her] was a choice of evils."[51] What other hard choices might "coerce" a person into entering a labor relation "involuntarily" remained to be explored.

If in Illinois the specific enforcement of a 40 year labor agreement did not render the labor involuntary so long as the agreement had been entered into voluntarily, such was not the case in Indiana. In 1821, the Indiana high court set aside the indenture of a black woman who, the court reported, had *"voluntarily* bound herself to serve . . . as an indented servant and house-maid for 20 years."[52] The court ruled that

[w]hile the [woman] remained in the service of the obligee without complaint, the law presumes that her service was voluntarily performed; but her application to the Circuit Court to be discharged from the custody of her master, establishes the fact that she is willing to serve no longer; and, while this state of the will appears, the law can not, by any possibility of intendment, presume that her service is voluntary . . . The fact then is, that the appellant is in a state of involuntary servitude; and we are bound by the Constitution, the supreme law of the land, to discharge her therefrom.[53]

Under the Indiana rule, labor became "involuntary servitude" the moment a person wanted to leave the relationship but was prevented from doing so by a judicial decree of specific performance, or by bodily seizure by an employer. Here, the legal right to withdraw from the labor relationship at any time the laborer wished marked the boundary between "free labor" and "involuntary servitude." The use of the legal remedies of specific performance or penal sanctions to enforce even a "voluntary" labor agreement turned the labor into "involuntary servitude." The issue implicitly left unresolved by the Indiana decision was whether a labor contract could be enforced through *any* legal remedy at all consistently with the proscription against "involuntary servitude." More fundamentally, the rule brought to the surface a fundamental problem with liberal commitments to freedom, which contained a basic, unresolvable contradiction between commitments to liberty of person and commitments to liberty of contract. Liberty of person under the rule required that one's contractual liberty be restricted. The rule deprived a person of the legal power to alienate labor irrevocably by contract.[54]

These opposing interpretive traditions, generated in the 1820s by the conflict over slavery in the Northwest Territory, persisted in American constitutional law throughout the nineteenth century. A definitive choice between them, surprisingly, was not made by the United States Supreme Court until the twentieth century. This is not to say that the views enjoyed equal popularity in the wider culture. It is fair to say that throughout the North, labor practices and ideas conformed, in the main, to the view set forth by the Indiana court. With the complete disappearance of white immigrant indentured servitude in the 1830s, the labor agreements of white adults were not subject to specific performance or to penal sanctions anywhere in the northern states, with one significant exception we discuss below. But there were only a few court opinions inscribing this view in constitutional law. One such was rendered by the Massachusetts Supreme Judicial Court in 1856. The court held that a *voluntary* labor contract amounted to a species of servitude akin to slavery if a worker was not free to leave before its expiration, and if the nature of the labor services and the place where they were to be performed were left to be determined unilaterally by the employer.[55] On the other hand, the Supreme Court of the New Mexico Territory, following the lead of the Territorial legislature, adopted the Illinois view of the legitimate scope of labor contract enforcement in an opinion it delivered in 1857.[56]

Even the Civil War did not lay the interpretive question definitively to rest. In 1867, Congress seemed to adopt the Indiana/Massachusetts interpretation of the term "involuntary servitude." The Anti-Peonage Act it passed that year under its powers to enforce the Thirteenth Amendment reached a labor relationship that was often entered into "voluntarily." But this statute was badly drafted and failed to resolve the old question. The lack of a definitive constitutional resolution of the interpretive question even at this date may help to explain why the United States Army, and in certain cases agents of the Freedmen's Bureau, could believe that they were introducing a "free labor" system into the South even as they went about providing for the criminal enforcement, in numerous cases, of the labor contracts of former slaves who came under their jurisdiction.[57]

The United States Supreme Court did not directly confront the issue until 1897, when a majority of the court adopted, not the Indiana/Massachusetts interpretation, as one might have expected,

but the Illinois/New Mexico interpretation of the term "involuntary servitude." The Indiana view, however, which was to triumph in
the twentieth century, survived in Justice Harlan's dissent. The
case of *Robertson v. Baldwin* arose when several merchant seamen
were arrested for deserting their ship in Oregon before it had completed its voyage, in breach of the contract they had signed to perform the duties of seamen during the entire voyage. The men were
detained by the local authorities until the ship was ready to sail,
and then they were placed on board against their wills. They refused to perform their duties, and when the ship returned to San
Francisco, they were arrested and charged with refusing to work in
violation of a federal statute governing merchant seamen. They
sued out a writ of habeas corpus asking that they be freed from
their confinement, arguing that the federal statute under which
they were being held violated the "involuntary servitude" provision of the Thirteenth Amendment.

The court upheld the validity of the statute on two grounds.
The first, broader ground is the more interesting one. The validity
of this statute, Justice Brown wrote for the court,

depends upon the construction to be given to the term "involuntary servitude." *Does the epithet "involuntary" attach to the word "servitude"
continuously, and make illegal any service which becomes involuntary at
any time during its existence; or does it attach only at the inception of
the servitude, and characterize it as unlawful because unlawfully entered
into?* If the former be the true construction, then, no one, not even a soldier, sailor or apprentice, can surrender his liberty, even for a day; and the
soldier may desert his regiment upon the eve of battle, or the sailor aban-
don his ship at any intermediate port or landing, or even in a storm at sea
. . . *If the latter, then an individual may, for a valuable consideration,
contract for the surrender of his personal liberty for a definite time and
for a recognized purpose, and subordinate his going and coming to the
will of another during the continuance of the contract;*—not that all such
contracts would be lawful, but that *a servitude which was knowingly and
willingly entered into could not be termed involuntary. Thus, if one
should agree, for a yearly wage, to serve another in a particular capacity
during his life, and never to leave his estate without his consent, the contract might not be enforceable for the want of a legal remedy, or might be
void upon grounds of public policy, but the servitude could not be properly termed involuntary* [emphasis added]. Such agreements for a limited
personal servitude at one time were very common in England [citing an
1823 English statute] . . . The breach of a contract for personal service has
not, however, been recognized in this country as involving a liability to

criminal punishment, except in the case of soldiers, sailors and possibly some others, nor would public opinion tolerate a statute to that effect.[58]

The majority correctly saw that criminal punishment for labor contract breaches was not nearly as anomalous as many people in the United States believed. It referred to recent English practice as a way of vindicating its choice of freedom of contract over freedom of person, its resolution of that unresolvable dilemma within liberalism. The court also placed its decision on a second ground. "[T]he [Thirteenth] amendment," Justice Brown wrote, "was not intended to introduce any novel doctrine with respect to certain descriptions of service which have always been treated as exceptional," merchant mariners constituting one of these exceptions.[59] In a blistering dissent, Justice Harlan offered this reply to the court's opinion:

The condition of one who contracts to render personal services in connection with the private business of another becomes a condition of involuntary servitude *from the moment he is compelled against his will* to continue in such service . . . [T]o require him, against his will, to continue in the personal service of his master is to place him and keep him in a condition of involuntary servitude.[60]

Harlan raised the spectre that

If congress under its power to regulate commerce with foreign nations and among the several states, can authorize the arrest of seamen who engaged to serve upon a private vessel, and compel him by force to return to the vessel and remain during the term for which he engaged, a similar rule may be prescribed as to employés upon railroads and steamboats engaged in commerce among the states . . . Again, as the legislatures of the States have all legislative power not prohibited to them . . . why may not the States, under the principles this day announced, compel all employés of railroads engaged in domestic commerce, and all domestic servants, and all employés in private establishments, within their respective limits, to remain with their employers during the terms for which they were severally engaged, under penalty of being arrested by some sheriff or constable, and forcibly returned to the service of their employers?[61]

Harlan, a southerner himself, may have realized that the majority's opinion could open the floodgates to this kind of legislation in the South. Immediately following the Civil War, a number of southern states had attempted to enact black codes, which contained provisions, among others, for the criminal punishment of labor contract breaches. These were greeted with an uproar in the North as attempts to reimpose slavery, and most of the codes were repealed or withdrawn, though some of these early laws survived.[62] With one eye on possible Northern reaction, in the 1880s Southerners began again to fashion a new set of laws calling for criminal punishment, now, in most cases, not directly for breach of labor contracts, but for acceptance of advances followed by failure to work out one's time. These so-called false pretense statutes proliferated in the 1880s and 1890s. But under the logic of *Robertson v. Baldwin*, such subtlety would not be necessary. Southerners could feel free to attack the problem of labor contract enforcement directly.[63]

Indeed, the majority's opinion echoed an opinion delivered by the South Carolina Supreme Court not too many years earlier. In *State v. Williams* it ruled that a South Carolina statute, which provided directly for the criminal punishment of labor contract breaches, did not violate the constitution's prohibition on "involuntary servitude."

If the general assembly sees proper to make the violation of a particular species of civil contracts a criminal offence, we are unable to discover in the provisions of the constitution anything which forbids such legislation. No person is required to enter into such a contract unless he chooses to do so; and if he does so, he must take the consequences affixed by the law to the violation of a contract into which he has voluntarily entered . . . We are unable to discover any feature of "involuntary servitude" in the matter. Everyone who undertakes to serve another in any capacity parts for a time with that absolute liberty which it is claimed that the constitution secures to all; but as he does this voluntarily, it cannot be properly said that he is deprived of any of his constitutional rights; and if he violates his undertaking he thereby of his own accord subjects himself to such punishment as the law making power may have seen fit to impose for such violation.[64]

The opinions in *Robertson v. Baldwin* and *State v. Williams* make apparent that the interpretive tradition developed in Illinois in the 1820s still possessed great vitality at the close of the nineteenth century, long after the Civil War. At the time *Robertson v. Baldwin* was decided in 1897, there were, in effect, two systems of contract law covering labor agreements in this country. The Southern one bore rough similarities to the contract system that had been in effect in Prussia and England not too many years before. The Northern one, in which neither specific performance nor penal sanctions were available for labor contract breaches, had a long history, and was supported by its own constitutional tradition which harked back to a decision of the Indiana high court. Under these two constitutional traditions, both systems could make out a plausible claim that they were "free labor" systems based on "free contract."

The truth seems to have been that the majority in *Robertson v. Baldwin* did not believe that its decision applied beyond the situation of merchant seamen. But this is interesting in and of itself, given that *Robertson v. Baldwin* was brought to the Supreme Court as a test case mounted by the seamen's union.[65] The decision produced a strong reaction among organized seamen. As the *San Francisco Examiner* put it: "According to the highest tribunal which can pass on the matter, the difference between a deep-water sailor and a slave is $15 per month."[66] Union leaders immediately launched a campaign in Congress to have the federal statute amended. Under intense pressure from the seamen's union, Congress did give the seamen half of what they wanted, amending the statute, but eliminating criminal penalties only for desertion in American ports, not for desertion in foreign ports.[67] The seamen's union continued to lobby Congress on and off for complete repeal of penal sanctions for more than a decade, until finally, in the La-Follette Seamen's Act of 1915, it achieved what it had been seeking.[68] The seamen's victory was primarily symbolic by this time, however, since ship owners had, for the most part, abandoned the use of penal sanctions even before *Robertson v. Baldwin* was decided.

The seamen continued to pursue their goal of repeal through the legislature, even after the Supreme Court had begun to hand down its first peonage decisions. In *Clyatt v. United States* (1905), a peonage prosecution brought by the federal government against a Florida employer for "forcibly" returning workers to his service and decided only eight years after *Robertson*, the court finally made a definitive choice between constitutional traditions, adopting the Indiana interpretation of the term "involuntary servitude." Justice Brewer writing for the court declared,

Peonage is sometimes classified as voluntary or involuntary, but this implies simply a difference in the mode of origin, but none in the character of the servitude. The one exists where the debtor voluntarily contracts to enter the service of his creditor. The other is forced upon the debtor by some provision of law. But peonage, however created, is compulsory service, involuntary servitude . . . A clear distinction exists between peonage and the voluntary performance of labor or rendering of services in payment of a debt. In the latter case the debtor, though contracting to pay his indebtedness by labor or service, and subject like any other contractor to an action for damages for the breach of contract, can elect at any time to break it, and no law or force compels performance or a continuance of the service.[69]

Though it was implicitly rejecting the view of the *Robertson* majority, the *Clyatt* court did not explicitly overrule *Robertson*. Rather, it limited the earlier case to its facts, adopting the second ground of the decision as the rule of the case, and then simply brushing the case aside. "We need not stop to consider," Justice Brewer wrote, "any possible limits or exceptional cases, such as the service of a sailor [citing *Robertson v. Baldwin*]."[70] In *Bailey v. Alabama*, decided in 1911, in which a worker appealed his conviction for breaching a labor agreement to the Supreme Court, the court struck down Alabama's false pretense statute under which the worker had been convicted as violative of the Anti-Peonage Act and the Thirteenth Amendment. Justice Hughes, building on the *Clyatt* opinion, declared that the Anti-Peonage Act "necessarily embraces all legislation which seeks to compel the service or labor by making it a crime to refuse or fail to perform it."[71]

Evidently, northern elites were of two minds on the question of penal sanctions for labor contract breaches. When it came to their use against helpless black people in the South, with its history of slavery but also with its distance from northern labor relations, northern elites felt inclined to invoke the Indiana tradition which had, after all, first been developed in a similar context. The peonage cases which found their way to the Supreme Court had been initiated by federal authorities and did not grow out of an indigenous movement of black workers. The people responsible for the attack on southern peonage were Progressives, committed to protecting the weak by reforming government and the legal system.

When the question of penal sanctions was posed as an abstract matter of contract law in a northern context, however, where penal sanctions applied to only a tiny portion of the white working population and no widespread working class opposition was likely, the resolution of the question seemed not to be quite so straightforward for these elites. Not only do we have the decision in *Robert-*

son v. *Baldwin* to point to, but during the first decade of the twentieth century, the legislatures of three northern states made their sympathy with the views contained in *Robertson* clear when they enacted false pretense labor contract statutes of their own, aimed at enforcing the labor agreements of white workers who had received transportation advances to remote lumbering, mining, or railroad construction sites. Minnesota enacted such a statute in 1901,[72] followed by Michigan in 1903[73] and Maine in 1907.[74] We do know that the Maine statute was enforced. Fifty or sixty cases were brought before one rural justice of the peace alone under the 1907 legislation.[75]

In his dissent in *Bailey v. Alabama*, Oliver Wendell Holmes suggested that the majority's opinion had been improperly swayed by the particular social context in which the case had arisen. "We all agree that this case is to be considered and decided in the same way as if it arose in Idaho or New York. Neither public document nor evidence discloses a law which by its administration is made something different from what it appears on its face, and therefore the fact that in Alabama it mainly concerns the blacks does not matter."[76] And he went on to explain how deeply problematical the majority's opinion was. "The Thirteenth Amendment," he wrote,

does not outlaw contracts for labor. That would be at least as great a misfortune for the laborer as for the man that employed him. For it certainly would affect the terms of the bargain unfavorably for the laboring man if it were understood that the employer could do nothing in case the laborer saw fit to break his word. But any legal liability for breach of contract is a disagreeable consequence which tends to make the contractor do as he said he would. Liability to an action for damages has that tendency as well as a fine. If the mere imposition of such consequences as tend to make a man keep to his promise is the creation of peonage when the contract happens to be for labor, I do not see why the allowance of a civil action is not, as well as an indictment ending in fine . . . I do not blink the fact that the liability to imprisonment may work as a motive when a fine without it would not, and that it may induce the laborer to keep on when he would like to leave. But it does not strike me as an objection to a law that it is effective. If the contract is one that ought not to be made, prohibit it. But if it is a perfectly fair and proper contract, I can see no reason why the State should not throw its weight on the side of performance.[77]

Holmes was correct, of course; all contract remedies operate to enforce agreements by presenting a breaching party with a choice between performing and some disagreeable alternative. To the extent that a party decides to perform labor in order to avoid the unpleasant alternative, that party may be said to have chosen the lesser evil "voluntarily," or to have chosen it under "coercion." Either characterization is available, but once we decide to characterize such a choice as "coerced," as the majority decision does in the case of criminal penalties, then there is no *logical* ground for saying that any similar choice is "voluntary." And we must conclude that labor contracts cannot be enforced through any legal remedy at all if they are not to violate the prohibition on "involuntary servitude."

Though Holmes is correct about all this, it does not seem to have bothered the majority in either *Clyatt* or *Bailey*, who blithely ignored the coercive effects of money damages for contract breach, presenting them, in fact, as the opposite of "compelled" performance. "A clear distinction exists," Justice Brewer wrote in *Clyatt*, "between peonage and the voluntary performance of labor or rendering of services in payment of a debt. In the latter case the debtor, though contracting to pay his indebtedness by labor or service, *and subject like any other contractor to an action for damages for breach of that contract, can elect at any time to break it, and no law or force compels performance or a continuance of the service* [emphasis added]."[78]

It is of course also true, as Holmes recognized, that certain alternatives to performance are less unpleasant than others, and fewer people will tend to choose to continue performance when confronted with them. But the performance of those who choose to avoid these unpleasant alternatives by rendering the labor service is no more "voluntary" than the labor service of those who choose to perform to avoid the unpleasant alternative of prison. The decision of the majority is, from a logical standpoint, arbitrary, a decision to draw a line through a continuum, and to call certain decisions to perform labor under certain kinds of threats "voluntary," and other decisions to perform labor under other kinds of threats "involuntary." In fact, the decision as to where to place such a line is not a decision about where coercion begins or ends in labor relations. It is a normative political decision about what kinds of hard choices we should continue to allow certain people to force other people to make, as the latter go about deciding whether to enter or to remain in a labor relation; and what kinds we should not permit.

There is no natural or logical marking point in this process. The peonage cases place criminal penalties for breaches of labor contracts on one side of the line and ordinary money damages on the other, without any explanation or justification of this particular line drawing. What should be the court's attitude toward a host of other possible contract enforcement mechanisms? On which side of the line shall we place a negative injunction, one prohibiting a sports super star from playing with any other team than his present one? The disagreeable alternative to continuing to render labor services may be to take up another calling in which the remuneration is a hundredth of his current salary. Is this alternative disagreeable enough so as to make the decision to play out the contract "involuntary servitude"? Suppose a negative injunction is phrased to prohibit the party from working anywhere other than for his present employer. The disagreeable alternative to performance would be living on welfare, if one could qualify, or perhaps starving. Is *this* alternative disagreeable enough so as to make the decision to continue in employment "involuntary servitude"? Under modern law, negative injunctions are constitutionally permitted. What about the case of an employer withholding a month's pay, payable only if a worker completes his contract term, and so forth?

In the peonage cases, the Supreme Court created the modern constitutional standard for free labor by rejecting an earlier constitutional tradition which had defined "free" labor differently. The court took this step as a result of its belief that it was essential to combat southern efforts to reimpose a form of servitude on black people. And it is to this moral and political decision that we must trace the origins of modern free labor in this country, just as we must trace the origins of modern free labor in England to a political and moral victory of the laboring classes.

The conception and practice of modern free labor did not arise as the result of the spread of liberal ideas, or the diffusion of "free" markets based on "free" contract. It was the result of a difficult political and moral resolution of a fundamental conflict within liberalism, between the commitment to freedom of contract and the commitment to freedom of person. Indeed, modern free labor does not represent the pure expression of a regime of free contract. It is, on the contrary, constituted by a regime of contract rules that restricts freedom of contract by prohibiting workers from alienating their labor irrevocably, in the interest of preserving their liberty of person.[79] Other resolutions of this fundamental conflict were possible, leading to regimes of free contract like those in place in England and Prussia or Illinois during the first two-thirds of the nineteenth century. It was only a set of contingent political events and changing moral standards that produced our modern free labor during the late nineteenth and early twentieth centuries.

≺ IV ≻

Modern Free Labor

But this does not conclude the story of modern free labor, for there was another movement to redefine "free" and "coerced" labor mounted at roughly the same time, which failed. It is not only to the peonage cases, but to these failed contemporaneous efforts that we must turn in search of the constitutional origins of modern free labor.

Recall that in its decision in *Phoebe v. Jay*, the Illinois court had to decide whether the labor contract at issue had been *entered* into "voluntarily." To do so the court examined the alternatives to signing that faced the black woman in that case. These were to sign or to be returned to slavery in another state. Under the circumstances, the court ruled that the decision to sign was "coerced," because the "only choice given [her] was a choice of evils."[80] But suppose that the only choice confronting a worker was to sign or to see one's children go hungry. Confronted with this hard choice, is the decision to enter a labor relation the "voluntary" choice of a lesser evil, or a "coerced" decision?

The same problem which infects the question of remedies for breach of contract infects the entire concept of "voluntary" contract at the core of liberalism. Liberal ideas require that only "voluntary" agreements be enforced. If an agreement is not voluntary it should not be enforced, and perhaps should not be allowed. Any regime of free contract, therefore, must have a set of rules for deciding how to distinguish "voluntary" from "coerced" agreements. But here again, from the standpoint of pure logic, that effort can only yield arbitrary results, or more precisely results that are the outcome of normative rather than logical judgments. During the late nineteenth and early twentieth centuries, an activist American labor movement confronted constitutional law with precisely this challenge, though the issue came before the Supreme Court in a different jurisprudential posture than the peonage cases.

During the final decades of the nineteenth century and the early decades of the twentieth, a number of states passed legislation which was designed to aid working people in various ways. One type of law limited the hours working people could agree to labor. The case of *Holden v. Hardy* arose in 1896 when the operator of a Utah mine was arrested under a Utah statute which prohibited employers from asking underground miners to work more than eight hours per day. The act declared that employers who violated this restriction were guilty of a misdemeanor.[81] The mine operator, it was charged, had "unlawfully required"[82] one of his miners to work ten hours a day. The employer admitted the facts set forth in the complaint, but answered that he was not guilty, because the miner had "voluntarily engaged his services for the hours per day alleged."[83]

The case was brought to the United States Supreme Court where the question was whether the statute violated both the mine operator's and the miner's liberty of contract by prohibiting them from voluntarily entering into contracts which provided for longer hours of work. Could Utah constitutionally restrict freedom of contract in this way? The Supreme Court upheld the law, primarily on the ground that the state had the power to restrict freedom of contract in cases in which it was legislating to protect the health or morals of its citizens. But Justice Brown, writing for the majority, as he had just a year earlier in *Robertson*, went further. He placed the decision upon a second ground, questioning whether contracts for longer hours were actually entered into "voluntarily" at all.

The legislature has also recognized the fact, which the experience of legislators in many States has corroborated, that the proprietors of these establishments and their operatives do not stand upon an equality, and that their interests are, to a certain extent, conflicting. The former naturally desire to obtain as much labor as possible from their employés, while the latter are often induced by the fear of discharge to conform to regulations which their judgment, fairly exercised, would pronounce to be detrimental to their health or strength. In other words, the proprietors lay down the rules and the laborers are practically constrained to obey them. In such cases self-interest is often an unsafe guide, and the legislature may properly interpose its authority.[84]

Brown came very close to saying that it was proper for the legislature to interpose its authority in this case because the contract in question was not truly "voluntary," but the result of duress: "induced by fear of discharge to conform to [employer] regulations"; "constrained to obey them." There was at this time a well-established tradition in both common law and equity, which, though strictly circumscribed in its doctrinal applications, nevertheless held that, as Lord Northington put it in the eighteenth century,

Necessitous men are not, truly speaking, free men, but, to answer a present exigency, will submit to any terms that the crafty may impose upon them.[85]

Just a few years before *Holden* was decided, the Illinois Supreme Court observed that usury statutes represented a justifiable interference with freedom of contract.

Usury laws proceed upon the theory that the lender and the borrower of money do not occupy toward each other the same relations of equality that parties do in contracting with each other in regard to the loan or sale of other kinds of property, and that *the borrower's necessities deprive him of freedom in contracting and place him at the mercy of the lender* [emphasis added] and such laws may be found on the statute books of all civilized nations of the world both ancient and modern.[86]

Alhough *Holden v. Hardy* and the cases we are about to discuss arose as Fourteenth Amendment freedom of contract cases, not as Thirteenth Amendment involuntary servitude cases, their implications for the issue of when labor was rendered as a result of "coercion" and when it was truly "voluntary" were clear. In *Robertson* and *Holden*, Justice Brown carved out a position for the court which permitted legislatures wide latitude in the remedies they could adopt to enforce labor contracts, so long as the contract had been entered into "voluntarily." At the same time, he narrowed the circumstances under which contracts would be considered to have been entered into "voluntarily," implicitly calling into question the "voluntariness" of a wide range of labor agreements.

During the following decade, the Supreme Court turned Brown's position on its head. In the peonage cases, it narrowed the remedies states could constitutionally make available for the enforcement of labor contracts. In *Lochner* and in a series of later cases which we will discuss below, it expanded the circumstances under which contracts would continue to be considered "voluntary," so that "threats" of the kind that Brown pointed to would no longer be recognized as "coercive," justifying a legislature's interference with freedom of contract. The story of the formulation of the constitutional standard of modern free labor is simultaneously the story of the restriction of remedies for contract breach, on the ground that such remedies produced "involuntary servitude," and the refusal to expand the universe of "choices among evils" that were to be considered "coercive" with respect to entry into or continuation in a labor relation. The final triumph in constitutional law of this broad definition of "voluntariness" was not, as one might imagine, the simple result of the triumph of laissez-faire constitutionalism, but of a significantly more complex process.

In *Lochner v. New York*, decided eight years after *Holden v. Hardy*, the court divided five to four, the majority holding that the kinds of threats Brown had pointed to were not "coercive." The majority had a clear understanding of what was at stake. The New York law at issue in Lochner limited hours of work for bakers. The case itself arose when a proprietor of a bakery was indicted and convicted of a misdemeanor for "requiring" his workers to work longer hours. Justice Peckham wrote for the majority in striking down the law:

There is nothing in any of the opinions delivered in this case, either in the Supreme Court or the Court of Appeals of the State, which construes the section, in using the word "required," as referring to any physical force being used to obtain the labor of an employé. It is assumed that the word means nothing more than the requirement arising from voluntary contract for such labor in excess of the number of hours specified in the statute. There is no pretense in any of the opinions that the statute was intended to meet a case of involuntary labor in any form . . . The mandate of the statute . . . is the substantial equivalent of an enactment that "no employee shall contract or agree to work," more than ten hours per day.[87]

In a later case, *Coppage v. Kansas*, Justice Pitney provided an extended analysis of this constitutional standard of "voluntariness." At issue was a Kansas statute making it "unlawful" for an employer "to coerce, require, demand or influence any person or persons to enter into any agreement . . . not to join . . . any labor organization or association."[88] Pitney wrote that the statute

uses the term "coerce," and some stress is laid upon this in the opinion of the Kansas Supreme Court. But, on this record, we have nothing to do with any question of actual or implied coercion or duress, such as might overcome the will of the employé by means unlawful without the act. In the case before us, the state court treated the term "coerce" as applying to the mere insistence by the employer, or its agent, upon its right to prescribe terms upon which alone it would consent to a continuance of the relationship of employer and employé . . . The evidence shows that it would have been to the advantage of Hedges [the employee], from a pecuniary point of view and otherwise, to have been permitted to retain his membership in the union, and at the same time to remain in the employ of the railway company . . . But aside from this matter of pecuniary interest, there is nothing to show that Hedges was subjected to the least pressure or influence, or that he was not a free agent, in all respects competent, and at liberty to choose what was best from the standpoint of his own interests. Of course, *if [Coppage] . . . was otherwise within his legal rights in insisting that Hedges should elect whether to remain in the employ of the company or to retain his membership in the union, that insistence is not rendered unlawful by the fact that the choice involved a pecuniary sacrifice to Hedges* [emphasis added].[89]

This particular choice among evils merely led the employee "to choose what was best from the standpoint of his own interests," given the set of choices with which his employer confronted him.[90] This kind of hard choice was one which Pitney thought employers should continue to be permitted to force workers to make, a hard choice which led to a "voluntary" rather than a "coerced" decision. Pitney went on to offer an elaborate justification for a broad definition of "voluntariness," and hence broad scope for freedom of contract, under conditions of unequal distribution of property.

[I]t is said by the Kansas Supreme Court . . . to be a matter of common knowledge that "employés, as a rule, are not financially able to be as independent in making contracts for the sale of their labor as are employers in making contracts of purchase thereof." No doubt, wherever the right of private property exists, there must and will be inequalities of fortune; and thus it naturally happens that parties negotiating about a contract are not equally unhampered by circumstances. This applies to all contracts, and not merely to that between employer and employé. Indeed a little reflection will show that wherever the right of private property and the right of free contract co-exist, each party when contracting is inevitably more or less influenced by the question whether he has much property or little, or none; for the contract is made to the very end that each may gain something that he needs or desires more urgently than that which he proposes to give in exchange.[91]

Whatever we might think of the legitimacy of Pitney's position, it is important to understand that it was not a simple matter for the court to maintain such a position, under the circumstances then prevailing. For during these years, organized labor was not without its own means of forcing employers to choose between pecuniary sacrifice and doing the will of their employees, and the Supreme Court was faced with a bit of a dilemma. Could such choices *not* be "coercive" when employers forced workers to make them, but "coercive" when unions forced employers to make them? Justice Pitney did not hesitate to resolve this dilemma by adopting flatly inconsistent positions.[92] In *Hitchman Coal & Coke Co. v. Mitchell*, Pitney, writing for the court, upheld an injunction against a labor union. One of the grounds upon which he placed the decision was that the *pressure* applied by the union to force the employer to *agree* to recognize the union was "coercive." The union's object, Pitney wrote, was

to alienate a sufficient number of the men to shut down the mine, to the end that *the fear of losses through stoppage of operations might coerce* [the employer] into "recognizing the union."[93]

Other members of the court, however, believed that the answer in the two situations had to be the same, but they divided over whether that answer should be yes, such actions were "coercive" in both kinds of cases and should be regulated by the state; or no, they were not, and the parties should be permitted to enter "voluntary" agreements under these kinds of pressures. Justices Day and Hughes took the former position, Justice Brandeis the latter. In *Coppage*, Day wrote,

It is constantly emphasized that the case presented is not one of coercion. But in view of the relative positions of employer and employed, who is to deny that the stipulation here insisted upon [agreement not to join a union] and forbidden by the law is essentially coercive? No form of words can strip it of its true character . . . [But now let us take] [a]n analogous case,—viewed from the employer's standpoint . . . Can the State, in the exercise of its legislative power, reach concerted effort of employés intended to coerce the employer as a condition of hiring labor that he shall engage in writing to give up his privilege of association with other employers in legal organizations [to promote their interests]?

I entirely agree that there should be the same rule for employers and employed, and the same liberty of action for each. In my judgment, the law may prohibit coercive attempts, such as are here involved, to deprive either of the free right of exercising privileges which are theirs within the law.[94]

But in his dissent in *Hitchman Coal*, Justice Brandeis adopted the opposite position. The two kinds of situations should indeed be treated in the same way, but neither should be recognized as "coercive" in law.

It is also urged that [the union is] seeking to "coerce" [the coal mine owner] to "unionize" its mine. But coercion, in a legal sense, is not exerted when a union merely endeavors to induce employees to join a union with the intention thereafter to order a strike unless the employer consents to unionize his shop. Such pressure is not coercion in a legal sense. The employer is free either to accept the agreement or the disadvantage. Indeed, the [employer's] whole case is rested upon agreements secured under similar pressure of economic necessity or disadvantage. If it is coercion to threaten to strike unless [the employer] consents to a closed union shop, it is coercion also to threaten not to give one employment unless the [worker] will consent to a closed non-union shop. The employer may sign the union agreement for fear that *labor* may not be otherwise obtainable; the workman may sign the individual agreement for fear that *employment* may not be otherwise obtainable. But such fear does not imply coercion in a legal sense.[95]

With the growing realization that the kinds of hard choices employers could sometimes force employees to make were similar in nature to the kinds of hard choices that organized employees could sometimes force employers to make, perceptions changed. Workers and employers were restored to a kind of plane of equality, at least in the abstract. Many unions wanted the courts to stop interfering as they waged economic war with their employers. It became increasingly difficult, under the circumstances, to portray these kinds of threats as threats which gave rise to "coerced labor" when employers made them. These apparent similarities were, in large measure, illusory, however. To workers, a pecuniary threat could mean spending the winter in the cold, without sufficient food, or perhaps losing one's home. It rarely meant that to employers. Nevertheless, the increasing acceptance in law of the power of organized labor during the first decades of the twentieth century helped finally to cement the position of the laissez-faire constitutionalists that economic coercion did not produce "coerced labor."

And so by this complicated path, we come to the constitutional origins of the modern American definition of free labor. Far from being the simple result of the triumph of free markets under a liberal state, modern free labor is the result of a complicated set of moral and political choices to restrict freedom of contract in some ways but not in others, a set of choices that were only finally inscribed in American constitutional law in the course of this century. Europeans followed their own quite different, but equally complex, path to a conception of "free" labor in the twentieth century. It is similar to the American in some ways, but also different in that it regards a vigorous social insurance system (which limits the disagreeableness of the alternatives to work which confront working people) as an essential component of a "free" labor system.

Precisely because the line between free and coerced labor is drawn on the basis of normative and political judgments, it can never be drawn finally and irrevocably. Whenever our Supreme Court is again confronted with a peonage prosecution in which a worker is shown to have given his labor under appalling working conditions, as in the recent Shackney and Kozminski cases with which we began this chapter, judges, even conservative judges, will be tempted to move the line subtly or not so subtly in order to redeem the promise of American justice. Simultaneously, they will fear that if they do so they will be placing the entire system of voluntary contract in question. How these tensions are resolved will depend upon who sits on the court, what political circumstances prevail in the country, and many other factors, all of which will determine whether the line dividing "coerced" from "free" labor will be moved again in the future as it has been moved in the past.

Race, Labor, and Gender in the Languages of Antebellum Social Protest

DAVID ROEDIGER

"You have been with us, too, for some years, and can fairly compare the twilight of rights, which your race enjoy at the North, with that 'noon of night' under which they labor south of Mason and Dixon's line. Tell us whether, after all, the half-free colored man of Massachusetts is worse off than the pampered slave of the rice swamps."
—Wendell Phillips's letter prefacing *Narrative of the Life of Frederick Douglass, an American Slave* (1845)

R ECENT SCHOLARS OF the nineteenth century, like the reformers they study, emphasize that African American slavery affected the visions and strategies of movements for the freedom of workers and of women in the antebellum United States. Indeed the rich historical literature on slavery and the idea of free labor, and the fine body of work on the roots of women's rights organizations and ideas in abolitionism, fully establish the mid-nineteenth century United States as illustrating Orlando Patterson's insight that Western ideas about freedom were "generated from the experience of slavery."[1] From "sex slavery," to "wage slavery" to "white slavery," slavery became what Barry Goldberg has called the "master metaphor" in the "language of social protest" and the *lingua franca* in which the women's, white labor, and abolitionist movements spoke to and past each other.[2]

But so pervasive was the slavery metaphor, and so balkanized is historical scholarship, that difficult issues surrounding its deployment remain unexplored. One such issue is timing. To regard, for example, the chattel slavery of Africans as unproblematically available as a touchstone against which to measure other oppression is to miss the accomplishment of mid-nineteenth century antislavery movements, which helped to make it such a touchstone. As David

Brion Davis writes, "For some two thousand years men thought of sin as a form of slavery. One day they would come to think of slavery as sin."[3] Moreover, the view that there were many "slaveries"—to vice, to passion, to drink, to the bank, and in politics, for example—continued well into the nineteenth century. For white workers and white women to so zealously contend that they were "no (or little) better off than slaves" was to enter into a dramatically changing and contested discourse which ultimately made chattel slavery into what Alice Felt Tyler called the "background for every crusade."[4]

A second issue is that an understanding of the slavery metaphor suffers from a tendency to study race, class, and gender separately (or, at best, in pairs) rather than in what Black feminist writers have called "their simultaneity."[5] Thus the very different grounds on which white, largely male, labor leaders and white, largely middle class, women's rights activists drew comparisons with Black slaves, the various conclusions which they drew from those comparisons, and their differing abilities to work in coalition with abolitionists, go unexplored. The languages of social protest used by Black abolitionists and by militant working class white women consistently fall through cracks in discussions of the slavery metaphor, examined neither for their own importances nor for what they can tell us about broader discourses and movements. When Davis writes that abolitionism was "always related to the need to legitimate free wage labor," we may wonder if he has fully considered whether such a claim could apply to Black abolitionist labor radicals like Britain's Robert Wedderburn, to David Walker, to John Brown, to Lowell's labor abolitionists, or even to a Frederick Douglass or a Lucretia Mott.[6]

Considering more broadly the varied rhetoric of slavery and freedom would also call into question a tendency of existing scholarship to accept the premises of the discourse it describes. One excellent study of abolition and women's rights describes their symbiosis as "natural," while most treatments of white labor and abolition are inordinately sympathetic to the antebellum view that reformers, "trapped in a zero-sum game," were bound to give "precedence" to one cause over the other.[7] But if we set the "sex slavery" and the "wage slavery" metaphors alongside each other, a more complicated picture emerges: the seemingly natural affinity of movements promoted by the former metaphor, like the "inevitable" hostility promoted by the latter metaphor, is precisely what needs to be explained. Indeed if we carry our examination of the trajectories of these languages of social protest through 1870 rather than stopping in 1860, the difficulties attendant to regarding any coalitions as "natural" emerge clearly, as abolition-feminist alliances fall apart and as former abolitionists lend significant support to radical labor movements.[8]

To initiate a discussion of what a "simultaneous" consideration of the slavery metaphor might mean for our historical understanding of visions of freedom; of the relation of those visions to the terms of labor, to white terror, and to party politics; and of the dynamics of coalition among the oppressed, I would like to begin modestly. This chapter turns on a consideration of several moments involving Frederick Douglass, using each as a point of entry to broader issues. It may be true that comparison of other oppressions with chattel slavery, whether that comparison involved the "wage system" or "conventional marriage," necessarily "diluted the charge that Negro slavery in the South was a system of exceptional and intolerable oppression."[9] However, the *logic* of discourse was not all that was at issue and, for a variety of reasons which this chapter explores, labor reformers' use of the slavery metaphor occasioned explosive opposition from abolitionists, while use of the same metaphor by women's rights advocates did not always do so. What follows attempts to survey and to account for the various patterns of resistance and accommodation to the slavery metaphor by Douglass and other abolitionists. It seeks to locate those patterns only partly in the idealization of free wage labor by abolitionists. In large part, it argues, opposition to slavery, and the need to build effective coalitions and arguments against it, undergirded both the questioning and the toleration of the slavery metaphor.

≺ I ≻

Douglass, Abolition, and the Challenge
to "Wage Slavery" Metaphors

In 1846, on an extended speaking tour in Britain, Douglass had substantial contact with Chartist radicals—masters at the use of the language of political, and to some extent wage, slavery to describe the plight of the British masses. In a marvelous account which flirts with the idea of a "natural" but tragically missed connection between labor radicals and abolitionists, Douglass's biographer William McFeely details the patterns and limits of contacts between Douglass and the Chartists. In the course of this discussion McFeely pauses to make the vitally important observation that in the corpus of Douglass's writings and speeches, the "metaphoric" usage of slavery is largely absent. Indeed after Douglass's bitter 1845 comparison of the fawning "slaves" of political parties with plantation slaves who curried favor from overseers and masters, such rhetoric is almost wholly missing from his writing.[10]

This silence was not Douglass's alone. Although free Blacks in the North were, by 1840, among the ranks of those denied the republican liberty of political participation, African American protests seldom employed and carefully circumscribed the slavery metaphor to describe this denial. In the appeal for political rights in the "Address of the New York State Convention to Their Colored Fellow Citizens," for example, the charge was to avoid "political slavery" by building on the fact of having been "relieved" from "chains and slavery," to continue progress to the "exalted privileges of a freeman," though the document once referred to Black New Yorkers as "political slaves" already. A similar 1848 appeal in Pennsylvania emphasized "we are not slaves," as it framed struggle historically: "Our fathers sought personal freedom—we now contend for political freedom." In an 1855 letter to Douglass, the abolitionist Uriah Boston went so far as to provide an annotated list of the free Blacks' advantages over slaves. While the idea that free Blacks were often only "nominally" so ran through the antebellum African American state convention movement and early Black nationalism, the slavery metaphor appeared far less frequently than in women's and white labor movement literature.[11] Firm distinctions between "enslavement" and "prejudice" recurred. Douglass even argued at times that the "low condition" of free Blacks in the North ought to claim abolitionists' attention because it was used to argue against emancipation and thus stood as a "stumbling block [to] the slave's liberation."[12]

This care to portray Southern slavery as *sui generis*, even while agitating against Northern oppression, must be seen as part of an abolitionist strategy properly designed to make chattel slavery the focus of moral outrage. But it is likewise important to stress that Black abolitionists, and especially runaway slaves who became abolitionists, occupied positions which enabled them to contribute to the shaping of such a strategy most forcefully. C. L. R. James's characterization of such figures as the "self-expressive presence . . . embodying in their persons the nationally traumatic experience of bondage and freedom [without whom] antislavery would have been a sentiment only,"[13] captures much. It suggests the monumental import, as matter of fact and as political statement, of a Frederick Douglass regarding his life as being divided into two distinct parts. In one he "experienced slavery"; in the other he became a "part of this living, breathing world."[14]

The remarkable 1850 "Letter to the American Slaves from Those Who Have Fled from American Slavery" made the same point more self-consciously. Slavery, its authors wrote in terms which find echoes in recent scholarship, was not just death but the experience of being "killed all the day long." It stood as "the curse of curses, the robbery of robberies, and the crime of crimes." The fact that before and, especially, after 1850, runaways necessarily feared capture and return to slavery sometimes made for a feeling, as Harriet Jacobs put it, of being still a "slave" in the North. But such realities, as well as the reality of racial discrimination in the North, also made the more common drawing of a sharp distinction between Southern bondage and the Northern "liability to be seized and treated as slaves," all the more impressive and vital.[15]

In July of 1843, John A. Collins, a Fourierist advocate of land re-distribution and the general agent of the American Anti-Slavery Society (AASS), scheduled an "anti-property" meeting in Syracuse at the same time that Douglass, Abby Kelley, and Charles Lenox Remond were to speak at an abolitionist gathering. When challenged, Collins agreed to appear at the abolition event and cancel the anti-property one. But what he said at the meeting distanced him from Remond and Douglass. Collins "quickly turned the audience's attention from the 3,000,000 of his countrymen held in slavery to the 800,000,000 people worldwide whom he described as living with the evils deriving from property." Abolition, on this view, was "a mere dabbling with effects." Remond responded by furiously reasserting the primacy of the evil of chattel slavery.

Douglass more coolly pledged to leave the projected tour on which he and Collins were to speak under AASS auspices, if Collins were not prevented from repeating his performance. As they waited for support from the AASS leadership in Boston, Douglass and Remond showed signs of implementing such a boycott, attending the National Convention of Colored Citizens, not a scheduled AASS convention, in Buffalo. The national leadership, after threatening to dock Douglass's pay, ultimately but hesitantly did side with Douglass and Remond, removing the unrepentant Collins as general agent.[16]

The Douglass-Collins conflict was an early salvo in an increasingly fierce battle. In the middle and later 1840s labor and land reformers attempted to show that landlessness and wage labor amounted to a "slavery" as vile as and more pervasive than Southern slavery. Abolitionists fiercely rejected "metaphoric uses" of slavery in such ways. The term "white slavery," and labor reform contentions that at most a "shade" of difference separated it from chattel slavery, had existed in the United States since the 1830s; William Lloyd Garrison had unsympathetically parried charges of abolitionist insensitivity to the white poor's plight during his 1840 trip to Britain for the World's Anti-Slavery Convention. "Have We No White Slaves?" read one leaflet he was handed there.[17] But the initial United States clash leading to an open rupture between abolitionists and those who styled themselves as opponents of "all slavery" had Douglass and Collins at its center. By 1847, Garrison was publishing words reflecting the "Down with all slavery, both chattel and wages" position in his abolitionist publication, The Liberator. However, they appeared only in its "Refuge of Oppression" column, which sourly reprinted proslavery propaganda. However strenuously such reformers as George Henry Evans, William West, and Horace Greeley insisted that they did not "hate chattel slavery less [but] wages slavery more," abolitionists insisted otherwise.[18]

The major exceptions in which Douglass and fellow abolitionists suggested that they might see white laboring people as being in a state of semi-slavery lay on the other side of the Atlantic. Wendell Phillips, for example, held out the possibility that political powerlessness and driven work made some British workers unfree. But in his case and that of others, when lack of freedom of aristo-

cratic Europe was admitted, the context was usually one designed
to make stronger the point that white American workers, enfran-
chised and mobile, could not be considered enslaved.[19] Reflections
on the oppression of increasingly landless, politically disempow-
ered, and colonized Ireland fit this pattern. In an antebellum autobiography, Douglass recounted a visit to Ireland in which the sor-
rowful music he heard convinced him that Irish peasants and
American slaves were trapped inside the same "wail." He credited
a speech on "Catholic emancipation" in Ireland, read while he was
still a slave in Baltimore, with giving a "tongue" to his antislavery
dreams. In attempting to recruit support for abolitionism in Ireland
and among Irish Americans (with considerable success in the former case and virtually none in the latter), abolitionists preached a
double "repeal," of United States slavery and of British oppression
in Ireland. In an 1846 letter to Garrison, Douglass wrote of his
need, as one "identified with one class of outraged, oppressed and
enslaved people," to speak out against the "misery and wretched-
ness of the Irish people."[20]

In praising the 1848 risings in Europe, Douglass singled out
"Ireland, ever chafing under oppressive rule" for its heroic determination to "be free or die." After the Civil War, with the need to
placate British antislavery opinion no longer in force, Douglass was
even more emphatic, welcoming the jeering of the "besotted" English royal family on tour in Ireland as "a very natural and genuine
exhibition of the feelings of the Irish people," reacting to the "oppression and despotism" of the English government. Writing at a
time when the land question was especially posed in the American
South as well as in Ireland, Douglass skewered British reformers
who had taken "safe and harmless pleasure" in agitating for abolition while ignoring Ireland. He singled out for praise the Irish revolutionary Jeremiah O'Donovan Rossa, connecting Rossa's exploits
with those of the anti-British rebels who mounted the Sepoy insurrection in India from 1857 to 1859 and the Gordon conspiracy in
Jamaica in 1865.[21]

Nonetheless, Douglass and other abolitionists stopped quite
short of characterizing British oppression of Ireland as enslavement. The analogy between such oppression and that of free Blacks
in the United States did have its appeals. But after such prolabor
papers as the *Voice of Industry* counted Irish famine deaths as

proof that wage slavery caused greater horrors than Black slavery, and after recruitment of Irish Americans to abolition had proven a failure, Douglass was firm in his denial. "The Irishman is poor," he reasoned in 1850, "but he is not a slave. He is still the master of his own body." The Irish multitude could assemble, press grievances, write, speak, and emigrate. American slavery, that "grand aggregation of human horrors," rendered its victims as mute, as the "silent dead." The escaped slave Harriet Jacobs added, "I would ten thousand times rather that my children should be the half-starved paupers of Ireland than to be the most pampered among the slaves of America."[22]

Accounting for the often splendid rage that energized abolitionist reaction to agitation over "white slavery" is made difficult by the consistent expressions of common ground by enemies of chattel slavery and those who extended the metaphor to white labor. Douglass termed land reform a "great project," for example, and answered pleas from supporters in a factory town that he pay more attention to poverty among whites by declaring deep sympathy for their cause.[23] He specifically lauded workers' mobilizations during the 1848 revolutionary upsurge in France and at times verged on proclaiming what the historian Waldo Martin has called a "utopian, quasi-Marxist unity" of Black and white workers. Phillips meanwhile insisted that "wages slavery [and] white slavery would be utterly unintelligible" to a typical audience of laboring people. But he added that "crowded cities" and "manufacturing towns" provided some exceptions and that the absence of women's rights especially burdened women workers. Garrison signed an 1858 letter of sympathy to a radical labor meeting with the salutation "Yours to break every yoke."[24]

Abolitionists, and especially Black abolitionists, did not deny the possibility of white slavery, but rather searched for literal instances of it (for example, in the history of "Saxon slavery" and in odd contemporary Southern cases showing chattel slavery among whites) which shook up complacencies about certain races being "fit" for slavery. Political slavery fostered by the "slave power" and the degradation of slaveholding women and nonslaveholding poor whites in the South were evoked in abolitionist writing quite before their use by the Republican Party. But such "white slavery" did not rest on wages.[25]

Conversely, land and labor reformers often avowed a hatred of slavery. Indeed recent scholars such as Eric Foner, Eric Lott, and Alan Dawley have found in the very "rhetoric of wage slavery" evidence of a critique of all slavery and even an "identification" of free workers with slaves. In the British case, appeals to and by the working class often turned on the inattention of some abolitionists to the problems of workers domestically. However, as Seymour Drescher and others have shown, there were also deep connections, at the levels of discourse and of mutual support, between labor and abolitionist mobilizations.[26] Some who used the "white slavery" metaphor, especially in areas with large numbers of organized women workers, took considerable care to specify that "chattel slavery is the worst degree of slavery" although "far from the only one." *The Voice of Industry*, the labor paper of the Lowell factory women and others, printed poems in homage to Garrison and careful analyses of the unsurpassed "depth of slavery" suffered by Douglass and his fellow slaves, alongside contentions that abolitionists needed to reserve at least "a tear" for white slaves. The great shoe strike at Lynn in 1860 was fought under the banner AMERICAN LADIES WILL NOT BE SLAVES, but a worker at a strike meeting there held, "We know we are not a quarter as bad off as the slaves of the South" who could not vote, complain, nor strike.[27] Moreover, we know that urban artisans participated actively, out of proportion with their number in the population, in supporting abolition campaigns, though their unions did not. And, of course, large sectors of the land reform and abolitionist movements did join eventually in political coalition under the Republican banner.[28]

Indeed so great are the overlaps of labor reform and abolition that we might well wonder why the two movements did not amicably agree to view the wage slavery metaphor, as some modern scholars have, as a "rhetorical device" not to be taken "literally" in any case. Why did the 1845 hopes of the radical reformers at *The Harbinger*, that the "Land and Labor Reform movements" and the "general Anti-Slavery movement" would come to see themselves as one, so consistently go unrealized amidst contention over the slavery metaphor?[29]

A key to the abolitionist opposition to wage/white slavery metaphors has already been suggested. It lies in the insistence of Black leaders, often escaped slaves or the children of runaways, that the line between slavery and wage labor—a difference central to their own life experiences—be kept distinct. The Douglass-Remond-Collins episode illustrates a broader tendency for Black abolitionists to criticize forcefully the extension of discourse regarding chattel slavery to other forms of economic oppression. When militants from Douglass to William Wells Brown directly challenged such metaphors—at times by advertising the job vacancy created by their having fled slavery and asking if any white workers wanted to fill the position—they functioned not just generically as abolitionists intervening in an important debate but also specifically as Black abolitionists reflecting on their own and their families' life histories. Often their experience was transatlantic, so that the daring runaway William Craft could report that he never met a poor person in Britain who "did not resent it as an insult" when his or her circumstances and those of American slaves were compared.[30]

The land and labor reformers' penchant for reporting their own life histories also complicated matters. George Henry Evans and Horace Greeley, the most prominent such reformers, openly described their evolution as one moving from a special opposition to Black slavery to the realization that many slaveries needed to be fought. They, and others, often added openly that this realization made chattel slavery a less pressing issue. Indeed they insisted that the allegedly more radical reforms they championed had to precede abolition in time. Lacking such prior changes, abolitionism was mere "substitutionism." Emancipation would leave the Black Southerner as "a slave still, though with the title and cares of a freeman," and as "a great loser by such a change." Evans opposed "the slavery of property" and "the slavery of the lash" but he and his followers were certain that the former would have to end first, and even held that land reform would set an egalitarian example for slaveowners to follow.[31] Liquidation of the struggle for the immediate abolition of slavery was thus not an abolitionist charge but the stated policy of labor and land reformers. On both sides, issues of timing and priority were openly debated. To regard, as Bernard Mandel does, Evans and his followers as "in favor of emancipation" but as adopting "tactics which required the subordination of the slavery question to the labor question," is to see the abstract position land reformers championed and to miss the fact that the implications of their position were anything but abstract.[32]

The forceful abolitionist rejection of the wage/white slavery metaphor also grew out of a history and a context in which the calling of white workers in the North *slaves* was forwarded not just by those who opposed "all slavery" but by those who supported Southern slavery. It was not merely that proslavery Southerners, including such very visible figures as John C. Calhoun, James Hammond, and George Fitzhugh, found Northern workers utterly degraded, but also that proslavery Northerners, including such labor reformers as Ely Moore, Theophilus Fisk, and Mike Walsh, did likewise.[33] The inability of opponents of "all slavery" to separate themselves from supporters of Southern slavery deepened abolitionist suspicions of the idea of "white slavery." It was not just that an Evans and a Walsh shared rhetorical habits but that Northern groups decrying all slavery often hosted proslavery advocates and at times entered political alliances with them. That the record of support for abolition by labor groups institutionally was so spotty and the record of trade union racism against Black workers was egregious also undermined claims of labor's universal opposition to oppression.[34]

The association of those who avowedly employed the slavery metaphor to attack all forms of oppression with those who did so to deflect attacks on chattel slavery did more than raise questions regarding sincerity, however. In republican America, working men and women did not relish being termed slaves or being called females "without virtue" by outsiders, though they themselves and their leaders might use such rhetoric.[35] Thus abolitionists who rejected the white slavery metaphor did not simply refuse to see the world as workers saw it. Douglass, after all, practiced his abolitionist appeals early on by trying various arguments out on white workers. He carefully crafted appeals to the republican pride and the aspirations of such workers who were perhaps more eager to hear of their distance from slavery than of their proximity to it. Those who rejected the "white slavery" metaphor were particularly well positioned to argue in defense of the reputation of white workers against proslavery Southerners whose disdain for degraded factory women and "greasy mechanics" was clear.[36]

Finally, the divorce between abolitionists and those opposing "white slavery" was ensured by the grounds on which labor and land reformers pressed comparisons designed to make the slavery metaphor plausible. Both of the two major comparisons made by opponents of "white slavery" flew fully in the face of abolitionist ideas, at the levels of facts and of values. The case for "white slavery" was first of all narrowly materialistic. White workers in the North, it was argued, from decidedly partial evidence, worked harder, for longer hours, and at a higher rate of exploitation then did slaves. Sometimes the alleged evidence came anecdotally and rhymed: "The niggers have their tasks, and when done they may spree it,/ But the jers [journeymen] they were asked to work as long as they could see it." At other junctures mathematical precision seemed possible, as in the contention that capital kept 9/11 of the Northern white worker's product, and far less of the slave's. Abolitionist arguments, strongly made by Douglass, for the much greater efficiency of free labor, became grist for the "white slavery" mill, in that they could be flipped over to suggest proportionally more exploitation in the North. The most used analogy regarding working conditions held that the slave resembled the horse owned by one owner, who took care not to work the animal to death, and the free laborer was like a horse for hire, whose renters cared nothing about his or her welfare in the long run.[37]

It was not simply that such material comparisons were wrong, from an abolitionist point of view, but that the narrow grounds for making the comparison undercut the indictment of chattel slavery. Focus on narrowly material concerns obscured the systematic terror of slavery, a theme which always framed abolitionist descriptions of bondage.[38] When labor reformers did stray beyond speculations about the hours and conditions of work and the return on labor, they curiously emphasized that slaves enjoyed the relative advantage of "mutual dependence" in the relations to owners. According to this fully unrepublican distinction, slavery was preferable because it provided "protection" while wage labor did not. Here again it was not just conclusions which were at issue, but the adoption of a terrain of comparison which did not sharpen attacks on "all slavery," but instead mitigated indictments of chattel slavery.[39] In its essentials, the extension of the slavery metaphor to white labor found its premises in the same view of slavery current in another institution in which white workers have been said to "identify" with slaves: the minstrel stage.[40]

≺ II ≻

Abolitionism, Feminism and the Limits of "Sex Slavery"

In 1848, Douglass stood forth for women's rights at the first national convention held in the United States on that subject. Reportedly the only African American man in attendance—no Black women participated—Douglass was also, according to Eleanor Flexner, the first and for a time the most significant male leader to support Elizabeth Cady Stanton's insistence that the Seneca Falls gathering stand unequivocally for women's suffrage.[41] During the twenty years before the Black abolitionist/women's rights alliance fell apart during Reconstruction debates over women's suffrage and constitutional change, Douglass enjoyed a deserved reputation as a leading male advocate of women's rights. If he occasionally wavered on women's property rights, he did not do so on the franchise. If he once suggested that earlier abolitionist splits over women's rights amounted to destructive contention over a "side issue," he could also place blame for the split squarely on abolitionists who made the "judgment [that] the American slave system, with all its concomitant horrors, is less to be deplored" than public reform activities by women.[42]

Douglass's feminism has drawn considerable attention from historians as a living embodiment of the historic connection between abolition and women's rights. That connection is so well known that it is unsurprising that it is at times seen as "natural." But when viewed in comparison to Douglass's (and other abolitionists') reaction to white labor reformers' use of the slavery metaphor, Douglass's position seems more in need of historical explanation. If he rose to combat notions of the "white slavery" of workers, he abstained from condemning the usage of "sex slavery" metaphors by women's rights campaigners.

Such usages pervaded reform discourse quite as insistently as did land and labor reformers' fixation on the "slavery" of some white workers. From very early in abolitionism, when the Grimké sisters signed their letters "Thy sister in the bonds of women and the slave," and when Margaret Fuller decried "even well-meant restrictions" placed on women by men as akin to slavery, women's leaders frequently used metaphors to describe their oppression. As Blanche Glassman Hersh observes, the "woman and slave" comparison was both an "effective rhetorical device" and a favorite one. Susan B. Anthony found a wife "the slave of the man she marries." Taking of a husband's name was seen as akin to the fastening of masters' names onto slaves.[43] Stanton's eloquent defense of a mother who took her child away from an abusive husband challenged abolitionist men to see the case as like the defense of runaway slaves. To Sarah Grimké, "the very being of a woman, like that of a slave, is absorbed in her master." For Stanton, the "free" woman resembled "the slave on the Southern plantation" in that she could "own nothing, sell nothing."[44]

The comparison of white women and slaves admitted charges of overstatement just as the white slavery metaphor did.[45] Nonetheless the metaphor thrived. It could explain why men opposed women's rights. Like slaveowners, they could not see their own roles as oppressors. It could explain why, as Douglass put it, "women have more and stronger prejudices" against women's rights than men. Like slaves, such white women allegedly had "been oppressed so long that [they] cannot appreciate the blessings of Liberty." Such a woman, as Lucretia Mott held, had learned the slave's lessons in subservience: "she hugs her chains."[46]

Douglass registered no objection to the slavery metaphor when white women's rights advocates applied it to themselves. It is true that during the late 1830s and early 1840s, bitter debates over women's rights and women's speaking to "promiscuous audiences" rent abolition and called into question Angelina Grimké's contention that "the rights of the slave [and] woman blend like the colors of the rainbow." Indeed Grimké's husband, the militant abolitionist Theodore Weld, sharply warned against mixing the "*lesser* work" of women's rights with the "*greater* work" of abolition. But after these early clashes, as women's rights advocates elaborated the slavery metaphor in the 1840s and 1850s, abolitionists could rarely be found insisting on giving priority to one of the two struggles. Despite a considerable record of exclusion and segregation of Black women by white feminists, and notwithstanding biting criticism from Sojourner Truth and others regarding the racial and class blindnesses of the women's movement, the slavery metaphor went unchallenged except on rare occasions. To understand why is to see how differently the metaphor was employed by women's rights advocates than it was by labor reformers and to appreciate how dif-

ferent were the relations of the two reform movements to abolitionism.[47]

A first major contrast between women's rights usage and labor
reform usages of the slavery metaphor lay in context. While labor
reformers lacked a substantial record of ongoing practical activity
on behalf of slaves, women's rights grew in large part out of abolition. This historical reality, as Hersh shows, was as much a part of
the logic of woman/slave metaphors as any specific set of comparisons.[48] Much early argument for extension of women's rights rested
squarely on recognizing and enhancing their activities as fighters
against slavery. In *History of the Condition of Women*, Lydia
Maria Child used the same methods and much of the same material as in her earlier comparative studies in *Appeal in Favor of That
Class of Americans Called Africans*. Indeed, as Carolyn Karcher
argues in her biography of Child, the antiracist agenda of *History of
the Condition of Women* remained more explicit than her feminist
one.[49] Discussion of white women's oppression often unfolded
alongside, not instead of, detailings of the horrors experienced by
slave women. Moreover, as Nancy Hewitt reminds us, a substantial number of female abolitionists eschewed advocacy of women's
rights altogether and did not press comparisons of slaves and themselves.[50]

At times, women's rights advocates bragged, as labor reformers
did not, of being "more fully identified with the slave," not just of
being in a similar plight.[51] Rarely, but significantly, they also argued for affinities between their own oppression and that of free
Blacks, with Stanton pronouncing "skin and sex" as the "scarlet
letters" of the antebellum United States. Nor, of course, did alliances with proslavery political forces undermine women's rights
organizations' usage of the slavery metaphor as they did in the case
of labor reformers. Not only did women bring no voting strength to
the table, but proslavery ideologues clearly tied the defense of patriarchy with their defense of slavery. Proslavery attacks on
women's rights, seen as a symptom of Northern degeneracy, were
at times repaid in kind. Thus when women's magazine editor Jane
Grey Swisshelm forcefully opposed the Fugitive Slave Law, the
proslavery editor George D. Prentice accused her of being both
wrong on slavery and "a man." Swisshelm began her reply with

Perhaps you have been busy
Horsewhipping Sal or Lizzie
Stealing some poor man's baby
Selling its mother, maybe.[52]

The content and the terrain of comparisons employed by women using the slavery metaphor also mattered greatly. Unlike white labor reformers, who often convinced themselves that their own oppression was more harsh than that of slaves, feminists almost always hedged and admitted significant differences. Women, especially wives, were degraded "almost to the level of the slave," were in "about the same legal position [as] the slave," and suffered disabilities "not very unlike the slave laws of Louisiana." Women's legal status was "pathetically suggestive" of slavery. When Lucy Stone's use of the slave metaphor to describe married white women once underwent mild challenge, she immediately allowed that chattel slavery "is a still lower depth."[53]

Thus in the use of slavery as a metaphor by women's rights advocates there was far less to challenge the hard-won insights into the differences between chattel slavery and other forms of oppression of a Douglass than there was in the rhetoric of those who discussed "white slavery." Nor did women's rights discourse carry anything like the labor reformers' strong implication that abolition was a cause necessarily fated to wait until other "slaveries" ended before it could be addressed.

Finally, the terrain on which women's rights advocates claimed comparability to chattel slavery was far more compatible with abolitionist appeals than were the arguments developed by land and labor reformers. This was the case largely because feminists and abolitionists both idealized what C. B. Macpherson has called "possessive individualism," while land reformers idealized the individual's possessions. The inability of white women and of slaves to possess and control their own labor, wages, property, and bodies made possessive individualism powerfully appealing to abolitionists and to women's rights advocates. The parallels between laws regarding slavery and those regarding married white women's property were substantial. The women's rights evocation of the slavery metaphor consistently addressed such parallels. These comparisons, unlike those mounted by land and labor reformers, utterly eschewed the construction of ersatz measures of rates of labor exploitation comparing slaves and other oppressed groups. Indeed there was little specific discussion of the labor, as opposed to the property, of married white women when connections to slavery were made.[54] Nor was the alleged protection of ill, disabled, and aged slaves brought forward as evidence that slaves were like, or privileged over, married white women. Abolition and women's rights supporters both sought to disarm such references to patriarchal beneficence.

In short, the land and labor reformers wanted the slavery metaphor to concentrate on paternalist protection and on bloodless considerations of rates of return on labor; the feminist writers left intact the abolitionists' insistence that stark realities of property and terror set slavery apart from free labor. On the issue of terror, the women's rights argument accommodated abolitionism in a particularly interesting and intricate way. As a number of feminist scholars have shown, the antebellum white women's movement tended not to make control over the physical bodies and the sexuality of married white women a public issue, although its leaders at times privately insisted on the centrality of just such control to women's freedom.

This silence, and at times self-censorship, left much space in women's rights discourse for the slave woman's imperiled body to stand in for consideration of white women's vulnerability to sexual coercion and terror. Consider, for example, S. E. P.'s remarkable 1839 poem "Appropriate Sphere of Woman," published in *The Liberator*:

> Tell me not of Woman's station,
> Tell me not we leave our "sphere,"
> When we urge by mild persuasion,
> Rights to every woman dear.
> When her back is stained and gory,
> When her tears in anguish flow,
> Shall we then not heed her story—
> Her sad tale of grief and wo?
> When her tend'rest ties are riven,
> For the sordid love of gold;
> And her children from her driven,
> "Human chattels" to be sold . . .
> Must we seek our lips to fetter,
> When our nature bids us plead?
> By our silence be the abetter,
> Causing woman's heart to bleed?

Evoking the slavery metaphor and then concentrating solely on the bodies of slave women, feminists made, and refused to give flesh to, a critical comparison. Thus Karen Sanchez-Eppler observes that abolitionist-feminist literature could "emphasize the similarities in the condition of women and slaves" even as its frequent use of the image of "the sexually exploited female slave betray[ed] an opposing desire to deny any share in this vulnerability."[55] While such psychological projection rightly has been read as evidence of a desire to avoid speaking, if not thinking, directly about the politically and personally difficult issue of sexual terror, it may also have reflected a desire to avoid making claims which made literal the slavery metaphor and put at risk abolitionist-feminist cooperation. In any case, the concentration of attention on the bodies of slave women in white feminist literature raised issues of slavery and terror which labor reformers' use of the slavery metaphor thoroughly suppressed.

≺ III ≻

The Burden of Slavery and the Roots of Division

This close consideration of the differences between labor reform and women's rights where the slavery metaphor is concerned has emphasized putting the discourse of each movement into counterpoint with abolitionism, and particularly with the African American abolitionism of Frederick Douglass. It suggests that while the abolitionists claimed chattel slavery as the greatest American evil, they did not simply reject any other claims of "enslavement." From the plight of the Irish to women's rights, Douglass and his colleagues could accommodate limited use of the slavery metaphor, if doing so promised to serve the interests of political coalition and if the particulars of the comparison did not vitiate the argument against slavery and/or cast abolition as a secondary reform which needed to wait its turn behind more fundamental ones. The existence of ongoing coalitions, or their absence, could also structure the ways in which the slavery metaphor was articulated, was tolerated, and was attacked. The stark distinction between abolitionists' acceptance of the slavery metaphor as used by women's rights advocates and fierce opposition to its use by land and labor reformers also suggests that some coalitions were more viable than others while slavery existed in a society taking off toward industrial capitalist expansion. Since both slavery and patriarchy violated the sanctity of property in one's own person, the meshing of their arguments was far less difficult than making abolitionism square with labor reform ideas.

Nonetheless, this bringing together of interactions between abolitionism and land reform and abolitionism and women's rights around the slavery metaphor does not support the extension to the antebellum United States of David Brion Davis's arguments concerning antislavery's contributions to the legitimation of wage labor. To argue that abolition and women's rights could find common ground because they were both bourgeois reform initiatives which validated capitalist labor relations misses the mark in several ways. Women's rights, in its evocations of the slavery metaphor and elsewhere, spoke little to the question of wage labor and it was by no means clear in 1850 that the logic of capitalist relations could successfully undergird even limited appeals for women's freedom. More critically, if we take Douglass (rather than an atypical capitalist reformer like Lewis Tappan) as central to abolitionism, it becomes properly difficult to suppose that the idealizing of the wage relationship formed any significant part of the core of the abolitionist political project. Certainly Douglass could be found singing the praises of "free" waged labor in the North. But he did so largely in response to proslavery, labor reform, and minstrel arguments which held chattel slavery to be less onerous and perilous than free labor. His goal, and that of abolitionists generally, was manifestly the ending of slavery, not the perpetuation of wage labor. When emancipation came, abolitionists often moved dramatically to positions critical of the wage system.[56]

The abolitionists' wholesale rejection of labor reformers' use of the slavery metaphor might, of course, be said to have had powerful consequences in legitimating wage labor, no matter what its strategic antislavery impetus. But one could easily counter that it was labor reform provocations and exaggerations in deploying the slavery metaphor which forced the abolitionists into strong defenses of wage labor. That the issue admits none but very highly subjective resolutions indicates how difficult it would have been to find an ideal middle position which effectively criticized wage labor while also acknowledging chattel slavery as the greater evil. No significant United States thinker or group managed to strike such a balance. This failure resulted from neither the abolitionists' blinkered middle class world view nor the narrowness of labor reformers. It resulted from the coexistence of slavery and wage labor, a coexistence bound to sow confusion and to work much more powerfully (but not naturally) to discredit the slavery metaphor and to legitimate the wage system than any abolitionist propaganda ever could.[57]

"We Did Not Separate Man and Wife, But All Had to Work": Freedom and Dependence in the Aftermath of Slave Emancipation

AMY DRU STANLEY

SINCE THE FOUNDING OF the republic, freedom and dependence have been paired as opposites in American thought. Yet at the heart of the revolutions of the nineteenth century—the abolition of slavery in the South and the rise of industrial capitalism in the North—lay the emergence of dependent wage labor. Almost simultaneously, although by vastly different social and political processes, chattel slaves and independent commodity producers were transformed into a class of hirelings. In both regions this transformation recast the meaning of freedom and gave rise to legal coercions at odds with the principles of free labor.[1]

In both regions, too, the contest over the making of this class turned in no small part on the question of dependent labor in the household.[2] My argument is that a central way that wage dependency was at once legitimated as freedom and condemned as slavery was in terms of housework. In both the South and the North, for both exponents and critics of the wage system, title to this quintessentially female brand of dependent labor was a crucial measure of freedom for men who owned nothing else but their own labor. Still, even after slave emancipation, it was unclear if this property right belonged equally to all men or if it presupposed race difference, along with differences of sex.

≺ I ≻

Free Labor and Criminal Dependence

Among slave emancipation's epic paradoxes was destroying the dependency relations at the heart of the Old South's social order while establishing wage dependency as the basis of a national free labor system. Freedpeople aspired not simply to negate the personal dominion of slave masters but in many instances to resist the impersonal discipline of voluntary wage contracts. In response, Yankee liberators designed a scheme of legal coercions to prompt them to sell their labor when the condition of being landless and hungry did not prove incentive enough. Rules outlawing "idleness" and "vagrancy"—classic proscriptions, inherited from early modern English law, that defined masterless persons subsisting outside wage contracts as criminally dependent and that forcibly extracted labor as punishment—were the cornerstone of this scheme. According to Oliver Otis Howard, the chief of the Freedmen's Bureau, the government's duty was not to "'feed the niggers in idleness'" as enemies of Reconstruction charged. Rather, he explained, in regard to those who would not enter or fulfill labor contracts, "At last I urged for such freedmen the use of the vagrant laws." His justification was that "wholesome constraint" would promote "larger independence."[3]

By defining the alternatives as either wage labor or unlawful dependence, the northern architects of freedom invalidated ex-slaves' efforts to construct livelihoods based on independent property ownership and self-employment. Yet, far from being anomalous, institutions of emancipation erected on forced labor and vagrancy decrees had counterparts throughout the world in nations implementing the abolition of slavery.[4]

While northern emissaries of freedom were suppressing "idleness" through compulsory labor, southern legislatures were pursuing a similar agenda through the infamous Black Codes enacted immediately after the war. Among their other provisions, the Codes required black persons to enter into year-long wage contracts and prohibited vagrancy. For example, the antebellum Mississippi vagrant law, which had punished with fines and imprisonment an Elizabethan array of deviants—"rogues and vagabonds, idle and dissipated persons, beggars, jugglers, or persons practicing unlawful games or plays, runaways, common drunkards, common night-walkers, pilferers, lewd, wanton, or lascivious persons"—was rewritten to govern "freedmen, free negroes and mulattoes . . . without lawful employment or business." The Alabama Black Codes defined a vagrant as a "stubborn or refractory servant; a laborer or servant who loiters away his time, or refuses to comply with any contract for any term of service without just cause." The penalty for black vagrants was hard labor in jails or on chain gangs; or they could be hired out to individual employers for a term of involuntary service. Though by the postbellum era white persons were not subject any longer to penal sanctions for breaking labor contracts and were not forced specifically to perform them, under many of the Black Codes ex-slaves were arrested for quitting work and either returned to their employers or imprisoned as vagrants.[5]

Northerners responded selectively to the coercions aimed at the freedpeople, crying out that the Black Codes, but not Yankee free labor policy, resurrected slavery. Writing to Senator Lyman Trumbull about the mindset of the "great mass of the southern people," a Union soldier stationed in Meridian, Mississippi, observed, "It is their hope, and intention, under the guise of vagrant laws, &c, to restore all of slavery but its name." Abolitionist leaders also condemned the Black Codes as a return to "practical Slavery." But though they objected to some aspects of the Freedmen's Bureau policy, they did not equate its forcible labor laws with bondage.[6]

It is hard to suppose that Yankees wholly overlooked the parallels between the Black Codes and their own rules for converting slaves into wage laborers. At least some bureau officers were troubled about imposing vagrancy sanctions on ex-slaves who were idle "from necessity" rather than choice, cautioning against punishments that replicated slavery. But for most northerners, the crucial difference between the two sets of ordinances lay in their racial character. Bureau law was formally blind to color, extending existing vagrant rules "made for free people" to former slaves. By contrast, northerners denounced the Black Codes for imposing extraordinary punishments on "account of color." South Carolina policy was a case in point. In January 1866 the bureau nullified the Black Codes in the name of equal rights, declaring that "all laws shall be applicable alike to all the inhabitants." The bureau's own rules, which withheld charity from the able bodied and authorized hiring out convicted vagrants to planters, expressly provided that rules "applicable to free white persons, will be recognized as the only vagrant laws applicable to the freedmen." In the Yankee worldview, it was not legal coercion that contravened free labor, but its unequal application based on race.[7]

The many complexities of freedom, dependence, and compulsion had been signalled by the 1864 report of the American Freedmen's Inquiry Commission, which led to the bureau's formation. Written by the antislavery reformers Samuel Gridley Howe, Robert Dale Owen, and James McKaye, who were appointed by the Secretary of War to study the transition from slavery to freedom, the report warned against governmental paternalism that would inadvertently restore bondage "under the guise of guardianship." It advised that former slaves must be "self-supporting," not protected or burdened by special laws for "colored people" but treated "as any other freeman." And though holding that only the market's "natural laws" should govern wage labor and that ex-slaves "should be subjected to no compulsory contracts as to labor," it recommended vagrancy laws "as apply equally to whites."[8]

The Commission's report endorsed principles and procedures already established by the Union Army. As early as 1862 army officials ordered that fugitive slaves must be saved from "idle and vicious habits . . . that they should work; and as they are yet too ignorant, thoughtless and improvident to think and act judiciously for themselves, they must be subjected to wholesome rules and restraints." Later military ordinances required former slaves to toil on plantations and commanded that transgressors must be arrested as vagrants and forced to work, sometimes specifying that all idle persons loitering around the camps, "either white or black," should be set at penal labor. The Freedmen's Bureau elaborated these precepts. "A man who can work has no right to a support by government or by charity," declared the bureau in 1865. As one Mississippi agent told the ex-slaves in his district, if "you are found idle you may be taken up and set to work where you will not like it." Through all the bureau's proclamations ran warnings that freedom forbade dependence and enjoined labor.[9]

Notably, these peculiar institutions of freedom took root not only in the South but also in the North, where wage labor was hardly unfamiliar. During the era of Reconstruction, reformers and statesmen dedicated to free labor strove to abolish the dependencies of pauperism as well as of chattel slavery. Throughout the North, state legislatures dominated by Republicans augmented older codes by passing harsh new vagrancy laws, which punished persons who wandered about lacking work and asking for charity with imprisonment and forced labor. Massachusetts led the way. In

1866, just a month after Congress voided the Black Codes through the Civil Rights Act, it adopted an "Act Concerning Vagrants and Vagabonds" that confined roving beggars to workhouses. Though existing legislation had outlawed a wide array of streetfolk, the new statute dwelled on the crime of begging. Fittingly, it was promoted by Samuel Gridley Howe, who had finished his southern tasks with the Freedmen's Inquiry Commission. Now, as director of the Massachusetts Board of State Charities, he advocated new law sentencing "sturdy beggars" to "enforced labor."[10]

Roughly a quarter of a century earlier, in the British Empire, there had also been striking simultaneity between colonial slave emancipation and the metropolitan enactment of the 1834 New Poor Law, which granted public charity to sturdy paupers only if they assented to enter a workhouse. Yet the sanctions against dependency and the labor compulsions that accompanied the American triumph of freedom were more extreme. For unlike the British "workhouse test," the American variant of poor law reform commanded the summary arrest and forced labor of beggars, denying dependent persons even the formal right of free choice.[11]

In shaping postbellum responses to dependency, the ideas of Edward Pierce, a Boston lawyer with impeccable antislavery credentials, were especially important. In both the South and the North, he held positions that clothed his views with state power. Appointed in 1862 by Secretary of the Treasury Salmon P. Chase to oversee the famous wartime experiment with free labor cotton cultivation in the Sea Islands of South Carolina, he explained his mission as both moral and economic. "I was to observe all about . . . the capacities and traits of the negroes—how they could best be managed, and kept from being demoralized in this *quasi* interregnum—how for that end they could best be organized for labor and so far as possible their moral nature addressed and their good will secured." Pierce's reports from the South outlined a plan of emancipation that fused free labor doctrine with a defense of legal coercion. Chief among the incentives to voluntary labor, he wrote, were "love of wages, of offspring, and family." But when these failed, he recommended "the workhouse or even the prison." He reported warning former slaves "that if they were to be free, they would have to work and would be shut up or deprived of privileges if they did not . . . I told them they must stick to their plantations and not run about and get scattered . . . we wanted them to stay on the plantations and raise cotton." Yet Pierce opposed the Black Codes, not only for discriminating against ex-slaves, but also for classifying the breach of labor contracts as a crime.[12]

On returning to Boston, Pierce joined Howe on the Massachusetts Charities Board and then became a state legislator. In 1872, echoing ideas he had advanced in Port Royal, he claimed that criminal law must force begging vagabonds to work, a punishment not "interfering with personal liberty." In 1875 he drafted and guided through to enactment a vagrancy law that authorized overseers of the poor to extract some type of work from alms seekers— "chopping wood, picking stones"—in exchange for food or a night's lodging. On the cotton plantations, he had abhorred idleness, claiming that "Nothing is found to discourage faithful laborers so much as to see the indolent fare as well as themselves." As a state official in the North, he declared that the vagrant "lacks any principle or purpose impelling him to labor," thereby requiring the "force of the criminal law." Just as he had proposed workhouses for freed slaves, so he aimed to exact work from Yankee beggars. On both sides of the Mason-Dixon line, he justified penal coercion in transforming dependent persons into free laborers.[13]

Enactments embodying convictions similar to Pierce's swept the country during the depression of the 1870s. Charity reformers and state officials joined in promoting involuntary pauper labor laws as a remedy for the growing number of impoverished and itinerant persons—legislation that coincided with scientific philanthropy's assault on "indiscriminate" private almsgiving and public outdoor relief. The New England states passed a series of stringent vagrancy or "tramp" acts during this era, as did Pennsylvania in 1871, 1876, and 1879. Illinois tightened its laws against vagabond beggars in both 1874 and 1877, requiring their punishment in jails or workhouses for up to six months, whereas the 1845 criminal code had provided that they be hired out at public auctions for no longer than four months' service. In New York the State Charities Aid Association pledged to force "lazy vagabonds to work" and drafted several bills resulting in an 1880 act punishing them at hard labor in penitentiaries, amending earlier rules that had sent them to poor houses. "Harsh as it may seem," Francis Wayland, the dean of the Yale Law School, told the 1877 Conference of

Charities, "when those who honestly desire employment, but can find nothing to do, are reduced to the necessity of begging from door to door, they must . . . be classed with those who are unwilling to labor." Thus dependency became synonymous with the wrongful refusal to labor.[14]

Each year thousands were confined in workhouses under the vagrancy laws. Labor reformers contended that the legislation violated personal liberty, but the courts rarely struck the statutes down as unconstitutional. One exception, significant in both its reasoning and its holding, was an 1876 Maine case. The case concerned a law authorizing overseers of the poor to commit to the workhouse "'all persons able of body to work, and not having estate or other means to maintain themselves, who refuse or neglect to do so.'" The state supreme court ruled that the law was an "arbitrary exercise of power" that violated the Fourteenth Amendment. Pointedly, the court drew a parallel between North and South—between impoverished whites and freed blacks. "If white men and women may be thus summarily disposed of at the north, of course black ones may be disposed of in the same way at the south; and thus the very evil which it was particularly the object of the fourteenth amendment to eradicate will still exist." The court interpreted the Maine vagrancy law as subverting the principles of emancipation.[15]

Yet, while underscoring the relationship between the rights of dependent citizens in the North and of former slaves in the South, even this ruling upheld involuntary pauper labor. It vacated the vagrancy conviction not because the law in dispute compelled work but because it did not require a judicial trial, thereby violating the guarantee of due process. The objection lay not "in the fact that . . . persons . . . may be restrained of their liberty," declared the Court. "Not in committing them to the workhouse, but in doing it without first giving them an opportunity to be heard." Just as Yankees distinguished the Black Codes from legal coercions to labor that were formally blind to color, so they vindicated forced labor, when rooted in proper legal process, on their own home ground. In both the North and the South the tenets of freedom distilled during slave emancipation barred people "not having estate" from subsisting without labor—either for wages or in exchange for alms. Yet prior to the vast social and ideological changes brought about by the contest over slavery, most Americans had stigmatized even voluntary wage labor as a form of dependence unfit for free men.[16]

<< II >>

Freedom and Housework—the South

The process by which wage dependency came to signify freedom was complex, grounded in new relations of property and labor as well as in changing moral and economic precepts; and it was protracted, emerging in the late eighteenth century, becoming decisive in the nineteenth, but still not wholly complete today. It went hand in hand with assertions of white racial prerogatives, but, paradoxically, gained extraordinary force with the rise of the abolition movement and the destruction of slavery. It was inseparable from the outlawing of dependency, defined as the abstention of the unpropertied from wage labor. And it was accelerated at the nineteenth century's end by a burgeoning culture of consumption that represented the gratifying of needs and desires, not the social relations of labor, as the measure of freedom. Absolutely central too, in redefining wage dependency as freedom, were rights claims based on sex—especially the claim that even free men who sold their own labor had a right to their wives' work at home. The two doctrines were tightly interwoven: that freedom meant toiling for wages and that dependent female labor belonged to hireling men but not to slaves.[17]

In the South, Edward Pierce was one of the first to enunciate these dual strains of free labor doctrine. "Where I came from all were free . . . we did not sell children or separate man and wife; but all had to work," he told ex-slaves on the Sea Islands plantations in 1862. "If they behaved well," he promised the men, "they should have wages, small perhaps at first . . . they should have better food, and not have their wives and children sold off." Thus he affirmed that black households would be as inviolate as those of white laborers, that freedmen's wives and children would not be commodities, that freedom protected the home from the market's incursions.[18]

Anxious that domesticity was something new for ex-slaves, which had to be taught just as much as thrift and industry, Pierce

lamented that they did not eat meals together at a family table and
that their houses and bodies were dirty. "Each one takes his hom-
iny, bread, or potatoes, sitting on the floor or a bench, and at his
own time. They say their masters never allowed them any regular
time for meals," he reported. "Whoever under our new system is
charged with their superintendence, should see that they attend
more to the cleanliness of their persons and houses, and that, as in
families of white people, they take their meals together at table."
Pierce heralded the arrival of female teachers who would visit former slaves' dwellings and meet with the women in order to "improve their household life." Worrying fastidiously about proper
meals and the cleaning of people and houses—as well as about
growing cotton—he equated freedom not only with home life but
with housework.[19]

Yet Pierce hardly exempted freedwomen from the injunction to
work for wages. He noted that on the plantations only the very old,
the very young, and the sick did not perform wage labor. Though
not listing how many wives numbered among the field hands, he
did explain that the term "half hand" included pregnant women.
Perhaps Pierce privately opposed this facet of free labor, for abolitionists had bitterly protested the economic exploitation of female
slaves, especially pregnant slaves and mothers who were forced to
suckle their infants in the cotton fields. But officially he voiced no
objections, tacitly endorsing the principle of freedwomen's wage
labor by calculating that if a man could work 300 days a year,
"each healthy woman could do about equally well." What he did
not figure was how she could do her field work while also taking
care of the cleaning and the family table that were as much tokens
of freedom as wage labor.[20]

The enshrinement of work and family life was entrenched in
antislavery thought, but abolitionists had not faced the actualities
of implementing free labor and profitably farming staple crops. It
was a commonplace of abolitionism to counter polemics about
wage slavery by contrasting the rights of the hireling—both at
work and at home—to the slave's situation. "May he not choose
his employer? May he not contract for his wages? . . . Is he chained
to the soil? . . . Can any power take from him his wife and his children?" These rights belonged to the "most degraded and dependent
free laborer," declared William Lloyd Garrison. "If the white labor-

ing men in America are *slaves* . . . they are Slaves that hold the
sceptre of Sovereignty in their own hands." Yet abolitionists did
not think to ask whether a free man's sovereignty would be diminished if his wife and children also worked for wages, as hirelings of
other men. Would this place him alongside the slave, who held
"the endearing relations of wife and child, at the beck of the ca-
price, the passion or the interest of a natural enemy"?[21]

For the most part, the Yankees who worked and traveled in the
South after the Civil War also avoided this question, even as they
celebrated domesticity and fussed about the sloppy housekeeping
of former slaves. The concern with the state of freedpeople's homes
was widespread, made central in discussions of freedom by both
men and women, black and white reformers, state officials and
missionaries from private relief agencies. As Sojourner Truth, who
taught former slaves "habits of industry and economy" as an agent
of the National Freedmen's Relief Association, explained the problem, "Many of them are entirely ignorant of housekeeping . . . they
all want to learn the way we live in the North."[22]

The famous fugitive slave Harriet Jacobs was still more emphatic in defining the home—and female labor within it—as a
touchstone of emancipation's progress. From a freedpeople's settlement in Alexandria, Virginia, where she served as a teacher, she
wrote in March 1864: "When we went round visiting the homes of
these people, we found much to commend them for. Many of them
showed marks of industry, neatness, and natural refinement. In
others, chaos reigned supreme. There was nothing about them to
indicate the presence of a wifely wife, or a motherly mother. They
bore abundant marks of the half-barbarous, miserable condition of
slavery, from which the inmates had lately come. It made me sad
to see their shiftlessness and discomfort; but I was hopeful for the
future." The tidy dwelling stood for civilized family life.[23]

Thus housework marked a home as free. In *The Freedmen's
Book*, a textbook used in freedpeople's schools, the antislavery
writer Lydia Maria Child linked dirty rooms and dirty clothes with
idleness and vagabondage, exhorting ex-slaves to be a model for
abolition throughout the world:

There are still many slaves in Brazil and the Spanish possessions. If
you are vicious, lazy, and careless, their masters will excuse themselves
for continuing to hold them in bondage, by saying: "Look at the freedmen

of the United States! What idle vagabonds they are! How dirty their cabins are! How slovenly their dress! That proves that negroes cannot take care of themselves, that they are not fit to be free." But if your houses look neat, and your clothes clean and whole, and your gardens well weeded, and your work faithfully done . . . then all the world will cry out, "You see that negroes *can* take care of themselves". . . . Thus, while you are serving your own interests, you will be helping on the emancipation of poor weary slaves in other parts of the world.

Child lingered particularly on the importance of sewing and flowers, remarking that clothes "that are clean and nicely patched . . . indicate that the wearer is neat and economical" and that roses and jasmine outside the home served as "an advertisement, easily read by all men, that the people who live there are not lazy, slovenly, or vulgar." A well-sewn patch, flowers at the door—these household tasks were emblems of a race fit for freedom.[24]

Home visits were as much errands of slave emancipation as of philanthropy among the northern poor. Elizabeth Hyde Botume, a Yankee schoolteacher in the Sea Islands, recounted her first visit to the "quarters" that "resembled huge wooden boxes," where each house was divided into four rooms, and each room was occupied by a family of up to fifteen persons. "I now came for the first time face to face with life in the 'one-roomed cabin.' Outwardly it represented the poorest and most meagre animal existence. In military order I began inspection at once, to marshal my forces and 'muster in' recruits." Though some aspects of the "quarters" recalled the infamies inventoried by abolitionists, others had changed. "The space before some of the doorways was swept clean, and sprinkled with white sand from the bluff. The clothes, just washed, were spread over the wild plum bushes, and the washtubs were turned on their sides against the house." Inside each room was a fireplace, a window, a row of bunks built into the wall, some benches, "and a pine table with 'piggins,' home-made cedar tubs, on it, completed the furniture." According to Botume, not the extent of family property, but rather the tidiness of the room, the "whiteness and cleanliness of table and piggins . . . indicated the character, I might say the social status, of the owner."[25]

It was axiomatic that the sewing, flower tending, cleaning, and cooking were the tasks of freedwomen. So the Tennessee head of the Freedmen's Bureau, Gen. Clinton B. Fisk, admonished former bondswomen. "Do not think of getting married until you know how to knit and sew, to mend clothes and bake good bread, to keep a nice clean house and cultivate a garden." In his *Friendly Counsels* for former slaves the Rev. J. B. Waterbury likewise wrote, "What do you think of a mother who keeps neither herself nor her children clean? Who likes to enter a cabin or cottage where the dirt has to be wiped off a seat before a decent man or woman can sit down upon it?" Botume reported instructing the freedwomen that "water, air, and sunshine were free. The superintendent would give them soap, and we would furnish needles and thread." The husbands of these women were urged to be respectably hardworking, but never to take up sewing and scrubbing.[26]

Yankees in the South represented not simply wage dependency, then, but dependent labor in the home as the essence of freedom. Indeed, their promise to the former slaves was that hireling work would support unpaid domestic work, that men would support women—not as in slave families, but as in idealized white families. Just days after Appomattox that was the message brought South by Republican statesmen. As Senator Henry Wilson declared to a gathering of black people in Charleston, South Carolina, "Freedom does not mean that you are not to work. It means that when you do work you shall have pay for it, to carry home to your wives and the children of your love." To the freedwomen in the same audience Congressman William D. Kelley stated, "Remember, my friends, that you are to be mothers and wives in the homes of free men. You must try to make those homes respectable and happy." As northerners habituated freed slaves to market incentives, they claimed the quid pro quo for a man's labor was a wife at home, an exchange at the heart of the Victorian domestic ideology of separate sexual spheres that portrayed the household as a realm set apart from the cash nexus.[27]

Yet freedwomen's fieldwork was as central to the Yankee emancipation program as were ideals of wifely housework, even though abolitionists had highlighted the conflict between domesticity and slave women's plantation labor. Almost from the war's start the Union Army had to deal with masses of destitute freedwomen who lived in or had fled to occupied territory as well as trailed the troops to be with their enlisted male kin. One response was to employ them in menial service for the army. But mostly their emancipators aimed to create order and curb dependence on government support by returning them to plantation labor, a policy that held sway throughout Reconstruction. As the Freedmen's Inquiry Commission advised, farming abandoned plantations would be "expedient and profitable . . . even though chiefly by women and children." Sometimes, therefore, scenes of free field labor were oddly—if unintentionally—reminiscent of abolitionist portraits of slavery. "It was not an unusual thing," wrote Botume, "to meet a woman coming from the field, where she had been hoeing cotton, with a small bucket or cup on her head, and a hoe over her shoulder, contentedly smoking a pipe and briskly knitting as she strode along. I have seen, added to all these, a baby strapped to her back." Only rarely did Yankee liberators expressly note the difficulty of mixing housework and fieldwork. "The women are mostly field-hands, and are entirely ignorant of domestic duties," wrote a Massachusetts teacher from her Virginia post in 1863. One freedpeople's textbook addressed the problem with rare candor:

All the members of your family have heretofore been accustomed to work in the field, or at some other labor . . . At present this cannot perhaps be changed. It is to be hoped, however, that the time will come when the wife and mother will be able to devote her whole time and attention to family and household duties, to the care of the house, keeping it tidy and clean, and to the training of her children . . . In this case the support of the family will rest on the husband and father.

Still, the advice was work and forbearance: "You must, however, wait patiently . . . Meanwhile let all the household keep on with labor and toil."[28]

In discounting all but wage labor as idleness, the Freedmen's Bureau denied the value of housework also instilled by apostles of free labor. It refused to discriminate by sex in enforcing the duty of work. "Do the women work in the field? Do they work indoors, and in what way?" inquired an 1866 bureau circular that was distributed to local agents supervising government plantations in Virginia. The responses reflected the bureau's program across the South. "It is impossible for the freedman to support himself and his family by working five days a week and keeping a wife and daughter in idleness," one agent declared. "Unless something is done by the Bureau in this county to induce the freedmen to make the female members of their families work in the crops next year there will be destitution amongst them." Other agents reported gathering together former slaves and lecturing on rights and duties in order to instill the principle that all family members should work. One sense in which the bureau did defer to domestic custom was by assuming the authority of husbands and fathers over the sale of freedwomen's labor.[29]

The bureau's views on freedwomen's industry were not all that different from the interests of ex-masters, though not overlaid with the same feelings of personal outrage. Yankee concerns about dependence and work discipline converged with southern efforts to reclaim the labor of entire black families. Planters appealed to the bureau to establish rules requiring wives to enter into labor contracts and return to the fields because men's work alone was not sufficient to raise the crop or worth enough for family subsistence. "Allow me to call your attention to the fact that most of the Freedwomen who have husbands are not at work—never having made any contract at all—Their husbands are at work, while they are as nearly idle as it is possible for them to be, pretending to spin—knit or something that really amounts to nothing," one planter complained at length to the bureau chief in Georgia.

Now these women have always been used to working out & it would be far better for them to go to work for reasonable wages & their rations . . . Say their husbands get . . . 13¢ per month and out of that feed their wives and from 1 to 3 or 4 children . . . It is impossible for one man to do this & maintain his wife in idleness without stealing . . . beside their labor is a very important percent of the entire labor of the South . . . I think it would be a good thing to put the women to work and all that is necessary to do this . . . is an order from you directing the agents to require the women to make contracts.

Reaffirming his ownership as a master, but also conceding the new terms of the labor contract, the planter stated he was "willing to carry my idle women to the Bureau & give them such wages as the Agent may think fair."[30]

Alternatively, he wondered whether the freed wives could be set to work for him under the vagrancy law: "Are they not in some sort vagrants as they are living without employment—and mainly without any visible means of support?" Used to having chattel labor fully at his own disposal, he both devalued the freedman's support of his wife and dismissed her spinning and knitting at home as doing nothing. In the planter's eyes, her housework simply represented a form of vagrancy. This view was widely shared across the South. Against the loss of their entitlements of race and property, former masters protested that freedwomen aimed "to play the lady and be supported by their husbands like the white folks." For them, the exchange of a husband's pay for a wife's dependent labor at home symbolized white supremacy, but when mirrored in black marriages was a sign of depravity.[31]

But in the eyes of former bondsmen, the right to be sole owners of their wives' labor was fundamental to freedom. Emancipation brought freedwomen's withdrawal from the fields, and though their own views went largely unrecorded, it is more than likely, despite all the evidence of family disputes, that most freedwomen shared their husbands' aspirations more than their ex-masters' interests. But between these two classes of men there was naked conflict over the ownership of freedwomen's labor. "When I married my wife," as a Tennessee freedman declared, "I married her to wait on me."[32] A legacy from the days of slavery, when forcible female work had gone hand in hand with forcible sex, this antagonism burst into the open after emancipation. For freedom emboldened husbands to assert their newfound rights by keeping their wives from serving two masters.

In laying claim to housework, freedmen thereby declared themselves slaves no more. Beyond owning themselves, most of them probably owned no other property but their wives' labor (and perhaps their children's). Though selling their own labor, they counted themselves free due to their wives' dependent work at home. Accordingly, they defied the claims of planters, which were based on land ownership. As one freedman reported, "I seen on some plantations . . . where the white men would drive colored women out in the fields to work, when the husbands would be absent from their home, and would tell colored men that their wives and children could not live on their places unless they work in the fields. The colored men would tell them . . . whenever they wanted their wives to work they would tell them themselves; and if he could not rule his own domestic affairs on that place he would leave it and go somewhere else. So the white people would tell them . . . I will be damn if niggers ain't got to work on my place or leave it." Former slaves and former masters echoed each other in the intensity with which both asserted title to freedwomen's labor. As one

North Carolina freedman, seeking his wife's return from her white employer's home, in this case against her own will, declared, "I consider her my property."[33]

Along with land ownership and political rights, constructing a family economy based on the husband's support took pride of place in the aims of many freedmen. This ideal did not bar a wife's productive labor as her husband's helpmeet, either in the unusual instance where they were wholly self-employed or in the common instance where they cultivated a garden plot at home, but it did run counter to her hiring by white employers. Responding to the Freedmen's Inquiry Commission's query—"What induces a colored man to take a wife?"—one South Carolina freedman explained that since emancipation, "there are more married than ever I knew before, because they have a little more chance to mind their families and make money to support their families." In earning their livelihoods, he testified further, "The people here would rather have the land than work for wages. I think it would be better to sort out the men and give land to those who have the faculty of supporting their families." At the war's end, freedmen in North Carolina told the state constitutional convention that their "first and engrossing concern" was being able to "provide shelter and an honorable subsistence for ourselves and families." Newly masters of their own households, freedmen affirmed both their husbandly rights and economic duties as they sought to replace slavery's reciprocities with those of marriage.[34]

That their liberators often had little insight into former slaves' home life is reflected in Whitelaw Reid's account of a typical "sermonizing talk" that he heard delivered in the Sea Islands during his famous postbellum tour of the southern states. The talk was "judicious," noted Reid, given by a northern minister "in a vein to which the negroes were accustomed," and concluding with a series of questions on the themes of labor and marriage, independence and dependence, male support and female housework:

"Well now, you know at the North people think you are starving beggars, dependent on the Government? . . . How many of you support yourselves?"

In an instant every adult in the crowd held up a hand . . .

"Now, before your masters ran away, you all say that your wives were not as attentive as they should be to the wants of the household; that they required a great deal of beating to make them do their work; that they

didn't mend your clothes and cook your meals. Perhaps freedom had made
them worse. All who say it has, hold up your right hands."
There was a great deal of sly chuckling among the men . . . Not a
hand, however, was raised.
"Well, now, I'd like to have the women tell me about the men. Are
they as good husbands as when they were slaves? . . . Do they work as
well, and make you as comfortable?" . . . [E]very woman's hand was
raised.

The point of this catechism was that freedom created good wives
and husbands. Yet in abjuring dependency, it did not reckon that
meals might be uncooked and clothes unmended because of work
rules imposed by southern planters and northern overseers of free
labor. Whitelaw Reid himself grew lyrical at the sight of freedwomen performing gang labor on a Mississippi cotton plantation:
"A quarter of a mile ahead of the plows a picturesque sight presented itself. Fifty women and children . . . were scattered along
the old cotton rows, chopping up weeds, gathering together the
trash that covered the land, firing little heaps of it, singing an occasional snatch of some camp-meeting hymn, and keeping up inces-
sant chatter . . . Most of them were dressed in a stout blue cot-
tonade; the skirts drawn up till they scarcely reached below the
knee . . . and gay-checkered handkerchiefs wound about their
heads." At dusk the gang left the fields, "looking as much like a
caravan crossing the desert as a party of weary farm-laborers." No
abolitionist tract—in contrasting southern cotton fields to northern
hearths—had ever called female slave labor picturesque.[35]
Among the essential pledges of freedom was that the marriages
of former slaves would never again be torn apart by sale, that abolition would end the traffic in human chattels that destroyed home
life. This had been the memorable promise of *Uncle Tom's Cabin*,
and northerners renewed it again and again after the war. As General Rufus B. Saxton, an Assistant Bureau Commissioner, asked of
freedmen in August 1865, "Could you rise . . . against a government which has given you a right to yourselves, your wives, and
children, and taken from you the overseer, the slave trader, the
auction block?" But earlier that summer, in one of Saxton's South
Carolina districts, a Union Army captain had issued orders to the
freedpeople that brought to light the ambiguities of this pledge in a
free market economy based on the wage labor of all who were fit to

work. "Remember that all your working time belongs to the man who hires you . . . [W]hen a husband and wife live on different places . . . this year, they have their crops planted on their own places and they must stay to work them. At the end of the year they can live together. Until then they must see each other only once in a while . . . Remember that even if you are badly off, no one can buy or sell you."[36] Even though the traffic in free labor did not occur on the auction block, it nonetheless eroded the freedman's right to his wife, for as a hireling her labor was bought by other men.

It was in light of the home and women's place within it that the black preacher Alexander Crummell sorrowfully gauged the progress of his race since abolition in an 1883 address to a freedmen's aid society. The freedwoman still lived in the "old plantation hut," beside the "master class, who still think her freedom was a personal robbery of themselves," he grieved. Emancipation Day had brought her "no invisible but gracious Genii who, on the instant, could transmute the rudeness of her hut into instant elegance, and change the crude surroundings of her home into neatness, taste, and beauty." For her, both home life and housework remained wishes unfulfilled. "With her rude husband she still shares the hard service of a field-hand . . . Her furniture is of the rudest kind. The clothing of the household is scant . . . She has rarely been taught to sew . . . [or] the habitudes of neatness, and the requirements of order." What Crummell still dreamed of was a world where women would be "helpers of *poor* men," creating "homes of Christian refinement" even in "the cabins of the humblest freedmen."[37]

Yet obstacles to this vision had been planted at the outset of emancipation. Without apology, the Freedmen's Inquiry Commission had ranked the value of labor above the stature of women as a gauge of cultural superiority. "It has been sometimes said, with much truth, that the grade of civilization in a nation may be measured by the position which it accords to woman. A stricter test is the degree of estimation in which labor is held there," the Commission moralized.[38] But, though speaking in universal terms, the Commission did not state whether the precepts governing the extraordinary circumstances of a race being liberated from slavery should also apply in the North, to white citizens reared in the faith that woman's place at home marked a fundamental difference between freedom and slavery.

≺ III ≻

Freedom and Housework—the North

After the Civil War the relationship between freedom and housework was as central to the question of wage labor's legitimacy in the North as in the South. In the antebellum era, with the rise of industrial capitalism, the economic value of unpaid housework had been denied by Yankee culture, which increasingly defined money as the sole index of all value. Nonetheless, many elite reformers and moralists had offered abundant practical advice about it and romanticized it as part of women's separate sphere.[39] What was new in the postbellum era was the ideological weight that housework—or, more precisely, its absence—bore in laboring men's critique of class relations in the North and the conditions of proletarian life. No less than former slaves, they viewed being divested of a wife's dependent labor at home as a betrayal of freedom, a betrayal rooted in the traffic in free labor as a market commodity and in the wage dependency of men.

The horror that filled abolitionist writing on home life under slavery echoed powerfully in Samuel Gompers's indictments of cigar making in tenement houses in Gilded Age New York City. In 1881 he toured working-class neighborhoods, documenting the misery of daily existence. The tenement cigar shop was worlds away from the cotton fields of the Old South, but the images of domesticity generated by antislavery and by labor reform were strangely alike. There were similar scenes of filthy, crude living quarters, and of households menaced by commodity production. But in Gompers's portrait, the family was not sacrificed on the altar of chattel slavery, but "to the Moloch of wage slavery."[40]

Gompers vividly described the state of the tenement homes that doubled as cigar workshops, where the hours of labor began before sunrise and lasted far into the night. Like other metropolitan investigators of the day, he explained that the object was "to see with our own eyes . . . the rooms in which people live and work, are born and die." He observed that in the typical tenement house each family occupied two or three small rooms, furnished with a worktable, a stove, a few wooden chairs, a bed, and some cheap pictures. "The filth, stench of tobacco, etc. are nauseating," for tobacco lay everywhere, drying on the floor, spread about the stove, piled next to the beds. "Our hope of finding something pleasant here was not fulfilled . . . in every room, tobacco, filth, and human beings, thrown together," he found. "The 'shop' has completely taken over the living quarters . . . [I]t is probably impossible to dream of anything but tobacco in this atmosphere." In these dwellings, Gompers aimed to discover what "the pursuit of the almighty dollar, through exploitation, oppression, and sacrifice of our fellow men, has created in our midst."[41]

To reveal how wage relations wholly contaminated the home, Gompers focused on the work of women. "In one room," he wrote, "we saw a mother who had just begun to nurse her child but had not interrupted her work of making wrappers. That is how people work in these factories; not a moment must be lost—the mother with the babe at her breast." In another shop on East Second Street, "a picture greeted us that seemed created to demonstrate the poison of tenement-house work: a young woman was sitting at the worktable, rolling cigars with her hands, her feet rocking a cradle in which lay a baby: the poor child was sick, terribly emaciated, and its shrunken features seemed to say: 'How can I stay alive in such a place?'" Surely these images were calculated to recall the appeals of antislavery.[42]

Indeed, Gompers presented the scene of the woman rolling cigars while rocking a cradle in a part of his survey titled "Slaves of the Tobacco Industry." Here, too, he despaired about family meals, suggesting that the food itself embodied the terms of bondage in the tenements. "The 'dinner' consisted . . . mainly of cooked or smoked sausage or something similar which does not need to be prepared first," he noted. "The housewife would lose too much valuable time cooking a meal; she has other work to do: making wrappers and rolling cigars."[43] The uncooked meals, the dirty rooms, and the sick children—all these figured as signs of the intrusion of commodity relations into northern homes, homes in which wage work defied free labor doctrine by affording housewives no time for housework.

The groundwork for Gompers's explorations had been laid a decade earlier in the surveys into working-class households conducted by the Massachusetts Bureau of Labor Statistics. Tenement life was a well-established field of urban inquiry, but the bureau surveys were among the first social scientific studies to ascribe disordered home life to the conditions of wage work. Just as Massachusetts was first to apply the lessons of slave emancipation regarding dependency and penal labor in the North, so it was also first to duplicate the scrutiny of ex-slave homes in Yankee tenements in order to test free labor's promise against the realities of wage dependency. But different groups of reformers pursued these northern variants of emancipation policy. While abolitionists turned charity officials rewrote the poor law, labor radicals acting as statisticians inaugurated the state inquiry into the relation between home life and wage labor. Edward Pierce had his counterpart in George McNeill, the first deputy chief of the labor bureau and a leader of the New England labor reform league. In its first report of 1870 the bureau stated its purpose of exploring "The Wage System and Its Results," starting with the "Homes of Low-Paid Laborers in the City of Boston." For the bureau, the home was the proving ground for the wage system.[44]

During three days in December 1869 the bureau's staff explored the Boston tenement district, inspecting premises inhabited by immigrants and native born, and by whites and blacks. In *"private affairs"* they sought data "upon the great question of Labor." They compiled inventories of destitute rooms, with only a few sticks of furniture, that resembled portraits of slave quarters. The rooms were sometimes "a marvel of neatness," they noted, but usually only as clean as "could be expected." More often than not they found that the husband's earnings were so low that the wife also worked for wages instead of attending to the "duties of the household . . . indicated by the whole family relation." While the men worked in a range of jobs, their wives mostly went out scrubbing or took washing and ironing into their homes, which hung all over the rooms drying. There were "dreadful pictures . . . of want and degradation"—of poverty that "emasculates home of all its quickening powers," the bureau stated. "The people in all the places we visited barely live." Thus the evidence gathered in these home visits was of free labor in crisis. Depicting wage dependency as "radically wrong" through images of men destitute of domesticity, the bureau pointed to the homes of the low-paid laborers whose wives were scrub women for other families.[45]

Many of the bureau's findings were common themes of labor protest. Since the rise of the labor movement, its spokesmen had claimed that male earnings must at least equal the cost of family survival and had condemned market relations that slashed wages below this minimum, thereby driving the entire household into paid work. As a New York City tailor declared in an 1860 tract that represented wage labor as "a state of slavery," the "Shylocks in the Free States . . . care not how many families they may ruin, so long as they can realize fortunes out of their blood and bones." Whereas abolitionists had defended free labor as the bedrock of domesticity, hirelings had maintained that the family life of poor men was just as precarious as the slave's.[46]

What was new in the bureau's argument was the stress it laid on housework in deploring wage labor and the plight of free men and their families.[47] The 1871 bureau report, which resumed the study of laboring households, featured exemplary testimony from one mule spinner about the conditions and relations of domestic economy—"an inside view of operative life at home." The mule spinner could be said to stand for all hireling men who had lost property in their wives' labor. He testified that his wife also worked at the mill six days a week, usually leaving at 6:20 in the morning and returning at 7:30 at night. Therefore he did much of the cooking and cleaning.

For breakfast we manage thus: I get up at 5 o'clock and let wife and children lie while I get the meal ready, then they get up, we eat and start for the mill.

Q. *You mean to say you get the breakfast and not she?* [emphasis added]

A. Yes, sir.

Q. Who gets the dinner?

A. We make it and put it in the pails over night, because we have no time in the morning. I take my dinner to the mill and eat it there, then I run home and do a little choring . . . to get ready for the night. I have bread and meat and a little pie,—the same as wife has. I get home at 7 o'clock, and help along supper until she gets home, and then it will take us both until half past 7 to get ready to commence on the supper.

Q. Is this the common way in which operatives in your town live?

A. Yes, sir.

Q. Through all the mills?

A. Yes, sir; those that have wives that go to the mill . . . I generally lay in bed until about 7 o'clock on Sundays . . . [T]hen it takes wife and me about all the time to wash, clean and scrub up the house, and cook the extra dinner for Sunday, so we can have a comfortable meal.

Q. When does your wife do the mending for the family?

A. She does it at night after we have had supper.

When asked if his wife had much "knowledge of household work," the mule spinner pointed out that factory girls could "only learn cooking, washing, mending and housework after they get home from the mill" and were not "as apt at these things as out-of-mill girls." As for childbirth—"How near their time of confinement have you known pregnant women to work in a mill?" asked the bureau—he stated that women stayed at their looms up to a few weeks before and returned a few weeks after.[48]

As noteworthy as the mule spinner's testimony were the bureau's questions. Less than a decade earlier the Freedmen's Inquiry Commission had interrogated freedmen about home life under slavery, asking if they had ever eaten "food together as families" and if masters had spared bondswomen "in the family way" or let them nurse their newborn children. Meanwhile, a range of Yankees had mourned former slaves' housekeeping, especially freedwomen's unproficiency. So too did the bureau concentrate on housework in investigating the wage system—incredulous that a husband would have to cook and clean at home. It decried "the desperate need of extra work from wife and children" and the poverty that "changed home into houses," arguing that a man's labor should be worth enough to support his family and enable his wife "to perform all the duties of the home." Thus the bureau undertook to document how free labor was destroying the household's natural dependencies. The mule spinner preparing the family breakfast before dawn did not much resemble the antislavery vision of laboring men clasping the "sceptre of Sovereignty" in their hands.[49]

Later bureau studies continued to explore free labor's effect on home life, providing a model for statisticians in other states. When the staff of the bureau was changed in 1873 amidst controversy over its alliance with labor reform, it came under the direction of Carroll Wright, a lawyer whose milieu was elite social science. By no means did Wright adopt the terms of the wage slavery argument. Nevertheless, the bureau surveys he carried out into the "Conditions of Work-ingmen's Families" used chattel slavery as a negative standard for gauging the rights of free men. The 1875 report declared that pre-cisely because the slave system had provided for the "bodily wants" of the "unhappy workers," the wage system must assure no less:

No one should receive such small compensation for his toil, that even when expended with economy and prudence, it fails to pay for his neces-sary cost of living . . . obliging him to overwork his wife with home and outside duties.

The bureau assailed the wife's wage work as "the most harmful wrong," conversely defending as "natural and just" the doctrine that a man's labor should sell for at least enough to support his family. It catalogued food, family belongings, and the cleanliness of rooms and persons, affirming the free labor ideal that even hireling men were entitled to be masters of a household of dependent per-sons. But its statistics showed this right was unrealized in a "ma-jority of cases."[50]

By the Progressive Era the concern with the relationship between wage work and family life had been embraced by a multitude of elite reformers and lawmakers. Their solution was to restrict and regulate the market in female labor, to formulate sex-specific protective laws. Anxious above all about wives' wage earning, they sharply differen-tiated between the status of women and of men at work. Seemingly, their values clashed with those espoused by the Yankees who had guided the transition to capitalism in the New South, for they ranked home life (or at least women's place at home) above the universal imperative to labor. Yet the difference in reform perspectives ulti-mately turned not on spoken ideas about gender, but on unspoken ideas about race—on the shared assumption that rights at home did not belong equally to the white working classes in the North and to black field hands in the South. Former slaves, concentrated in farm labor and domestic service, fell outside the system of protective law sought by Progressives.[51] No less than after slavery's downfall, race qualified the principle of female dependence in the household, a principle that, by the turn of the century, had come to justify govern-ing wage labor in the interest of home life.

In the age when free labor triumphed over chattel slavery, rela-tions of personal dependency evoked intense ideological conflict in both the North and the South. At law, the stakes of the matter had been made clearcut. From Port Royal to Boston, the distinction between depending on wages as freedom and depending on alms as unfreedom—states of dependence once conflated in republican thought—was starkly drawn by criminal law and upheld through penal labor. Lending moral weight to the law's rules were free labor tenets distilled during the long contest over slavery and emancipation. According to those tenets, a man was free not because he owned productive property and thereby escaped wage dependence, but because, even as a hireling, he owned property in his wife as well as in himself. As antislavery statesmen proclaimed during debates over the Thirteenth Amendment, explaining what household property abolition would not touch, "A husband has a right of property in the service of his wife."[52] Freedom, presumably, would absolutely guarantee the traditional dependencies of marriage.

At the war's end, Yankee moralists and lawmakers taught no doctrine more steadfastly than the counterpoint between freedom and dependence. But both ex-slaves and northern labor responded to wage relations in ways that exposed the perplexities of this doctrine. Though in form their responses differed, as did the particular social conditions they confronted, both former bondsmen and men who had never been chattel maintained that the circumstances of free labor subverted their property rights in their wives' labor. It was in the free market, not the slave auction, they argued, that wives were now sold off, forced to earn wages by serving other men. Using antislavery guidelines, these men declared themselves unfree.

Thus housework emerged as a central issue in postbellum strife over the legitimacy of free labor and the nature of dependence. An extraordinarily broad range of Americans appraised the free wage system in terms of the unpaid cooking, scrubbing, and mending done by wives. Even as capitalism's emphasis on commodity production and money income rendered housework's economic value invisible, its cultural value expanded, asserted not only in tributes to woman's sphere but in debates over slavery and freedom that transcended regional boundaries. However, that value dissolved where differences of race hedged the property rights of free men at home.

Free Labor, Law, and
American Trade Unionism

DAVID BRODY

IT WOULD BE A CONTRADICTION in terms to speak of a trade union of slaves or serfs. Indeed, the rise of trade unionism is entwined in the great arc of free labor development that is the common history of all the western industrializing countries. Yet the
condition of freedom, essential though it be, stands in an uneasy
relationship to trade unionism. The problem, as the English jurist
A. V. Dicey framed it a century ago, is that individual liberty encompasses "the right of combined action," but this right threatens
individual liberty. This dilemma "is at bottom always and everywhere the same," but not its resolution, since, in principle, there is
no way to bring "into harmony two essentially conflicting rights,
namely the right to individual freedom and the right of association." The most that can be achieved is a "rough compromise,"
which manifestly each country must find for itself.[1] In this chapter,
I want to explore how, in the domain of employment, the United
States grappled with Dicey's "theoretically insoluble problem"
and, more particularly, why the rough compromise it arrived at so
burdened the reception of trade unionism in American labor law.

≺ I ≻

The Invention of Free Labor

In the beginning, of course, the notion of free labor was itself a
contradiction in terms. In early English law, work was compulsory
for every able-bodied person without visible means of support, and
the terms of employment—wages, worktime, length of service—
were matters of state policy. The Statute of Artificers (1563) codi-
fied these medieval labor rules definitively just a half century be-

fore English settlement in America began. Although not automatically subject to its jurisdiction, the colonies, having no other model to draw on, treated the Tudor industrial code as their starting point for labor regulation. But because the administrative structures were so much looser—the colonial governments, for example, never duplicated the royal oversight of wage-fixing by the English justices of the peace—the history of colonial labor regulation is clouded, embedded in the court records of townships, parishes, and counties. Thanks to the indefatigable study of those local records by Richard B. Morris many years ago,[2] however, we have a good idea of how closely colonial practice conformed to and then, very quickly, diverged from the Tudor industrial code. In its specifics, that divergence reflected colonial conditions, but the breakdown of labor regulation also sprang from an ideological shift that was experienced on both sides of the Atlantic.

The medieval idea of labor as a resource of the community, and hence at communal command, gave way to the idea of labor as a kind of private property conveyed by mutual agreement from the worker to the employer. The doctrinal principle underlying that great shift was what C. B. Macpherson has called "possessive individualism"—the conviction arising out of the seventeenth-century English revolution that man is born free and that "freedom is proprietorship of one's own person and capacities."[3] For labor, the implications of possessive individualism were ambiguous because, in the name of his freedom, the worker sold the labor in himself to another. As Robert J. Steinfeld remarks, there was "a deep tension between the idea that social order was composed of naturally equal, essentially uniform, autonomous individuals and the notion that the labor agreement, which involved the selling of one's most basic property, the property in one's own energies, left some individuals under the control of other individuals, in a sense as their property."[4] The resolution of that tension came not by retreating from the first idea but by redefining the second, so that labor entered into voluntarily, by contract, became, definitively and absolutely, "free"—hence the title of Steinfeld's book on which I am relying here, "The Invention of Free Labor."

Of the constraints on labor imposed by the Tudor industrial code, Steinfeld fastens on the provision that subordinated the worker's personal freedom to the employer's claim to his or her services. Under the Statute of Artificers, workers could be compelled to perform agreed-upon services on pain of imprisonment. This principle crossed the Atlantic along with the rest of the English labor code and was routinely enforced by colonial courts in the early years. But it seems by the early eighteenth century to have lapsed for laborers and artisans, and within another half century, for hired servants as well.[5]

In England, by contrast, the coercive enforcement of labor agreements remained robust. The law in fact became more effective during the eighteenth century because of supplementary bills applying to specific trades. In 1823 a new master and servant law reaffirmed criminal sanctions for breach of labor contracts, and until far into the nineteenth century Engish workers were routinely prosecuted and imprisoned under that provision of the law.[6] On the Continent, restrictions on mobility tended to be enforced administratively. Belgian and French workers were by law required to carry a *livret*, or work passport, showing that they had fulfilled their obligations to previous employers. Swedish workers were prohibited from changing jobs except at a specified annual break period, and anyone without work could be prosecuted for being "unprotected" and assigned to compulsory service.[7] In central and eastern Europe, the heavy hand of the police reinforced the constraints on labor mobility. "An atmosphere of permanent suspicion and surveillance" pervaded mid-century Germany, writes Jurgen Kocka, burdening traveling journeymen "under the elaborate system of passports, obligatory travel records, work licenses, and prohibitions" and for practical purposes making any movement dependent on the assent of their employers.[8] In Prussia, as part of the liberalizing economic reforms of 1845, industrial employment became contractual, but with penal sanctions against workers who violated their agreements.

If the range of freedom was greater in America, so paradoxically was the range of servitude. It was not from a sense of superiority over Europe but from contradictions inside their own country that Americans began to arrive at a final definition of free labor. The biggest contradiction arose from the curse of slavery. In itself, however, slavery was not problematic because, as an involuntary condition, it was clearly distinct from free labor, and doubly distinct because it was reserved exclusively for blacks. But slavery was not

America's only system of bondage. Roughly half the immigrants arriving from Europe before the 1820s came as indentured servants, bound to service under terms markedly harsher than those generally countenanced by the Tudor code. For practical purposes, indentured servants were the property of the owner of their indentures. They could be moved, sold, or rented; and if they ran off, they were subject to pursuit and forceable return. This was, indeed, a major function of colonial law enforcement. Yet indentured servitude fell within the bounds of possessive individualism, since it was conceived to be a contractual arrangement freely arrived at between consenting individuals.

What indentured servitude revealed was that, into the years of the early republic, Americans still had not divested themselves of the received assumption that, in Steinfeld's words, "legal freedom (and unfreedom) were not absolute matters but matters of degree." The particular form that this belief took in America was not that all labor was in some degree unfree, but rather that, between freedom and unfreedom, there might exist a third state. Indentured servants occupied, as a court said in 1793, "a middle rank between slaves and freemen."[9] The bias of indentured servitude, however, was toward freedom—voluntary servitude, not partial slavery.

That bias shifted, ironically, because of the liberating impact of the American Revolution. The movement to emancipate the slaves in the northern states invoked indentured servitude as a key check on the process. The first beneficiaries—the children born after the state laws went into effect—would be held in bondage as indentured servants until full maturity, generally age 28. Still more compromising were the uses slaveholders found for indentured servitude when they moved to free states. Their lawyers held that indentures entered into by slaves were good contracts because of the consideration received in being delivered from slavery. Steinfeld cites a series of Pennsylvania decisions accepting this appalling line of reasoning.[10] The effect, however, was to call into question the very rationale on which indentured servitude depended, namely, that it was *voluntary*.

There already was, in the Northwest Ordinance of 1785, a legal scaffolding for proceeding on this front. This was the conception of involuntary servitude, which, along with slavery, was proscribed in the states created under mandate of the Northwest Ordinance. In

The Case of·Mary Clark, a Woman of Color (1821), the Supreme Court of Indiana tested indentured servitude against that constitutional provision. Mary Clark was a free black, not a former slave; an adult, not a minor; and she had freely consented to serve for twenty years. Was the contract she had signed binding on her? No, the Court ruled, because she would then be "in a state of involuntary servitude." The condition of free labor required, no matter what the terms of agreement, that employment be "at the will of the employee."[11]

As indentured servitude collapsed into impermissible involuntary servitude, the notion of freedom as a matter of degree also became impermissible. This, says Steinfeld, was the moment of invention, conjuring out of the crisis over indentured servitude the American doctrine of free labor. What was invented, it is important to recognize, had little to do with the exercisable rights of wage workers. After all, they had been enjoying the freedom to depart long before the courts declared that they had that right by law. Nor can it be said, even about indentured servitude, that the legal impact was substantial, since by then immigrants were no longer coming to America as indentured servants. The succeeding case law on contract enforcement is likewise scant because the employment practice that rubbed against the right of departure—the time contract—began to disappear after midcentury. It was supplanted by employment at-will, the contractual apotheosis of free labor: if the worker's right to leave was absolute, so was the employer's to dismiss him or her.

In Europe, specific performance began to be abandoned half a century after *Mary Clark*. It took a robust campaign by the emerging labor movement for England to repeal criminal sanctions for breach of employment contracts by act of Parliament in 1875. Prussia had done the same for industrial workers six years earlier. France ended the law requiring work passports in 1890. Across Europe (and in Canada and Australia) the laws enforcing labor contracts were gone by the early twentieth century.

In light of this history, the rejection of enforceable agreements by the American courts might be seen merely as the opening chapter in an international movement against contractual constraints on workers. But within that common history the differences of meaning bear emphasis. Much more than in America, workers in

Europe gained an actual expansion of personal freedom from the abolition of coercive performance. On the other hand, that particular advance had comparatively little ideological resonance in Europe or, at least, not a resonance picked up by the historians of European labor. And this in turn suggests, as a third point of difference, the potency of law in the processes of ideological formation in America. The right to depart, Steinfeld's work implies, served in this way: it was the core legality underpinning a conception of free labor that imagined American labor relations as a universe of independent and equal individuals. Very much in America's encounter with trade unionism turned on this ideo-legal formulation.

We can better appreciate the relationship between law and ideology by attending to a speech delivered by Henry Williams, a Taunton lawyer, in the debate over the secret ballot at the Massachusetts constitutional convention of 1853:

In a free government like ours employment is simply a contract between parties having equal rights. The operative agrees to perform a certain amount of work in consideration of receiving a certain amount of money. The work to be performed is, by the contract, an equivalent for the money paid. The relationship, when properly entered into, is therefore one of mutual benefit. The employed is under no greater obligation to the employer than the employer is to the employed . . . In the eye of the law, they are both freemen—citizens having equal rights, and brethren having one common destiny.[12]

Williams's speech is illuminating in at least three ways. First, it offers a spacious account of the law of free labor, at the core of which was the principle of equal rights: the law treats, without distinction, employers and workers alike. Their relationship is likewise governed by an equality of obligation, no more and no less than the terms of contract. The law of free labor, however, extends beyond employment and encompasses the equal rights of workers as "freemen" and "citizens," a precocious achievement (for white males) of the early American republic.[13] All this was in larger terms appropriate, politically, "in a free government like ours" and, socially, between classes that are "brethren having one common destiny."

Second, there is what one might call the pseudo-reality of law revealed in Williams's speech. He speaks as if he is describing a world of free and equal individuals. But Williams knows that not to be the case. On the contrary, he says, the employment relationship is cruelly unequal, exposing workers to coercion by employers and imperiling the democratic process. "The practice of intimidation has become with us an evil of great magnitude," but it is an evil not easily dealt with "because every man has a right to employ, or to dismiss from his employment, whom he pleases."[14] We have mistaken one face of the law for another. The law is real, of course, invoked every day by myriad citizens going about the business of life. But the law also describes an imagined world—in this instance, of free and equal workers—that encompasses what these same citizens valued and wanted to believe to be true. It is in this particular sense that law can be called ideological; and, more specifically, that the law of employment translates into the ideology of free labor.

Third, from Williams's speech we get a suggestion of the utility of law as ideology. Williams invokes it as a kind of resource, mobilized to advance the case he is making, which is, in this instance, the adoption of the secret ballot. Others might have different cases to make, but, insofar as they were arguing about labor, the ideology of free labor would serve in the same way. Thus Williams's chief protagonist, Otis P. Lord of Salem, accuses him of undermining the independence vital to a system of free labor. The secret ballot "is, in its nature, calculated to, and actually does, diminish the self-respect of the voter" by assuming his cowardice and need for protection from his employer. "Any such imputation . . . is unworthy of them. They are not a craven, miscreant class of men, who are afraid to look upon the face of day to vote."[15]

For purposes of this chapter, the question is how free-labor ideology—for which Williams's words provide the text—was mobilized in the nation's encounter with trade-union organization, which was, of course, how workers themselves responded to the imbalance of power that was Williams's true subject.

< II >

The Reception of Trade Unionism

No state regime ever welcomed the onset of working-class organization. Across Europe the first response was outright repression. In

France the Chapelier Act of 1791 declared gatherings of workers "riotous" meetings whose participants would be "dispersed by force" and be subjected to severe punishment. The penal code of 1810 outlawed any "coalition on the part of the workingmen to cease work at the same time, to forbid work in a shop, to prevent the coming or leaving before or after certain hours, and in general, to suspend, hinder or make dear labor."[16] The Federal Congress of German States in 1840 unified the policies of its members against workers "who have committed offenses against the State Government through participation in illicit combinations, journeymen's societies, and boycotts" and declared strikes "rebellious disturbances against the constituted authorities." Prussia's Industrial Code of 1845 prohibited meetings of workers to obtain better conditions and required that workers' societies of any kind receive police authorization.[17] Even in Britain, where labor combinations were criminal conspiracies under the common law, Parliament saw fit to enact Combination laws from 1721 onward covering specific occupations and, in the Combination acts of 1799 and 1800, making the statutory ban against trade unionism universal.

Such laws were unknown in America. Not that condemnation was lacking of the early journeymen's unions as "self-created societies," illicit, substituting "the power of associations or parties for the authority of law," and gaining "unrighteous advantages by means of disciplined and confederated numbers."[18] The response to that threat, moreover, drew openly and unapologetically on English sources. Only what was taken came not from the statutes, but from the common law.

In 1806, the mayor's court of Philadelphia, Moses Levy presiding, heard for the first time a case[19] charging American workers—in this instance, the city's journeymen shoemakers—with criminal conspiracy. The common law, Levy instructed the jury, "says there may be cases in which what one man may do without offence, many combined may not do with impunity," depending on the objective. "If the purpose to be obtained, be an object of individual interest, it may be fairly attempted by an individual," but not by "many . . . combining for the attainment of it."[20] In the case before him, the shoemakers had undertaken to raise the prices on their work. Any one of them might freely have done this, and so indeed might the entire group, if such was "individually the opinion of all." The conspiracy was "that they were bound down by their agreement, and pledged by mutual engagements to persist in it, however contrary to their own judgment."[21] The essence of the crime, therefore, was the fact of association, the rules and obligations welding workers into a collective body. There is no other way of reading Levy's holding than as a condemnation of trade unionism per se and not different, in principle, from the repressive standard then prevailing across Europe.

The reality was, of course, otherwise, which was why the common law on which Levy drew had not sufficed in Britain. The Combination acts afforded the advantage of summary justice, enabling the authorities to move swiftly and certainly against strikers, without the indictments, pleadings, and trial by jury encumbering common law proceedings. Summary action bespoke in part the advanced state of British industrialism: the early Combination laws targeted the modernizing trades and were generally triggered by industrial strife,[22] for which there was no American counterpart at least until the 1830s. But the British sense of urgency was also politically inspired. There, as on the Continent, unauthorized confederacies were perceived as inherently subversive, affronting the authority of the Crown and, in the shadow of the French Revolution, deemed so dangerous that they called forth the sweeping Combination acts of 1799 and 1800, with imprisonment at hard labor for infractions of the law. All that the Philadelphia shoemakers got was a fine of eight dollars plus costs, preceded by the prosecutor's opening assurances that, beyond establishing the illegality of their actions, he had "no wish to punish these men" and, on the contrary, intended "to shield [them] from any disagreeable consequences from a conviction."[23]

The vantage point of 1806 does not, as it turns out, offer us a fair glimpse on the future. In 1824, the British Combination acts were repealed en masse, and a year later prosecution for common-law conspiracy (which had incautiously also been struck out) was reinstated, but exempting meetings and agreements to fix wages and hours and, for those purposes, effectively legalizing trade unionism. Once American courts arrived at that place, the law of labor conspiracy in the two countries became aligned and, one might have expected, likely to develop along parallel lines. In fact, had it been up to the British courts, that would have happened. But Parliament intervened, and curbed the judicial assault on trade union power. After the climactic Conspiracy and Protection Act of 1875, the resort to criminal conspiracy by the courts in labor disputes finally ceased, and they were disarmed, a conclusion reinforced by the Trade Disputes Act of 1906 overruling the Taff Vale decision and, as John V. Orth observes, "positively stripp[ing]" the British courts of jurisdiction over the law of labor.[24]

From the standpoint of 1806, one might better have expected that outcome in the United States, for here the standing of the common law itself had been ambiguous. In the colonies, the common law had only slowly been implanted, and, as one scholar has noted, "even far down into the [eighteenth] century . . . legal administration was in the hands of laymen in many of the provinces," while in New England, the "subsidiary force of the common law was plainly denied."[25] Regarding labor conspiracy, no authenticated case has been found for the colonial era, notwithstanding that labor conspiracy had been recognized in English common law since 1721.[26] With independence, moreover, English common and statutory law lapsed and it took affirmative action, state by state, to re-establish it. The issue was bitterly contested, dividing federalists and republicans, and in fact dominating Pennsylvania politics just as the conspiracy indictments came down against the Philadelphia shoemakers in 1805. Their lawyers argued strenuously that no legal basis existed in Pennsylvania for the indictments.[27]

Moses Levy would have none of it. He directed the jury to ignore, as immaterial and improper, the defense's claim "that the spirit of the revolution and the principle of the common law are opposite in this case" or that applying it "would operate an attack on the rights of man." The foundation of justice, pronounced Levy, was the common law, far more than the legislature, whose enactments are only the "temporary emanations" of a "fluctuating political body." The common law "regulates with a sound discretion most of our concerns in civil and social life. Its rules are the result of the wisdom of the ages." Only those who knew it intimately, and in its entirety—the inner sanctum of lawyers—were "competent judges of it." The courts, in their "laborious" pursuit of justice, ought never be impugned, because "from that moment the security of persons and property is gone."[28]

Because Levy's views prevailed—an echo, of course, of the more general triumph of law in the American polity that Christopher Tomlins has been pondering[29]—American labor law became for the next century preeminently a judicial prerogative and, unlike Britain, out of reach of Levy's "fluctuating political bod[ies]." Judge-made labor law, more than any other proximate fact, distinguishes the state regulation of unions in America from that of Britain, or indeed, any European country until far into the twentieth century.[30]

Still, Levy's criminalization of trade unions clearly would not do, not in republican America, with its citizen workers and enshrined rights of assembly. Almost at once the courts began to scramble to more defensible grounds. In the next conspiracy trial, against New York shoemakers who had struck to enforce their rule against working alongside expelled members, the judge acknowledged their "right to meet and regulate their concerns, and to ask for wages, and to work or refuse," but he found "the means they used were of a nature too arbitrary and coercive, and . . . went to deprive their fellow-citizens of rights as precious as any they contend for."[31] Thus, only three years after *Commonwealth v. Pulis*, the chink was already opening through which lawful combination might slip. But what, in Britain, well-placed Benthamite parliamentarians initiated with dispatch in 1824, took in America the labors of the courts in several state jurisdictions over three and a half decades[32] and the mounting crisis of the 1830s to bring forth, in *Commonwealth v. Hunt* (1842),[33] the definitive opinion of the chief justice of Massachusetts, Lemuel Shaw.

The essence of the charge against the Boston bootmakers in the case under appeal before him, Shaw wrote, was

that the defendants and others formed themselves into a society, and agreed not to work for any person, who should employ any journeyman or other person, not a member of such society, after notice given him to discharge such workman.

The manifest intent of the association is, to induce all those engaged in the same occupation to become members of it. Such a purpose is not unlawful.[34]

With these words Shaw put American unionism on the right side of the law.

But unions were not thereby quit of the conspiracy law incubus.

On the contrary, Shaw's purpose was to defend the integrity of that legal system and to fix labor activity securely under the scrutiny of the courts. In the law of labor conspiracy, however, the court wielded too flawed an instrument. The precedents, as they came down to him, did not enable Shaw to frame "any definition or description . . . which shall identify this offense—a description broad enough to include all cases punishable under this description, without including acts which are not punishable."[35] The problem, distinguishing Massachusetts from Britain, was that there was no equivalent in Massachusetts (or any other American state) for the statutory wage controls whose violation had figured in the foundational English case, *Rex v. Cambridge Tailors* (1721). Shaw's remedy was technical, focusing as it did on the sufficiency of the indictment. Shaw agreed with the brilliant defense counsel Robert Rantoul that, inasmuch as conspiracy was a criminal act, it required indictments as rigorous as those applying in criminal cases generally. The gist of Shaw's masterly argument—brought off, as Walter Nelles remarks, with "an old-style technical rigor"[36]—was to demonstrate, point by point, how the indictment in the case before him fell short of that standard. On that specific ground, Chief Justice Shaw reversed the lower court and discharged the bootmakers.

Embedded in this technical argument, however, was Shaw's meditation on the nature of labor conspiracy itself—"a question of great importance to the Commonwealth." On two central issues, he laid down conclusions that rightly qualify *Commonwealth v. Hunt* as the base-line decision for the American law of trade unionism.

One involved the question of power, which, as Shaw noted, indubitably was why workers associated themselves in unions.[37] Critical to everything else was his rejection of injury to others as a sufficient test of criminal conspiracy. Suppose a group of neighbors, burdened by the high price of bread, induced a rival baker to set up shop.

The effect would be to diminish the profit of the former baker, and to the same extent impoverish him. And it might be said and proved, that the purpose of the associates was to diminish his profits, and thus impoverish him, though the ultimate and laudable object of the combination was to reduce the cost of bread to themselves and their neighbors. The same

thing may be said of all competition in every branch of trade and industry;
and yet it is through that competition, that the best interests of trade are
promoted.[38]

Trade unions, Shaw was suggesting, fell within this competitive
ambit, striving for ends in themselves laudable (including, specifically, higher wages, a point Shaw made by dictum, since no wage
demand was involved in *Commonwealth v. Hunt*), but using
means that, as in all marketplace competition, might have impov-
erishing consequences for others. The crucial test had to do with
the means: if criminal, by force or fraud, or unlawful, by violating
the legal rights of others, then a union might "be stamped with the
character of conspiracy."[39] But so would any other association, and
that was the crucial point, normalizing trade unions as economic
actors and treating them like any other combination in an enter-
prising society that presumed that progress sprang from the clash
of competing interests.[40] In fact, *Commonwealth v. Hunt* proved
controlling not in any subsequent labor case, but in business disputes.[41]

Commonwealth v. Hunt was a lodestar, secondly, for what it
had to say about free labor, and more specifically, about the balance Shaw struck between the liberties of the individual worker
and the associative interests of the group. *Commonwealth v. Hunt*
was deeply, one might say peculiarly, infused by the terms of free
labor. This had first of all to do with the facts of the case, which
arose from the complaint by a journeyman, Jeremiah Horne, that
he had been deprived of employment by the action of the Boston
bootmakers' society. Compulsion of his employer, Jeremiah Wait,
was actually not at issue, since Wait testified that, although he
"did not feel at liberty to employ any but society men," he had not
been "injured or oppressed" by the union's demand and, on the
contrary, was the beneficiary of the good workmanship and steady
habits inculcated by the union. He had, in fact, done his best to
persuade Horne to make his peace with the bootmakers' society.
Nor had Horne evidently suffered material injury, since he had
found other work at one of the smaller shops where the closed shop
was not enforced. So, to a peculiar degree, *Commonwealth v. Hunt*
was about his freedom to work.[42]

As for Shaw, he framed his opinion very much within those
same free labor terms. Thus, he noted, "it would have been a very

different case" had the indictment stated "that Wait was under obligation, by contract, for an unexpired term of time, to employ and
pay Horne."[43] Inducing a breach of contract—the signature right of
the free worker—would have caused Shaw to find against the
bootmakers' society. It was likewise a free labor perspective that
informed Shaw's crucial distinction between American and English
standards for conspiracy indictments. He trod familiar ground here:
the reception of English law after the Revolution had always disal-
lowed what was unsuited to republican states. But consider his examples: "all those laws of the parent country" regulating wages,
settling paupers, and enforcing apprenticeship—all, of course, laws
inappropriate to a land of free labor.[44] What Shaw was, in fact, bent
on determining was a law of collective action that was appropriate
to a land of free labor.

"The case supposes that these persons were not bound by contract, but free to work for whom they please, or not work, if they so
prefer. In this state of things, we cannot perceive, that it is criminal
for men to agree together to exercise their own acknowledged
rights, in such a manner as best to subserve their own interests,"
including by an agreement "that when they were free to act, they
would not engage with an employer, or continue in his employment, if such an employer, when free to act, should engage with a
workman, or continue a workman in his employment, not a member of the association."[45] At this point, the circle closed between
free labor and union power, for what justified privileging the bootmakers' society over the journeyman Horne was that the association needed "to induce all those engaged in the same occupation to
become members of it" so as to gain the power to carry out its
laudable purposes.

≺ III ≻

Questions of Power

The Boston bootmakers' society that Chief Justice Shaw had contemplated was an informal, locally organized body, still rooted in
the artisanal world of pre-industrial America. Its postbellum successors, however, seemed far less benign, linked as they were into a
nationalizing trade union movement and endowed with ever more

formidable resources for confronting their employers. On another front, meanwhile, the Knights of Labor was developing a potent capacity for organizing on a community and industry-wide basis. In the 1880s, as Knights assemblies and craft unions grew prodigiously, a wave of strikes swept the country, and a new tactic, the boycott, suddenly emerged, mobilizing labor's power against "unfair" employers with devastating effect and sparking sympathy strikes across the railroad system. To the judges in their courtrooms, the boycott seemed like the opening gun of social revolution—"a reign of terror, which, if not checked, and punished in the beginning by the law, will speedily and inevitably run into violence . . . and mob tyranny."[46]

In this crisis, what *Commonwealth v. Hunt* had achieved came undone, and so briefly did the Olympian calm with which the bench normally read the law. The labor boycott was of that class of acts, like a conspiracy to seduce a minor female, so "destructive of the happiness of individuals and the well being of society" as to justify proscription even in the absence of an applicable statute or common-law offense. Thus, in *State v. Stewart*, one of several defining state appellate rulings at the height of the labor crisis of the mid 1880s, the Vermont Supreme Court declared itself not bound to find criminal conspiracy only when labor combinations "promote[d] objects or adopt[ed] means that [were] *per se* indictable." It was enough that the ends promoted or means employed be *"per se* oppressive, immoral or wrongfully prejudicial to the rights of others."[47] Presuming labor's actions to be uniquely ruinous of the public interest, the courts discarded what had been fundamental in *Commonwealth v. Hunt*, namely, that union power was in law indistinguishable from the power exerted by any other combination, or, as a major textbook put it in 1880, that "[we] cannot indict employees who combine, without indicting capitalists who combine."[48]

The courts had little trouble, of course, distinguishing capitalists from workers when it came to actions on the ground. Under the rubric of criminal means, a ready instrument was at hand for redefining the limits of permissible conduct during strikes and boycotts. The contrast with Britain is especially exact here, because in both countries laws were enacted against the expansive court reading of criminal means; but whereas in Britain "molestation" and "obstruction" gave way in 1875 to statutorily specified strike offenses, thereby ending judicial discretion in this realm,[49] in America the anticonspiracy laws of Pennsylvania and New York never overrode the authority of the courts to decide what "intimidation" meant. The results are evident in the judge's instructions to the jury in the prosecution of New York bakery strikers in 1886: regarding circulars, how many days they were distributed and "whether they contain appeals to the passions or are otherwise inflammatory"; whether, in the absence of direct threats, the strikers maintained "an attitude of imtimidation"; or whether their numbers might be taken to be intimidating. Any one of these would suffice for a conviction (and, as happened in this case, ten to thirty days in jail).[50] What emerged was a remarkable case law of strike conduct, distinct from the criminal code, and aiming at "a species of intimidation that works upon the mind rather than the body [and is] quite as dangerous, and generally altogether more effective, than acts of actual violence."[51]

On a second front, the courts swept out the defenses set forth in *Commonwealth v. Hunt* for the exercise of trade union power. Thus, in *State v. Donaldson* (1867), the originating case in the postbellum generation of conspiracy prosecutions, the judge saw only "the purpose of oppression and mischief,"[52] where, on the same showing of facts (save the employer's receptiveness), *Hunt* had seen a lawful union effort to strengthen itself. By demanding the dismissal of nonunion workers, the union was seeking to control the employer's business. This was the crux of it—that unions had no lawful right to strengthen themselves by what the courts defined as injury to or interference with an employer's business. In *State v. Glidden* (1887), arising from a boycott to oust nonunion printers from a Connecticut newspaper, the judge rejected the defendants' claim that they intended only to better their own conditions. Whatever their ultimate purpose, he ruled, their "direct and primary object must be regarded as the destruction of the [newspaper's] business."[53]

The finishing touches on this assault on *Hunt's* formulation came from the pen of William Howard Taft in *Moores v. Bricklayers' Union* (1889). Injury to others, Taft acknowledged, resulted whenever economic actors competed, but unions differed from other competitors, because in the unions' case, the injury done was "without cause or excuse," and hence showed malice. "The remote motive of wishing to better their condition by the power so acquired, will not . . . make any legal justification." *Moores* enabled employers to sue for damages, but its significance in the development of civil conspiracy was overshadowed by the larger message it conveyed condemning union exertions of power as acts of malice.[54]

Swift and mighty as this judicial response was, it did not in fact rescue boycotted employers: they could be destroyed before their antagonists felt the bite of the law. The situation was very like Britain's a century earlier, when common-law conspiracy had also proved wanting against an aroused working class. But where the British authorities had turned to Parliament for summary justice via the Combination acts, their American successors only reached deeper into the bag of common law for the right instrument. This was the injunction, a restraining order issued by an equity court to provide a remedy where no adequate relief was available at law. Injunctions could be granted instantly, at the court's discretion and, as an initial order, requiring no hearing or even notice to the affected persons. But such restraining orders, issuing from equity proceedings, applied only in very limited, well-specified circumstances, namely, repeated trespass or irreparable damage to real property. Undeterred, the courts forthwith expanded the definition of protectable property to encompass the business enterprise, in its entirety and all its activities, with strikers "clearly trespassers" by virtue of the disruptions they caused to business operations.[55] Within a few years, and with scant regard for precedent, the courts manufactured a new law of the labor injunction, driven by the conviction that, without pushing aside long-settled rules of equity, the boycotted employer "is certainly remediless, because an action at law, in most cases would do no good, and ruin would be accomplished before an adjudication would be reached."[56]

The impact was simply devastating. The injunction abruptly halted the boycott drive and, beyond that, disrupted what might have been America's one chance to build a working-class movement comparable to the movements then taking shape in Europe. So potent was the injunction, in fact, that it in practice replaced criminal proceedings in labor disputes. Conspiracy doctrine remained good law, but after the mid-1890s it was effectively superceded by summary restraining orders, which had undertaken the law's work of suppressing strikes and boycotts done (in the new language of labor conspiracy) with "a malicious intent to injure and destroy the complainant's business."[57]

The labor injunction was also the bridge by which the federal courts joined the legal assault on trade unionism. They had, in fact, been the first courts to use labor injunctions, initially to shield railroads in receivership (and hence court-controlled) from strikes; then, with the Interstate Commerce Act (1887), against sympathy strikes more generally as obstructions of commerce; and finally, against strikes and boycotts construed to be conspiracies in restraint of trade under the Sherman Antitrust Act (1890). In the great Pullman boycott of 1894, the federal injunction was unveiled in all its might, immobilizing the strike officers and sending their leader Eugene V. Debs to prison for contempt of court. From this point onward, moreover, state and federal jurisdictions increasingly overlapped, with the federal courts holding that, under the diverse citizenship provision of the Constitution, they could entertain labor cases even absent a federal violation if the parties were citizens of different states. All it took was an out-of-state third party (conniving of course with the "defendant" employer) coming forward with a claim to a material interest in the dispute. So advantageous did the federal jurisdiction prove to be that, over the next 30 years, roughly two-thirds of all labor cases, mostly of local provenance, came to the federal courts.[58]

The labor movement was cast down, to use William Forbath's apt phrase, into "semi-outlawry."

An injunction against picketing could vanquish a strike, but for every picket line enjoined, many more were broken up without court decisions by local officials who invoked the illegality of picketing, boycotts, organizing, and closed-shop strikes. The courts had woven a powerful web of associations between strikers' use of economic "coercion" and their use of brute physical force, between popular images of criminal conspirators and the legal construction of virtually all secondary actions as conspiracies in restraint of trade, and between picketing in any fashion and threats of violence.[59]

The victory was, in a sense, too complete. "Defy the law," a union leader urged a mass meeting of striking Chicago printers in 1905. "Judge-made law is not good law." In its distress, the embattled AFL was driven onto the path of civil disobedience. "Con-

tempt of court" is "obedience to law," proclaimed Samuel Gompers, who showed himself as good as his word by defying the
Buck's Stove injunction and courting a year in jail.[60] The precious
consent that law required thus, jeopardized, the courts sought to
shore up by appealing to that other strand of *Commonwealth v.
Hunt*—the law of free labor.

≺ IV ≻

The Utility of Free Labor

The conspiracy decisions of the 1880s sometimes included among
proscribed combinations those "designed to coerce workmen to become members, or to interfere with, obstruct, vex, or annoy them
in working, or in obtaining work, because they are not members, or
in order to induce them to become members."[61] From this reading
sprang a minor line of case law, contra *Hunt*, establishing the right
of a discharged worker to sue for damages, as, for example, an engi-
neer did after being ousted from his job because of a closed-shop
agreement between the brewery union and an employers' association. The New York Court of Appeals found in his favor, ruling in
Curran v. Galen (1897) that he had been unlawfully deprived "of
his constitutional right freely to pursue a lawful avocation, under
conditions equal to all."[62] But this right was ringed by limitations—
by whether, for example, he could have joined the union had he
chosen to do so, or whether other suitable work was to be had—and
seems rarely to have been asserted by aggrieved nonunion workers.
Curran was reversed in 1905.[63] The paramount legal issue in
closed-shop case law was not whether the closed shop violated the
rights of nonunion workers, but whether the employer agreed to it.
  This was the crux of the matter, and, for practical purposes, so
it had been ever since the revival of conspiracy law after the Civil
War. The language of *State v. Donaldson* (1867), the first important
conspiracy case to surface after *Hunt*, is telling on that score: the
closed shop that the defendants sought "cannot in any event be advantageous to the employee" but "must always be hurtful to the
employer," who "in the presence of a coalition of his employees
. . . must submit."[64] Later judges knew better than to privilege the
employer's rights in this bald way, but that in fact was where the

law had real bite: that when workers "combine . . . to prevent an employer from employing others by threats of a strike, they combine to accomplish an unlawful purpose."[65]

The closed shop was, in reality, preeminently about power relations. Listen, for example, to Abraham Bisno, a "walking delegate" for the Chicago garment workers.

We could not have an organization at all unless we had an organization that was competent to protect the individual member from being thrown out of employment for being a union man . . . So when these men demand that the union be recognized to the extent of employing no other people except members of their union, this is essential to the very existence of their organization. It is a life-and-death question with them.[66]

And so, on the other side, it was to employers. By resisting the closed shop, they resisted collective bargaining. What the landmark conspiracy cases of the 1880s mainly vindicated was the employer's interest in a struggle over unionization, not the rights of individual workers in deference to the law of free labor.

And when it came to the injunction, not even the pretense of deference could be sustained. The essential doctrinal maneuver was, as we have seen, to redefine property so as to encompass the business enterprise, which included the flow of work and the employer's relations with his workers. Inducing them to quit work became a form of enjoinable trespass on the employer's "property." There was some precedent for this in existing law, but from a strand utterly antithetical to free labor—the feudal law of master and servant, under the head of "enticement." The first efforts at enjoining strikes had, indeed, run aground on just that claim, resting as it did "upon the theory that such servants had not freedom of action which is conceded to that class at the present day." The judge was "disinclined to extend, by any judgment of mine, the doctrine of recovery for enticing away servants where, both in fact and theory, the person enticed is a free agent to come and go as he will, responsible only, like other persons, for the violation of his contract or his duty."[67] In overcoming such scruples, later courts revealed how little the doctrine of free labor actually counted in the law of labor conspiracy and injunctions that came down on American trade unionism.

Where free labor did hugely figure was as ideology, as I have defined it, an imagined world of free and equal workers. Thus, in an

1887 debate on the tumultuous labor crisis, it was Colorado Senator Henry Teller's conviction that

no laboring man for a moment should surrender [the right of free contract], either to the State, to his fellow-workmen, or to capital. His labor is valuable to him only as it is at his uncontrolled disposal, both as to whom he will sell it, and when he will sell it. Any interference by his fellow workmen of the same trade or any other in the disposal of his labor is an invasion of his right . . . The difference between a slave and a freeman consists mainly in the fact that the freeman may freely dispose of his labor . . . oñ the terms fixed by himself.[68]

The labor conspiracy cases are replete with this language of free labor, going back, indeed, to the very first, when, having described how the Philadelphia shoemakers disciplined their ranks, Moses Levy burst out indignantly: "Is this freedom? Is it not restraining, instead of promoting the Spirit of '76?"[69]

Then, and long after, Levy's republican cry of freedom might have encompassed the self-employed as well as wage workers. In the *Slaughter-House Cases* (1873), Forbath reminds us, Justice Field invoked "the right of free labor" on behalf of New Orleans butcher-entrepreneuers against a state-mandated stockyards monopoly. But while Field's dissent eventually became ruling doctrine, his invocation of free labor in defense of entrepreneurial rights fell silent and, Forbath finds, played no part in the succeeding line of due-process cases restraining the states' regulation of labor conditions. With the rise of a permanent working class, the language was no longer of the free laborers' right to "the fruits of their labor," but only of their freedom to sell their labor to "those who might be disposed to employ them."[70]

In the conspiracy cases, the essential task was to enfold this hard truth within the law's repressive project, first, by invoking the glories of freedom of contract, in which

every owner of property may work it as he will, by whom he pleases, at such wages, and upon such terms as he can make; and every laborer may work or not, as he sees fit, for whom, and at such wages, as he pleases; and neither can dictate to the other how he shall use his own, whether of property, time, or skill[71]

and, second, by utilizing the elastic definition of property as everything of "exchange value" now taking hold generally in American jurisprudence, and vividly voiced, for example, by *State v. Stewart*:

"The labor and skill of the workman, be it of high or low degree,
the plant of the manufacturer, the equipment of the farmer, the investment in commerce, are all in equal sense property," and all
equally to be protected from "the anathema of secret organization[s] of men combined for the purpose of controlling the industry
of others."[72]

How free labor ideology, so formulated, was mobilized against
"the anathema of secret organizations" is best seen in the work of
the American Anti-Boycott Association (AABA), which was formed
in 1903 by two Danbury hat manufacturers threatened by a union
boycott. By this time, the boycotting strategy had entered a new,
more sophisticated phase, operating through a nationwide trade union network and targeting unfair employers in multiple local markets. The AABA's purpose was to defend this class of threatened
firms by spreading the costs of litigation and developing the legal
expertise to challenge the boycott. The undertaking ended trium-
phantly in *Loewe v. Lawlor* (1908), which declared "We Don't Pa-
tronize" campaigns to be conspiracies in restraint of trade under
the Sherman Act (and subjected the Danbury members to triple
damages). The economic roots of this case were in the cutthroat
soft-hat market, pitting the marginal operator Loewe against the
Hatters' Union's efforts to take wages out of competition and stabi-
lize the industry. The closed-shop clause was, in Loewe's case, not
exactly incidental, since some employees evidently stood to lose
their places if he signed the contract, but his decision to fight the
union was dictated by his situation as a marginal, low-cost competitor.

Audiences could scarcely have drawn that conclusion. The
AABA presented itself as champion of the open shop, cloaked in
the Declaration of Independence and standing for "the free rights of
every American citizen." The closed shop had to be resisted, said
the AABA attorney Daniel Davenport, because "every man, I don't
care who he is, has implanted in his heart the deep seated love of
liberty." Davenport inveighed against trade unionists for excluding
"others from the opportunity to work, although those others are of
the same condition in life as themselves and have nothing but
their hands and their dexterity by which to live and support their
families." To drive home his point, Davenport described the abuse
of a respectable young woman ("any man would have been proud

to call her sister or daughter") who had tried to go to work during the recent Chicago packinghouse strike of 1904.

They seized that girl, they rolled her in the mud, they disfigured her, and they subjected her person to indignities not fit to be described in your presence.

The incident had made Davenport's "blood boil."[73]

In our postmodernist age, historians are disinclined to be skeptical of such pronouncements or, at any rate, to regard them as true as anything else that is said or written. So it may bear mentioning that the one great case in which the law of free labor did figure centrally—*Commonwealth v. Hunt*—was devoid of the cant of free labor dogma. Indeed, what most provoked Chief Justice Shaw were the "qualifying epithets, (as 'unlawful, deceitful, pernicious,' &c.)," larding the indictment and the partisan bent of the lower court proceedings.[74]

Had employers wanted to make the law of free labor determining, all that was needed was for them to heed Shaw's advice and sign their employees to time contracts. This, however, they declined to do, far preferring the freedom of at-will employment and content with the legal protections they already enjoyed. To this generalization, one exception stands out.

From the 1870s onward, many firms required workers to sign "ironclads" (better known, in later years, as yellow-dog contracts) stating that, as a condition of employment, they would not join a union or, alternatively, not strike or otherwise engage in concerted activity regarding working conditions. The yellow-dog was a good contract, consistently upheld by the courts against state laws seeking to declare it illegal. But for many years the effect was strictly atmospheric, inasmuch as, in practice, the employer's only recourse against breach of contract was discharge (which was his absolute right anyway).[75] In 1907, however, the Hitchman Coal & Coke Company bethought itself to seek an injunction, on the grounds that the organizing activity of the United Mine Workers amounted to inducing breach of contract by its miners. When the Supreme Court finally upheld the company's application in 1917, freedom of contract and the injunction fused into an extraordinary defense against unionization.

The Court justified its decision on familiar free labor grounds:

The same liberty which enables men to form unions, and through the union to enter into agreements with employers willing to agree, entitles other men to remain independent of the union and other employers to agree with them to employ no man who owes any allegiance or obligation to the union . . . Plaintiff, having in the exercise of its undoubted rights established a working agreement between it and its employees, with the free assent of the latter, is entitled to be protected in the resulting status, as in any other legal right.[76]

Out in the coal fields, where nonunion contracts proliferated (and acquired their "yellow-dog" designation), operators boasted that they were upholding "a principle of democracy." And miners, if they bothered to read the contracts they were signing, would have seen that they were affirming "the preservation of the right of individual contract, free from interference or regulation by others, and payment in proportion to service."[77]

In 1927 *United Mine Workers v. Red Jacket* upheld an injunction that effectively ordered the United Mine Workers away from all of southern West Virginia, a district of hundreds of mines and 40,000 miners. The presiding circuit court judge, John J. Parker, paid for *Red Jacket* by forfeiting his elevation to the Supreme Court three years later. In the Senate confirmation battle, Judge Parker had many defenders (and the defense that he was bound by *Hitchman*), but only one Senator defended the yellow-dog contract. It was, in fact, indefensible. And the judicial system, for defending it, suffered a remarkable moral collapse. The courts had overreached themselves.

≺ V ≻

The Imprint of the Old Order

On March 23, 1932, Congress passed the Norris-LaGuardia Anti-Injunction Act. Norris-LaGuardia declared the yellow-dog contract unenforceable in the federal courts and withdrew from them jurisdiction to issue injunctions in most labor disputes. For the well-specified exceptions, the law laid down rigorous procedural and evidentiary protections. Norris-LaGuardia was an act of demolition, sweeping out the worst of the judge-made labor law and preparing the ground for a new regime of statutory labor-relations law. Norris-LaGuardia took note of "the aid of governmental authority for owners of property to organize in the corporate and other forms of ownership association." Because of the resulting imbalance, "the individual worker is commonly helpless to exercise actual liberty of contract and to protect his freedom of labor, and thereby to obtain acceptable terms and conditions of employment." These were remarkable words, recapitulating *Commonwealth v. Hunt*'s disdain for the unequal legal treatment of capital and labor, but now marshalling the language of free labor more forcefully on behalf of solidarity. "Under prevailing economic conditions," said Norris-LaGuardia, free workers will want to act collectively because only in that way can they exercise "actual freedom of contract."

In the National Labor Relations [Wagner] Act of 1935, what Norris-LaGuardia asserted in principle received the force of law. The heart of the Wagner Act was Section 7:

Employees shall have the right to self-organization, to form, join, or assist labor organizations, to bargain collectively through representatives of their own choosing, and to engage in concerted activities, for the purpose of collective bargaining or other mutual aid or protection.

This declaration of rights was implemented by an array of unfair labor practices: employers could not interfere with, restrain, or coerce employees in the exercise of their rights; dominate or interfere with labor organizations; discriminate against employees to discourage union membership; or refuse to bargain with representatives of their employees.

The law might have stopped at this point—Norris-LaGuardia had contemplated nothing further—but for the stormy labor history of the early New Deal's National Recovery Administration, out of which came the decision that the state had to take charge of the process of determining representation for purposes of collective bargaining. The result was a preferred bargaining structure based on "exclusive representation"—one union for all the workers in a plant or other "appropriate" unit—and the principle of majority rule in the choice by workers of representatives, with the minority, in good democratic fashion, obliged to submit to the majority. It was similarly the impotence of the NRA labor boards that instructed the authors of the Wagner Act in the need for a National Labor Relations Board amply endowed with investigative and enforcement powers.

In its time, the Wagner Act was celebrated (or, alternately, reviled) as the most radical law of the New Deal era. Its passage helped spark the greatest surge of labor organizing in American history. Formidable industrial unions emerged, millions of workers joined up, and, in the postwar era, collective bargaining became a national institution governing the labor relations of the booming industrial economy. At its height in the mid-1950s, organized labor represented eighteen million workers, a third of the entire American labor force. In such basic industries as steel, automobiles, and mining, union coverage was virtually total. But slowly and then, as the economy foundered in the 1970s, precipitously, the unions lost ground until in the private sector they stand today roughly where they did before the New Deal, with scarcely one worker in ten a union member.

The law, it turns out, is not what it seemed. We can track its impotence in the rising incidence of unfair labor practice charges against employers, which amounted to a few thousand a year in the mid 1950s, but 35,000 in 1980; or in the failure rate of unions in representation elections, which rose above 50 percent, notwithstanding that unions almost never petition for an election without signed cards from a good majority of the workers they are seeking to represent; or in the fact that, when they do prevail, unions fail one time in three to get a first contract, notwithstanding that the law requires the employer to negotiate in good faith with them.[78] Workers are fired every day for union activities, and nonunion workers know it. In a 1991 poll, 79 percent thought it "very" or "somewhat" likely that workers would be fired for trying to organize a union; half of these respondents believed that, if they participated, they themselves would be fired.[79] Had such a poll been taken before the advent of the Wagner Act, the results would likely not have been far different. In that convergence of past and present, I find my concluding text. For what I want to argue for is the staying power of the old order and its imprint, only now fully visible, on the failing collective-bargaining law of our own time.

It might have seemed, in such a law, that claims of solidarity would take precedence. That, most certainly, was what the authors of the Wagner Act had intended. We can see their hand, for example, in the omission from the law's Section 7 rights of the right of workers (acknowledged in original Norris-LaGuardia language) not to associate; in the provision that, once a majority elected a bargaining agent, every worker in the unit had to accept representation by that agent; and in the absence of any acknowledgment that workers might be coerced by labor organizations. More fundamental was "self-organization"—first of the Section 7 rights—which the law's authors intended as the doctrinal underpinning for the collectivist bent of the law. For a heady time, it seemed as if they had solved the riddle of freedom and solidarity. Workers were free, but they would express that freedom collectively and reap the benefits of "actual freedom of contract." A labor law based on that premise would surely bring forth a great and powerful union movement. And, for one generation, it did.

Then, with the sweeping Taft-Hartley amendments of 1947, the hard truth set in, signalled by the reinsertion in Section 7 of the worker's right "to refrain from any and all [concerted] activities."[80] From this language followed the "right-to-work" provision in the amended law. The Wagner Act had expressly permitted the union shop where it derived from an agreement between the employer and a union certified as exclusive bargaining agent. Now, in Section 14(b), Taft-Hartley invited the states to exempt themselves from that provision. In right-to-work states, nonunion workers acquired stronger rights of nonassociation (but not of individual bargaining) than they had ever enjoyed under the pre–New Deal legal regime, since in no circumstances (not even by the assent of their employers) could they now be required to join a union in order to keep a job. More remarkable, although less noticed, was Taft-Hartley's assault on the law's conception of self-organization: new unfair labor practices protected workers from coercion by labor organizations; employers received the right to participate in representation campaigns; and the secret election became mandatory for certification. In the eyes of the law, the worker had become just a voter making a choice between collective and individual bargaining. The mandated collective-bargaining structure was not altered, nor, despite fierce denunciations by the labor movement, was the unionized sector visibly damaged. Taft-Hartley was craftier, striking not at the edifice of collective bargaining, but at the sustaining premises of solidarity. In that endeavor, it succeeded, setting in motion in the name of individual rights and free choice the corrosive forces that ate away at the law and rendered it in our own time an empty bulwark of labor's collective rights.

Taft-Hartley was a political event and, in that sense, fixed in the chronology of the postwar reaction against the New Deal: the Republicans, having retaken the Congress in 1946, had the votes to pass Taft-Hartley and override President Truman's veto. But, in concept, Taft-Hartley was the Wagner Act's relentless companion from the first.[81] Literally hundreds of Congressional bills (not to mention hostile hearings) preceded Taft-Hartley. It was only a matter of time, and the right political conditions, before Taft-Hartley or something very like it would prevail. The Wagner Act was vulnerable to Taft-Hartley from birth, and here too, in its vulnerability, we find the imprint of the old order.

On the main question—on the worker's right to organize—the Supreme Court had long since taken its stand. The lead case was *Adair v. U.S.* (1908), declaring unconstitutional a provision of the Erdman Act (1898) that forbade railroads from discharging employees for union membership. *Adair* rested squarely on liberty of contract and its companion, free labor.

The right of the employe to quit the service of the employer, for whatever reason, is the same as the right of the employer, for whatever reason, to dispense with the services of such employe . . . Any legislation that disturbs that equality is an arbitrary interference with liberty of contract which no government can justify in a free land.[82]

Adair served, in turn, as the legal grounding for the yellow-dog contract.

Everyone in labor's camp agreed on the vileness of the yellow-dog contract, but they disagreed about how to kill it. The AFL leaders wanted a frontal attack that challenged *Adair*'s espousal of liberty of contract and seized the banner of free labor for their own cause. They assailed the yellow-dog contract as "fully as destructive of human liberty as a condition of peonage," conducive of "economic servitude," and, altogether, "as un-American as peonage or slavery."[83] The legal experts, citing the failed rights language of the Clayton Anti-Trust Act (1914), demurred. They regarded *Adair* as authoritative, so that, rather than being declared illegal because (as the AFL argued) it violated the worker's freedom, the yellow-dog contract became merely unenforceable, and the injunction, rather than being declared inapplicable to labor disputes because (as the AFL argued) labor was not property, became restricted. Norris-LaGuardia was high legislative craft, but witness also to an insurmountable case law: in the estimation of Norris-LaGuardia's authors, the rights-based act that the AFL wanted would never have prevailed against *Adair*.

The Wagner Act, however, required a different maneuver, inasmuch as it met *Adair* head on. The solution was supplied by Oliver Wendell Holmes, who in his dissent to *Adair* had argued that the employer's liberty was not being fundamentally challenged: protecting union workers from discrimination constituted "in substance, a very limited interference with freedom of contract, no more."[84] So, still less, did the interference by the Wagner Act, since the law that Mr. Justice Holmes was defending had made discharge of union workers a criminal offense, while in the Wagner Act it was only an unfair labor practice, the remedy for which was, in discharge cases, reemployment with backpay (minus interim earnings), and, on other violations, an NLRB order to cease and desist and, where appropriate, restoration of the status quo. Taft-Hartley, astute as always, drove home the inferiority of labor's rights when it outlawed secondary boycotts, for which, in defense of their property rights, employers were entitled to automatic injunctive relief and standing to sue for damages and legal costs. Unions boycott employers at their peril; little is at risk when employers violate workers' rights.

At the time, of course, the authors of the Wagner Act had in mind the urgent business of getting the Wagner Act past the Supreme Court, which they did, to the general consternation of conservatives, in *NLRB v. Jones and Laughlin* (1937). They were content that *Adair* be left intact (as it remains to this day, still authoritative on at-will employment) and that their law be excepted from *Adair*. The Court's exact words were that *Adair* was "inapplicable to legislation of this character."[85] Here, too, the hand of Mr. Justice Holmes could be seen. If, on "an important ground of public policy" Congress chose to intrude on liberty of contract, "the Constitution does not forbid it, whether this court agrees or disagrees with the policy pursued."[86] Holmes was the high priest of legal realism, and in *Adair* (and many other celebrated opinions) he was striking a blow at judicial formalism. Following Holmes, the New Deal progressives regarded a labor law not grounded in inalienable rights as a positive achievement. Far better that it be recentered, as their mentor had said in *Vegelahn v. Guntner* (1896), on "considerations of policy and social advantage."

Norris-LaGuardia, in fact, did just that: it curbed the yellow-dog contract and labor injunction because they were contrary to "public policy," which was that workers not be denied the benefits of collective bargaining. In the Wagner Act, the affirmation of collective bargaining became more assertive. Its practice and procedure were to be "encouraged," in part because this was what the constitutional argument for the law demanded—collective bargaining reduced the industrial strife that obstructed interstate commerce—and in part because the Great Depression had brought forth an economic rationale for collective bargaining: its absence "tends to aggravate recurrent business depressions, by depressing wage rates and the purchasing power of wage earners in industry and by preventing the stabilization of competitive wage rates and working conditions within and between industries."

These propositions, remnants of early New Deal corporatism, are still in the labor law, but no politician would dream of espousing them in our globalized, free-market age. Nor, in broader terms, does public policy today, or for the quarter century past, actually correspond to the declared policy of the labor law that collective bargaining is good for the country. Thus, if we look at how the law today works rather than at what it professes, a "union-free environment" has as much legitimacy as, and in actual fact holds a decided advantage over, collective bargaining. At the law's nadir in the Reagan era, the NLRB chairman himself was heard to say that "collective bargaining frequently means monopoly, the destruction of the marketplace."[87] It may have been quixotic, as the legal realists believed, for the AFL to prefer a labor law grounded in the inalienable rights of free labor, but the alternative has been a labor law grounded only in the shifting sands of public policy.

In the old days, a keyword in labor's vocabulary had been "recognition." It referred to the standing a union attained on entering contractual relations with an employer. In granting recognition, the employer acknowledged the union's power; and, overtly or not, the process leading to collective bargaining constituted a power struggle. The primary function of labor law was to police this struggle, which it did, as we have seen, with unabashed and ultimately reckless disregard for labor's cause. With the advent of the Wagner Act, the keyword became "certification," meaning a union's official standing as exclusive bargaining agent (and the employer's correlative obligation to negotiate with it). This was the essence of the New Deal's collective-bargaining revolution: the state had undertaken to replace equations of power with a rule of law, which consisted, of course, of the provisions of the Wagner Act. So long as employers consented, that revolution held, but once they regrouped and counterattacked, the fragility of that rule of law stood forth, and so, I am suggesting, did the imprint of the old legal regime. By centering itself, as it had to do, on the rights of workers, the modern labor law was reproducing the free labor premises of the old regime, and hence reproducing, within its own confines, the abiding American tension between freedom and solidarity.

No trade unionist would want to return to the days of yellow-dog contracts and wholesale labor injunctions. But the evil that they did at least had the virtue of clarity. The oppression of workers today is mostly invisible, masked within the processes of a law that speaks in the language of labor's rights. The labor movement has demanded reform for many years, but as the more fundamental problems in the law have emerged, it has become less apparent just how to deal with them. In any case, the weakened movement lacks the necessary political clout, and will have all it can do to preserve the one provision of the law with which management is dissatisfied—the prohibition against dominating labor organizations (Section 8a[2]), which, be it noted, is also the one bar to employer interference not about individual rights. In the meantime, some unions are beginning to vote with their feet. They are boycotting NLRB elections, organizing workers directly, and pressuring employers for voluntary recognition. In acting in an old-fashioned way, of course, they are inviting an old-fashioned response, which now includes even a revival of labor conspiracy via a federal racketeering law that the courts have begun to apply against vigorously fought strikes.[88]

All this suggests an unstable future for the collective bargaining law. But there is nothing unstable about the underlying dynamics that, ever since the earliest craft unions, rendered the law of labor a burden on American trade unionism. It would be implausible, of course, to attribute the failure of the modern labor law to an obscure Indiana decision back in 1821 declaring that the woman of color Mary Clark could not be held to her indenture because that

constituted involuntary servitude. Yet the free labor doctrine embraced by *Mary Clark*, unimpeachable though it be, is also surely
implicated in the peculiar disfavor in which the claims of solidarity are held, even in a law whose declared purpose is the encour-
agement of collective bargaining.

Social Mobility, Free Labor, and the American Dream

CLAYNE POPE

NO IDEAL OR MYTHOLOGY is more central to the interpretation of the American experience than that related to social
mobility. "Rags to Riches; shirt sleeves to shirt sleeves; born in a
log cabin; streets paved with gold; go west young man; give me
your tired, your poor, your huddled masses"—the list could go on
and on. The fact that we refer to one or another expression of upward mobility as the American Dream with Abraham Lincoln as
the principal icon demonstrates how central this mythology is to
American self-description. Those leading cheers for America exalt
mobility while those leading the criticism point to the absence of
upward movement. Some celebrate examples of scrambles to the
top while others demand that the government make the mythology
more true. Regardless of one's position, the view of America is colored by a personal view of the reality of social mobility in contrast
to the myth. Those who believe America has delivered on its promise of mobility write approvingly of American opportunities and
institutions. Those who believe the American dream is bogus concentrate on the immobilities and demand significant social change.

Because the mythology of American mobility is a mythology of
extremes, histories, social commentaries, or descriptions from literature seem puzzlingly contradictory. Scholars remind us that
myths contain profound elements of truth if they are properly interpreted while believers in a myth reassure one another with
mountains of selective evidence. So it is with the American myth
of social mobility: somewhere within the rhetoric of a land of
boundless opportunity or a country ruled by rapacious capitalists
lies the truth. Unfortunately, the central importance and exaggera-
tion of the social mobility myth make that reality difficult to find

and even more difficult to interpret. This chapter will argue that the rise of free labor has been accompanied by a high degree of social mobility which has generally been undervalued.

The basic building blocks for the mythology are well known. America was born out of opportunity. A frontier of unsettled land (non-Europeans were ignored), sometimes of questionable value and sometimes with hidden riches in gold, minerals, or fuels, was here for the taking for three centuries. Only after the closing of the frontier, noted by Frederick Jackson Turner's influential essay in 1893, did land recede from center stage in the description of American mobility.[1] Inevitably linked to the land was internal and international migration. Tied to both the clearing and settlement of new land and westward migration, whether from Europe or the East Coast, was the notion of sacrifice by the first generation to benefit future generations. Beyond land settlement, but often tied to it, was the notion of labor scarcity and the opportunity to move up the occupational ladder. By the middle of the nineteenth century, movement up that ladder was linked to education—first common schools; then, sequentially in the twentieth century, widespread diffusion of high school, extensive use of the GI bill, and a push for universal access to higher education in community and state colleges.

But the most basic of building blocks of the American dream is the institution of free labor. Without the ownership of self, embodied in free labor, the idea of social mobility and individual economic progress would be difficult to envision.[2] This linkage between free labor and social mobility is the central focus of this chapter.

Many of the constraints binding the location, wages, and working conditions of labor have been eliminated or loosened with remarkable speed over the past two centuries, making the American dream a possibility. The slave trade from Africa to the Americas, slavery throughout the world, serfdom, indentured servitude, and compulsory performance of labor have all passed from being dominant institutions to non-existence or obscurity. Slavery and related institutions are now relegated to geographical backwaters or to isolated incidents elsewhere in the world. The right of labor to bargain freely for better terms and working conditions is well entrenched throughout much of the world. Access to education and training, though not readily available to all, has been expanded to near universality in developed countries and to growing availability in many developing countries. Indeed, the changes in the institutions of labor have been so dramatic in the past two centuries that the term "free labor" is no longer seen as a clarion call for reformers or political leaders.

These expansive or positive forces for mobility were countered by the barriers of discrimination and by closed political and economic systems. Ethnicity, race, and gender have stood as immobilizing attributes that have made the American dream seem cruelly hollow to some. Group differences in income, wealth, occupation, or other measures of status are an ever-present reminder of rigidities. The growing size of business enterprises and the appearance of new business giants have kept alive the question of unequal power between employee and employer.

Some institutions have had ambiguous effects on social mobility. Government has been perceived as both a provider of opportunity (for example, publicly provided primary and secondary education, cheap higher education) and a reinforcer of immobility (support for school segregation, Jim Crow laws). Technological change has been seen as both the creator of opportunity through new industries (picture Henry Ford in his bicycle shop or Bill Gates tinkering with DOS) and the destroyer of niches that some had managed to carve out (the decline of the family farm, the disappearance of passenger rail traffic, the substitution of computers for clerks and secretaries). Labor unions have been seen both as a vehicle for workers to make a decent wage and accumulate the basic trappings of the American dream and as a barrier for the entry of the disadvantaged into higher paying skilled employment.

Although the social mobility myth is central to our understanding of American history and much time and energy goes into comparing actual experience to one or another version of the myth, even a rough consensus about actual social mobility eludes us.[3] Data that trace individuals and their economic activity through time are rare and usually beset by problems of selection bias. Basic conceptual and measurement issues have yet to be resolved. Perhaps, most important, a frame of reference to gauge how much mobility would be enough does not exist. Yet the American dream continues to occupy a more or less permanent central position in the interpretation of American history because social mobility embodies much of what we care about regardless of our own sense of the myth and the reality.

The task of isolating the effect of free labor institutions upon economic well-being and social mobility is not easy given the numerous changes that have occurred in all areas of society. Introductory economics classes handle such complexities by invoking terms like *ceteris paribus* (holding everything else constant). History does not work that way. Rather there are confounding influences that must be separated. At the same time that labor institutions were becoming more open and free, technological change, capital accumulation, investment in education, and other factors combined with the institution of free labor in promoting economic growth.[4] Health as measured by life expectancy, morbidity, height, or other nutritional measures also improved dramatically.[5] All of these changes make it impossible to measure with precision the effect of changing labor institutions upon social mobility and economic well-being. Not all improvement in material conditions should be attributed to the new and more open labor institutions. But it is clear that the institutional changes affecting labor did matter.

There is no necessary theoretical link between free labor institutions, high economic growth, and social mobility of labor. Each of these conditions could, in principle, exist without the others. But there is a necessary link between the efficient allocation of labor and economic growth. Labor is, by far, the most important resource of an economy. Reallocation of labor that is being put to the wrong task will bring substantial gain in productivity. For example, the movement of labor off farms to urban areas increased productivity throughout industrializing western Europe and North America by shifting labor from farming, a relatively low productivity sector, to manufacturing, a high productivity sector. This reallocation of labor was essential for high rates of economic growth, given the differences in productivity in the two sectors. Similarly, movement of farmers from less productive land in New England to more productive land in the Midwest increased agricultural output for the United States in the nineteenth century. But the conclusion that these reallocations of labor could not have been accomplished with unfree labor does not necessarily follow. Those individuals controlling coerced labor might have been even more responsive to productivity differentials between the city and the countryside or between regions.[6] Certainly, incentives seem central to economic efficiency and growth. But incentives may be implemented within coerced labor. One of the important results of the Fogel and Engerman analysis of the antebellum South was their conclusion that an economy organized around slavery could be comparatively more productive than a free economy.[7] Once there were examples in which slavery or coercion yielded a larger output than that possible with free labor, the economic consequences of free labor became an empirical question to be addressed by historical evidence. This chapter focuses on description of empirical trends in economic well-being, with particular reference to the United States and on empirical measures of social mobility.

<< I >>

Material Well-Being in the Period with
Free Labor Institutions

Economists tend to reduce measurement of material well-being to the average level of consumption or income in a nation with some attention to the distribution of consumption or income. But trends in other measures affecting well-being—such as life expectancy, nutritional status, and the amount of leisure time—are also worth examination. Because a consistent quantitative series for any measure of economic well-being over a long time period is rare, economic and social historians have often resorted to indirect measurement of trends. For example, measurements of height, often available in military records, provide insight into trends in nutrition, work capacity, and health.[8] While it would be useful to have a single summary measure of economic well-being, no current measure, including the ubiquitous GDP per capita, captures all of the influences on the comfort and welfare of society.

Table 1 summarizes different trends in measures related to levels of economic well-being in the United States for the past two centuries. These trends do not follow each other closely for all time periods. For example, height and adult life expectancy decline in the antebellum period while gross domestic product (GDP) per

TABLE I

Trends in Measures of Economic Well-Being in the United States

Year	GDP per capita 1840 prices	GDP per capita 1958 prices	Height (inches' white males)	Males White	Males Black and other	Females White	Females Black and other	Hours worked (manufacturing, weekly hours)
1800	$78		67.9	46		48		a
1830	90		68.3	45		45		
1850	111		67.1	41		40		
1860	135		67.0	41		42		a
1870		$ 531						
1900		1011	67.7	42	35	44	37	59
1930		1490	68.2	46	36	49	37	42
1950		2342	69.7	50	44	55	47	40.5
1970		3555		50	45	57	52	39.8

SOURCES: GDP per capita estimates: Thomas Weiss, "U.S. Labor Force Estimates and Economic Growth, 1800–1860," in Robert E. Gallman and John J. Wallis, eds., American Economic Growth and Standards of Living before the Civil War (Chicago, 1992); Historical Statistics of the United States from Colonial Times to the Present (Washington D.C., 1975), 224. Heights: Calculated from Figure 2.3 in Richard H. Steckel and Dora Costa, "Long-Term Trends in U.S. Health, Welfare and Economic Growth," in Richard H. Steckel and Roderick Floud, eds., Health and Welfare during Industrialization (Chicago, 1997), 51. Life Expectancy: Clayne Pope, "Adult Mortality: A View from Family Histories," in Claudia Goldin and Hugh Rockoff, eds., Strategic Factors in Nineteenth Century American Economic History (Chicago, 1992), 277, and Historical Statistics, 56. Hours: Historical Statistics, 169–70.

[a]Stanley Lebergott suggests that the work day was initially 13 hours in antebellum factories, but had fallen to 10 hours a day by 1860. Stanley Lebergott, The Americans: an Economic Record (New York, 1984), 68.

capita increases. However, when considered over the two-century span, the measures summarized—output per capita, height, life expectancy, work week—do show a strong pattern of improvement in the average level of economic well-being. These measures leave little doubt that the level in the latter part of the twentieth century is much higher than it was in the nineteenth century. The precise contribution of changes in labor institutions to this improvement is not known, but it seems reasonable to conclude that the gradual shift from coerced to free labor with strong incentives to invest in human capital added significantly to this dramatic growth.

Even though estimates of GDP per capita do not extend back to the colonial period, we know that modern growth rates (beyond a half to one per cent per annum) were not possible for extended periods before the nineteenth century. Extrapolating growth rates of one percent or higher backward into the colonial period would quickly lead to zero income.[9] Since 1800, however, growth in output per worker, ignoring short-run fluctuations, has been quite steady. For the United States, output per worker has roughly doubled every 40 years since 1840. The growth between the Revolution and 1840 appears to have been somewhat slower, but still substantial, likely doubling in 75 years.

The sustained growth in GDP per capita in both the nineteenth and twentieth centuries makes it difficult to argue that any specific change in labor institutions is reflected in an obvious change in the growth rate of income per capita. Growth in the antebellum period when slavery and vestiges of compulsory service were present was strong, but so was growth in the early twentieth century when labor was much more free to contract and organized labor was more powerful.

The growth enjoyed by the antebellum South with a substantial part of its workforce in slavery illustrates the tenuous link between labor institutional change and economic growth. GDP per capita grew faster between 1840 and 1860 for the South (1.7 percent per annum) than the North (1.3 percent per annum).[10] Southern growth was due, in part, to the movement of slaves from the Old South to the New South. Slave labor moved from low productivity regions, such as the South Atlantic, to high productivity regions such as the Lower Mississippi Valley and Texas. Labor movement in the North during the antebellum period seemed paradoxical as northern labor moved from the high income sector of the Northeast to the lower income sector of the Midwest. This shift of labor in the North was linked to expectations of higher agricultural productivity to come in the Midwest. (It may also be the case that income in the North for the antebellum period did not capture the full investment in land clearing that should have been added to output.) These paradoxical shifts illustrate the possibility that the masters of coerced labor will respond efficiently to incentives while the movement of free labor may appear to be unresponsive to productivity differences. Free labor will, of course, consider more than productivity, and will incorporate satisfaction or utility into the decision-making process.

Table 2, which summarizes growth in income for European countries, supports the conclusion that economic growth was wide-

TABLE 2

Growth in Per Capita GDP

(1990 dollars)

Year	France	Germany	Italy	Sweden	UK	Canada
1820	$1218	$1112	$1092	$1198	$1756	$893
1870	1858	1913	1467	1664	1986	1620
1900	2849	3134	1746	2561	2899	2758
1913	3452	3833	2507	3096	3482	4213
1950	5221	4281	3425	6738	5513	7047
1973	12940	13152	10409	13494	11694	13644
1992	17959	19351	16229	16927	17412	18159

SOURCE: Angus Maddison, *Monitoring the World Economy 1820–1992* (Paris, 1995), 23.

NOTE: Cross country comparisons are sensitive to assumptions about exchange rates. Estimates for GDP in the nineteenth century are subject to more error than are later estimates.

spread in developing countries in the nineteenth and twentieth centuries. Leaving aside the controversy over the immediate effect of the Industrial Revolution, there is a general upward trend in per capita GDP accompanied by broad variation in the pace of economic development across countries. With the exception of Italy, GDP per capita more than doubled from 1820 to 1900. Growth was generally even more impressive in the twentieth century in spite of the dislocation and trauma of two world wars and the economic disaster of the Great Depression. Unless the distribution of income grew markedly more unequal in these countries over these two centuries, the material well-being of laborers in Europe increased significantly. Other measures of well-being confirm this increase in living standards.

When other data sources are poor, trends in adult height may provide evidence of trends in the standard of living, especially health and food consumption, and in productivity. Completed height is determined by a variety of factors including genetic inheritance, food supplies, and energy expended in work. Food supplies provide calories, vitamins, and minerals for gross nutrition while work, disease, and other claims on nutrients influence net nutrition, which will in turn determine body growth. Because the genetic basis of most populations does not change rapidly, completed height produces a measure of the nutritional status of a population which reflects the disease environment and abundance of food. Consequently, upward trends in adult height will be associated with increased economic well-being.

The United States population achieved modern heights very early, with some decline in the early nineteenth century followed by growth in adult heights through to the present. Adult heights in European countries have grown markedly over the past two and a half centuries. Heights of British adult males increased by about 10 cm from 1750 to 1950 while the heights of working-class teenagers increased by 29 cm.[11] Heights in France grew steadily from 1800 to the present. David Weir estimates male's height at age 20 rose from less than 164 cm in 1800 to 172 cm after World War II.[12] Similar growth in heights occurred in other European countries. Stature of adult males increased by 12 cm in Sweden between 1820 and 1965 and by about 10 cm in the Netherlands between 1818 and 1940.[13] The substantial increases in heights for Europe and the smaller increases in the United States reflect improvement in the biological capacities of the population in both areas. Clearly, the period of free labor has been a period of improving health and well-being for common people. The general upward trend in adult heights suggests that calories and nutritional status were distributed such that heights were moving closer to genetic potential. Certainly consumption of calories became more equal through time.[14]

Increases in life expectancy reinforce the conclusion of substantial increase in the average level of well-being during the development of free labor. Infant mortality has declined substantially, as has adult mortality. Life expectancy at age twenty for the white population increased from 44 years for cohorts born right after the American Revolution to 56 additional years today.[15] Exact trends in life expectancy at birth are difficult to estimate in the United States before 1900 because of the frequent underrecording of infant deaths. Undoubtedly, the improvement in life expectancy at birth has been even larger than the improvement for adult ages because of the sharp decline in infant mortality in the last 150 years. Rough estimates of infant mortality suggest rates have fallen from one of every eight infants dying in the first year of life in the antebellum period to a current rate of one out of 120.[16] Patterns of life expectancy would be much the same for most fully-developed countries, with large improvements in life expectancy in poorer countries in the post–World War II period. Consequently, the trend in life expectancy, like the trends in height and GDP per capita, shows dramatic improvement as labor institutions have become more free.

Gains in life expectancy in Europe were similar to the gains in the United States. Life expectancy at birth in Sweden moved from 39 years in 1820 to 74 years by 1965. Life expectancy at birth in England increased from about 36 years in the last quarter of the eighteenth century to 75 years in the last quarter of the twentieth century. Age-specific mortality rates for France moved downward rapidly in the late eighteenth century and early nineteenth century, then slowly downward for the rest of the nineteenth century, followed by more rapid downward progress in the twentieth century.[17]

Work might be considered a temporary form of slavery when the firm or employer has control over the laborer. The amount of time each day subject to "wage slavery" has declined. A typical work week in manufacturing was 60 hours in 1860 compared with less than 40 hours today.[18] Extended vacation time for labor is largely a twentieth-century phenomenon, with most of the increase in extended time off work coming in the post–World War II period.

Part of the process of development may be seen as a shift of goods from being extraordinary, reserved for the wealthy, to becoming ordinary, available almost universally.[19] With few exceptions, goods and, to a lesser extent, services go through a process of becoming ordinary. Indoor plumbing, everyday consumption of meat, changes of clothing and shoes, automobiles, television sets, and restaurant meals are just a few examples of goods that have gone from markers of the wealthy to everyday availability for most people. The past two centuries have been marked by a continual shift of large numbers of goods and services from luxuries consumed only by the wealthy to mass consumption. Table 3 reviews these trends. In the twentieth century, automobiles, television, and telephones rapidly became widespread. Consumption of food became much more varied, with less reliance on beef and grains.

The above summary of trends in GDP per capita, adult height, life expectancy, leisure time, and consumption of ordinary goods does not prove that the shift from coerced labor to free labor pro-

TABLE 3

Trends in Consumption of Selected Goods in the United States

Year	Automobiles per household	Consumption of poultry per capita (pounds)	Households with television set (percent)	Households with telephone (percent)
1910	0.02	15.5	—	—
1940	0.79	17.0	—	37
1950	0.92	24.7	9	62
1970	1.41	49.5	81	87
1990	2.02	82.4	98	93

SOURCE: *Historical Statistics of the United States;* U.S. Bureau of the Census, *Statistical Abstract of the United States: 1995* (Washington, 1995).

duced dramatic improvements in the economic well-being of most ordinary people. But these trends are consistent with such a conclusion. It certainly seems unlikely that the changes in labor institutions summarized in the chapters in this volume caused reductions in productivity and material well-being which have been hidden by the economic growth caused by technological change, capital accumulation, and other contributors to increased productivity. Indeed, the massive investment in education, one of the most important sources of productivity growth, would probably have been much more difficult under a coerced labor regime. Hence, the links between more free labor, more economic growth, and more social mobility seem strong. The similar patterns of growth for most industrializing countries suggest that the development of free labor contributed to economic growth and mobility.

≪ II ≫

Trends in the Distribution of Measures
of Economic Well-Being

There is no logical reason that an upward trend in the average of some measure of economic well-being such as output per capita or life expectancy would necessarily improve the well-being of all laborers and their families. It is possible that the gains increasing the average accrued to owners of capital or land while leaving laborers in the same or even a deteriorating condition. However, the sheer size of the gains in life expectancy, other health measures, and

GDP per capita makes the possibility of stagnation or increasing impoverishment of labor highly unlikely. There seems little doubt that all segments of society have benefited materially from the increases in the average level of well-being. The extent of those benefits does, however, depend on the changes in the distribution of material outcomes. If a distribution were to become more unequal at the same time that the average improved, the disadvantaged segments of society might experience little gain. But it strains credibility to argue the "increasing average, but more unequal" case for the material well-being of labor over the past two centuries. The benefits from improved GDP per capita, life expectancy, and health, coupled with more leisure time and wider consumption of ordinary goods, have been shared broadly enough to improve the lot of even the poorest of most societies.

Most attention to the distribution of economic rewards has concentrated on the distributions of income and wealth while changes in the distribution of life expectancy, leisure time, and specific dimensions of consumption have been overlooked.[20] This particular emphasis is unfortunate because it appears that the overlooked distributions have become more equal over time while the distributions of income and wealth remain the most unequal distributions, exhibiting little tendency to change. Consequently, the emphasis on income and wealth measures exaggerates inequality and misses important trends toward egalitarian outcomes.

The most important egalitarian trend over the past two centuries has been in life expectancy. The dramatic gains in life expectancy have been shared so broadly that the distribution of life expectancy is much more equal today than in the past. For a cohort born around the American Revolution, the 20 percent of the population that lived the longest lived over 40 percent of all the years lived by that cohort.[21] For a cohort born in the post–World War II period, the 20 percent living the longest will only live about 24 percent of all the years lived by the cohort. (Note that perfect equality would imply that the longest lived quintile lived 20 percent of the years.) Fifty percent of the cohort born at the time of the Revolution would die by about age 40. Today 50 percent of a cohort would not die until roughly age 75. Because of high infant mortality two centuries ago, the quintile with the shortest lives lived about 1 percent of all cohort years, compared to 14 percent of all cohort years for the shortest-lived quintile of a modern cohort. The shortest-lived quintile lived only 5 percent as long as the longest-lived quintile. In contrast, the shortest-lived quintile today lives about three-fourths as long as the longest-lived quintile.

The above data would describe the general experience in developed countries over the past two centuries. While it is still unfortunately true that there are differences in life expectancy by race, gender, income level, and class, those differences, with the exception of the gender difference which favors women and is probably biologically based, are diminishing.[22] In short, there has been a dramatic reduction in the inequality of mortality. Height differences by class are also falling.

Distributions of consumption, education, and leisure have also contributed to increased equality as the level of well-being increased. This diminishing inequality is an indirect result of the rise in the average level of consumption and output per capita. As income per capita increases, many goods, especially those that contribute significantly to health and life expectancy, become widely available. Previous luxuries became common. By overemphasis on the new luxuries, the egalitarian trends are often overlooked.

The distributions of income and wealth, on the other hand, have remained stable with a high degree of inequality even though per capita averages of income and wealth are increasing.[23] There are fluctuations in the level of inequality, but discernible trends that are sustained for long periods of time are not evident. For the United States, the richest 10 percent of the population held 56 percent of the wealth in 1776 and 62 percent in 1962.[24] The poorest half of the population has consistently held no net wealth. Income is not as unequally distributed as wealth, but, like wealth, the distribution has been stable showing little or no move toward more equality. For the twentieth century, the richest 5 percent of families has received 15 to 20 percent of income for most of the century.[25]

To sum up, the past two centuries, marked by increasing freedom for labor to move, make contracts, bargain collectively, and challenge the prerogatives of employers, have seen increasing levels of economic well-being and a narrowing of some aspects of the distributions of material rewards of society. But there is also the issue of mobility *within* the distributions of income, wealth, occupations, and other measures of rewards, as well as across generations. The issue of social mobility is central because of the weight given to upward mobility in judging the degree of economic justice of a society or economy.

≺ III ≻

Social Mobility and Institutional Change

Social mobility is an outgrowth of changes in social institutions and of purposeful action by individuals trying to get ahead. Individuals possess or acquire attributes that may help or hinder their economic progress. Institutional change, in turn, shifts the impact that particular characteristics might have. The list of attributes that could influence one's economic position would include age, occupation, education, intelligence, location, household composition, skills, ethnicity or race, gender, work ethic, preferences for risk-taking, previous choices, and family background. Other variables could no doubt be added. It is possible to divide these attributes into those that are due to individual choice and those that are fixed or beyond individual influence.[26] Clearly, there are variables that may be fixed in some instances, but considered amenable to choice in others.

The time frame considered is important in this regard. For very short time periods, all attributes are fixed. When the time period is lengthened, occupation, education, location, and household composition are all amenable to change and could move an individual, household, or family upward or downward within the economic distribution. Other characteristics such as race or ethnicity, gender, family background, and age are not subject to choice. Individual mobility results from the particular choices made and from the relative importance of changeable attributes and immutable attributes. The choice made will be influenced by the cost and rewards of those choices.

Fixed attributes and those under some individual control often interact with one another. For example, the returns to a particular occupation may be influenced by how long a person has been in a particular location, by age, or by cognitive ability. The advantages of education are influenced by race and gender. Consequently, interpretation of individual choices and their effects on social mobility is often difficult.

Concentration on individual characteristics and their returns may lead to overlooking the importance of changes in institutions or aggregate forces as factors in social mobility. Institutional changes would include changes in the legal environment, in government (taxes, expenditures, agencies, and programs), in propensities to discriminate, and in educational opportunities. Aggregate forces would be embodied in market shifts or macroeconomic trends. Changes in institutional and market contexts may alter the costs of acquiring valuable attributes such as education or skills. These changes may also affect the returns to, or costs of, attributes whether or not these attributes are immutable or subject to decision-making by the individual. For example, a study by Butler, Heckman, and Payner found that the earnings of African Americans in South Carolina changed after 1964 when the Civil Rights Act opened high-paying manufacturing jobs in textiles to African Americans.[27] Holding all else constant, they argue that the equal opportunity provisions of that act promoted social mobility for African Americans, at least in South Carolina. In other words, the discrimination cost of an immutable attribute, race, had been decreased by the institutional change reflected in the 1964 legislation. David Galenson and his co-authors have found that Irish and German immigrants in New York and Boston faced greater disadvantages than similar immigrants in Chicago or Indianapolis.[28] This East-West difference may be due to the more attractive market for laborers in the West or to the lack of a native-born advantage in a recently settled region. The basic point here is that institutional influences may be examined through the changing costs or returns to particular characteristics.

To sum up this interpretive framework, the level and the course of social mobility for individuals and groups will be determined by the interaction of individual choices about attributes under their control, other individual attributes which cannot be changed, the influence of institutions and institutional change upon the costs and returns to particular characteristics, and market forces that are the accumulation of many elements, including individual decisions.

One approach to studying the influence of changing labor insti-

tutions on social mobility is to examine the effect of those institutions on the economic return to either the choice variables such as
education that were under the control of individuals or to the fixed
characteristics such as gender or race. How did abolition of compulsory service affect the return to education or to migration
within the country? Or, how did laws enabling more effective collective bargaining affect the costs of being an African American? In
addition to the institutional changes covered in this volume, key
changes include land policies that encouraged rapid settlement by
small farmers, free immigration, ever-diminishing costs of transportation, rising public investment in education, and increase in
the scale of business enterprises. Taken together, these institutional changes created an environment where individual decision-
making could, and did, generate substantial economic and social
mobility as measured either by household mobility across time or
by intergenerational mobility.

Inexpensive land played a central role in social mobility in the
nineteenth century. United States land policy encouraged westward expansion and settlement by large numbers of people on their
own land, in contrast to a policy that favored absentee ownership
of large tracts. Inexpensive land gradually became cheaper, culminating in the Homestead Act which, however, was more a symbol
of this cheap land policy than a fundamental change. Cheap land
drew millions of immigrants and native-born migrants westward to
farms and to frontier cities. In frontier communities, many unskilled laborers and even some skilled laborers moved into farming.
Furthermore, western cities grew at very rapid rates, becoming centers for farm-related manufacturing as well as transportation hubs
connecting farms and the East. The indirect effect of inexpensive
land on earnings of urban workers was also positive. Cheap land
made labor relatively scarce, putting consistent upward pressure on
wages. Thus, the cheap land policy opened up opportunities for migrants and non-migrants alike.

Inexpensive land was one of the primary attractions for immigrants from abroad. There is no clear consensus on the extent to
which antebellum immigration, dominated by Irish and German
immigrants, reduced wages and opportunities for natives. Goldin,
as well as Hatton and Williamson, argues that immigration reduced wages at the beginning of the twentieth century. In contrast,

Joseph Ferrie has found little effect of antebellum immigration on native-born wages before the Civil War. On the other hand, Robert Margo and Robert Fogel have each argued that immigration did squeeze the wages of native artisans. Ferrie argues that this effect was limited to the Northeast, especially its large urban centers.[29] The effect of immigrants on the economic fortunes of natives was less than many expected because duration in a local economy had a positive effect on economic status.[30] Studies at the city and county level have found a significant return to duration in growing communities. That is, the early arrivers enjoy a strong economic position, and natives rather than immigrants tended to be the early arrivers. Those who came early often reaped economic advantage through capital gains on land and returns from specialized knowledge of local market conditions.

There can be no question that the frontier with its open land created social mobility in the United States, as well as in other countries—among them Canada, Australia, Argentina, and other South American countries. But it would be an error to place too much emphasis on land or land policy as a source for social mobility. Land was of diminishing importance as industrialization moved forward. Other institutional changes such as low-cost access to education assumed more importance as land and land policy assumed less importance.[31]

The dramatic fall in transportation costs over the past two centuries has made it possible for people to move to new opportunities with higher productivity at low cost. A labor market that started out highly unintegrated at the beginning of the nineteenth century was largely integrated into a single market by the beginning of the twentieth century. The lands of the Midwest would have provided a much smaller opportunity for social mobility had transportation costs not declined so precipitously. The growth of western cities like Chicago, Milwaukee, and Minneapolis was driven by these lower transportation costs. Migration has continued to be important in the twentieth century, with movement of African Americans northward seeking higher incomes, better schooling, and less discrimination. There have also been large movements of population westward, especially to California and to the Sunbelt generally. As jobs have become more specialized, the low costs of communication and of relocation have continued to be important.

Investment in education, increasingly supported by public fund-
ing throughout the nineteenth and twentieth centuries, formed the
basis for social mobility for population cohorts in the late nineteenth and early twentieth centuries.[32] Attendance rates in 1860,
including those of students in private schools, were about 60 percent for the free population in the nation as a whole.[33] While there
were differences between East and West, the country was investing
more heavily than in earlier periods though clearly well below the
rates realized in the twentieth century. Frontier cities such as Chicago responded to the political power of immigrants and invested
heavily in schools acceptable to Catholic immigrants.[34] How important education was to social mobility in the nineteenth century
has not been well established. But it is hard to see how more widespread literacy and basic education could inhibit social movement.

In the twentieth century, education became a primary source of
social mobility. High school graduation rates move from about 30
percent in 1925 to about 48 percent on the eve of World War II.[35]
Investment in high school continued to grow after the war and
there were substantial increases in graduation rates for minorities.
In 1940, only 7 percent of the adult African American population
had completed high school, compared to 73 percent today.[36] The
immediate post–war period was marked by an explosion in enroll-
ment in higher education fueled by the GI bill. Increases in college
graduation rates grew through the rest of the twentieth century,
especially among minorities. The number of bachelor degrees
awarded rose from about 5 percent of the population age 23 in 1945
to over 18 percent in 1950. The rate grew to 22 percent in 1970 and
has risen to about 30 percent today.[37] Education has performed the
work in the twentieth century that the frontier performed in the
nineteenth century.

The rise of large-scale business has been one of the most important institutional changes of the past two centuries. However, its
effect on social mobility has not been studied extensively. Large-
scale business is closely associated with job specialization, which
has increased the rate of return to investment in education or on-
the-job training. On the other hand, large-scale business gave enterprises additional economic power, which could be used to limit
the growth of wages and other dimensions of the terms of labor.
Labor unions could, to a degree, offset this economic power. The

effect of large-scale enterprise on social and economic mobility is unclear.

To sum up, the primary institutional changes in the United States occurring in the nineteenth and twentieth centuries promoted social mobility. The settling of the frontier, the predominant population movement to the West with ancillary movements both north and south, increased investment in education, and increased job specialization combined to create an environment of social mobility. None of these institutional changes meant that all, regardless of race, gender, ethnicity or class, had equal opportunity. Barriers to upward mobility were present, but institutional changes sponsored by government reduced the costs that were associated with the fixed characteristics of gender and race. To be sure, the costs were present through the past two centuries, but they were falling.[38] Of course, many did not move up the economic ladder, but the opportunities embodied in the American dream were at least partially available to much of the population.

< IV >

Empirical Studies of Social Mobility

Before we consider the empirical record on social mobility, there are questions of measurement that require recognition if not resolution. Quantification of social mobility leads to a set of issues. What is the appropriate unit of measurement (for example individual, household, or family) for social mobility? What type of change (occupation, income, wealth, socioeconomic status) should be a measure of social mobility? How does time enter into the measurement of social mobility? Should we be interested in social mobility through time for a particular household or should we be interested in movement across generations? Should stochastic or random movements up or down be treated as part of social mobility? How do we determine a frame of reference for comparison; how do we know whether a given amount of movement represents a small or large amount of social mobility? And is social mobility always a relative measure or does absolute growth in income, wealth, and consumption represent a crucial aspect of mobility?

The unit of interest in the measurement of economic mobility shifts from family to household to individual to group depending on the question of interest. We are often interested in the relative positions of groups—Irish and German immigrants in 1860 compared to native-born; women's earnings as a percentage of male wages; the economic position of African Americans relative to others. In other instances, individuals or households are the focus. What is the relative position of a household in 1860 compared to 1870? The relative position of families across generations often becomes the focus. What percentage of sons of unskilled workers move to occupations with higher socioeconomic status?

Alternative measures of upward or downward social mobility may be used. The most common measures have been household wealth or a scale of occupational status. Income, earnings, and home ownership have also been used. Each measure has advantages and weaknesses. Occupation has the advantage that it is widely available and often present when names occur in records. Most households and most adult males have occupations, so that all linked units can be included in measurement. Occupations are not as likely to be as transitory as levels of wealth or income. But occupational classification carries a strong burden of ambiguity, especially in the nineteenth century. Is the occupational move from a carpenter to a clerk a move up or down the ladder? More to the point, what can possibly be done with comparisons between farming and other occupations? The occupation of farming has members in nearly every strata of wealth or status, from subsistence to landed gentry. How can we interpret a move from wheelwright to farmer? Do we interpret three decades of farming as evidence of economic immobility? Obviously not. Consequently, occupation is most useful as a measure of mobility in an urban setting. Even then ambiguities remain. In studies of nineteenth-century Utah, we found considerable occupational change within the usual classifications (for example, moving from a carpenter to a brick mason within the skilled labor grouping). And these changes of occupation within a class were associated with significant changes in wealth and income.

Wealth may be a better measure of social mobility in the countryside than occupation. Wealth is measured as a continuous variable. Wealth also appears to be more permanent than income. But wealth may be a poor measure of mobility in urban areas, especially large cities, because most urban households do not own wealth. The wealth problem in the city is somewhat analogous to the occupational class of farmer in rural areas. What does one make of the social mobility of households who report no wealth in two succeeding censuses? Clearly, some non-wealth holders could and did experience social mobility, because of income growth and the accumulation of household goods that may or may not have been reported as wealth. One of the most serious weaknesses with the use of wealth as a measure of social mobility is the exclusion of "human capital" from wealth data. Human capital, including investment in education, on-the-job training, or better health, will be reflected in increased income, but is not valued directly in wealth holdings.

In short, there is no unambiguous and universal way to measure social mobility. Status is a perception of others. Occupations are often self-reported. Wealth omits a large share of the population with widely differing levels of consumption. Time is a necessary dimension of studies of social mobility, yet time also presents some difficulties for measurement, confounding the effects of aging, cohort influences, and general economic growth. Consequently, some measured mobility may be due to the life cycle or to general economic growth.

One of the more difficult problems in the measurement of social mobility concerns the interpretation of random or stochastic processes that create change and the appearance of social mobility even though there has been no underlying change in the opportunities or barriers that promote mobility. Yearly incomes or earnings may fluctuate widely even though permanent incomes or earnings are unchanged. Should mobility due to transitory changes be viewed the same as mobility due to occupational change or to a change in long-term economic prospects?

A core problem is the establishment of a frame of reference for comparison. Comparisons may be made over time or across countries. Suppose that we compare wealth for households in 1860 and 1870 and find that 29 percent of households move up or down two quintiles. Do we conclude that is substantial mobility or evidence of rigidity? There are no obvious benchmarks to use.

Finally, there is the question of the treatment of general improvement in living conditions. We generally think of economic mobility in terms of relative movement or the absence of strong barriers between particular economic classes. Should we also consider improvement in living conditions without a change in relative position or occupational class as social mobility? If social mobility is confined strictly to relative movements, then someone moves down for every move upward. If economic progress is measured in terms of some absolute standard of living, then social mobility is expanded, and all could benefit.

These thorny measurement issues leave us with no generally accepted measure of social mobility. Rather there are a variety of measures that may be used to gain a general assessment of the level of social mobility. Here we will consider four measures—occupational change over the life cycle, occupations of fathers and sons, wealth mobility of a household over time, and, finally, wealth of fathers compared with wealth of sons.

For the past two centuries, the United States economy has been characterized by a modest degree of career mobility, with many, if not most, individuals moving up the occupational ladder over their lifetime. Part of this upward movement was due to the shift in the distribution of occupations toward white collar occupations. Unskilled laborers, both farm and non-farm, made up 30 percent of the labor force in 1900, but only 6 percent of the labor force of 1970.[39] Over the same time period, occupations classified as professional, technical, managerial, or proprietorial were rising from 10 to 23 percent. Consequently, the probability of higher status employment increased as a person aged because of the shift toward higher status occupations through time. In other words, upward mobility will be greater than downward mobility. In addition to this cause of upward mobility, the life cycle itself produces upward job mobility. As people age, they accumulate knowledge and skill enabling them to secure higher status positions. Some individuals will move up in skill from say an ordinary carpenter to a finish carpenter dealing with cabinetry or wood decoration. Others will move to a supervisory position as a foreman or supervisor. A few may move into the ranks of the white collar or entrepreneur.

The empirical studies of mobility in the nineteenth century, such as those by Stephan Thernstrom, Clyde and Sally Griffen, and Peter Knights as well as the classic study of the twentieth century by Peter Blau and Otis Duncan, find substantial career mobility.[40] If one considers a simple matrix of four occupational groupings—high white collar, low white collar, skilled, low manual—and follows a Boston sample of men born between 1850 and 1859, one finds about 28 percent of workers moved up to a "higher" occupational classification between first and last job classification while only 10 percent moved to a lower classification. For Poughkeepsie, the similar figures for men born between 1820 and 1850 were 29 percent and 7 percent respectively.[41] The twentieth century has also been marked by career mobility. Only 16 percent of men whose first job was classified as laborer remained in that occupation. Over a fifth of the laborers moved to white collar occupations.

Intergenerational mobility was even more substantial. In both the nineteenth and twentieth centuries, the sons of men with blue collar occupations often moved up the occupational ladder. There have been a large number of studies of intergenerational mobility measured by occupational change within cities or communities. Generally about half of the sons of unskilled or semi-skilled laborers moved into either skilled or white collar occupations. For example, Stephan Thernstrom found 39 percent of the sons of blue collar workers were in white collar occupations in 1880. Samples for 1890 and 1910 produced results of 43 percent and 39 percent, respectively. Between 14 and 20 percent of the sons moved into skilled occupations, leaving just less than half of the sons of unskilled and semi-skilled laborers remaining in the same occupational class.

Similar results were obtained by Blau and Duncan in their large-scale nation-wide study of mid-twentieth century social mobility. Slightly over half of the sons of unskilled and semi-skilled laborers moved into skilled or white collar occupations.[42] The most notable exception to this general pattern of significant upward occupational mobility was found by Thernstrom in Newburyport, Massachusetts. There only 29 percent of sons moved into skilled or white collar occupations. Thernstrom did find substantial upward mobility in Newburyport in home ownership, but little occupational change. Undoubtedly, there was some selection bias in the Newburyport sample. Because Newburyport was not experiencing vigorous economic growth, achievement-minded sons may have migrated to better prospects in Boston or elsewhere, leaving those more contented with lower skilled occupations in Newburyport.

Nevertheless, the Newburyport example is a reminder of local limits on social mobility.

It is important to note that there was also substantial intergenerational mobility in Europe. William Sewell found considerable and rising mobility in Marseille between 1820 and 1870. The sons of artisans and of unskilled and maritime workers often moved into the bourgeoisie. By 1869, 24 percent of the sons of artisans were upwardly mobile, while 12 percent of the sons of unskilled workers moved into the bourgeoisie. Others found less intergenerational mobility and no evidence of a trend toward more mobility.[43] Hartmut Kaelble, who surveyed a number of studies of social mobility for selected American and European communities, came to three basic conclusions. There was no clear evidence that the United States had more social mobility though there were more cities with impressive upward mobility in the United States. On both sides of the Atlantic, there was substantial variation in the rates of social mobility, with some communities very stratified and others open. Finally, the American studies showed less downward mobility than the European studies, a result probably reflecting somewhat more rapid economic progress in the United States.[44]

Studies of wealth mobility also support the general conclusion of upward mobility. As households are followed over time, the richest and poorest households tend to remain in the extreme tails of the wealth distribution while households in the middle of the distribution exhibit more mobility. For example, Richard Steckel sampled households in the 1850 and 1860 censuses.[45] He found that 48 percent of those with no real estate in 1850 also had no real estate in 1860. Of those in the richest decile of the wealth distribution, 46 percent stayed in that richest decile. Of households in the middle of the distributions, deciles 4 through 8, there was significant movement up and down within the distribution. Nearly 40 percent of households moved at least two deciles from their 1860 position. Donald Schaefer and Joseph Ferrie have also found substantial wealth mobility in their studies of migration and wealth accumulation in the nineteenth century.[46]

Frontier economies were especially marked by economic mobility. Curti and his co-authors found substantial wealth mobility in their classic study of Trempeleau County, Wisconsin. Similar results were also found for Appanoose County, Iowa, and for

Utah.[47] The Utah data provide an illustration of the high level of mobility on the American frontier. In a comparison of households found in the censuses of 1860 and 1870, researchers found that 65 percent of the households in the poorest quintile of the wealth distribution in 1860 had moved out of that quintile in 1870. Thirty-eight percent of these households moved up at least two quintiles and had to triple their wealth to do so.[48] There was a high degree of income mobility as well. In comparisons of income distributions ten years apart, researchers also found that less than one-third of households remained in the same quintile of the distribution. About one-third of the households moved two quintiles or more.[49] Mobility measured by wealth or income changes appears to capture more movement than mobility measured by occupational change.

Studies of the wealth or income of fathers and sons have also documented mobility.[50] Studies have found substantial "regression toward the mean" such that a father's wealth 10 percent above the mean wealth of the sample resulted in a son's wealth that was only 2 to 7 percent above the mean. Just as tall parents will have children who are taller than the average, but shorter than their parents, the children of wealthy parents will be wealthier than the average, but not as wealthy as their parents. There is even more regression with earnings or income where a 10 percent advantage for a father will only yield a 1 to 3 percent advantage for the son. Clearly, wealthy parents confer an advantage for the next generation, but that advantage is dissipated after a generation or two.

≺ V ≻

Conclusion

The evidence on social mobility supports a view that the last two centuries have been a time of extraordinary economic opportunity for individuals living in the United States and much of Europe. Health and life expectancy have improved dramatically and become much more equally shared. Consumption of calories, shelter, consumer durables, and leisure time have increased and also become more equally shared. Distributions of income and wealth have not moved significantly toward either more equality or more inequality, though there was some decline in the inequality of income earlier in the twentieth century followed by some increase in inequality toward its end. However, earnings and incomes have grown steadily, and that growth has been widely shared: the distributions of income and wealth are quite constant. There has been significant intergenerational mobility as evidenced by both occupational change and wealth accumulation.

In spite of these impressive gains in economic opportunity, society seems perpetually dissatisfied with that achievement and impatient with the record of social progress. The dissatisfaction is, in large part, a direct result of the successes of economic opportunity. Economic growth and economic mobility bring into bold relief any easily identifiable group whose economic position is inferior to that of others in society. African Americans, Native Americans, Hispanics, immigrants, and households headed by women have consistently had lower incomes, lower socioeconomic status, and less wealth. While all of these groups have been able to improve their standard of living and their general economic condition and have seized economic opportunities, their income and earnings have been discernibly different from others. These group differences are a constant reminder that inequality still exists and that there are clear limits on economic opportunity for some. Every step forward highlights those left behind.

The strides made toward more equal distribution of the material rewards of society make the remaining inequalities more obvious and less tolerable. Widespread consumption of common goods such as food and increases in the quality of housing make the absence of those goods for some an affront to the good order of society. When most of the population has plenty of food and many are trying to eat less, hunger, not to mention malnutrition, is not acceptable to the general populace. The push to diminish the inequality may be vigorous and partially successful, but it will simply highlight the remaining inequality.

In a fundamental way, the mythological American dream, to some degree shared by many societies, sets the stage for the economic opportunity of the last two centuries to be considered limited and unacceptable. The myth promised much more than could ever be delivered by a real society. It promised economic opportunity unconstrained by one's initial starting place or historical context. Economic outcomes were to be entirely the result of effort and ability, an ideal never realized or even approached. Thus, the myth was an ever-present reminder of what had not been accomplished. On the other hand, the myth of the American dream was the natural outcome of a society in which labor was increasingly free and economic growth was spreading many of the benefits widely. The social mobility of the past two centuries reinforces and entrenches the myth as an unmet standard for economic justice.

＜＞

REFERENCE MATTER

<>

Notes

This introduction is based upon the discussions at the two conferences held on this volume, and I wish to acknowledge the help provided by all the participants, including the three discussants at the first conference—Robert E. Gallman, David Montgomery, and Douglass C. North. In addition, for help in planning these conferences I wish to thank Ava Baron and Richard W. Davis. I have benefited from comments made on an early draft of this paper by Seymour Drescher, David Eltis, Sarah Pomeroy, and Robert Steinfeld.

1. There may have been early exceptions to this, by groups willing to accept a low standard of living, with their wants "easily satisfied." See Marshall Sahlins's discussion of hunter-gatherers in "The Original Affluent Society," in his *Stone Age Economics* (New York, 1972), 1–39. For a related argument, that the Industrial Revolution emerged with increased wants and increased working time and effort, see Jan deVries, "The Industrial Revolution and the Industrious Revolution," *Journal of Economic History* 54 (June 1994): 249–74.

2. M. I. Finley has commented that "in the context of universal history, free labour, wage labour, is the *peculiar* institution." "For most of the millennia of human history in most parts of the world . . . labour for others was normally performed under compulsion, because of superior force or of status or of such conditions as debt." "A Peculiar Institution?" *Times Literary Supplement* 3887 (July 2, 1976): 819–21. Two astute observers of the late eighteenth century noted the relative absence of free labor at that time. Adam Smith claimed that slavery had been abolished "in only a small part of Europe" and some parts of America. *Lectures on Jurisprudence* (Oxford, 1978; Reports of 1762–1763 and 1766, Glasgow University Library), 181. Arthur Young estimated that over 95 percent of the inhabitants of the world lived under "arbitrary governments," living as "miserable slaves of despotic tyrants." Arthur Young, *Political Essays* (New York, 1970; first pub. 1772), 19–22. Few at this time argued for the general freeing of slaves.

3. For comparisons of slavery and serfdom, see Stanley L. Engerman, "Slavery, Serfdom and Other Forms of Coerced Labor: Similarities and Differences," in M. L. Bush, ed., *Serfdom and Slavery: Studies in Legal Bondage* (London, 1996), 18–41.

4. Also suggestive is the long duration of British acts controlling labor (and some non-labor) matters under the rubric of master and servant, before the later change to employer and employee.

5. See Jerome Blum, *The End of the Old Order in Europe* (Princeton, NJ, 1978); and Stanley L. Engerman, "Emancipations in Comparative Perspective: A Long and Wide View," in Gert Oostinde, ed., *Fifty Years Later: Antislavery, Capitalism and Modernity in the Dutch Orbit* (Leiden, 1995), 223–41.

6. There were, of course, aberrations even in the western world in the twentieth century, as exemplified by the Soviets and their satellites, and by Nazi Germany; and not all nations have been interested in attaining the goal of freedom for its inhabitants. While these societies did have forced labor, in the Russian case of their own nationals, for neither the Soviets nor the Nazis was the primary purpose of forced labor based upon economic needs. Some specific industries, such as construction and mining, relied on forced labor in the Soviet Union. In general this accounted for only a small part of the Soviet national output, although this share no doubt exceeded that from forced labor in Nazi Germany. The continuing range of labor and other problems has meant that the Anti-Slavery Society remains actively involved throughout the world. For some earlier post–World War II background, see C. W. W. Greenidge, *Slavery* (London, 1958), as well as the many current publications of the Anti-Slavery Society.

7. Thus the innovations related to sugar production led to the development of the plantation using the gang system of labor, among the most distasteful forms of working conditions for free labor.

8. Defining political freedom in different societies goes beyond the ability of many in the population to vote. If wealth and other factors give differential power to influence elections to certain groups, then the precise meaning of democratic politics may be unclear. This distinction was drawn upon in the debates about the extent of democracy, even among whites, in colonial America. See, for example, the survey by John M. Murrin, "Political Development," in Jack P. Greene and J. R. Pole, eds., *Colonial British America: Essays in the New History of the Early Modern Era* (Baltimore, 1984), 408–56.

9. William Blackstone stated, in regard to property in Negro "servants," who were bought when captives, that "accurately speaking, that property consists rather in the perpetual *service*, than in the *body* or *person*, of the captive," *Commentaries on the Laws of England*, vol. 2: *On the Rights of Things* (Chicago, 1979; first pub. 1766), 402. A similar distinction was made by several proslavery advocates in the antebellum South, most prominently by Henry Hughes in his system of warranteeism. See Douglas Ambrose, *Henry Hughes and Proslavery Thought in the Old South* (Baton Rouge, LA, 1996).

10. The term *herrenvolk* democracy has been used to define the cases of cross-class coalitions against outsider groups. For an explanation of the origins of *American Slavery, American Freedom* in colonial Virginia, see

the book of that title by Edmund S. Morgan (New York, 1975). Similarly, freedom for males was often argued while advocating limited rights for women and children.

11. Indeed, one of the paradoxes of slavery and serfdom is that its end on economic grounds, as with the later years of the Roman Empire, should leave laborers at subsistence, with no choice but to work, so that freedom comes about with everyone at subsistence—a work or starve position. For various presentations of this point see H. J. Nieboer, *Slavery as an Industrial System: Ethnological Researches* (New York, 1971; first pub. 1910), 417–27; George Tucker, *Progress of the United States in Population and Wealth in Fifty Years* (New York, 1964; first pub. 1855), 108–18; and M. I. Finley, *Ancient Slavery and Modern Ideology* (New York, 1980), 123–49.

12. Adam Smith, *The Wealth of Nations* (Oxford, 1976; first pub. 1776), bk. 5. For expansions on this point see Jacob Viner, "Adam Smith and Laissez Faire," *Journal of Political Economy* 35 (April 1927): 198–232; and Nathan Rosenberg, "Some Institutional Aspects of the Wealth of Nations," *Journal of Political Economy* 68 (Dec. 1960): 557–70.

13. The extent to which the desired degree of exploitation varied, depending upon the income wanted by the lords, was noted by Max Weber. In his chapter on the manor in medieval times Weber comments that "the mode of life of the lord was little different from that of the peasant. Thus 'the walls of the stomach set the limits to his exploitation of the peasant' as Karl Marx observed." Max Weber, *General Economic History* (New York, 1961; first pub. 1927), 67.

14. The literature of the eighteenth century pointed to the dangers of individuals becoming slaves to their "passions," an argument for a more rational approach to life. On the discussion of passions more generally, see Albert O. Hirschman, *The Passions and the Interests: Political Arguments for Capitalism before its Triumph* (Princeton, NJ, 1977). This concern with "the loss of power of autonomous action" can be traced back to the Greek Stoics, as shown by Peter Garnsey, *Ideas of Slavery from Aristotle to Augustine* (Cambridge, 1996), 128–52. Several centuries later Augustine claimed, in effect, that "slavery was unavoidable, for we are slaves either of God or of sin." Garnsey, *Ideas of Slavery*, 206–19.

15. Orlando Patterson, *Freedom*, vol. 1: *Freedom in the Making of Western Culture* (New York, 1991). Patterson (xiii) states that "the basic argument of this work is that freedom was generated from the experience of slavery," and that the concept had developed in the West.

16. See the writings of David Brion Davis, in particular *Slavery and Human Progress* (New York, 1984). It would appear that the western definition of freedom emerged before the great expansion of New World slavery.

17. On this, see in particular, Finley, *Ancient Slavery*, 67–92, and Orlando Patterson, *Slavery and Social Death: A Comparative Study* (Cambridge, MA, 1982). For a discussion of the changing historical nature of who was considered an outsider, see William McKee Evans, "From the

Land of Canaan to the Land of Guinea: The Strange Odyssey of the Sons of Ham,'" *American Historical Review* 85 (Feb. 1980): 15–43.

18. On this, see David Eltis, "Europeans and the Rise and Fall of African Slavery in the Americas: An Interpretation," *American Historical Review* 98 (Dec. 1993): 1399–1423. A similar pattern can also be seen in the settlement of Asia.

19. For early antislavery arguments, based on economic and other grounds, see Thomas Wiedemann, *Greek and Roman Slavery* (Baltimore, 1981), particularly 135–53; and Peter Garnsey, *Ideas of Slavery*. See also Finley, *Ancient Slavery*, 90–92, 132–42. Smith drew upon the comments of several Roman observers on the unprofitability of slavery. *Wealth of Nations*, 387–88.

20. Jean Drèze and Amartya Sen have drawn attention to the issue of "female deprivation and gender bias" in the developing nations today. Their comparisons suggest that such deprivation is less, "the greater autonomy . . . (in terms of land rights, access to gainful employment, control over property, freedom of movement, etc.)." Jean Drèze and Amartya Sen, *Hunger and Public Action* (Oxford, 1989), 50, 54.

21. For related discussions see William E. Forbath, "The Ambiguities of Free Labor: Labor and the Law in the Gilded Age," *Wisconsin Law Review* 4 (1985): 767–817; and Jonathan A. Glickstein, "Pauperism, Chattel Slavery, and the Ideological Construction of Free Market Labor Incentives in Antebellum America," *Radical History Review* 69 (Fall 1997): 114–59. While different political economists of the time stressed one or the other of the aspects of the free labor ideology, in general most of the views since Smith have been for the long run in the positive or "optimistic" direction.

22. These restrictions can be found in Locke, who links them in one sentence, since man did not have "the Power of his own life." John Locke, *Two Treatises of Government* (New York, 1965; first pub. 1690), 325–26, 311. For a discussion of English attitudes toward suicide in the early modern period, see Michael MacDonald and Terence R. Murphy, *Sleepless Souls: Suicide in Early Modern England* (Oxford, 1990), 144–75. For a brief discussion of the quite broad and extensive phenomenon of self-enslavement, see Patterson, *Slavery and Social Death*, 129–31. The consistent treatment of debt bondage and of convict labor, both based on actions taken by individuals, is rather complex.

23. See Max Weber, *The Agrarian Sociology of Ancient Civilizations* (London, 1976), 96. A similar point was made for Rome by Cicero, who in describing hired manual laborers, commented "in their case the very wage they receive is a pledge of their slavery." To Cicero, however, this meant that slaves and employees must be treated similarly, with justice. Cicero, *De Officiis* (Cambridge, MA, 1990; first written 43 B.C.), 153, 45. See also John Crook, *Law and Life of Rome* (Ithaca, NY, 1967), 192–200. For a survey of pre-modern attitudes toward work see the chapter entitled "Work as Slavery" in P. D. Anthony, *The Ideology of Work* (London, 1977), 15–38. For a more recent analysis, focusing on the problems of defining the

length of tenure, see J. Philmore, "The Libertarian Case for Slavery," *Philosophical Forum* 14 (Fall 1982): 43–58, while legal aspects are discussed in Stewart E. Sterk, "Restraints on the Alienation of Human Capital," *Virginia Law Review* 79 (Mar. 1993): 383–460.

24. See the work of Robert Steinfeld on this issue. The various distinctions imaginable, as well as those made in law, between voluntary and involuntary labor were a major theme in the writings of Robert L. Hale. In *Freedom Through Law: Public Control of Private Governing Power* (New York 1957), 192, he states that "no labor is 'involuntary'—not even that of a slave," since "it is performed through the voluntary muscular movement of the laborer, who chooses to perform it in order to avoid something worse." And, also, "all labor is 'involuntary' unless performed for the sheer pleasure of it." He had earlier discussed similar issues in "Force and the State: A Comparison of 'Political' and 'Economic' Compulsion," *Columbia Law Review* 35 (Feb. 1935): 149–201, commenting (161) that "labor is often performed for others under fear of starvation. The [Supreme] Court has never recognized this as a violation of the Thirteenth Amendment." Famine, leading to voluntary slavery, as occurred in Asia and Africa during the modern era, and in Europe in early modern times, and the problems of the twentieth century Holocaust and related cases pose the problem of whether enslavement is the most serious evil to be imagined.

25. Sir James Steuart, *An Inquiry into the Principles of Political Economy*, 2 vols. (Chicago, 1966; first pub. 1767), 52.

26. The discussions about policies for the transition from slavery or serfdom to free labor often dealt with the importance of increasing the desire to consume on the part of the ex-slaves or ex-serfs, thus permitting high levels of labor input and national output without the need for physical or legal compulsion. The definition of subsistence is, of course, rather uncertain, varying considerably over place and time. It should consider length of life, ability to reproduce, and the ability to undertake hard labor, among numerous items.

27. For a model of serfdom based on this contention, see Nicholas Georgescu-Roegen, "Economic Theory and Agrarian Economics," *Oxford Economic Papers* 12 (Feb. 1960): 1–40.

28. Among the standard objections to modern factory methods of production, which lower prices and make goods available to more individuals, are its impact on the living standards of artisans, the effects on aesthetics of the shift from personal hand production to machine output, and the changing working and living conditions with the shift from rural to urban residence, and farm to factory labor.

29. For a description of this process in England, see David W. Galenson, "The Rise of Free Labor: Economic Change and the Enforcement of Servant Contracts in England, 1351–1875," in John A. James and Mark Thomas, eds., *Capitalism in Context: Essays on Economic Development and Cultural Change in Honor of R. M. Hartwell* (Chicago, 1994), 114–37.

30. See also the various sources in regard to slave and Russian serf labor compared to free labor cited in Adam Hodgson, *Remarks During a Journey Through North America* (New York, 1823), 291–330. The debate on incentives covered not only coerced vs. free labor but time-wages vs. piece-wages. See, for example, James Anderson, *Observations on Slavery* (Manchester, 1789), 7–11. An interesting earlier discussion of wage incentives (first brought to my attention by Sherwin Rosen) was provided by Xenophon. Xenophon, when providing laborers with clothing and footwear in kind, had some articles made better than the others so as to be able to "reward the better workers with superior garments." He also claimed that "slaves need some good thing to look forward to no less, in fact, even more than free men so that they may be willing to stay." Sarah B. Pomeroy, *Xenophon, Oeconomicus: A Social and Historical Commentary* (Oxford, 1994), 177, 133.

31. In some cases of the emancipating of slaves in the Americas, there was discussion of having the slaves, not taxpayers, compensate the slave owners. In no case, however, was this done. Manumissions often meant that slaves did purchase their freedom from their owners, often at market valuations. See Stanley L. Engerman, "Pricing Freedom: Evaluating the Costs of Emancipation and of Manumission" in Verene Shepherd, ed., *Working Slavery, Pricing Freedom* (Kingston, Jamaica, 1999).

32. See the discussion by Stanley L. Engerman, "The Land and Labour Problem at the Time of the Legal Emancipation of British West Indian Slaves," in Roderick A. McDonald, ed., *West Indies Accounts: Essays on the History of the British Caribbean and the Atlantic Economy in Honour of Richard Sheridan* (Kingston, Jamaica, 1996), 297–318.

33. On the Russian serf emancipation see the chapter by Peter Kolchin in this volume, as well as Evsey D. Domar, "Were Russian Serfs Overcharged for their Land by the 1861 Emancipation?: The History of One Historical Table," *Research in Economic History* Supplement 5 (1989), 429–39. Stevens advocated giving confiscated land to the ex-slaves, since they would not have been able to buy or rent at market prices. He believed that the Russian emancipation compelled landowners to provide land "not at a full price, but a nominal price." *Congressional Globe* (39th Congress, 1st session, 1866), 658–59.

34. On the impact of the perception of relatively rapid growth in free labor societies see, in addition to the writings of Davis cited above, Howard Temperley, "Capitalism, Slavery, and Ideology," *Past and Present* 75 (May 1977): 94–118.

CHAPTER I

1. Seymour Drescher, *Capitalism and Antislavery: British Mobilization in Comparative Perspective* (London, 1986), 16–17; Robert W. Fogel, *Without Consent or Contract: The Rise and Fall of American Slavery* (New York, 1989), 343; Russell Blaine Nye, *Fettered Freedom: Civil Liberties and the Slavery Controversy, 1830–60* (East Lansing, MI, 1963), 304. Quotes are from Southern newspapers.

2. See the useful discussion in John Thornton, *Africa and Africans in the Making of the Atlantic World* (Cambridge, 1992), 206–11.

3. David Brion Davis, *The Problem of Slavery in Western Culture* (Ithaca, NY, 1966); M. I. Finley, *The Ancient Economy* (Berkeley, 1973), 70–83; William Bouwsma, "Liberty in the Renaissance and Reformation," in R. W. Davis, ed., *The Origins of Modern Freedom in the West* (Stanford, 1995).

4. Column 1 shows African arrivals in the Americas, column 3 shows European departures. Almost all European migrants went to the areas of the Americas where their own country held sovereignty. If column 3 is adjusted for deaths in transit—probably no more than 5 percent of those embarking in Europe at this time on average—then the sum of columns 1 and 3 yields total immigration into each national jurisdiction in the Americas.

5. David Galenson, *White Servitude in Colonial America: An Economic Analysis* (Cambridge, 1981), 1–15.

6. W. R. Scott, *The Constitution and Finance of English, Scottish and Irish Joint-Stock Companies to 1720*, 3 vols. (Cambridge, 1910), 2: 20, 246.

7. Barbadians' claims are in "Address of the Assembly of Barbados to Oliver Cromwell," Sept. 1653, British Library, Egerton MSS., 2395, f. 175. For the Levellers' argument for slavery see Gerard Winstanley, *The law of freedom in a platform . . . Wherein is declared, what is kingly government and what is commonwealth's government* (London, 1652).

8. Davis, ed., *Origins*, 180–90.

9. For a fuller discussion of this issue and the relevant references see David Eltis, "Gender and Slavery in the Early Modern Atlantic World" (unpublished ms, 1997).

10. For the "patriarchal construction of 'civil society'" in the early modern era, and the implication that individualism was premised on the conception of women as non-persons see, inter alia, Carole Pateman, *The Sexual Contract* (Stanford, 1988). Quote is from 143.

11. J. R. Ward, *British West Indian Slavery, 1750–1834* (Oxford, 1988).

12. Paul Lovejoy, *Transformations in Slavery: A History of Slavery in Africa* (Cambridge, 1983), 1–22; Suzanne Miers and Igor Kopytoff, eds., *Slavery in Africa: Historical and Anthropological Perspectives* (Madison, WI, 1977), 3–77; Thornton, *Africa and Africans*, 72–97.

13. Robert J. Steinfeld, *The Invention of Free Labor: The Employment Relation in English and American Law and Culture, 1350–1870* (Chapel Hill, NC, 1991), 55–93; Ann Kussmaul, *Servants in Husbandry in Early Modern England* (Cambridge, 1981).

14. Fogel, *Without Consent or Contract*, 60–80; Elizabeth Fox-Genovese and Eugene D. Genovese, *The Fruits of Merchant Capital: Slavery and Bourgeois Property in the Rise of and Expansion of Capitalism* (New York, 1983), 34–60; David Eltis, *Economic Growth and the Ending of the Transatlantic Slave Trade* (New York, 1987), 185–204.

15. Compare the occupational distributions of the slave labor force in the British West Indies in 1834 in Barry Higman, *Slave Populations of the British Caribbean* (Baltimore, 1984), 47–48 with those in Britain in 1841 in B. R. Mitchell, *British Historical Statistics* (Cambridge, 1988), 104.

16. Steinfeld, *The Invention of Free Labor*, 15–54.

17. John Iliffe, *The African Poor: A History* (Cambridge, 1987), 1–94, and especially the comparative introduction on 1–8 concludes that the poor in England and Africa had in common the fact they could rely only on their own resources. This may have been the case in Africa where the poor (and we might add the potentially enslavable) were often the kinless, but not in England. Iliffe argues for a different type of poverty in Africa, but his evidence for widespread poverty in pre-colonial Africa is incontrovertible. Taken together with the evidence of famine in twentieth-century Africa, it suggests that the mesh of the kin-based safety net was larger and the net itself set—of necessity—considerably lower than in Europe, though he does not himself make this point. For a view of pre-colonial Africa as less stratified socially than Europe and colonial Africa see Jack Goody, *Cooking, Cuisine and Class* (Cambridge, 1982). Poverty in most parts of Asia was of a different order of severity from Europe, and I have been able to find no scholar who argues to the contrary or can point to a non-European state-based, palliative system.

18. Interpretations of the evolution of Western economic dominance that stress the critical role of private property rights usually set up a polarity between private property rights on the one hand and common property resources on the other, with the former being classed as "western." For a well-known example see Douglass C. North and Robert Paul Thomas, *The Rise of the Western World: A New Economic History* (Cambridge, 1973). In fact, group or corporate rights—a hybrid in terms of the above polarity—have been the global norm, a norm to which the Western world has returned in a sense since the advent of widespread business incorporation in the nineteenth century. Most post-neolithic societies—Western or not—must have drawn a very small share of their total income from common property resources.

19. Philip Curtin et al., *African History* (Boston, 1978), 156–71; Miers and Kopytoff, *Slavery in Africa*, 3–77. For some interesting parallels in one context in the Americas see William A. Starna and Ralph Watkins, "Northern Iroquoian Slavery," *Ethnohistory* 38 (Jan. 1991): 34–57.

20. Orlando Patterson, *Freedom*, 3 vols. (New York, 1991-), 1: *Freedom in the Making of Western Culture*, 20–44.

21. If slavery is defined more restrictively in terms of a "slave society" in Moses Finley's sense, then the description "peculiar" remains apt, be-

cause, as noted above, there have been only five such societies. See his "A Peculiar Institution," *Times Literary Supplement*, July 2, 1976, p. 819. But Finley also notes how unusual was the Greek practice of incorporating "peasantry and urban craftsmen into the community . . . as full members" (p. 821).

22. See the discussion of these issues in S. L. Engerman, "The Atlantic Economy of the Eighteenth Century: Some Speculations on Economic Development in Britain, America, Africa and Elsewhere," *Journal of European Economic History* 24 (1995): 146–57.

23. Stanley L. Engerman, "Coerced and Free Labor: Property Rights and the Development of the Labor Force," *Explorations in Entrepreneurial History* 29 (1992): 1–29; and see the several essays in John Brewer and Roy Porter, eds., *Consumption and the World of Goods* (London, 1993).

24. Christopher Hill, "Pottage for Freeborn Englishmen: Attitudes to Wage Labor in the Sixteenth and Seventeenth Centuries," in H. Feinstein, ed., *Socialism, Capitalism and Economic Growth: Essays Presented to Maurice Dobb* (Cambridge, 1967), 338–50; Eric Foner, *Free Soil, Free Labor, Free Men: The Ideology of the Republican Party Before the Civil War* (New York, 1970), 11–29; Eltis, *Economic Growth*, 17–28.

25. A. W. Coats, "Changing Attitudes to Labour in the mid eighteenth Century," *Economic History Review* 11 (1958–59): 35–51; Engerman, "Coerced and Free Labor"; Jan de Vries, "Between Purchasing Power and the World of Goods: Understanding the Household Economy in Early Modern Europe," in Brewer and Porter, eds., *Consumption and the World of Goods*, 85–132.

26. James Axtell, *Beyond 1492: Encounters in Colonial North America* (New York, 1992), 125–51, esp. 128–29; Thornton, *Africa and Africans*, 43–71.

27. Steinfeld (*The Invention of Free Labor*, 138–72) argues that antislavery and a rising awareness of slavery helped create the modern concept of a free labor force. This was undoubtedly true, but the counter effect—that the changing nature and apparent success of free labor (free in the modern sense) helped create and shape antislavery—seems on balance to have been the stronger of the two effects. Antislavery in Steinfeld's argument appears as a deus ex machina. For possessive individualism see C. B. Macpherson, *The Political Theory of Possessive Individualism: Hobbes to Locke* (Oxford, 1962).

28. Howard Temperley, "Capitalism, Slavery and Ideology," *Past and Present* 75 (1977): 94–118 and "Anti-Slavery as a Form of Cultural Imperialism," in Christine Bolt and Seymour Drescher, eds., *Anti-Slavery, Religion and Reform: Essays in Memory of Roger Anstey* (Folkeston, Kent, 1980), 336–50; Eltis, *Economic Growth*.

29. Charles Verlinden, *The Beginnings of Modern Colonization: Eleven Essays with an Introduction* (Ithaca, NY, 1970); William D. Phillips, *Slavery from Roman Times to the Early Atlantic Slave Trade* (Minneapolis, 1984), 66–88; Davis, *Slavery and Human Progress*, 51–82.

30. Galenson, *White Servitude*, 141–68; Hilary Beckles, *White Servitude and Black Slavery in Barbados* (Knoxville, TN, 1989); H. A. Gemery and J. S. Hogendorn, "The Atlantic Slave Trade: A Tentative Economic Model," *Journal of African History* 15 (1974): 223–46; Stuart B. Schwartz, *Sugar Plantations in the Formation of Brazilian Society* (Cambridge, 1985), 15–27, 51–72.

31. For the Dutch case see Herbert H. Rowen, "The Dutch Republic and the Idea of Freedom," in David Wootton, ed., *Republicanism, Liberty and Commercial Society, 1649–1776* (Stanford, 1994), 310–40, esp. 336–37.

32. As Seymour Drescher has pointed out (*Capitalism and Antislavery*, 18–20, and "The Ending of the Slave Trade and the Evolution of European Scientific Racism," *Social Science History* 14 [1990]: 415–50), both the proslavery and antislavery campaigns in England in the late eighteenth and early nineteenth centuries were relatively free of the biological racism that became prevalent in the mid-nineteenth century. Prior to the 1820s the abolitionist literature conveyed a strong sense that any cultural differences between Europeans and Africans were to be explained by the ravages of the slave trade. Yet there is also a sense that Africans were at an earlier stage of development than Europeans—most clearly expressed in Henry Brougham's *An Enquiry into the Colonial Policy of the European Powers* 2 (Edinburgh, 1803): 507–18, which embodied the stages model of human development popular in the eighteenth century.

33. Timothy Joel Coates, "Exiles and Orphans: Forced and State Sponsored Colonizers in the Portuguese Empire, 1550–1720," (unpub. PhD thesis, Univ. of Minnesota, 1993); Leslie Choquette, *Frenchmen into Peasants: Modernity and Tradition in the Peopling of French Canada* (Cambridge, MA, 1997), 273–76; "Order of the Council of State," Sept. 10, 1651, in W. Noel Sainsbury, ed., *Calendar of State Papers, Colonial Series* 1 (London, 1860): 360.

34. See most recently the essays by Nigel Bolland, Lucia Lamounier, and Mary Turner in Mary Turner, ed., *From Chattel Slaves to Wage Slaves: The Dynamics of Labour Bargaining in the Americas* (London, 1995).

35. Chap. 6 below.

36. T. E. J. Wiedmann, *Slavery* (Oxford, 1987), 3–6.

37. Edmund S. Morgan, *American Slavery; American Freedom* (New York, 1975), 338–87; Duncan J. McCleod, *Slavery, Race and the American Revolution* (Cambridge, 1974), 62–108, 183–84.

38. Davis, *Slavery and Human Progress*, 279–320.

39. As a test of this see the sections on "Slavery" and "Colonies" of the index and catalogue of the *Goldsmith's-Kress Library of Economic Literature: A Consolidated Guide*, 4 vols. (Woodbridge, CT, 1976–77). The coverage before the mid-eighteenth century can only be described as thin.

40. Patterson argues for an implicit bargain in Solonic Greece between slaveowners and non-slaves. The latter tolerated the manumission of slaves (which was a way of reinforcing the slave system), because non-

slaves were assured of a measure of personal and civic freedom (*Freedom*, 64–81). There are parallels here with Edmund Morgan's argument for an implicit alliance between rich and poor whites in Virginia against African slaves, though the Greek case appears to lack the ethnic element (*American Slavery American Freedom*, 295–337).

41. Steinfeld, *Invention of Free Labor*, 163–72.

CHAPTER 2

I am grateful to the participants in the Terms of Labor project and to the Working Class group of the Pittsburgh Center for Social History for their incisive and helpful suggestions. I would also like to offer particular thanks to Stanley Engerman, Van Beck Hall, and Michael Jimenez for careful readings of earlier drafts of this chapter.

1. See Robert J. Steinfeld, *The Invention of Free Labor: The Employment Relation in English and American Law and Culture, 1350–1870* (Chapel Hill, NC, 1991); and id., "The Myth of the Rise of Free Labor: A Critique of Historical Stage Theory" (forthcoming). The controlling distinction was that a "free-man" had the proprietary right to sell future limited actions ("service") for a limited duration. See John Locke, *Two Treatises of Government*, Peter Laslett, ed. (Cambridge, 1970), 2, sec. 85. Locke's "laws of nature" explicitly precluded anyone from purchasing rights in persons as opposed to rights in actions. It remains doubtful whether Locke extended this law to the Caribbean (See ibid., 1, sec. 130).

2. For overviews, see Robin Blackburn, *The Overthrow of Colonial Slavery, 1776–1848* (London, 1988); David Eltis, *Economic Growth and the Ending of the Transatlantic Slave Trade* (New York, 1987); Robert William Fogel, *Without Consent or Contract: The Rise and Fall of American Slavery* (New York, 1989), pt. 2.

3. See William A. Green, *British Slave Emancipation: The Sugar Colonies and the Great Experiment, 1830–1865* (Oxford, 1976), chap. 7.

4. Charles Buxton, *Slavery and Freedom in the West Indies* (London, 1860), title page. Buxton's summary had already been published as "The West Indies as They Were and Are," *Edinburgh Review* 109 (1859): 216–36.

5. M. I. Finley, *Ancient Slavery and Modern Ideology* (New York, 1980), 90. Aristotle, *The Politics of Aristotle*, trans. Ernest Barker (Oxford, 1948), bk. 1; Christopher J. Berry, *The Idea of Luxury: A Conceptual and Historical Investigation* (Cambridge, 1994), 46–58.

6. Sir Thomas Smith, *De Republica Anglorum* (1583; rept. Cambridge, 1906), 46; Jean Bodin, *The Six Books of A Commonwealth*, ed. K. D. McRae (Cambridge, 1996), 135–37.

7. P. K. O'Brien and S. L. Engerman, "Exports and the Growth of the British Economy from the Glorious Revolution to the Peace of Amiens," in *Slavery and the Rise of the Atlantic System*, Barbara Solow, ed. (New York, 1991), 207.

8. See, inter alia, S. Drescher, *Capitalism and Antislavery: British Mobilization in Comparative Perspective* (New York, 1987), 1–12; id., "The Long Goodbye: Dutch Capitalism and Antislavery in Comparative Perspective," in Gert Oostindie, ed., *Fifty Years Later: Antislavery, Capitalism and Modernity in the Dutch Orbit* (Leiden, 1995), 25–66; David Eltis, *Economic Growth*, chap. 1.

9. Drescher, *Capitalism and Antislavery*, 12–24.

10. Anthony J. Barker, *The African Link: British Attitudes to the Negro in the Era of the Slave Trade, 1550–1807* (London, 1978), 98–99. See also, David Eltis, "Europeans and the Rise and Fall of African Slavery in the Americas: An Interpretation," *American Historical Review* 98 (1993): 1399–1423; John Thornton, *Africa and the Africans in the Making of the Atlantic World, 1400–1680* (Cambridge, 1992).

11. Drescher, *Capitalism*, 22–24; id., "Capitalism and Abolition: Values and Forces in Britain, 1783–1814," in Roger Anstey and P. E. H. Hair, eds., *Liverpool, The African Slave Trade, and Abolition* (Bristol, 1976), 167–95.

12. Sir James Steuart, *An Inquiry into the Principles of Political Economy*, 2 vols. (London, 1767), 1:227.

13. Drescher, *Capitalism*, chap. 2; id., "Long Goodbye," 49–50; David Brion Davis, *The Problem of Slavery in the Age of Revolution, 1770–1823* (Ithaca, NY, 1975), chap. 10; Sue Peabody, *"There Are No Slaves in France": The Political Culture of Race and Slavery in the Ancien Régime* (New York, 1996).

14. Bruce A. Ragsdale, *A Planter's Republic: The Search for Economic Independence in Revolutionary America* (Madison, WI, 1996).

15. Benjamin Franklin, "Observations Concerning the Increase of Mankind," in L. W. Labaree, ed., *The Papers of Benjamin Franklin* 4 (New Haven, CT, 1961): 229–30.

16. Berry, *Luxury*, 142–73, on Hume and Smith.

17. Adam Smith, *Lectures on Jurisprudence*, ed. R. Meek, D. Raphael, and P. Stein (Indianapolis, 1982), 185; id., *Wealth of Nations*, ed. R. H. Campbell, A. S. Skinner, and W. B. Todd (Indianapolis, 1981), 22–23.

18. Smith, *Wealth of Nations*, 387–88, 398. Abolitionists later frequently alluded to the high overhead costs of managing slaves. In an overall evaluation of plantation costs in 1833, however, one of the Colonial Office policy architects dismissed the "managerial-costs" argument with a single sentence: "What capitalist in any country carries on a manufacture with fewer hired superintendents for every hundred of laborers than the sugar planter?" [Henry Taylor] "Colonial Office, January 1833. Memo: for the Cabinet," Co884/1, 58. [Hereafter Taylor, "Memorandum."]

19. Smith, *Lectures*, 186–87.

20. Smith, *Wealth of Nations*, 70.

21. *Adam Smith's An Inquiry into the Nature and Causes of the Wealth of Nations: A Concordance*, Fred R. Glahe, ed. (Lanham, MD, 1993). Early abolitionists mentioned the presence of indentured laborers to refute the idea of the impossibility of using European field labor in the

Caribbean. They were less anxious to discuss its subsequent yielding to slave labor.

22. Smith, *Wealth of Nations*, 98.

23. Ibid., 99. Defenders of the slave trade confidently appealed to the authority of Hume and Smith in defense of their system. See S. Drescher, "Capitalism and Abolition," in *Liverpool*, 195 n. 49.

24. James Ramsay, *Objections to the Abolition of the Slave Trade, with Answers* (London, 1788), 8; Thomas Clarkson, *Essay on the Impolicy of the African Slave Trade* (London, 1788); id., *The History of the Rise, Progress and Accomplishment of the Abolition of the African Slave Trade by the British Parliament*, 2 vols. (London, 1808), 1:86.

25. See *Morning Chronicle* Sept. 15, Oct. 3, 1785; *London Chronicle* Sept. 29, Oct. 4, 1785; Ramsay, *Objections*, 8–9.

26. Ibid., 104.

27. William Wilberforce, *A Letter on the Abolition of the Slave Trade* (London, 1807), 144, 210.

28. Ibid., 104.

29. See, inter alia, Stanley L. Engerman and David Eltis, "Economic Aspects of the Abolition Debate," in Christine Bolt and Seymour Drescher, eds., *Anti-Slavery, Religion and Reform: Essays in Memory of Roger Anstey* (Hamden, CT, 1980), 284–85; Jonathan A. Glickstein, *Concepts of Free Labor in Antebellum America* (New Haven, CT, 1991); Davis, *Slavery in the Age of Revolution, 1770–1823*, 346–54; Howard Temperley, "Capitalism, Slavery and Ideology," *Past and Present* 75 (1977): 94–118; id., "Anti-Slavery as a Form of Cultural Imperialism," in Bolt and Drescher, eds., *Anti-Slavery, Religion and Reform*, 335–50; David Eltis, *Economic Growth*, 20–24.

30. See e.g. Wilberforce, *Letter*, 254.

31. Seymour Drescher, "People and Parliament: The Rhetoric of the British Slave Trade," *Journal of Interdisciplinary History* 20 (1990): 561–80.

32. Roger Anstey, *The Atlantic Slave Trade and British Abolition, 1760–1810* (Atlantic Highlands, NJ, 1975), 256. For the various valuations of capital invested in the British West Indies, see Seymour Drescher, *Econocide: British Slavery in the Era of Abolition* (Pittsburgh, PA, 1977), 22–23.

33. Wilberforce, *Letter*, 257.

34. *Hansard's Parliamentary Debates*, 1st ser. vol. 9 (Mar. 17, 1807), cols. 142–46.

35. H. Brougham, *An Inquiry into the Colonial Policy of the European Powers*, 2 vols. (Edinburgh, 1803), 2:60–140 and 310–14; and Wilberforce, *Letter*, 259.

36. See, inter alia, Eltis, *Economic Growth*, 22; David Brion Davis, *Slavery and Human Progress* (New York, 1984), 189–91.

37. Dean Tucker, *Reflection on . . . Great Britain and Ireland* (London, 1785), quoted in F. O. Shyllon, *James Ramsay: The Unknown Abolitionist* (Edinburgh, 1977), 77.

38. Seymour Drescher, *Econocide: British Slavery in the Era of Abolition* (Pittsburgh, PA, 1977), 114–19.

39. Ibid., 76–83.

40. See David Eltis, *Economic Growth*, 20; and Sidney W. Mintz, *Sweetness and Power: The Place of Sugar in Modern History* (New York, 1985), 61–73.

41. See e.g. Wilberforce, *Letter*, 262–64.

42. Drescher, *Capitalism and Antislavery*, 78–79; Clare Midgley, "Slave Sugar Boycotts, Female Activism and the Domestic Base of British Anti-Slavery Culture," *Slavery and Abolition* 17 (1996): 137–62.

43. Drescher, *Capitalism and Antislavery*, 243; J. Stephen, *Crisis of the Sugar Colonies* (London, 1802), 185–89. Stephen's estimates of St. Domingue's production under Toussaint L'Ouverture are still regarded as reliable. See Mats Lundahl, "Toussaint L'Ouverture and the War Economy of Saint-Domingue, 1796–1802," *Slavery and Abolition* 6 (1985): 122–38.

44. *Parliamentary Debates* 19 (Apr. 4, 1811), col. 710.

45. Drescher, *Econocide*, 156–59.

46. J.-B. Say, *Traité d'economie politique*, 2 vols. (Paris, 1814), 1:283. For a similar conclusion about sugar and slavery from an English economist's perspective, see J. R. McCulloch, *The Principles of Political Economy*, 4th ed. (London, 1849), pt. 3, chap. 2, sec. 2, 437–39. McCulloch was one of Britain's most popular political economists between the opening of the campaign for gradual emancipation in 1823 and the ending of colonial apprenticeship in 1838. See also S. Drescher, "Cart Whip and Billy Roller: Antislavery and Reform Symbolism in Industrializing Britain," *Journal of Social History* 15 (1981): 3–24, esp. 5–6. Characteristically, Jeremy Bentham subscribed precisely to Smith's comparison of free and slave labor, but never doubted abolition's unprofitability to the slaveowners. Despite decades of friendly relations with Wilberforce, Bentham offered no public support whatever to the campaign for gradual abolition in the 1820s. See Lea Campos Baralevi, *Bentham and the Oppressed* (New York, 1984), 154–56.

47. Adam Hodgson, *A Letter to M. Jean Baptiste Say on the Comparative Expense of Free and Slave Labor*, 2d ed. (London, 1823), 60.

48. See Montifort Longfield, *Lectures on Political Economy* (Dublin, 1834), 71 (*Parliamentary Debates*, 2d ser., vol. 18 [1828], cols. 1026–27); and Wilmot-Horton, *First Letter to the Freeholders of the County of York, on Negro Slavery: being an inquiry into the claims of the West Indians for equitable compensation* (London, 1830), 7.

49. B. W. Higman, "Slavery and the Development of Demographic Theory in the Age of the Industrial Revolution," in James Walvin, ed., *Slavery and British Society* (London, 1982), 164–94.

50. See, inter alia, *The Petition and Memorial of the Planters of Demerara and Berbice on the Subject of Manumission, examined* (London, 1827), 21–48.

51. Sir J. R. Wilmot Horton, *Speech in the House of Commons, March*

6, *1828, with notes and appendix* (London, 1828), app. B, p. 73; Alexander MacDonnell, *Considerations on Negro Slavery* (London, 1824), 62–68. While some historians assume that the "consumer revolution" was well under way by the eighteenth century, others date its spread to the working classes after 1850. See E. Hobsbawm, *Industry and Empire* (Harmondsworth, 1968), 74.

52. MacDonnell, *Considerations*, 63, 69; Horton, *Speech*, 73; Gilbert Mathison, *A Critical View of the West India Question . . . In a letter addressed to the Right Hon. Robert Wilmot Horton* (London, 1827), 77–78.

53. See David Geggus, "Haiti and the Abolitionists: Opinion, Propaganda and International Politics in Britain and France, 1804–1838," in *Abolition and its Aftermath: The Historical Context, 1790–1916*, David Richardson, ed. (London, 1985), 113–40; David Eltis, "Abolitionist Perceptions of Society after Slavery," in James Walvin, ed., *Slavery and British Society 1776–1846* (London, 1982), 195–213.

54. Drescher, *Capitalism and Antislavery*, chaps. 5–6. See also Harriet Martineau, *Tale of Demerara, Illustrations of Political Economy* (London, 1832); Josiah Conder, *Wages or the Whip* (London, 1833), discussed by Patricia Hollis, "Anti-Slavery and British Working-Class Radicalism," in Bolt and Drescher, eds., *Anti-Slavery*, 294–315. See also Davis, *Slavery and Human Progress*, 189, 214–22; and Thomas C. Holt, *The Problem of Freedom: Race, Labor, and Politics in Jamaica and Britain, 1832–1938* (Baltimore, 1992), 48–53. On slave motivations, see Michael Craton, *Testing the Chains: Resistance to Slavery in the British West Indies* (Ithaca, NY, 1982), 300–304. Before British emancipation the French revolutionary colonial experience also indicated a high probability of partial or total withdrawal from plantation agriculture unless limited by coercive restraints.

55. George Thompson, *Speech on Colonial Slavery . . . at . . . Manchester*, Aug. 13, 1832, quoted in Drescher, *Capitalism*, 266 n. 1. For Henry Taylor, at the Colonial Office, the strength of popular demands was such that immediate emancipation without any compensation seemed to be a real possibility by the beginning of 1833. The West Indians' only hope lay with those classes and politicians who valued property, legality, and political economy. See Taylor, "Memorandum," 62–63.

56. On the Bill's development and passage, see Holt, *Problems of Freedom*, 42–50; and Green, *British Slave Emancipation*, chap. 4. Thomas Fowell Buxton specifically invoked the automatic and immediate efficacy of wages among free men as insuring adequate labor. See *Parliamentary Debates*, 3d ser. vol. 10 (June 10, 1833), col. 517.

57. For the abolitionists on sugar protection, see inter alia, *Second Report of the Committee of the Society for the Mitigation and Gradual Abolition of Slavery* (London, 1825), 26–33; *Anti-Slavery Reporter* 12 (May 31, 1826): 185–87.

58. J. R. Ward, *British West Indian Slavery, 1750–1834: The Process of Amelioration* (Oxford, 1988), 249.

59. Green, *British Slave Emancipation*, chap. 9; Hugh Tinker, *A New*

System of Slavery: The Export of Indian Labor Overseas, 1830–1920 (London, 1974); David Northrup, *Indentured Labor in the Age of Imperialism, 1834–1922* (New York, 1995); P. C. Emmer, ed., *Colonialism and Migration: Indentured Labor Before and After Slavery* (The Hague, 1986).

60. Howard Temperley, *White Dreams Black Africa: The Antislavery Expedition to the Niger, 1841–1842* (New Haven, CT, 1991); Pieter Emmer, "The Ideology of Free Labor and Dutch Colonial Policy, 1830–1870," in Oostindie, ed., *Fifty Years Later*, 207–22. The "Cultivation System" required laborers to cultivate export crops for a certain number of days each year.

61. Davis, *Slavery and Human Progress*, 179–81, 199.

62. Drescher, *Econocide*, 127–29, 174–77; Howard Temperley, "Eric Williams and Abolition: The Birth of a New Orthodoxy," in Barbara L. Solow and Stanley L. Engerman, eds., *British Capitalism and Caribbean Slavery: The Legacy of Eric Williams* (Cambridge, 1987), 229–57.

63. See J. R. Ward, *British West Indian Slavery*, 249 ff.

64. William A. Green, *British Slave Emancipation*, 165, 306. Green emphasizes British antislavery's radicalization after Emancipation, in placing "highest emphasis on the protection of freedmen's liberty, not the maintenance of export levels." See also Green, "Was British Emancipation a Success?," in *Abolition and its Aftermath: The Historical Context, 1790–1916*, David Richardson, ed. (London, 1985), 183–202, esp. 199 n. 36.

65. See Howard Temperley, *British Antislavery, 1833–1870* (London, 1972), 137–67; Ruth Dudley Edwards, *The Pursuit of Reason: The Economist 1843–1993* (London, 1993), 19–20; and C. Duncan Rice, "'Humanity Sold for Sugar!' The British Abolitionist Response to Free Trade in Slave-Grown Sugar," *Historical Journal* 13 (1970): 402–18. Rice notes that sugar free traders always remained a minority in the movement (416), but Temperley correctly concludes that the split depreciated the once formidable powers of popular mobilization (*British Antislavery*, 161).

66. *Hansard's Parliamentary Debates*, 3d ser. vol. 88 (Aug. 13, 1846), col. 662.

67. Northrup, *Indentured Labor*, 21, fig. 2.1. In the 1850s, the British colonies received 61 percent of indentured servants.

68. Temperley, *British Antislavery*, 141–51; Ward, *British West Indian Slavery*, 263.

69. Smith, *Wealth of Nations*, 400.

70. See Ian Duffield, "From Slave Colonies to Penal Colonies: The West Indian Convict Transportees to Australia," *Slavery and Abolition* 7 (1986): 25–45; Drescher, *Capitalism and Antislavery*, chap. 6; id., "Cart Whip and Billy Roller," 3–24; id., "The Ending of the Slave Trade and the Evolution of European Scientific Racism," *Social Science History* 14 (1990): 415–50; Jonathan A. Glickstein, *Concepts of Free Labor in Antebellum America* (New Haven, CT, 1991). On comparative living standards in Britain and the West Indies, see Green, *British Slave Emancipation*, 198n, and J. R. Ward, *British West Indian Slavery*, 263, 286–88.

71. See, for example, *Condition of the Slave not Preferable to that of the British Peasant, from the evidence before the Parliamentary Committees on Colonial Slavery* (London, 1833). On the historiography, see Thomas Bender, ed., *The Antislavery Debate: Capitalism and Abolitionism as a Problem in Historical Interpretation* (Berkeley, 1992); and S. Drescher, "The Antislavery Debate" (review essay) in *History and Theory* 32 (1993): 311–28.

72. *Anti-Slavery Reporter* 23 (Apr. 30, 1827): 356. See also *The Petition and Memorial of the Planters of Demerara and Berbice on the Subject of Manumission, Examined* (London, 1827), 41.

73. See, above all, David Brion Davis, *Slavery in the Age of Revolution*, chaps. 8 and 9, passim.

74. See, inter alia, ibid., esp. 349–57; 453–68; Bender, *The Antislavery Debate*, passim; and Drescher, "*The Antislavery Debate*," 320–29. On agricultural laborers, see Peter Karsten, "'Bottomed on Justice': A reappraisal of Critical Legal Studies Scholarship Concerning Breaches of Labor Contracts by Quitting or Firing in Britain and the U.S., 1630–1880," *American Journal of Legal History* 34 (1990): 213–61, esp. 217–21; David H. Morgan, *Harvesters and Harvesting, 1840–1900: A Study of the Rural Proletariat* (London, 1982), 124–33.

75. Temperley, *British Antislavery*, 93–110.

76. Herman Merivale, *Lectures* (London, 1861), 300, 353. Eric Williams invoked Merivale's economic premises to explain the rise of the British slave system in the seventeenth and eighteenth centuries (*Capitalism and Slavery*, Chapel Hill, NC, 1944), 7. Based upon those same premises, however, Merivale radically rejected economic explanations for the fall of that slave system in the nineteenth century.

77. Merivale, *Lectures*, 303 (Merivale's emphasis) and 307–8, 565. See also note 56 above.

78. On indentured servants see Dharma Kumar, "Colonialism, Bondage and Caste in British India," in Martin A. Klein, ed., *Breaking the Chains: Slavery, Bondage, and Emancipation in Modern Africa and Asia* (Madison, WI, 1993), 112–30, esp. 125. The volume of migrants from India from 1834 until the termination of indentured service in 1916 is calculated from Kingsley Davis, *The Population of India and Pakistan* (Princeton, NJ, 1951), 98–99. The interhemispheric flow of Asian indentured labor (about one million) was far smaller than its African counterpart, but the flow of Asians within Asia and to Africa was also largely in the form of indentured service. As Pieter Emmer notes, "Production of sugar and coffee in Asia and Africa for export overseas was feasible only in case labor could be subsidized or forced to work below market prices or in case the consumer market was protected." See Emmer, "The Price of Freedom: The Constraints of Change in Postemancipation America," in *The Meaning of Freedom: Economics, Politics, and Culture after Slavery*, Frank McGlynn and Seymour Drescher, eds. (Pittsburgh, PA, 1992), 23–47, esp. 26–28. On the implications of indentured servitude for the question of slav-

ery's competitive viability in the Americas, see also Martin Klein, "Slavery, the International Labour Market and the Emancipation of Slaves in the Nineteenth Century," in Paul E. Lovejoy and Nicholas Rogers, eds., *Unfree Labour in the Development of the Atlantic World* (London, 1994), 197–220, esp. 206–7.

79. J. E. Cairnes, *The Slave Power: Character and Probable Designs* (London, 1862). Karl Marx agreed completely with Howick, Merivale, and Cairnes that the terms of labor were utterly different in newly developing colonies from those in more densely populated areas. See Karl Marx, *Capital* vol. 1, trans. Samuel Moore and Edward Aveling (Moscow, n.d.), 770. Although cautious about the difficulties of comparison, in view of changing taxes and overhead costs, Thomas Holt also concluded that "strictly speaking, it may have been cheaper to run a slave than to hire a free worker" in Jamaica (Holt, *Problem of Freedom*, 124 ff.). This assessment is consistent with the findings of economic historians of the Americas. For a recent hemispheric summary, see Laird Bergad et al., *The Cuban Slave Market, 1790–1880* (New York, 1995), 143–54.

80. See Alexis de Tocqueville, *Democracy in America*, 2 vols. (New York, 1945), 1:376 ff.

81. Merivale, *Lectures*, 336–48. By the end of the 1850s, British West Indian sugar exports had virtually regained their pre-emancipation levels (see Green, *British Slave Emancipation*, 246). Charles Buxton, recalculating from the low point of the early 1840s, viewed the post–1846 rise in exports as a vindication of the decisive success of *two* "great" experiments, British slave emancipation and British free trade. (See Buxton, "The West Indies as they were and are," 229.) *The Edinburgh Review* illustrates the continued volatility of assessments of free vs. slave labor in the 1860s. See [Meadows Taylor,] "Cotton Culture in India," *Edinburgh Review* 115 (1862): 478–509; [Harriet Martineau,] "The Negro Race in America," *Edinburgh Review* 119 (1864): 203–42; [P. W. Clayden,] "The Reconstruction of the American Union," *Edinburgh Review* 123 (1866): 524–56. On the outcome of free labor "experiments" by Northern capitalists and abolitionists, see Richard H. Abbott, *Cotton and Capital: Boston Businessmen and Antislavery Reform, 1854–1868* (Amherst, MA, 1991), 87–88.

82. See Frank McGlynn and Seymour Drescher, eds., *The Meaning of Freedom: Economics, Politics and Culture After Slavery* (Pittsburgh, PA, 1992).

83. Merivale, *Lectures*, 337.

84. Ibid., 340. From the perspective of many economic historians of the United States South, a central theme "remains the failure of the free labor system to live up to the hopes of either its Republican spokesmen or the freedmen themselves." (See Peter Kolchin, "The Tragic Era? Interpreting Southern Reconstruction in Comparative Perspective," in McGlynn and Drescher, eds., *The Meaning of Freedom*, 291–311, esp. 293–94.)

85. The line between slave and free labor has blurred in slave historiography. See, inter alia, Mary Turner, ed., *From Chattel Slaves to Wage*

Slaves: The Dynamics of Labour Bargaining in the Americas (Kingston, Jamaica, 1995), 11; Mark D. Smith, "Old South Time in Comparative Perspective," *American Historical Review* 101 (1996): 1432–69. Noneconomic historians now seem as skeptical about Adam Smith's view of the universal superiority of free labor as was Merivale. See, e.g., Michael Twaddle, "Visible and Invisible Hands," in *The Wages of Slavery: From Chattel Slavery to Wage Labour in Africa, the Caribbean and England* (1993) (a special issue of *Slavery and Abolition*), 1–12, esp. 10–11.

86. On the relation of the abolition of slavery to abolitions of other unfree labor systems see, inter alia, Stanley Engerman, "Emancipations in Comparative Perspective: A Long and Wide View," in Oostindie, *Fifty Years Later*, 223–41; and Drescher, "Reflections," in ibid., 243–61, esp. 254–59. For an extensive overview of the complex impact of British emancipation on European consciousness see Davis, *Slavery and Human Progress*, 168–226.

CHAPTER 3

I would like to thank the other *Terms of Labor* authors, as well as my colleagues Michelle Lamarche Marrese and David Shearer, for reading an earlier draft of this chapter and providing helpful suggestions for strengthening it.

1. For changing perceptions of unfree and free labor, see David Brion Davis, *Slavery and Human Progress* (New York, 1984); Robert J. Steinfeld, *The Invention of Free Labor: The Employment Relation in English and American Law and Culture, 1350–1870* (Chapel Hill, NC, 1991); and Jonathan A. Glickstein, *Concepts of Free Labor in Antebellum America* (New Haven, CT, 1991). The best delineation of the "free labor" ideology that swept much of the West in the mid-nineteenth century remains Eric Foner's study of the northern United States, *Free Soil, Free Labor, Free Men: The Ideology of the Republican Party Before the Civil War* (New York, 1970). The historical literature on emancipation is vast. For broad overviews, see Jerome Blum, *The End of the Old Order in Rural Europe* (Princeton, NJ, 1978); and Robin Blackburn, *The Overthrow of Colonial Slavery, 1776–1848* (London, 1988). For surveys of Russian emancipation, see P. A. Zaionchkovskii, *Otmena krepostnogo prava v Rossii*, 3d ed. (Moscow, 1967); Daniel Field, *The End of Serfdom: Nobility and Bureaucracy in Russia, 1855–1861* (Cambridge, MA, 1976); L. G. Zakharova, *Samoderzhavie i otmena krepostnogo prava v Rossii, 1856–1861* (Moscow, 1982); B. G. Litvak, *Russkaia derevnia v reforme 1861 goda: Chernozemnyi tsentr, 1861–1895 gg.* (Moscow, 1972); and N. M. Druzhinin, *Russkaia derevnia na perelome: 1861–1880 gg.* (Moscow, 1978).

2. The quotation is from A. D. White, "The Development and Overthrow of the Russian Serf-System," *Atlantic Monthly* 10 (Nov. 1862): 549. For other examples of foreign free labor critiques of Russian serfdom, see M. P. D. de Passenans, *La Russie et l'esclavage, dans leurs rapports avec*

la civilisation européene; ou de l'influence de la servitude sur la vie do-mestique des russes (Paris, 1822); and Laurence Oliphant, *The Russian Shores of the Black Sea* (New York, 1970; originally New York, 1852), 59–64. "Enlightened" Russians also endorsed the free labor critique of serf-dom, often from the safety of exile abroad. See N. Tourgueneff, *La Russie et les russes*, 3 vols. (Brussels, 1847), 2:110–12, 117; and A. P. Zablotskii-Desiatovskii, "O krepostnom sostoianii v Rossii" (1844), in his *Graf P. D. Kiselev i ego vremia: Materialy dlia istorii imperatorov Aleksandra I, Nikolaia I i Aleksandra II* (St. Petersburg, 1882), 4:271–344.

3. Stevens speech, quoted in Eric Foner, *Nothing But Freedom: Emancipation and Its Legacy* (New York, 1983), 8; J. Lang, *Results of the Serf Emancipation in Russia* (New York, 1864); White, "The Development and Overthrow of the Russian Serf-System," 549–52. On American percep-tions of Russian emancipation, see Anna Babey, *Americans in Russia, 1776–1917: A Study of the American Travelers in Russia from the Ameri-can Revolution to the Russian Revolution* (New York, 1938); she notes (68) that most American travelers to Russia in the 1860s and 1870s were northerners who "felt that Russia deserved high praise for achieving peaceably what republican and democratic America could attain only after violent bloodshed, and were unaware of the many hardships besetting the recently freed serfs."

4. See C. L. R. James, *The Black Jacobins*, 2d ed. (New York, 1963); and Carolyn Fick, *The Making of Haiti: The Saint Domingue Revolution from Below* (Knoxville, TN, 1990).

5. For early enunciation of the argument that, by engaging in a massive "general strike" during the Civil War, southern slaves forced the Federal government to move against the peculiar institution, see W. E. B. DuBois, *Black Reconstruction in America, 1860–1880* (New York, 1935), 55–83. Recently, this interpretation has received renewed elaboration; see, espe-cially, Ira Berlin et al., *Slaves No More: Three Essays on Emancipation and the Civil War* (New York, 1992); and Barbara J. Fields, "Who Freed the Slaves?" in Geoffrey C. Ward, *The Civil War: An Illustrated History* (New York, 1990), 178–81. But for a response cautioning against exaggerating the slaves' "self-liberation," see James M. McPherson, "Who Freed the Slaves?" in McPherson, *Drawn with the Sword: Reflections on the Ameri-can Civil War* (New York, 1996), 192–207. For a recent study of a slave rebellion that fuelled antislavery sentiment in Britain and thereby has-tened the British decision for emancipation, see Emilia Viotti da Costa, *Crowns of Glory, Tears of Blood: The Demerara Slave Rebellion of 1823* (New York, 1994).

6. For graphic illustration of peasant unrest in pre-reform Russia, see the first four volumes of a massive documentary series on the "peasant movement" under the general editorship of N. M. Druzhinin: S. N. Valk, ed., *Krest'ianskoe dvizhenie v Rossii v 1796–1825 gg.: Sbornik dokumen-tov* (Moscow, 1961); A. V. Predtechenskii, ed., *Krest'ianskoe dvizhenie v Rossii v 1826–1849 gg.: Sbornik dokumentov* (Moscow, 1961); S. B. Okun',

ed., *Krest'ianskoe dvizhenie v Rossii v 1850–1856 gg.: Sbornik dokumentov* (Moscow, 1963); and S. B. Okun', ed., *Krest'ianskoe dvizhenie v Rossii v 1857-mae 1861 gg.: Sbornik dokumentov* (Moscow, 1963).

7. For elaboration of this contrast in independence, see Peter Kolchin, *Unfree Labor: American Slavery and Russian Serfdom* (Cambridge, MA, 1987), chaps. 1–3.

8. See, especially, David Moon, *Russian Peasants and Tsarist Legislation on the Eve of Reform: Interaction Between Peasants and Officialdom, 1825–1855* (London, 1992); Field, *The End of Serfdom*; and Zakharova, *Samoderzhavie i otmena krepostnogo prava v Rossii.*

9. Quotations are from Larissa Zakharova, "Autocracy and the Reforms of 1861–1874 in Russia: Choosing Paths of Development," in Ben Eklof, John Bushnell, and Larissa Zakharova, eds., *Russia's Great Reforms, 1855–1881* (Bloomington, IN, 1994), 30; Penza province nobleman Nikolai Charykov, "Ob uluchshenii byta pomeshchich'ikh krest'ian v Penzenskoi gubernii," in *Zhurnal zemlevladel'tsev* no. 7 (July, 1858), 123; and Prince S. V. Volkonskii, "Nekotoryia zamechaniia otnositel'no uluchsheniia byta pomeshchich'ikh krestian," *Trudy vysochaishe uchrezhdennoi Riazanskoi Uchenoi Arkhivnoi Komissii* 6 (1891): 34. See, also, Field, *The End of Serfdom*, 42–43, 77–89, 166; Terence Emmons, *The Russian Landed Gentry and the Peasant Emancipation of 1861* (Cambridge, 1968), 55, 245; Zaionchkovskii, *Otmena krepostnogo prava*, 72, 78–79, 84–85, 95–97, 112–16. On emancipation in the Baltic provinces, see Edward C. Thaden with Marianna Foster Thaden, *Russia's Western Borderlands, 1710–1870* (Princeton, NJ, 1984); 104–9, 133–37; David Kirby, *The Baltic World, 1772–1993: Europe's Northern Periphery in an Age of Change* (London, 1995), 62–64; Blum, *The End of the Old Order in Rural Europe*, 228–30. On Austrian and Prussian emancipation, see sources cited below in note 19.

10. The quotation is from Geroid Tanquary Robinson, *Rural Russia Under the Old Regime: A History of the Landlord-Peasant World and a Prologue to the Peasant Revolution of 1917* (New York, 1949), 65. The government distributed 220,000 copies of the manifesto, 190,000 copies of the general act of emancipation, and 140,000 copies of the local act covering Great Russia, New Russia, and Belorussia; some provincial officials published and circulated additional copies on their own. Because of the far-flung nature of the Russian empire, promulgation of the manifesto took almost a month, beginning in Moscow and St. Petersburg on March 5 and ending in Kishinev on April 2; a few copies of the voluminous emancipation legislation typically accompanied the manifesto, but most arrived several days—or even weeks—later. See "Iz obzor deistvii Ministerstva vnutrennikh del po zemskomu otdelu s 1 ianvaria 1861 po 19 fevralia 1863 g.," in M. Lur'e, ed., "Reforma 1861 g. i krest'ianskoe dvizhenie," *Krasnyi arkhiv* 35 (1936), no. 2:64–65; and E. A. Morokhovets, ed., *Krest'ianskoe dvizhenie v 1861 godu posle otmeny krepostnogo prava* (Moscow, 1949), which contains accounts prepared by special imperial aides-de-camp sent to the provinces to help maintain order during emancipation.

11. The full text of the various emancipation acts can be read in the *Polnoe sobranie zakonov Rossiiskoi Imperii*, 2d ser., 55 vols. (1825–81), vol. 36 (1861), nos. 36,650 (the manifesto) and 36,657–36,675; for a convenient collection of the most important provisions, see V. A. Fedorov, ed., *Padenie krepostnogo prava v Rossii: Dokumenty i materialy*, vol. 2, *"Polozheniia 19 fevralia 1861 goda" i russkoe obshchestvo* (Moscow, 1967), 7–63. For an English version of Alexander's emancipation manifesto, see Basil Dmytryshyn, ed., *Imperial Russia: A Source Book, 1700–1917*, 2d ed. (Hinsdale, IL, 1974), 270–75.

12. Fedorov, *Padenie krepostnogo prava*, 30–34. On the post-emancipation operation of this new rural administration, see Druzhinin, *Russkaia derevnia na perelome*, 25–44; A. P. Korelin, *Dvorianstvo v poreformennoi Rossii 1861–1904 gg.: Sostav, chislennost', korporativnaia organizatsiia* (Moscow, 1979), 180–96; Korelin, "Institut predvoditelei dvorianstva: O sotsial'nom i politicheskom polozhenii dvorian," *Istoriia SSSR*, 1978, no. 3 (May-June): 31–48; James I. Mandel, "Paternalistic Authority in the Russian Countryside, 1856–1906" (Ph.D. diss., Columbia Univ., 1978), 73–123; Jerman W. Rose, "The Russian Peasant Emancipation and the Problem of Rural Administration: The Institution of the *Mirovoi Posrednik*" (Ph. D. diss., Univ. of Kansas, 1976); N. F. Ust'iantseva, "Institut mirovykh posrednikov v otsenke sovremennikov (Po materialam gazety 'Mirovoi posrednik')," *Vestnik Moskovskogo universiteta*, ser. 8, Istoriia, 1984, no. 1, 64–75; Natalia F. Ust'iantseva, "Accountable Only to God and the Senate: Peace Mediators and the Great Reforms" (trans. Ben Eklof), in Eklof et al., eds., *Russia's Great Reforms*, 161–80; P. N. Zyrianov, "Sotsial'naia struktura mestnogo upravleniia kapitalisticheskoi Rossii (1861–1914 gg.)," *Istoricheskie zapiski* 107 (Moscow, 1982): 273–95.

13. As this suggests, emancipation did not abolish either the collective life or the administrative authority of village and commune that had long characterized rural Russia; see below, sect. III.

14. The owners were also prohibited from requiring more than three days per week of labor from men or two days from women, as well as from arbitrarily converting peasants' money dues into labor obligations. Quotations are from Fedorov, ed., *Padenie krepostnogo prava*, 14 and 35.

15. In the nonblack-earth region, the maximum size of allotments ranged from 3 to 7 *desiatiny* per soul (1 *desiatina* = 2.7 acres); in the more fertile black-earth region, the corresponding range was 2.75 to 6 *desiatiny*; in the steppe region, prescribed allotments varied from 3 to 12 *desiatiny*. See Fedorov, ed., *Padenie krepostnogo prava*, 44–55. On the drafting and implementation of statutory charters, see Druzhinin, *Russkaia derevnia na perelome*, 45–49; and L. R. Gorlanov, "Akty i protokoly mirovykh posrednikov kak istochnikov realizatsii reformy 1861 g. (Po materialam Kostromskoi gubernii)," *Istoriia SSSR*, 1972, no. 2, 118–25. Russian censuses traditionally counted only males among the mass of the "registered" population subject to the "soul tax," and estates were measured by the number of *male* souls they contained. Normally, the total peasant popula-

tion of any estate was therefore approximately twice the number of its souls.

16. Fedorov, ed., *Padenie krepostnogo prava*, 37–38. According to Ministry of Internal Affairs statistics, 73,195 charters covering 68.6 percent of the former serfs had been verified by January 3, 1863. (An additional 22,105 charters had been drafted and were waiting to be put into effect.) Of these, 36,413 had received the signatures of peasant representatives and 36,782 had not. Peasants on large estates, however, were particularly likely to reject charters; as a result, the unsigned charters covered estates containing 3,913,178 souls, while the signed charters covered holdings with only 2,834,716 souls. See *Otmena krepostnogo prava: Doklady Ministrov vnutrennikh del o provedenii krest'ianskoi reformy 1861–1862* (Moscow, 1950), 282.

17. Fedorov, ed., *Padenie krepostnogo prava*, 39–44. The government undertook special measures to secure peasant loyalty in the western provinces, where the Polish Revolution of 1863 created widespread unrest. Three imperial decrees of 1863 transferred all peasants in Vil'no, Grodno, Kovno, Minsk, Vitebsk, Kiev, Podolia, and Mogilev provinces from temporarily-obligated status to that of peasant proprietors, ended all remaining *barshchina* obligations, and reduced the *obrok* fees defined in statutory charters 20 percent; see Fedorov, ed., *Padenie krepostnogo prava*, 55–57.

18. For the decrees of 1881 and the manifesto of 1905, see ibid., 59–63. On the pace, process, and terms of redemption, see Zaionchkovskii, *Otmena krepostnogo prava*, 233–59, 293; Litvak, *Russkaia derevnia v reforme 1861 goda*, 326–99; and Druzhinin, *Russkaia derevnia na perelome*, 63–74, 260–63.

19. In its gradual implementation, its concern for the financial remuneration of noble landowners, and its provision that peasants would receive land but would have to pay for that land—and therefore in effect for their own freedom—the Russian settlement resembled earlier peasant emancipations that began in Prussia in 1807 and in Austria in 1848 (as well as in Prussian- and Austrian-controlled Poland). See Robert M. Berdahl, "Paternalism, Serfdom, and Emancipation in Prussia," in Erich Angermann and Marie-Luise Frings, eds., *Oceans Apart? Comparing Germany and the United States* (Stuttgart, 1981), esp. 40–44; Jerome Blum, *Noble Landowners and Agriculture in Austria, 1815–1848: A Study in the Origins of the Peasant Emancipation of 1848* (Baltimore, 1948), esp. 237–46; Blum, *The End of the Old Order in Rural Europe*, passim; Stefan Kieniewicz, *The Emancipation of the Polish Peasantry* (Chicago, 1969), 58–71, 133–39; and Steven Mintz, "Models of Emancipation During the Age of Revolution," *Slavery and Abolition* 17 (Aug. 1996), esp. 7–8.

20. For emphasis on the unique nature of post-emancipation Reconstruction in the southern United States, see Foner, *Nothing But Freedom*, esp. chap. 1; and Thomas J. Pressly, "Reconstruction in the Southern United States: A Comparative Perspective," *OAH Magazine of History* 4 (Winter 1989): 14–34. For examples of contrasts between the South and

specific New World societies, see Reid Andrews, "Black and White Workers: Sao Paulo, Brazil, 1888–1928," *Hispanic American Historical Review* 68 (1988): 491–524; and Rebecca J. Scott, *Slave Emancipation in Cuba: The Transition to Free Labor, 1860–1899* (Princeton, NJ, 1985), 285. For the suggestion of parallel Russian and American "reconstructions," see Peter Kolchin, "Some Thoughts on Emancipation in Comparative Perspective: Russia and the United States South," *Slavery and Abolition* 11 (Dec. 1990): esp. 357–63.

21. Noting the "exceptionally full documentation" of emancipation in the United States South, the editors of the Freedom and Southern Society Project declared that "as far as is known, no comparable record exists for the liberation of any [other] group of serfs or slaves"; Berlin et al., *Slaves No More*, xiii. The documentary record on the process of and responses to Russian emancipation—including statutory charters, redemption agreements, peasant petitions, reports (and subsequent recollections) of various government officials ranging from peace mediators to the minister of internal affairs, statistical reports put out by provincial agencies, and responses to various economic, legal, and ethnographic surveys—must rank a close second. For a small sample of such records, see *Otmena krepostnogo prava*, which contains reports from the minister of internal affairs; E. A. Morokhovets, ed., *Krest'ianskoe dvizhenie 1827–1869 godov* 2 (Moscow, 1931), which contains reports of the political police; Morokhovets, ed., *Krest'ianskoe dvizhenie v 1861 godu*, which contains reports of special imperial emissaries, one of whom was sent to each province to help preserve order immediately after emancipation; *Mirovoi posrednik* [*The Peace Mediator*], a bi-weekly newspaper published from January 1862 through June 1863; Okun', ed., *Krest'ianskoe dvizhenie v Rossii v 1857-mae 1861 gg*; and L. M. Ivanov, ed., *Krest'ianskoe dvizhenie v Rossii v 1861–1869 gg.: Sbornik dokumentov* (Moscow, 1964). A recent bibliographical work lists 604 primary sources published on Russian emancipation (as well as 1,405 secondary sources published down to 1989); see L. G. Zakharova, L. R. Gorlanova, and A. T. Topchii, comps., *Otmena krepostnogo prava v Rossii: Ukazatel' literatury (1856–1989 gg.)* (Tomsk, 1993).

22. Generalizations on the nature of Russian serfdom in this and the following two paragraphs are based on my *Unfree Labor*.

23. The tenth census, in 1858, counted 463,968 male noblemen and 11,338,042 male serfs, yielding a ratio of 24.4 serfs per nobleman; peasants (including those owned by the state and crown) constituted 83.0 percent of the population, while noblemen formed 1.6 percent. By contrast, the ratio of slaves to members of slaveowning families in the southern United States in 1860 was 2.1; blacks (slave and free) constituted 34.4 percent of the southern population, while members of slaveowning families constituted 15.7 percent. The Russian countryside was a peasant world: 80.8 percent of serfs belonged to masters holding more than 200 peasants (male and female), whereas only 3.3 percent had owners with 40 or fewer serfs; in the United States, only 2.4 percent of slaves were held in units of 200 or

more and the great majority—75.1 percent—were held in units of under 50. See Kolchin, *Unfree Labor*, 51–57.

24. It is not the existence but the level of this economic activity that distinguished Russian serfdom from American slavery, for "internal" or "slave" economies also developed in the Americas; in much of the Caribbean, slaves grew their own food on "provision grounds," which provided the basis for considerable commercial activity. The slaves' internal economy in the southern United States was most extensive in the low country of South Carolina and Georgia but rarely reached the "proto-peasant" level of the Caribbean; even so, it has attracted increasing historical attention. See, e.g., Ira Berlin and Philip D. Morgan, eds., *Cultivation and Culture: Labor and the Shaping of Slave Life in the Americas* (Charlottesville, VA, 1993); Roderick A. McDonald, *The Economy and Material Culture of Slaves: Goods and Chattels on the Sugar Plantations of Jamaica and Louisiana* (Baton Rouge, LA, 1993); Betty Wood, *Women's Work, Men's Work: The Informal Slave Economies of Lowcountry Georgia* (Athens, GA, 1995); and Larry E. Hudson, Jr., *To Have and To Hold: Slave Work and Family Life in Antebellum South Carolina* (Athens, GA, 1997).

25. In six representative black-earth provinces, for example, 50.1 percent of the peasants received reduced allotments, 6.7 percent received increases, and 43.2 percent had the size of their holdings unchanged; see Litvak, *Russkaia derevnia v reforme 1861 goda*, 152–53. Recent studies of Novgorod and Petersburg provinces have found reductions of 26.9 percent and 34.1 percent, respectively, in the overall size of peasant allotments according to the statutory charters; see A. Ia. Degtiarev, S. G. Kashchenko, and D. I. Raskin, *Novgorodskaia derevnia v reforme 1861 goda: Opyt izucheniia s ispol'zovaniem EVM* (Leningrad, 1989), 134; and S. G. Kashchenko, *Reforma 19 fevralia 1861 goda v Sankt-Peterburgskoi gubernii* (Leningrad, 1990), 132.

26. According to Litvak (*Russkaia derevnia v reforme 1861 goda*, 279–87), the average *obrok* per soul in six black-earth provinces fell 11.4 percent, from 8.19 rubles to 7.26 rubles, with payments increasing in 4 districts, decreasing in 69, and unchanged in one. For comparisons of pre- and post-emancipation peasant payments per *desiatina* of allotment land, see statistics in Degtiarev, Kashchenko, and Raskin, *Novgorodskaia derevnia v reforme 1861 goda*, 140–44; Kashchenko, *Reforma 19 fevralia 1861 goda v Sankt-Peterburgskoi gubernii*, 137–39; Litvak, *Russkaia derevnia v reforme 1861 goda*, 287.

27. Report of N. G. Kaznakov, May 24, 1861, in Morokhovets, ed., *Krest'ianskoe dvizhenie v 1861 godu*, 94. For examples of similar reports from other provinces, see ibid., 106, 113; and *Otmena krepostnogo prava*, 68, 73. But for the view that spring cultivation was proceeding normally, see Baron F. F. Vintsengerode's report of June 15, 1861, to Alexander II from Tambov province; Morokhovets, ed., *Krest'ianskoe dvizhenie v 1861 godu*, 235.

28. The average size of allotments provided in the statutory charters

varied according to local conditions; although the charters produced a leveling of the disparities that had existed in pre-emancipation allotments, average figures hide variations that continued to exist within given localities. In Russia as a whole, the average size of peasant allotments ranged from less than 1 to more than 10 *desiatiny* per soul, but 76.5 percent of peasants received holdings of between 2 and 6 *desiatiny* per soul; see Zaionchkovskii, *Otmena krepostnogo prava*, 244. In Novgorod province, the average allotment was 5.9 *desiatiny* per soul, with 91 percent of peasants receiving allotments of 4–6 *desiatiny* per soul; see Degtiarev, Kashchenko, and Raskin, *Novgorodskaia derevnia v reforme 1861 goda*, 134–37. In St. Petersburg province, the average holding was 4.8 *desiatiny* per soul, with 82 percent of peasants receiving 4–6 *desiatiny*; Kashchenko, *Reforma 19 fevralia goda v Sankt-Peterburgskoi gubernii*, 132, 192. Measured by peasant *household*, of course, holdings were much larger: in Riazan province they averaged 11.6 *desiatiny* and in Orel province 13.2 *desiatiny*; Litvak, *Russkaia derevnia v reforme 1861 goda*, 274–75. Over time, as the population grew, the size of allotments per soul shrank: thus, in the Saratov district of Saratov province, the average allotment size in 1883 was 3.9 *desiatiny* per official soul, as counted in the tenth census on the eve of emancipation, but 3.1 *desiatiny* when measured according to "actual" souls at the time; see *Sbornik statisticheskikh svedenii po Saratovskoi gubernii* 1 (Saratov, 1883), sec. 1, 24–31.

29. See the description of work done "out of respect" in Cathy A. Frierson, ed., *Aleksandr Nikolaevich Engelgardt's Letters from the Countryside, 1872–1887* (New York, 1993), 55–59. Most Soviet historians followed Lenin in portraying *otrabotka* as a backward remnant of the old order that gradually yielded to a more progressive wage labor system; see V. I. Lenin, *The Development of Capitalism in Russia: The Process of the Formation of a Home Market for Large-Scale Industry* (Moscow, 1956; orig. 1899), 190–262. On migrant labor, see especially Timothy Mixter, "The Hiring Market as Workers' Turf: Migrant Agricultural Laborers and the Mobilization of Collective Action in the Steppe Grainbelt of European Russia, 1853–1913," in Esther Kingston-Mann and Timothy Mixter, eds., *Peasant Economy, Culture, and Politics of European Russia, 1800–1921* (Princeton, NJ, 1991), 294–340. For other kinds of out-village migration, see below, sec. III.

30. The quotation is from Frierson, ed., *Aleksandr Nikolaevich Engelgardt's Letters from the Countryside*, 38–39. On peasant purchases and rental of noble lands, see Druzhinin, *Russkaia derevnia na perelome*, 136–46; Peter Gatrell, *The Tsarist Economy, 1850–1917* (London, 1986), 110–15; Korelin, *Dvorianstvo v poreformennoi Rossii*, 54–68, 77–129, 270–76; and Seymour Becker, *Nobility and Privilege in Late Imperial Russia* (DeKalb, IL, 1985), 31–43, 108–14, 171–74. For the "peasantization" of agriculture, see Teodor Shanin, *Russia as a "Developing Society": The Roots of Otherness: Russia's Turn of Century, Volume I* (New Haven, CT, 1986), esp. 136–56 (statistics 137). In some fertile black-earth provinces, the de-

cline in noble landholding was relatively modest. In Saratov province, for example, the number of landholding nobles decreased from 335 to 254 (24.2 percent) between 1867 and 1883, but the amount of land they owned only decreased from 331,692.5 to 267,746 *desiatiny* (19.3 percent); the average landholding per nobleman thus increased from 921.5 to 1,052 *desiatiny*. See *Sbornik statisticheskikh svedenii po Saratovskoi gubernii* 1 (Saratov, 1883), sec. 1, 12–16. For statistics on landholding among blacks in the southern United States, see Loren Schweninger, *Black Property Owners in the South, 1790–1915* (Urbana, IL, 1990), esp. 146–80. On the absenteeist orientation of Russian serfholding noblemen, see Kolchin, *Unfree Labor*, pt. 1. On the transformation of the post-emancipation nobility, see below, sec. III.

31. The quotation is from editor M. M. Shevchenko's introduction to *Krest'ianskoe dvizhenie v Voronezhskoi gubernii (1861–1863 gg.): Dokumenty i materialy* 1 (Voronezh, 1961): 5. In six black-earth provinces, *pomeshchiki* received an average of 38.50 rubles per *desiatina* for land that on the open market averaged 36.46 rubles per *desiatina*, a subsidy of 5.6 percent; including interest, peasants eventually paid a total of 63 rubles per *desiatina* for this land; see Litvak, *Russkaia derevnia v reforme 1861 goda*, 377–78, 388.

32. A significant dualism has marked Soviet evaluations of emancipation. Even while noting its exploitative nature and stressing the serfholding survivals that pervaded the new era, historians have typically seen emancipation as a "most important event, a 'watershed,' a 'turning point'" in Russian history that made possible the subsequent development of a capitalist order; L. G. Zakharova, "Samoderzhavie, biurokratiia i reformy 60-kh godov XIX v. v Rossii," *Voprosy istorii*, 1989 (no. 10), 3. The one-tenth estimate is from Shanin, *Russia as a "Developing Society,"* 140. Average land prices in European Russia increased from 13 rubles per *desiatina* in the 1850s to 47 rubles in the 1890s and 93 rubles in 1905–6; see Becker, *Nobility and Privilege in Late Imperial Russia*, 43–44. As a result of a doubling of land prices in six black-earth provinces between the 1860s and the late 1880s, by 1887 the value of peasant land exceeded not only the principal of the original redemption loans but also the total of redemption payments, including interest; see Litvak, *Russkaia derevnia v reforme 1861 goda*, 394–95.

33. Between 1861 and 1913, Russia's per capita income decreased from 22 to 21 percent of Britain's, 41 to 32 percent of Germany's, and 47 to 39 percent of France's. Russia's appallingly high infant mortality rate declined slightly during those years, from 267 to 245 per 1,000 births, but this modest drop of 8.2 percent was far less than that achieved by Britain, Germany, France, Italy, Spain, or Sweden. Russia's exceptionally high mortality and fertility rates did not begin sustained declines until the second half of the 1890s. See Peter Gatrell, *The Tsarist Economy, 1850–1917* (London, 1986), 30–138 (statistics: 32–34); Paul R. Gregory, *Before Command: An Economic History of Russia from Emancipation to the First*

Five-Year Plan (Princeton, NJ, 1994); David M. Heer, "The Demographic Transition in the Russian Empire and the Soviet Union," *Journal of Social History* 1 (Spring 1968): 208–9; and Ansley J. Coale et al., *Human Fertility in Russia Since the Nineteenth Century* (Princeton, NJ, 1979), 15–16, 20–21. As late as 1887–96, 432 of every 1,000 babies born in Russia did not survive to age 5; see David L. Ransel, "Infant Care Cultures in the Russian Empire," in Barbara Evans Clements et al., eds., *Russia's Women: Accommodation, Resistance, Transformation* (Berkeley, 1991), 114–15.

34. On the Caribbean, see Stanley L. Engerman, "Economic Adjustments to Emancipation in the United States and British West Indies," *Journal of Interdisciplinary History* 13 (1982): 191–220; Foner, *Nothing But Freedom*, 8–38; Frank Moya Pons, "The Land Question in Haiti and Santo Domingo: The Sociopolitical Context of the Transition from Slavery to Free Labor, 1801–1843," in Manuel Moreno Fraginals et al., eds., *Between Slavery and Free Labor* (Baltimore, 1985), 181–214; Robert K. Lacerte, "The Evolution of Land and Labor in the Haitian Revolution, 1791–1820," *The Americas* 34 (1978): 449–59; and Thomas C. Holt, *The Problem of Freedom: Race, Labor, and Politics in Jamaica and Britain, 1832–1938* (Baltimore, 1992), 115–76. For statistics on economic growth in the southern United States, see Gavin Wright, *Old South, New South: Revolutions in the Southern Economy Since the Civil War* (New York, 1986), 30–138. For an overview of southern industrialization, see James C. Cobb, *Industrialization and Southern Society, 1877–1984* (Chicago, 1984).

35. W. Bruce Lincoln, *The Great Reforms: Autocracy, Bureaucracy, and the Politics of Change in Imperial Russia* (DeKalb, IL, 1990); L. G. Zakharova et al., eds., *Velikie reformy v Rossii 1856–1874* (Moscow, 1992); Eklof et al., eds., *Russia's Great Reforms*; Terence Emmons and Wayne S. Vucinich, eds., *The Zemstvo in Russia: An Experiment in Local Self-Government* (Cambridge, 1982). For parallels between the Great Reforms in Russia and Reconstruction in the United States—as well as for the contrast with other post-emancipation societies—see Kolchin, "Some Thoughts on Emancipation in Comparative Perspective," esp. 354–59.

36. Quotations are from Becker, *Nobility and Privilege in Late Imperial Russia*, 154; and Anatole Leroy-Beaulieu, *The Empire of the Tsars and the Russians*, 3 vols., translated from the third French edition by Z. A. Ragozin (New York, 1969), 1:395. For differing views of the transformation of the nobility, see Roberta Thompson Manning, *The Crisis of the Old Order in Russia: Gentry and Government* (Princeton, NJ, 1982); G. M. Hamburg, *Politics of the Russian Nobility, 1881–1905* (New Brunswick, NJ, 1984); Alfred J. Rieber, "The Sedimentary Society," in Edith W. Clowes et al., eds., *Between Tsar and People: Educated Society and the Quest for Public Identity in Late Imperial Russia* (Princeton, NJ, 1991), 356–58; Gregory L. Freeze, "The Soslovie (Estate) Paradigm and Russian Social History," *American Historical Review* 91 (Feb. 1986): 14, 25–35; and Korelin, *Dvorianstvo v poreformennoi Rossii*. On the pre-reform nobility, see S. A. Korf, *Dvorianstvo i ego soslovnoe upravlenie za stoletie 1762–1855 godov* (St. Petersburg, 1906).

37. For statistics on the decline of noble landowning, as well as on the increase in land prices, see the sources cited above in notes 28 and 30. The quotation is from Becker, *Nobility and Privilege in Late Imperial Russia*, 154.

38. Quotation from Daniel Field, "The Year of Jubilee," in Eklof et al., eds., *Russia's Great Reforms*, 41.

39. See Ben Eklof, *Russian Peasant Schools: Officialdom, Village Culture, and Popular Pedagogy, 1861–1914* (Berkeley, 1986); and Jeffrey Brooks, *When Russia Learned to Read: Literacy and Popular Literature, 1861–1917* (Princeton, NJ, 1985). For early Ministry of Internal Affairs reports on peasant enthusiasm for education, see *Otmena krepostnogo prava*, 43, 77, 92, 99, 109, 114, 150, 169, 188. By the end of 1862, former serfs were attending 270 "literacy schools" in Kaluga province; see *Pamiatnaia knizhka Kaluzhskoi gubernii na 1862 i 1863 gody, izdannaia Kaluzhskim Gubernskim statisticheskim komitetom* (Kaluga, 1863), 145. Despite such educational efforts, however, 60.7 percent of rural men and 86.6 percent of rural women remained illiterate in 1897; see B. N. Mironov, "Literacy in Russia, 1797–1917: Obtaining New Historical Information through the Application of Retrospective Prediction Methods," *Soviet Studies in History* 25 (Winter 1986–87): 89–117, statistics 106–7 (originally published as "Gramotnost' v Rossii 1797–1917: Poluchenie novoi istoricheskoi informatsii s pomoshch'iu metodov retrospektivnogo prognozirovaniia," *Istoriia SSSR*, 1985, no. 4, 137–53).

40. The number of peasant *otkhodniki* (departers), who received temporary passes to leave their villages for work elsewhere, surged during the last third of the nineteenth century, especially in the less fertile non-black-earth region. In the 1860s, an average of 1,233,400 such passes were issued per year in European Russia; in the 1870s the number was 4,730,400; in the 1880s, 6,211,400; and in the 1890s, 7,775,600. See Jeffrey Burds, "The Social Control of Peasant Labor in Russia: The Response of Village Communities to Labor Migration in the Central Industrial Region, 1861–1905," in Kingston-Mann and Mixter, eds., *Peasant Economy, Culture, and Politics of European Russia*, 52–100 (statistics: 56–57); N. A. Iakimenko, "Agrarnye migratsii v Rossii (1861–1917 gg.)," *Voprosy istorii*, 1983, no. 3, 17–32; and Mixter, "The Hiring Market as Workers' Turf." In Iaroslavl' province, 130,908 persons (out of a total population of 996,124) were away from home in 1865 on passes ranging from 1 month to 3 years in duration; since these *otkhodniki* included few women and children, the proportion of the adult male migrants must have been close to 50 percent. See *Trudy Iaroslavskago gubernskago statisticheskago komiteta* 3 (Iaroslavl', 1866): 53.

41. Historians disagree on the extent of peasant stratification; Soviet historians, following Lenin, traditionally emphasized its prevalence and saw it as an index of the decomposition of the peasantry into two antagonistic rural classes (bourgeois and proletarian); Lenin's populist opponents, by contrast, portrayed the peasant village as relatively undifferentiated.

For an introduction to the historiography of this debate, see Lenin, *Development of Capitalism in Russia*, 50–189; and Esther Kingston-Mann, "Marxism and Russian Rural Development: Problems of Evidence, Experience, and Culture," *American Historical Review* 86 (Oct. 1981): 731–52. Recent Western scholars have cautioned—correctly I believe—against overemphasizing the degree of peasant stratification. See, e.g., Daniel Field, "Stratification and the Russian Peasant Commune: A Statistical Inquiry," in Roger Bartlett, ed., *Land Commune and Peasant Community in Russia: Communal Forms in Imperial and Early Soviet Society* (New York, 1990), 143–64; and Heinz-Dietrich Lowe, "Differentiation in Russian Peasant Society: Causes and Trends, 1880–1905," ibid., 165–95.

42. The quotation is from N. L.-V., "Markitanty," in *Pamiatnaia knizhka Kaluzhskoi gubernii na 1862 i 1863 gody*, 195. Recent research makes clear the increased burdens that male outwork placed on women, but also suggests some real benefits, including reduced childbearing, supplementary income, and enhanced authority. For differing evaluations, see Rose Glickman, "Peasant Women and their Work," in Ben Eklof and Stephen Frank, eds., *The World of the Russian Peasant: Post-Emancipation Society and Culture* (Boston, 1990), 50–57; Barbara Engel, "The Woman's Side: Male Outmigration and the Family in Kostroma Province," ibid., 65–80; Christine D. Worobec, "Victims or Actors? Russian Peasant Women and Patriarchy," in Kingston-Mann and Mixter, eds., *Peasant Economy, Culture, and Politics*, 184–87; Christine D. Worobec, *Peasant Russia: Family and Community in the Post-Emancipation Period* (Princeton, NJ, 1991), 33; Burds, "The Social Control of Peasant Labor in Russia." On the less common *women* outworkers, see Judith Paillot, "Women's Domestic Industries in Moscow Province, 1880–1900," in Clements et al., eds., *Russia's Women*, 163–84.

43. The quotation is from Anatole Leroy-Beaulieu, *The Russian Peasant* (Sandoval, NM, 1962), 63, condensed from his *The Empire of the Tsars* (1881–89). See also Stepniak, *The Russian Peasantry: Their Agrarian Condition, Social Life and Religion* (New York, 1888), 74; and Donald Mackenzie Wallace, *Russia on the Eve of War and Revolution* (New York, 1962; from rev. 1912 ed.; first ed. 1877), 264. For typical complaints about the harmful effects of family divisions, see N., "O krest'ianskikh semeinykh razdelakh v Voronezhskoi gubernii," *Voronezhskii iubileinyi sbornik v pamiat' trekhsotletiia g. Voronezha* (Voronezh, 1886), 331–35; Aleksandr Novikov, *Zapiski zemskago nachal'nika* (St. Petersburg, 1899), 20–23; and Frierson, ed., *Aleksandr Nikolaevich Engelgardt's Letters from the Countryside*, 163–68, 172–83. For a good recent examination of the subject, see Cathy A. Frierson, "Razdel: The Peasant Family Divided," *The Russian Review* 46 (1987): 35–52.

44. Kolchin, *Unfree Labor*, passim.

45. Edgar Melton, "Proto-Industrialization, Serf Agriculture and Agrarian Social Structure: Two Estates in Nineteenth-Century Russia," *Past and Present* 115 (May 1987): 69–106. For an overview of the extent and limitation of such stratification, see Kolchin, *Unfree Labor*, 336–43.

46. During the past decade, there has been a surge in scholarly attention (much of it Western) devoted to Russian peasants during the late nineteenth century; one of the most noteworthy themes to pervade these works has been the persistence of traditional peasant ways. See, e.g., Stephen P. Frank, "Popular Justice, Community and Culture among the Russian Peasantry, 1870–1900," *Russian Review* 46 (1987): 239–65; Cathy Frierson, "Crime and Punishment in the Russian Village: Rural Concepts of Criminality at the End of the Nineteenth Century," *Slavic Review* 46 (Spring 1987): 55–69; Worobec, *Peasant Russia*; Kingston-Mann and Mixter, eds., *Peasant Economy, Culture and Politics*; Boris Mironov, "The Russian Peasant Commune after the Reforms of the 1860s," trans. Gregory L. Freeze, *Slavic Review* 44 (Fall 1985): 438–67. For an interesting earlier collection of Soviet essays emphasizing the same theme, see Sula Benet, ed. and trans., *The Village of Viriatino: An Ethnographic Study of a Russian Village from Before the Revolution to the Present* (Garden City, NY, 1970; originally Moscow, 1958). For a fascinating—and condescending—contemporary description of traditional village life in the late nineteenth century, see Olga Semyonova Tian-Shanskaia, *Village Life in Late Tsarist Russia*, ed. David L. Ransel (Bloomington, IN, 1993).

47. See V. A. Aleksandrov, *Sel'skaia obshchina v Rossii (XVII-nachalo XIX v.)* (Moscow, 1976), quotation 176; and Kolchin, *Unfree Labor*, esp. 201–6.

48. The quotation is from Rieber, "The Sedimentary Society," 345. For the emancipation legislation on village administration, see Fedorov, ed., *Padenie krepostnogo prava v Rossii*, 16–27. On the post-emancipation commune, see, especially, Mironov, "The Russian Peasant Commune"; G. A. Alekseichenko, "Prigovory sel'skikh skhodov kak istochnik po istorii krest'ianskoi obshchiny v Rossii vtoroi poloviny XIX veka (Po materialam Tverskoi gubernii)," *Istoriia SSSR*, 1981, no. 6, 111–25; A. N. Anfimov and P. N. Zyrianov, "Nekotorye cherty evoliutsii russkoi krest'ianskoi obshchiny v poreformennyi period (1861–1914 gg.)," *Istoriia SSSR*, 1980, no. 4, 24–41; L. I. Kuchumova, "Sel'skaia pozemel'naia obshchina evropeiskoi Rossii v 60–70-e gody XIX v.," *Istoricheskie zapiski* 106 (Moscow, 1981): 323–47; Francis M. Watters, "The Peasant and the Village Commune," in Wayne S. Vucinich, ed., *The Peasant in Nineteenth-Century Russia* (Stanford, 1968), 133–57.

49. Samuel C. Ramer, "Traditional Healers and Peasant Culture in Russia, 1861–1917," in Kingston-Mann and Mixter, eds., *Peasant Economy, Culture, and Politics*, 207–32; Eklof, *Russian Peasant Schools*, 254–82. Statistics show enormous disparities between school attendance of boys and girls: in Iaroslavl' province in 1865, for example, 3,484 peasant boys and 521 girls attended school; see *Trudy Iaroslavskago gubernskago statisticheskago komiteta*, 60–61. Similar disparities existed in literacy rates. In 1883, the literacy rate stood at 14.1 percent for male peasants in Saratov district of Saratov province, but only 4.2 percent for females; in the province's more remote Tsaritsynskii district, 11.2 percent of male but

only 0.25 percent of female peasants were literate. See *Sbornik statisti-cheskikh svedenii po Saratovskoi gubernii* 1 (Saratov, 1883), sec. 3, summary table, p. 3, and 2 (Saratov, 1884), sec. 3, p. 33. See also, Mironov, "Literacy in Russia," passim.

50. Quotations are from Frank, "Popular Justice, Community and Culture among the Russian Peasantry," 245, 259. See also Frierson, "Crime and Punishment in the Russian Village," and Peter Czap, Jr., "Peasant-Class Courts and Peasant Customary Justice in Russia, 1861–1912," *Journal of Social History* 1 (Winter 1967): 149–78.

51. Quotations are from Minister of Justice Count V. N. Panin to Ober-prokuror of the Church Synod Count A. P. Tolstoi, Nov. 24, 1860, in Z. Gurskaia, ed., "Tserkov' i reforma 1861 g.," *Krasnyi arkhiv* 72 (1935), no. 5:183; and report of estate steward P. P. Abramov to *pomeshchik* Zybin, March 21, 1861, Makar'evskii district, Nizhnii Novgorod province, in Okun', ed., *Krest'ianskoe dvizhenie v Rossii v 1857-mae 1861 gg.*, 408. On distribution of the emancipation legislation and reports of the imperial emissaries, see sources listed in note 10 above.

52. For a perceptive analysis of "naive monarchism," and the suggestion that it may at times have been a clever ploy in dealing with authorities, see Daniel Field, "The Myth of the Peasant," in Field, ed., *Rebels in the Name of the Tsar* (Boston, 1976), 208–15.

53. Report of Orenburg province Governor G. S. Aksakov to Minister of Internal Affairs P. A. Valuev, March 13, 1862, in Ivanov, ed., *Krest'ianskoe dvizhenie v Rossii v 1861–1869 gg.*, 204. For immediate responses to emancipation, see documents in I. Kuznetsov, ed., "Semdesiat piat' let nazad (19 fevralia 1861 g.)," *Krasnyi arkhiv* 44 (1936), no. 1:5–36; Morokhovets, ed., *Krest'ianskoe dvizhenie v 1861 godu* (for reports of the imperial emissaries); *Otmena krepostnogo prava* (reports of the minister of internal affairs); and Okun', ed., *Krest'ianskoe dvizhenie v Rossii v 1857-mae 1861 gg.* For the continuing dispute over the meaning of emancipation, see documents in Ivanov, ed., *Krest'ianskoe dvizhenie v Rossii v 1861–1869 gg.*; P. A. Zaionchkovskii, ed., *Krest'ianskoe dvizhenie v Rossii v 1870–1880 gg.: Sbornik dokumentov* (Moscow, 1968); *Krest'ianskoe dvizhenie v Voronezhskoi gubernii (1861–1863 gg.); Krest'ianskoe dvizhenie v Voronezhskoi gubernii (1864–1904 gg.): Sbornik dokumentov* (Voronezh, 1964); Morokhovets, ed., *Krest'ianskoe dvizhenie 1827–1869 godov* 2 (for reports of the secret police); and P. Sofinov, ed., "Krest'ianskoe dvizhenie v kontse XIX v. (1881–1894 gg.)," *Krasnyi arkhiv* 89–90 (1938), nos. 4–5:208–57.

54. Report of peace mediator Astaf'ev to Governor of Voronezh, Oct. 23, 1861, *Krest'ianskoe dvizhenie Voronezhskoi gubernii* 1:49; report of Ostrogozhskii district *ispravnik* Golovinskii to Governor of Voronezh province, Nov. 3, 1861, ibid., 50. For numerous similar confrontations, see the documents listed above in note 53. Government officials credited the peace mediators with helping to restore rural calm, but did not always

agree on whose interests they were serving. Minister of Internal Affairs Valuev, for example, noted that the governor of Riazan province complained that "some mediators bias their decisions to the benefit of the *pomeshchiki*," but that others complained that the mediators were "always and intentionally taking the side of the peasants against the *pomeshchiki*"; see his report of Sept. 1, 1861, in *Otmena krepostnogo prava*, 67. Governors also varied in their handling of disturbances, but—like the vast majority of noble officials—most found it difficult to understand peasant aspirations even when sympathetic to their plight. For a governor (of Nizhnii Novgorod province) who showed unusual sympathy for peasants, blaming much of the peasant unrest on "the *pomeshchiki* themselves, and where not them, their stewards," see report of July 20, 1861, ibid., 50; even he, however, pointed to the peasants' "inaccurate understanding of the new legislation" as a major source of trouble. For the very different comments of a hardline official, who heaped praise on local *pomeshchiki*—"they answer the wild behavior of the peasants with magnanimity"—and advocated harsh repression to tame "the peasants' moral backwardness," see report of Rear-Admiral I. S. Unkovskii to Alexander II on Chernigov Province, April 18, 1861, in Morokhovets, ed., *Krest'ianskoe dvizhenie v 1861 godu*, 252.

55. Letter with unintelligible signature to Manager of the Third Department N. K. Shmit, May 7, 1879, in Zaionchkovskii, ed., *Krest'ianskoe dvizhenie v Rossii v 1870–1880 gg.*, 367. See similar reports in ibid., 330–31, 342, 367, 371, 372–74, 378–80, 380–81, 402. For police documents on peasant disturbances in the 1880s and 1890s, see Sofinov, ed., "Krest'ianskoe dvizhenie v kontse XIX v. (1881–1894 gg.)."

56. *Kolokol*, no. 9 (Aug. 15, 1858), 67; no. 101 (June 15, 1861), 845–48 (article written by Herzen's collaborator N. P. Ogarev); and no. 102 (July 1, 1861), 853–54. (Pages of *Kolokol* numbered consecutively within each annual volume, in 11-vol. reprint series, Moscow, 1962–64.) On the exuberance followed by disillusionment among radical intellectuals, see Abbott Gleason, *Young Russia: The Genesis of Russian Radicalism in the 1860s* (New York, 1980), 79–113; and Franco Venturi, *Roots of Revolution: A History of the Populist and Socialist Movements in Nineteenth Century Russia*, trans. Francis Haskell (New York, 1964), 1–330, passim.

57. The noble reaction was closely linked to government acts of 1889 and 1890, the first of which introduced the office of land captains (*zemskie nachal'niki*), made up of local noblemen who would supervise peasant life and preserve rural order, and the second of which sharply reduced peasant participation in *zemstvo* assemblies. On the noble reaction see Becker, *Nobility and Privilege in Late Imperial Russia*, 58–107, 130–34; Hamburg, *Politics of the Russian Nobility*, 99–101; Korelin, *Dvorianstvo v poreformennoi Rossii*, 254–70; Zyrianov, "Sotsial'naia struktura mestnogo upraveleniia kapitalisticheskoi Rossii," 263–72. On land captains, see Thomas S. Pearson, *Russian Officialdom in Crisis: Autocracy and Local*

Self-Government, 1861–1890 (Cambridge, 1989), 164–209, and "The Origins of Alexander III's Land Captains: A Reinterpretation," *Slavic Review* 40 (Fall 1981): 384–403, which challenges the notion of a noble reaction; George Yaney, *The Urge to Mobilize: Agrarian Reform in Russia, 1861–1930* (Urbana, IL, 1982), 49–143; Mandel, "Paternalistic Authority in the Russian Countryside," 178–385; Corinne Gaudin, "Les Zemskie načal'niki au village: Coutumes administratives et culture paysanne en Russie 1889–1914," *Cahiers du Monde Russe* 36 (July-Sept. 1995): 249–72; David A. J. Macey, "The Land Captains: A Note on their Social Composition, 1889–1913," *Russian History/Istoire Russe* 16 (1989), nos. 2–4:327–51; and A. A. Liberman, "Sostav instituta zemskikh nachal'nikov," *Voprosy istorii,* 1974, no. 8, 201–4.

58. On persistent but unsuccessful efforts to "reform" Russian village life, see Yaney, *The Urge to Mobilize;* Francis William Wcislo, *Reforming Rural Russia: State, Local Society, and National Politics, 1855–1914* (Princeton, NJ, 1990); Macey, *Government and Peasant in Russia;* Pearson, *Russian Officialdom in Crisis;* and Mandel, "Paternalistic Authority in the Russian Countryside." This reform impulse was closely linked to a new interest in peasant life and character that led to a variety of ethnographical and economic surveys; for the results of two such surveys, the first co-sponsored by the Free Economic Society and the Russian Geographic Society in the late 1870s and the second conducted by the Ethnographic Bureau in the 1890s, see *Dokumenty po istorii krest'ianskoi obshchiny 1861–1880 gg.* (Moscow, 1983); and B. M. Firsov and I. G. Kiseleva, eds., *Byt velikorusskikh krest'ian-zemlepashtsev: Opisanie materialov etnograficheskogo biuro kniazia V. N. Tenisheva (na primera Vladimirskoi gubernii)* (St. Petersburg, 1993). On varied and changing perceptions of Russian peasants, see Cathy A. Frierson, *Peasant Icons: Representations of Rural People in Late Nineteenth-Century Russia* (New York, 1993).

59. For the challenge by Western scholars to the traditional view that most peasants faced increasing hardship, poverty, and exploitation, see James Y. Simms, Jr., "The Crisis in Russian Agriculture at the End of the Nineteenth Century: A Different View," *Slavic Review* 36 (Sept. 1977): 377–98; Elvira M. Wilbur, "Was Russian Peasant Agriculture Really That Impoverished? New Evidence from a Case Study from the 'Impoverished Center' at the End of the Nineteenth Century," *Journal of Economic History* 43 (Mar. 1983): 137–44; Stephen G. Wheatcroft, "Crisis and the Condition of the Peasantry in Late Imperial Russia," in Kingston-Mann and Mixter, eds., *Peasant Economy, Culture, and Politics of European Russia,* 128–72; and Steven L. Hoch, "On Good Numbers and Bad: Malthus, Population Trends and Peasant Standard of Living in Late Imperial Russia," *Slavic Review* 53 (Spring 1994): 41–75. But for a very different view, see Shanin, *Russia as a "Developing Society,"* 140–49.

60. I have developed this theme, from somewhat different perspectives, in two essays: "Some Thoughts on Emancipation in Comparative Perspec-

tive," esp. 359–66; and "The Tragic Era? Interpreting Southern Reconstruction in Comparative Perspective," in Frank McGlynn and Seymour
Drescher, eds., *The Meaning of Freedom: Economics, Politics, and Culture after Slavery* (Pittsburgh, PA, 1992), 291–311.

61. Kolchin, "The Tragic Era?," 291–94. The quotation is from Frederick Law Olmsted, *The Cotton Kingdom: A Traveller's Observations on
Cotton and Slavery in the American Slave States* (New York, 1861),
1:106. Many southern blacks became convinced that there would be a
general redistribution of land on Christmas, 1865 or New Year's day,
1866, a conviction that in turn gave birth to widespread fears among
southern whites that the freedpeople were planning a massive uprising.
See Dan T. Carter, "The Anatomy of Fear: The Christmas Day Insurrection Scare of 1865," *Journal of Southern History* 42 (August 1976): 345–64;
and Steven Hahn, "'Extravagant Expectations' of Freedom: Rumour, Political Struggle, and the Christmas Insurrection Scare of 1865 in the
American South," *Past & Present* 157 (Nov. 1997): 122–58.

62. In the latest comprehensive survey of Reconstruction, Eric Foner
notes that "the term 'revolution' has reappeared in the most recent literature as a way of describing the Civil War and Reconstruction" and concludes that "like a massive earthquake, the Civil War and the destruction
of slavery permanently altered the landscape of Southern life." Eric Foner,
Reconstruction: America's Unfinished Revolution, 1863–1877 (New York,
1988), xxiv, 11. On transformation as a theme in the history of Russian
emancipation, see many of the sources cited above in notes 29, 32, 35, 36,
38, 39, 40, and 41.

63. Wallace, *Russia on the Eve of War and Revolution*, 338–39; Leroy-
Beaulieu, *The Empire of the Tsars and the Russians* 1:450–52.

64. Aleksandr Nikitenko, *The Diary of a Russian Censor*, abr., ed., and
trans. Helen Saltz Jacobson (Amherst, MA, 1975), 344–45 (Feb. 4, 1871),
281 (Mar. 16, 1864), 345 (Feb. 4, 1871), 357 (Jan. 14, 1873), 367 (Jan. 20,
1875), 361 (Aug. 2, 1873), 360 (July 14, 1873).

65. On the southern freedpeople's preference for sharecropping over
wage labor, see Peter Kolchin, *First Freedom: The Responses of Alabama's
Blacks to Emancipation and Reconstruction* (Westport, CT, 1972), 30–55;
Ralph Shlomowitz, "The Origins of Southern Sharecropping," *Agricultural History* 53 (July 1979): 557–75; Gerald David Jaynes, *Branches Without Roots: Genesis of the Black Working Class in the American South,
1862–1882* (New York, 1986), 141–90; and Lynda J. Morgan, *Emancipation
in Virginia's Tobacco Belt, 1850–1870* (Athens, GA, 1992), 187–96. On the
Jamaican freedpeople's flight from the plantations, see Holt, *The Problem
of Freedom*, 115–76. The behavior of the Jamaican freedpeople proved so
troubling to British abolitionists that, in David Brion Davis's words, they
"could not conceal their disappointment or hide their fear that blacks
were somehow predisposed to the cardinal sin of idleness"; Davis, *Slavery
and Human Progress*, 226.

CHAPTER 4

I am most grateful to Peter Coclanis for his encyclopedic grasp of references; to my fellow authors and colleagues on the Terms of Labor project—with special acknowledgment to Amy Dru Stanley, Robert Steinfeld, David Roediger, David Brody, and David Montgomery—for their searching criticisms and suggestions; and to Susan Levine, as ever, for her editorial judgment.

1. Evsey D. Domar, "The Causes of Slavery or Serfdom: A Hypothesis," *The Journal of Economic History* 30 (Mar. 1970): 18–32.

2. See, e.g., David Brion Davis, *Slavery and Human Progress* (New York, 1984), 11.

3. Joseph Dorfman, *The Economic Mind in American Civilization: 1606–1865* 1 (New York, 1946): 404–9, 426.

4. Ibid., 185–86.

5. Ibid., 456–59; on the outlines of classical liberalism and individualism, firmly elaborated by the close of the eighteenth century, see E. J. Hobsbawm, *The Age of Revolution, 1789–1848* (New York, 1962), 278–84.

6. Garrett Ward Sheldon, *The Political Philosophy of Thomas Jefferson* (Baltimore, 1991), 72–78. In his "Proposed Constitution for Virginia" (1776), Jefferson stipulated a minimum appropriation of fifty acres to "every person of full age" (Sheldon, *Political Philosophy*, 74).

7. David Brion Davis, *The Problem of Slavery in Western Culture* (Ithaca, NY, 1966), 445.

8. Gordon S. Wood, *The Radicalism of the American Revolution* (New York, 1991), 171.

9. Billy G. Smith, *The "Lower Sort": Philadelphia's Laboring People, 1750–1800* (Ithaca, NY, 1990), 7

10. Wood, *Radicalism*, 277.

11. Michael Merrill and Sean Wilentz, eds., *The Key of Liberty: The Life and Democratic Writings of William Manning, "A Laborer," 1747–1814* (Cambridge, MA, 1993).

12. Wood, *Radicalism*, 283–85, quotation 285.

13. Jonathan A. Glickstein, *Concepts of Free Labor in Antebellum America* (New Haven, CT, 1991), 2.

14. Robert J. Steinfeld, *The Invention of Free Labor: The Employment Relationship in English and American Law and Culture, 1350–1870* (Chapel Hill, NC, 1991), 147–72, 185–87, quotation 156.

15. Glickstein, *Free Labor*, 9.

16. Ibid., 32.

17. Ibid., 55; Alexis de Tocqueville would draw on a similar logic in warning of the effects of manufacturing on the worker: "it may be said of him that in proportion as the workman improves, the man is degraded . . . The master and the workman have then here no similarity, and their differences increase every day . . . the one is continually, closely, and necessarily dependent upon the other and seems as much born to obey as that

other is to command. What is this but aristocracy?" *Democracy in America* 2 (New York, 1945): 168–69.

18. Glickstein, *Free Labor*, 70, 92.

19. Eric Foner, *Free Soil, Free Labor, Free Men: The Ideology of the Republican Party Before the Civil War* (New York, 1970), 11–13.

20. Ibid., 17.

21. Ibid., 23.

22. Eugene D. Genovese, *The World the Slaveholders Made: Two Essays in Interpretation* (New York, 1969), 118–31, 165–94. As Fitzhugh said: "A half million died of hunger in one year in Ireland—they died because in the eye of the law they were the equals, and liberty had made them the enemies, of their landlords and employers. Had they been vassals or serfs, they would have been beloved, cherished and taken care of by those same landlords and employers." From Fitzhugh, *Slavery Justified, by a Southerner*, 1850, as quoted in Eric L. McKitrick, ed., *Slavery Defended: The Views of the Old South* (Englewood Cliffs, NJ, 1963), 38.

23. Glickstein, *Free Labor*, 666.

24. Ibid., 19, 145; For elaboration on Herrenvolk democracy, see George M. Fredrickson, *The Black Image in the White Mind: The Debate on Afro-American Character and Destiny, 1817–1914* (New York, 1971).

25. Byllesby, as quoted in Sean Wilentz, *Chants Democratic: New York City and the Rise of the American Working Class, 1788–1850* (New York, 1984), 165 and passim, 145–71.

26. Glickstein, *Free Labor*, 123–30. Nathaniel Hawthorne, for one, was notably unconvinced by Brook Farm's "ascetic utopianism": "A man's soul," he said, "may be buried and perish under a dung-heap or in a furrow of the field, just as well as under a pile of money." Glickstein, 134.

27. Ibid., 101; Dorfman, *Economic Mind* 2 (New York, 1946): 635.

28. Wilentz, *Chants Democratic*, 242.

29. David R. Roediger, *The Wages of Whiteness: Race and the Making of the American Working Class* (New York, 1991), 46–47, 72–73, 144–45.

30. Jeanne Boydston, *Home and Work: Housework, Wages, and the Ideology of Labor in the Early Republic* (New York, 1990), 99, 154–55.

31. Glickstein, *Free Labor*, 182; Boydston, *Home and Work*, 162–63.

32. Eric Foner, *Reconstruction: America's Unfinished Revolution, 1863–1877* (New York, 1988), 103–4.

33. William E. Forbath, "The Ambiguities of Free Labor: Labor and the Law in the Gilded Age," *Wisconsin Law Review*, 1985, 767–817, quotation 768–69.

34. Ibid., 773–80.

35. Andrew Carnegie, *Triumphant Democracy* [1885], as quoted in Leon Fink, ed., *Major Problems in the Gilded Age and the Progressive Era* (New York, 1993), 2.

36. Rev. Alexander Lewis, *Manhood-Making: Studies in the Elemental Principles of Success* (1902), quoted in Fink, *Major Problems*, 9. For elabo-

ration on this theme, see Judy Hilkey, *Character Is Capital: Success Manuals and Manhood in Gilded Age America* (Chapel Hill, NC, 1997).

37. David Montgomery, *Beyond Equality: Labor and the Radical Republicans, 1862–1872* (New York, 1967), 30.

38. See, e.g., Chester McArthur Destler, *American Radicalism, 1865–1901* (Chicago, 1966).

39. Henry George, *Progress and Poverty* as quoted in Leon Fink, ed., *Major Problems*, 7.

40. Garrison as quoted in Dorfman, *Economic Mind* 3:147.

41. Omaha Platform of the People's Party of America, as reprinted in Fink, *Major Problems*, 183.

42. Leon Fink, *Workingmen's Democracy: The Knights of Labor and American Politics* (Urbana, IL, 1983), 7.

43. W. Fitzhugh Brundage, *A Socialist Utopia in the New South: The Ruskin Colonies in Tennessee and Georgia, 1894–1901* (Urbana, IL, 1996), 7–19. The Ruskin colonists, who were each paid the same for a day's labor, substituted labor certificates representing "crystallized labor time in goods" for "the kind of money the capitalist system requires, the kind that BREEDS and enslaves the human race" (110–11).

44. Montgomery, *Beyond Equality*, 238–39.

45. Philip S. Foner, *American Labor Songs of the Nineteenth Century* (Urbana, IL, 1975), 222–24; Roy Rosenzweig, *Eight Hours For What We Will: Workers and Leisure in an Industrial City, 1870–1920* (New York, 1983), 1.

46. Gompers and Haywood as cited in Daniel T. Rogers, *The Work Ethic in Industrial America: 1850–1920* (Chicago, 1978), 156. To be sure, even within organized labor circles, the movement for the universal eight-hour day based on claims of free citizenship did not receive unanimous support. P. M. Arthur, head of the Brotherhood of Locomotive Firemen, for example, denounced the campaign as a demand for "two hours more loafing about the corners and two hours more for drink." Cited in Rogers, *Work Ethic*, 158.

47. Dorfman, *Economic Mind* 3:160–88; Leon Fink, "'Intellectuals' versus 'Workers': Academic Requirements and the Creation of Labor History," *American Historical Review* 96 (Apr. 1991): 395–421.

48. Ely as quoted in Fink, "Intellectuals," 399.

49. Adams (1886) as quoted in Dorfman, *Economic Mind* 3:166–67.

50. Dorfman, *Economic Mind* 3:167.

51. Mary O. Furner, "Social Scientists and the State: Constructing the Knowledge Base for Public Policy, 1880–1920," in *Intellectuals and Public Life: Between Radicalism and Reform*, ed. Leon Fink, Stephen T. Leonard, and Donald M. Reid (Ithaca, NY, 1996), 145–81.

52. Patten, as quoted in Dorfman, *Economic Mind* 3: 184–85.

53. Furner, "Social Scientists," 162.

54. Kathryn Kish Sklar, *Florence Kelley and the Nation's Work: The Rise of Women's Political Culture, 1830–1900* (New Haven, CT, 1995), 258.

55. Steward as quoted in Rogers, *Work Ethic*, 159–60.

56. Gunton as quoted in Dorfman, *Economic Mind* 3: 127. On Gunton and consumer strategies, see Daniel Horowitz, *The Morality of Spending: Attitudes Toward Consumer Society in America, 1875–1940* (Baltimore, 1985), 30–49.

57. Text of NLRA as quoted in Charles J. Morris, ed., *The Developing Labor Law: The Board, the Courts, and the National Labor Relations Act* (Washington D.C., 1971), app. A, 895.

58. William Leach, *Land of Desire: Merchants, Power, and the Rise of a New American Culture* (New York, 1993), 231–44, quotation 237.

59. William Serrin, *Homestead: The Glory and Tragedy of an American Steel Town* (New York, 1992), 304.

60. Haywood, as quoted in Leach, *Land of Desire*, 189.

61. David Montgomery, *Workers' Control in America: Studies in the History of Work, Technology, and Labor Struggles* (New York, 1979), 98.

62. Ibid., 102.

63. Jacquelyn Dowd Hall, "Disorderly Women: Gender and Labor Militancy in the Appalachian South," in Ellen Carol DuBois and Vicki L. Ruiz, eds., *Unequal Sisters: A Multi-Cultural Reader in U.S. Women's History* (New York, 1990), 303.

64. Lewis quoted in Serrin, *Homestead*, 205.

65. Paul Krause, *The Battle for Homestead, 1880–1892: Politics, Culture, and Steel* (Pittsburgh, 1992), 215–26, quotation 220.

66. Daniel J. Clark, *Like Night & Day: Unionization in a Southern Mill Town* (Chapel Hill, NC, 1997).

67. Charlotte, NC, *Observer*, May 13, 1995.

CHAPTER 5

1. *United States v. Shackney*, 333 F.2d 475 (1964), 476.

2. Ibid., 477.   3. Ibid., 478.

4. Ibid., 479–80.   5. Ibid., 485–86.

6. Ibid., 486.

7. See *United States v. Ingalls*, 73 F. Supp. 76 (S.D. Calif., 1947).

8. *United States v. Shackney*, 333 F.2d 475 (1964), n. 17.

9. Ibid., 486.

10. Ibid., 487. Friendly did say, however, that "if something was sought or obtained for withdrawing such a threat [the threat of deportation], the maker could be successfully prosecuted under state blackmail or extortion statutes" (486). In this case, of course, something was obtained for withdrawing the threat, labor services. The distinction between an employer "extorting labor services," which would also bring the "awful machinery of the criminal law" into play against him, and "coercing" another into "involuntarily" laboring for him is not altogether clear to me.

11. Ibid., 487.

12. Ibid., 487.

13. *Union Pacific Ry. Co. v. Public Service Commission*, 248 U.S. 67 (1918), 70.

14. John Dawson, "Economic Duress—An Essay in Perspective," *Michigan Law Review* 45 (1947): 267.

15. *United States v. Kozminski*, 487 U.S. 931 (1987), 935.

16. Ibid., 944.

17. Ibid., 947–48.

18. Justice Brennan's concurring opinion makes this point forcefully. "Although it is heartening that the Court recognizes that strange environs and the lack of money, maturity, education, or family support can establish the coercion necessary for involuntary servitude, labeling such coercion 'physical' is at best strained and (other than making the legislative history fit the Court's statutory interpretation) accomplishes little but the elimination of whatever certainty the 'physical or legal coercion' test would otherwise provide" (ibid., 958 n. 5).

19. Ibid., 948.

20. She quotes from the same language in Friendly's opinion that we quote above, ibid., 950.

21. Ibid., 959 (concurring opinion of Justice Brennan).

22. "My reading of the statutory language as not limited to physical or legal coercion is strongly bolstered by the legislative history" (ibid., 957; concurring opinion of Justice Brennan).

23. Ibid., 959 (concurring opinion of Justice Brennan).

24. Ibid., 960 (concurring opinion of Justice Brennan).

25. Ibid., 961 (concurring opinion of Justice Brennan).

26. Ibid., 962–63 (concurring opinion of Justice Brennan).

27. Ibid., 950–51.

28. Though it is obviously a matter of some controversy, I use the term "European" here as including "British."

29. Thomas Haskell, "Capitalism and the Humanitarian Sensibility, pt. 2," *The American Historical Review* 90 (1985): 553–55. In certain cases penalties for contract breach did become more severe in the eighteenth century. In England, maximum penalties for contract breach by certain categories of workers were increased from one month's imprisonment in the sixteenth century to three months' imprisonment in the eighteenth century. But I think that in general the term "important" would be more accurate than the term "severe."

30. Douglass C. North, *Institutions, Institutional Change and Economic Performance* (Cambridge, 1990), 33–35.

31. See, for example, James Edward Davis, *The Master and Servant Act, 1867* (London, 1868), 7.

32. *Gesetzsammlung für die Königlichen Preußischen Staaten 1845* (hereafter *PGS*), "Gewerbeordnung," 41–78. Freedom of trade, however, was repealed four years later in 1849, and not reestablished in Prussia until the Industrial Law of 1869, enacted by the North German Confederation.

33. *PGS*, "Gewerbeordnung," §§ 134, 145.

34. Ibid., § 184.

35. *Bundesgesetzblatt des Norddeutschen Bundes, 1869,* "Gewerbeordnung," no. 26, 245–82, § 154.

36. See, for example, 4 Geo. IV., c. 34, § III (1823).

37. Sidney and Beatrice Webb, *The History of Trade Unionism* (London, 1920), 250–51 n. 2.

38. *Judicial Statistics, England and Wales,* 19 vols. (London, 1858–76); see also Daphne Simon, "Master and Servant," in John Saville, ed., *Democracy and the Labour Movement* (London, 1954), 186 n. 2.

39. F. M. L. Thompson, *The Rise of Respectable Society, A Social History of Victorian Britain, 1830–1900* (London, 1988), 31.

40. *Select Committee on Master and Servant,* 1866, XIII, Qs.1379–81, 1408, Simon, "Master and Servant," 194.

41. The Reform Act of 1867 extended the suffrage to many town artisans.

42. Frederic Harrison, "Tracts for Trade Unionists—No.I," in Edmund Frow & Michael Katanka, eds., *1868, Year of the Unions: A Documentary Survey* (New York, 1968), 141–42.

43. Fry (Lord Justice), in *De Francesco v. Barnum,* 45 Ch. D. 430 (1890), 438.

44. The Northwest Ordinance of 1787, Article VI.

45. Richard Morris has argued that the practice of criminally enforcing the labor agreements of white adult hired workers continued in at least one slave state, Maryland, up until the 1830s or 40s, though his evidence would appear to be inconclusive. See Richard Morris, "Labor Controls in Maryland in the Nineteenth Century," *The Journal of Southern History* 14 (1948): 391–92.

46. Massachusetts, Rhode Island, Virginia, North and South Carolina, and Maryland were among the colonies in which there is evidence that "hired servants" could be compelled to perform their agreements; see Robert Steinfeld, *The Invention Of Free Labor* (Chapel Hill, NC, 1991), 47–51.

47. 1 Ill. (Breese) 268 (1828).

48. Ibid. See also the concurring opinion of Justice Thomas in *Sarah, a woman of color v. Borders,* 4 Scam. 341 (Ill., 1843), 347.

49. 1 Ill. (Breese) 268 (1828).

50. Ibid., 269.

51. Ibid., 270.

52. *The Case of Mary Clark, a woman of color,* 1 Blackf. 122 (Ind., 1821), 123.

53. Ibid., 126.

54. On this contradiction, see Guyora Binder, "Substantive Liberty and the Legacy of the Fuller Court" (unpub. ms. in author's possession), § VI. (30.); and Frank H. Knight, *Freedom & Reform: Essays in Economics and Social Philosphy* (Indianapolis, 1982), 78–79.

55. *Parsons v. Trask,* 73 Mass. (7 Gray) 473 (1856), 478.

56. *Jaremillo v. Romero,* 1 N.M. 190 (1857). The territorial legislature

had enacted a series of statutes which criminalized the breach of certain "voluntary" labor agreements.

57. Eric Foner, *Reconstruction, America's Unfinished Revolution, 1863–1877* (New York, 1988), 55, 166–67. Later Reconstruction governments, however, which embraced the more common northern conception of free labor, resisted the pressure of planters who wanted legislation enacted to enforce the performance of labor contracts, 372–73. But when Reconstruction ended, many Southern states began cautiously to enact contract enforcement laws.

58. *Robertson v. Baldwin*, 165 U.S. 275 (1896), 280–81.

59. Ibid., 282.

60. Ibid., 301.

61. Ibid., 302–3.

62. William Cohen, *At Freedom's Edge: Black Mobility and the Southern White Quest for Racial Control, 1861–1915* (Baton Rouge, LA, 1991), 28–37; see also Foner, *Reconstruction*, 199–200. When they attempted to justify these laws in the face of this northern reaction, some southerners pointed out that they "had been modeled on army and Freedmen's Bureau labor regulations" (Foner, *Reconstruction*, 208).

63. Southern legislatures also framed these statutes as false pretense statutes in many cases, it seems, to circumvent state constitutional prohibitions on imprisonment for debt.

64. *State v. Williams*, 32 S.C. 123 (1889), 126.

65. Hyman Weintraub, *Andrew Furuseth, Emancipator of the Seamen* (Berkeley, 1959), 35.

66. Quoted ibid., 35.

67. Ibid., 43.

68. Ibid., 120–21, 134.

69. *Clyatt v. United States*, 197 U.S. 207 (1905), 215.

70. Ibid., 216.

71. *Bailey v. Alabama*, 219 U.S. 219 (1911), 243.

72. *General Laws of Minnesota for 1901*, chap. 165, 212–13.

73. *Michigan Compiled Laws*, §§ 408.582–408.583.

74. *The Revised Statutes of Maine* (1917), chap. 128, § 12.

75. John Clifton Elder, "Peonage in Maine," a manuscript report sent to the Attorney General of U.S., National Archives, Record Group #60 Dept. of Justice File # 50–34–0, p. 13.

76. *Bailey v. Alabama*, 219 U.S. 219 (1911), 245–46.

77. Ibid., 246–47. In *The Common Law* (Boston, 1881) published 30 years earlier, Holmes had argued just the opposite, that the availability of money damages as a sole remedy for most contract breaches saved labor contracts from becoming contracts of servitude.

78. *Clyatt v. United States*, 197 U.S. 207 (1905), 215–16.

79. See Binder, "Substantive Liberty," VI (30); and Knight, *Freedom and Reform*, 78–79.

80. *Phoebe v. Jay*, 1 Ill. (Breese) 268 (1828), 270.

81. *Holden v. Hardy*, 169 U.S. 366 (1898), 380.
82. Ibid., 367.
83. Ibid.
84. Ibid., 397.
85. *Vernon v. Bethell*, 2 Eden 110 (1762), 113.
86. *Frorer v. People*, 141 Ill. 171 (1892).
87. *Lochner v. New York*, 198 U.S. 45 (1905), 52.
88. *Coppage v. Kansas*, 236 U.S. 1 (1915), 6.
89. Ibid., 8–9.
90. Ibid., 9.
91. Ibid., 17.
92. This was pointed out by Robert Hale many years ago in *Freedom Through Law* (New York, 1952), 72–73.
93. *Hitchman Coal & Coke v. Mitchell*, 245 U.S. 229 (1917), 248.
94. *Coppage v. Kansas*, 236 U.S. 1 (1915), 38–39 (Day and Hughes dissenting).
95. *Hitchman Coal & Coke v. Mitchell*, 245 U.S. 229 (1917), 271 (Brandeis dissenting).

CHAPTER 6

1. Thanks to Tiya Miles, Deirdre Murphy, and Gaye Johnson for assistance with this chapter and to Richard Davis, Stanley Engerman, Douglass North, Robert Gallman, David Montgomery, Amy Dru Stanley, Seymour Drescher, Robert Steinfeld, and Leon Fink for friendly criticisms.
2. Barry Goldberg, "'Wage Slaves' and White 'Niggers'," *New Politics*, 2d ser., 3 (Summer, 1991): 68.
3. David Brion Davis, *The Problem of Slavery in Western Culture* (Ithaca, NY, 1966), 90.
4. Goldberg, "'Wage Slaves,'" 68; Jonathan A. Glickstein, *Concepts of Free Labor in Antebellum America* (New Haven, CT, 1991), 208 and 445.
5. I have been most influenced by the use of "simultaneity" in drafts of Tera Hunter's *To 'Joy My Freedom: Southern Black Women's Lives and Labors After the Civil War* (Cambridge, MA, 1997); see also Rose Brewer, "Theorizing Race, Class and Gender: The New Scholarship of Black Feminist Intellectuals and Black Women's Labor," in Abena Busia and Stanlie James, eds., *Theorizing Black Feminisms: The Visionary Pragmatism of Black Women* (London, 1993), 16.
6. David Brion Davis, "Reflections on Abolitionism and Ideological Hegemony," in Thomas Bender, ed., *The Antislavery Debate: Capitalism and Abolitionism as a Problem in Historical Interpretation* (Berkeley, 1992), 162.
7. Blanche Glassman Hersh, "'Am I Not a Woman and a Sister?' Abolitionist Beginnings of Nineteenth-Century Feminism," in Lewis Perry and Michael Fellman, eds., *Antislavery Reconsidered: New Perspectives on the Abolitionists* (Baton Rouge, LA, 1979), 252. See also Hersh, *The Slav-*

ery of Sex: Feminist-Abolitionists in America (Urbana, IL, 1978); on the labor-abolitionist front, see Philip S. Foner, *History of the Labor Movement in the United States*, 10 vols. (New York, 1947–19), 1:273; Marcus Cunliffe, *Chattel Slavery and Wage Slavery: The Anglo-American Context, 1830–1860* (Athens, GA, 1979), 27; Goldberg, "'Wage Slaves'," 67.

8. Ellen DuBois, *Feminism and Suffrage: The Emergence of an Independent Woman's Suffrage Movement in America* (Ithaca, NY, 1978); Amy Dru Stanley, "Conjugal Bonds and Wage Labor: Rights of Contract in the Age of Emancipation," *Journal of American History* 75 (Dec. 1988): 471–500; Timothy Messer-Kruse, "The Yankee International: Marxism and the American Reform Tradition" (Ph.D. diss., Univ. of Wis.-Madison, 1994).

9. Davis, "Abolitionism and Ideological Hegemony," in Bender, ed., *The Antislavery Debate*, 173.

10. William S. McFeely, *Frederick Douglass* (New York, 1991), 140–41; Frederick Douglass, *Narrative of the life of Frederick Douglass, An American Slave* (New York, 1986, originally 1845), 56–57.

11. "Address of the New York State Convention to Their Colored Fellow Citizens," *Colored American*, Nov. 21, 1840; "An Appeal to the Colored Citizens of Pennsylvania," repr. in Philip S. Foner and George E. Walker, eds., *Proceedings of Black State Conventions, 1840–1865*, 2 vols. (Philadelphia, 1979), 1:126–27. See also 1:234 for an 1850 Ohio convention's opposition to "iron manacles for the slave [and] unjust written manacles for the free." For Uriah Boston's December 1855 letter to Douglass, see C. Peter Ripley, ed., *The Black Abolitionist Papers*, 5 vols. (Chapel Hill, NC, 1985–92), 4:323–25.

12. Philip S. Foner and Ronald L. Lewis, eds., *Black Workers: A Documentary History from Colonial Times to the Present* (Philadelphia, 1989), 112–14 and 122. See also "The Objects of the African Civilization Society" (1859) in Sterling Stuckey, ed., *The Ideological Origins of Black Nationalism* (Boston, 1972), 182. For the contrary and unsupported view that "As for the Negro workers, there was little question in their minds or anyone else's that there was little to choose between their conditions and those of slaves," see Bernard Mandel's often valuable *Labor: Free and Slave* (New York, 1955), 228.

13. C. L. R. James, "The Atlantic Slave Trade and Slavery: Some Interpretations of Their Significance in the Development of the United States and the Western World," in John R. Williams and Charles Harris, eds., *Amistad 1* (New York, 1970): 142. See also John Ashworth, *Slavery, Capitalism and Politics in the Antebellum Republic 1* (Cambridge, 1995): 4; and for a recent analysis resembling James's in its conclusions and its Hegelianism, Leonard Cassuto, "Frederick Douglass and the Work of Freedom: Hegel's Master-Slave Dialectic in the Fugitive Slave Narrative," *Prospects: An Annual of American Cultural Studies* 21 (1996), esp. 248–49.

14. Douglass, in his speech to the 1855 Negro convention in Troy, New York, as reprinted in Foner and Walker, eds., *Black State Conventions*

1:95. Douglass held to this sharp demarcation after slavery as well. See his "My Escape to Freedom," *Century Magazine* 23 (Nov. 1881): 125–31. For a fuller account of Douglass and free labor, see David Roediger, "Why Douglass Knew: An Afterword" in Roediger and Martin Blatt, eds., *The Meaning of Slavery in the North* (forthcoming).

15. For the 1850 letter, see Foner and Walker, eds., *Black State Conventions* 1:44–50; Jacobs, *Incident in the Life of a Slave Girl* (New York, 1988, originally 1861), 290; see also Philip S. Foner and Ronald L. Lewis, eds., *The Black Worker: A Documentary History from Colonial Times to the Present*, 8 vols. (Philadelphia, 1978–84), 1:182–83; Foner and Walker, eds., *Black State Conventions* 2:97 and 103. Douglass himself acknowledged his continuing liability to reenslavement by allowing friends to buy his freedom, while he was in Britain and contemplating return to the North in the United States in 1846. See Philip S. Foner, ed., *The Life and Writings of Frederick Douglass*, 5 vols. (New York, 1950–75), 1:72–73.

16. The quotes as well as the account are from McFeely, *Douglass*, 104–8, except "mere dabbling with effects," which is from Davis, "Abolitionism and Ideological Hegemony," in Bender, ed., *The Antislavery Debate*, 173.

17. McFeely, *Douglass*, 141 on "metaphoric uses"; David Roediger, *The Wages of Whiteness: Race and the Making of the American Working Class* (New York, 1991), 65–77; Cunliffe, *Chattel Slavery and Wage Slavery*, 16–17.

18. The "Down with all slavery, both chattel and wages" phrasing is a formulation of the land reformer William West, a supporter of George Henry Evans. See Eric Foner, "Abolition and the Labor Movement in Antebellum America," in id., *Politics and Ideology in the Age of the Civil War* (New York, 1980), 70–72; Philip S. Foner and Herbert Shapiro, eds., *Northern Labor and Antislavery: A Documentary History* (Westport, CT, 1994), 19; Davis, "Abolitionism and Ideological Hegemony," in *Antislavery Debate*, 133; Noel Ignatiev, *How the Irish Became White* (New York, 1995), 79–83.

19. *The Liberator*, July 9, 1847.

20. Douglass, *My Bondage and My Freedom* (Chicago, 1970, originally 1855), 76; "Douglass to Friend Garrison," Feb. 26, 1846, repr. in Foner, ed., *Life and Writings* 1:138–42; Douglass, *Narrative*, 83–84. On abolitionism and Irish Americans, see Ignatiev, *Irish Became White*, 8–31; Gilbert Osofsky, "Abolitionists, Irish Immigrants and the Dilemmas of Romantic Nationalism," *American Historical Review* 80 (Oct. 1975): 889–906.

21. John W. Blassingame et al., eds., *The Frederick Douglass Papers: Speeches, Debates and Interviews*, ser. 1, 5 vols. (New Haven, CT, 1982), 3:139; Ignatiev, *Irish Became White*, 9; Foner, ed., *Life and Writings* 4:266–67. See also, however, Blassingame et al., eds., *Douglass Papers* 5:275–78 and 367–68.

22. Quotations from Blassingame et al., eds., *Douglass Papers* 2:258–59; Jacobs, *Incidents*, 49. See also ibid. 2:293 for an Irish/free Black compari-

son. Foner and Shapiro, eds., *Northern Labor and Antislavery*, 10–13 and 22–24.

23. Foner, ed., *Life and Writings* 1:188; Blassingame et al., eds., *Douglass Papers* 2:307.

24. Waldo Martin, *The Mind of Frederick Douglass* (Chapel Hill, NC, 1984), 127; Herbert Aptheker, *Abolitionism: A Revolutionary Movement* (Boston, 1989), 36 and 43; Phillips, "The Question of Labor," *The Liberator*, July 9, 1847, as repr. in Foner and Shapiro, eds., *Northern Labor and Antislavery*, 6–7. Garrison is quoted in Messer-Kruse, "The Yankee International," 64–65.

25. On abolitionist interest in "Saxon slavery" and other historical examples of white bondage, see Daniel J. McInerney, *The Fortunate Heirs of Freedom: Abolition and the Republican Thought* (Lincoln, NE, 1994), 40–42; and Mia Bay's impressive *The White Image in the Black Mind* (forthcoming); Frederick Douglass, *My Bondage and My Freedom* (Chicago, 1970, originally 1855), 162; Martin, *Mind of Frederick Douglass*, 128; William and Ellen Craft, *Running a Thousand Miles for Freedom* (New York, 1969, originally 1860), 4–7.

26. Eric Foner, "Workers and Slavery," in Paul Buhle and Alan Dawley, eds., *Working for Democracy: American Workers from the Revolution to the Present* (Urbana, IL, 1985), 23; Eric Lott, *Love and Theft: Blackface Minstrelsy and the American Working Class* (Oxford, 1993), 200; Alan Dawley, *Class and Community: The Industrial Revolution in Lynn* (Cambridge, MA, 1976), 65. When Foner writes that the early labor movement's values were "obviously incompatible with the institution of slavery," the assumption is that defense of white privilege was not such a central value. On Britain, see esp. Seymour Drescher, "Cart Whip and Billy Roller: Antislavery and Reform Symbolism in Industrializing Briain," *Journal of Social History* 15 (Sept. 1981): 3–24.

27. *Voice of Industry*, May 7, 1847 and Sept. 25, 1847; Foner and Shapiro, eds., *Northern Labor and Antislavery*, 213; Philip S. Foner, ed., *The Factory Girls* (Urbana, IL, 1977), 279–81; for the Lynn quotes, Mary H. Blewett, *Men, Women, and Work: Class, Gender, and Protest in the New England Shoe Industry, 1780–1910* (Urbana, IL, 1988), 132, and Foner, *Labor Movement* 1:274. Clearly some labor organizations took the form of their appeals from abolitionism. See Philip S. Foner, ed., *American Labor Songs of the Nineteenth Century* (Urbana, IL, 1975), 68–69; Foner and Shapiro, eds., *Northern Labor and Antislavery*, xiv. For the British case, see Drescher, "Cart Whip and Billy Roller," 3–24. The emphasis in the United States on voting as differentiating white workers from slaves recurs interestingly. It unfolds in a context in which suffrage reformers had prevailed in early- and middle-nineteenth century campaigns to extend voting rights to propertyless adult white males by arguing that dependence inhered in "natural" categories of gender, age, and race rather than in non-possession of property. Such arguments clearly existed in considerable tension with ideas about wage slavery, which implied that the adult

white males without property were dependent. See Robert Steinfeld, "Property and Suffrage in the Early American Republic," *Stanford Law Review* 41 (Jan. 1989): 335–76.

28. Aptheker, *Abolitionism*, 35–49; Edward Magdol, *The Anti-Slavery Rank and File: A Social Profile of the Abolitionist Constituency* (Westport, CT, 1986); Bruce Levine, *The Spirit of 1848: German Immigrants, Labor and the Coming of the Civil War* (Urbana, IL, 1992), esp. 149–51 and 187–88; John Jentz, "Artisans, Evangelicals and the City: A Social History of Abolition and the Labor Movement" (Ph.D. diss., CUNY, 1977); Foner, "Abolitionism and the Labor Movement," 72. The support of *organized* labor's rank and file for abolition remains difficult to gauge. Anecdotal and statistical evidence, the latter mainly from analyses of petition signatures, shows a strong artisan base with some factory worker support. But it is possible that these signatures came as much or more from workers disinclined to unionism. See Roediger, *Wages of Whiteness*, 80–87. More broadly on abolition and the working class, see Betty Fladeland, *Abolitionists and the Working Class Problems in the Era on Industrialization* (Baton Rouge, LA, 1984); and Robin Blackburn, *The Overthrow of Colonial Slavery, 1776–1848* (London, 1988).

29. Foner and Shapiro, eds., *Northern Labor and Antislavery*, 147 and 213; Foner, "Workers and Slavery," 22; Ignatiev, *Irish Became White*, 79.

30. Douglass, *Narrative*, 138–40 and 145; *Liberator*, Dec. 1, 1837 and Apr. 28, 1848; *National Era*, May 21, 1857; Philip S. Foner, *History of Black Americans from the Emergence of the Cotton Kingdom to the Eve of the Compromise of 1850* (Westport, CT, 1983), 477–78; Ripley, ed., *Black Abolitionist Papers* 1:467.

31. Greeley found the chattel slaves' oppression less "proximate" and Evans, less pivotal. See *Working Man's Advocate*, July 6, 1844; Philip S. Foner, *American Socialism and Black Americans* (Westport, CT, 1977), 8–9; *Voice of Industry*, Aug. 21, 1845; John R. Commons et al., *Documentary History of Labor in the United States*, 10 vols. (Cleveland, OH, 1910), 7:211–13; (Lynn) *The Awl*, Aug. 23, 1845. Philip S. Foner and Herbert Shapiro graciously made available to me copies of the materials which went into their edited *Northern Labor and Antislavery*. See also Cunliffe, *Chattel Slavery and Wage Slavery*, 21; and Roediger, *Wages of Whiteness*, 77–80.

32. Mandel, *Labor: Free and Slave*, 229. On priority, see Foner and Shapiro, eds., *Northern Labor and Antislavery*, 9; Ignatiev, *Irish Became White*, 80–81; Norman Ware, *The Industrial Worker, 1840–1860* (Chicago, 1964, originally 1924), 225.

33. See Roediger, *Wages of Whiteness*, 75–77; Foner, ed., *Factory Girls*, 278; Ignatiev, *Irish Became White*, 69; Cunliffe, *Chattel Slavery and Wage Slavery*, 1; Wilfred Carsel, "The Slaveholders' Indictment of Northern Wage Slavery," *Journal of Southern History* 6 (Nov. 1940): 510–16.

34. Foner, ed., *Factory Girls*, 107; Roediger, *Wages of Whiteness*, 75–76.

35. Mandel, *Labor: Free and Slave*, 228 n. 57; Roediger, *Wages of*

Whiteness, 83–85. On the defense of the virtue of factory women against proslavery propagandists, see Harriet H. Robinson, *Loom and Spindle: Or Life Among Mill Girls* (New York, 1989), 196–98; Ware, *Industrial Worker*, 93–94; Foner, ed., *Factory Girls*, 81 and 83. The last-named contains an atypically frank discussion of sexual harassment in the mills, but also holds that slave women had masters to "protect" them. See also Benita Eisler, ed., *The Lowell Offering: Writings by New England Mill Women* (New York, 1977), 188–89.

36. Roediger, *Wages of Whiteness*, 80–87; Frederick Douglass, *Life and Times of Frederick Douglass* (New York, 1982, repr. of 1892 edition), 214; cf. Paul Gilroy, *The Black Atlantic: Modernity and Double Consciousness* (Cambridge, MA 1993), xiii; and n. 31 above.

37. Philip S. Foner, ed., *American Labor Songs*, 69. The song continued with a reference to the origins of union agitation for the ten-hour day lying in white workers desiring their own "abolition" societies after seeing the many "friends" of the "blackee." Eric Foner, "Workers and Slavery," in Buhle and Dawley, eds., *Working for Democracy*, 22; on the mathematical formulations, Roediger, *Wages of Whiteness*, 77; Foner and Shapiro, eds., *Northern Labor and Antislavery*, 15 and 23. On Douglass, see his *Narrative*, 148; *Life and Times*, 207–11; and *Bondage and Freedom*, 310. On the horses' comparison, see e.g., *Working Man's Advocate*, June 22, 1844; *The Awl*, Oct. 29, 1845.

38. See Karen Sanchez-Eppler, *Touching Liberty: Abolition, Feminism, and the Politics of the Body* (Berkeley, 1993); Gilroy, *Black Atlantic*, 117–20.

39. *Young America*, Feb. 7, 1844; Foner and Shapiro, eds., *Northern Labor and Antislavery*, 23 and 186.

40. For a reading of the extent, logic, and limits of such identification in minstrelsy, see Lott, *Love and Theft*, passim.

41. Flexner, *Century of Struggle: The Woman's Rights Movement in the United States* (New York, 1973), 76; Martin, *Mind of Frederick Douglass*, 146–52; Foner, ed., *Douglass* 1:320–21; Shirley J. Yee, *Black Women Abolitionists: A Study in Activism, 1828–1860* (Knoxville, TN, 1994), 140.

42. Blassingame et al., eds., *Douglass Papers* 2:451; Foner, ed., *Douglass* 1:321; Aptheker, *Abolitionism*, 87.

43. Hersh, "'Am I Not a Woman and a Sister?'" in Perry and Fellman, eds., *Antislavery Reconsidered*, 265; Flexner, *Century of Struggle*, 67.

44. Hersh, *Slavery of Sex*, 196 and 200; Sarah Grimké, *Letters on the Equality of the Sexes and Other Essays*, Elizabeth Ann Bartlett, ed. (New Haven, CT, 1988), 73; Antoinette Brown Bartlett and Susan B. Anthony, "Debates on Marriage and Divorce," in Mari Jo Buhle and Paul Buhle, eds., *The Concise History of Women's Suffrage: Selections from the Classic Work of Stanton, Anthony, Gage, and Harper* (Urbana, IL, 1978), 189; Ellen DuBois, ed., *The Elizabeth Cady Stanton–Susan B. Anthony Reader* (Boston, 1992), 48.

45. The most brilliant study of such changes remains Jeanne Boydston,

Home and Work: Housework, Wages and the Ideology of Labor in the Early Republic (New York, 1990); see also Rowland Berthoff, "Conventional Mentality: Free Blacks, Women and Business Corporations as Unequal Persons, 1820–1870," *Journal of American History* 76 (Dec. 1989): 753–84.

46. DuBois, ed., *Stanton-Anthony Reader*, 47–49 and 50; Grimké, *Letters on Equality*, 48; Blassingame et al., eds., *Douglass Papers* 2:451; Lucretia Mott, *Her Complete Sermons and Speeches*, Dana Greene, ed. (New York, 1980), 155, 213, and 232–33; Buhle and Buhle, eds., *Concise History*.

47. On exclusion, see Yee, *Black Women Abolitionists*, 140–41; on Truth, see Nell Irvin Painter, *Sojourner Truth, A Life, A Symbol* (New York, 1996), 227. For Grimké and Weld, see Katharine Du Pre Lumpkin, *The Emancipation of Angelina Grimké* (Chapel Hill, NC, 1974), 120 and 121. See also Aileen S. Kraditor, *Means and Ends in American Abolitionism: Garrison and His Critics on Strategy and Tactics, 1834–1850* (New York, 1969), chap. 3.

48. Hersh, "'Am I Not a Woman and a Sister?'" 252; Jean Fagan Yellin, *Women and Sisters: The Antislavery Feminists in American Culture* (New Haven, CT, 1989); Ellen Carol DuBois, "Outgrowing the Compact of the Fathers: Equal Rights, Woman Suffrage and the United States Constitution, 1820–1878," *Journal of American History* 74 (Dec. 1989): 840.

49. In 1837, Angelina Grimké exposed the threat of women becoming "white slaves of the North" if prejudice barred them from speaking out against slavery. See Hersh, *Slavery of Sex*, 196. On Child, see Carolyn Karcher, *The First Woman of the Republic: A Cultural Biography of Lydia Maria Child* (Durham, NC, 1994), 221–25; and David A. J. Richards, "Abolitionist Feminism, Moral Slavery and the Constitution," *Cardozo Law Review* 18 (Nov. 1996), esp. 784–85.

50. Aptheker, *Abolitionism*, 82; Hersh, *Slavery of Sex*, 197; DuBois, ed., *Stanton-Anthony Reader*, 84–85; Nancy A. Hewitt, "On Their Own Terms: A Historiographical Essay," in Jean Fagan Yellin and John C. Van Horne, eds., *The Abolitionist Sisterhood: Women's Political Culture in Antebellum America* (Ithaca, NY, 1994), 23–30.

51. DuBois, ed., *Stanton-Anthony Reader*, 69.

52. Ibid., 83; Emily Collins, "Reminiscences," in Elizabeth Cady Stanton, Susan B. Anthony, and Matilda J. Gage, eds., *History of Woman Suffrage*, 2 vols. (Salem, NH, 1985, originally 1882), 1:93; Alice Felt Tyler, *Freedom's Ferment* (New York, 1994), 439, quoting Swisshelm; Clement Eaton, "The Resistance of the South to Northern Radicalism," *New England Quarterly* 8 (1935): 218–19.

53. DuBois, ed., *Stanton-Anthony Reader*, 48; Buhle and Buhle, eds., *Concise History*, 73; Grimké, *Letters on Equality*, 72; Mott, *Complete Sermons and Speeches*, 157; Hersh, *Slavery of Sex*, 1977.

54. C. B. MacPherson, *The Political Theory of Possessive Individualism: Hobbes to Locke* (Oxford, 1962). On property, gender, and abolition, see Amy Dru Stanley, "Home Life and the Morality of the Market," in

Melvyn Stokes and Stephen Conway, eds., *The Market Revolution in America: Social, Political, and Religious Expressions, 1800–1880* (Charlottesville, VA, 1996), 88–90. On gender, race, slavery, and law, see Cheryl Harris, "Finding Sojourner's Truth: Race, Gender and the Institution of Slavery," *Cardozo Law Review* (forthcoming).

55. S. E. P., "Appropriate Sphere of Woman," *The Liberator*, Feb. 1, 1839, 20, as quoted in Matt Martin, "Nature, Gender and Political Action in the Women's Poetry: *The Liberator*, 1837–1847" (MA paper, Univ. of Minnesota, 1997). Sanchez-Eppler, *Touching Liberty*, 22; Hersh, *Slavery of Sex*, 197–98; Aptheker, *Abolitionism*, 79.

56. Douglass, *Narrative*, 148. Messer-Kruse's "Yankee International," *passim*, is indispensable on the post-emancipation evolution of many abolitionists toward labor radicalism and on the antebellum roots of that evolution.

57. This point is elaborated in Roediger, *Wages of Whiteness*, 87.

CHAPTER 7

1. See Amy Dru Stanley, "Beggars Can't Be Choosers: Compulsion and Contract in Postbellum America," *Journal of American History* 78 (Mar. 1992): 1265–93.

2. On the changing meanings of dependence and independence, and the significance of wage labor and housework in these changing ideological configurations, see Nancy Fraser and Linda Gordon, "A Genealogy of *Dependency*: Tracing a Keyword of the U.S. Welfare State," *Signs* 19 (Winter 1994): 309–36, esp. 312–19.

3. Oliver Otis Howard, *Autobiography of Oliver Otis Howard: Major General, United States Army* (2 vols., New York, 1907), 2:214, 247, 221. See Eric Foner, *Reconstruction: America's Unfinished Revolution, 1863–1877* (New York, 1988); Julie Saville, *The Work of Reconstruction: From Slave to Wage Laborer in South Carolina. 1860–1870* (New York, 1994).

4. See Wilhelmina Kloosterboer, *Involuntary Labour Since the Abolition of Slavery: A Survey of Compulsory Labour Throughout the World* (Leiden, 1960); Thomas C. Holt, "'An Empire over the Mind': Emancipation, Race, and Ideology in the British West Indies and the American South," in *Region, Race, and Reconstruction: Essays in Honor of C. Vann Woodward*, ed. J. Morgan Kousser and James M. McPherson (New York, 1982), 283–313; Frederick Cooper, *From Slaves to Squatters: Plantation Labor and Agriculture in Zanzibar and Coastal Kenya, 1890–1925* (New Haven, CT, 1980).

5. U.S. Congress, Senate, *Laws in Relation to Freedmen*, Sen. Exec. Doc. no. 6, 39 Cong., 2d Sess. (1866–67), quotes at 192, 170. See Robert J. Steinfeld, *The Invention of Free Labor: The Employment Relation in English and American Law and Culture, 1350–1870* (Chapel Hill, NC, 1991); Leon Litwack, *Been in the Storm So Long: The Aftermath of Slavery* (New York, 1979), 319–21, 367–71.

6. Letter of C. E. Lippincott to Lyman Trumbull, Aug. 29, 1865, Lyman Trumbull Papers, Library of Congress; "The Report of General Schurz," *National Anti-Slavery Standard*, Dec. 30, 1865; and see "South Carolina Re-Establishing Slavery," *Liberator*, Nov. 24, 1865. For critiques of bureau policy, which were targeted in particular at Gen. Joseph S. Fullerton, the bureau chief in Louisiana, see, for example, "Fullerton's Folly," *National Anti-Slavery Standard*, Nov. 18, 1865. On abolitionists' support for the bureau, see James M. McPherson, *The Struggle for Equality: Abolitionists and the Negro in the Civil War and Reconstruction* (Princeton, NJ, 1964), 178–91, 341, 349–50.

7. U.S. Congress, House, *Orders Issued by the Commissioner and Assistant Commissioners of the Freedmen's Bureau*, House Exec. Doc. no. 70, 39th Cong., 1st Sess. (1865), pp. 95, 52; U.S. Congress, House, *Report of the Commissioner of the Freedmen's Bureau*, House Exec. Doc. no. 1, 39th Cong., 2d Sess., 1866, p. 741; David Montgomery, *Citizen Worker: The Experience of Workers in the United States with Democracy and the Free Market during the Nineteenth Century* (New York, 1993), 85–86. And see Harold M. Hyman, ed., *The Radical Republicans and Reconstruction, 1861–1870* (New York, 1967), 218–19, 281; Foner, *Reconstruction*, 149–51, 153–55. During the war the Union Army had also barred idleness among both black and white refugees.

8. U.S. Congress, Senate, *Report of the Secretary of War . . . Communicating the Final Report of the American Freedmen's Inquiry Commission to the Secretary of War*, 38th Cong., 1st Sess., Sen. Exec. Doc. no. 53 (1864), 109–10. See Holt, "'An Empire over the Mind,'" 293–95.

9. Ira Berlin et al., eds., *Freedom: A Documentary History of Emancipation, 1861–1867*, ser. 1, vol. 3, *The Wartime Genesis of Free Labor: The Lower South* (New York, 1990), 380–82, 419, 316–18; U.S. Congress, House, *Orders Issued by the Commissioner and Assistant Commissioners of the Freedmen's Bureau*, 155; U.S. Congress, Senate, *Message of President Communicating Reports of Assistant Commissioners of the Freedmen's Bureau*, Sen. Exec. Doc. 27, 39 Cong., 1st Sess. (1865), pp. 36–37.

10. Mass. Stat. ch. 235, pp. 229–30 (1866); Massachusetts Board of State Charities, *Annual Report* 2 (1866): xcviii-ix. See Mass. Gen. Stat. chap. 165, sec. 28, p. 820 (1860).

11. See David Brion Davis, *Slavery and Human Progress* (New York, 1984), 122, 340, n. 26; Gertrude Himmelfarb, *Idea of Poverty: England in the Industrial Age* (New York, 1984), 164–68.

12. Berlin et al., eds., *Freedom* 3:152, 147, 144, 143, 131; See George F. Hoar, "Edward Lillie Pierce," *Proceedings of the American Antiquarian Society* 12 (Oct. 1897): 197–210; Willie Lee Rose, *Rehearsal for Reconstruction: The Port Royal Experiment* (New York, 1976), 21–62; McPherson, *The Struggle for Equality*, 159–72.

13. *Seventh Annual Report of the Board of State Charities of Massachusetts* (Boston, 1871), 7; *Eighth Annual Report of the Board of State Charities of Massachusetts* (Boston, 1872), 20, 30; "An Act Concerning

Vagrants," Mass. Stat. ch. 70 (1875), pp. 648–49; Berlin et al., eds., *Freedom* 3:199.

14. New York State Charities Aid Association, *Third Annual Report* (New York, 1875), 24; Francis Wayland, "The Tramp Question," in *Proceedings of the Fourth Annual Conference of Charities* (Boston, 1877), 118. See Samuel Levitt, "The Tramps and the Law," *Forum* 2 (Oct. 1886): 190–200; *Sixth Annual Conference of Charities* (1879), 24–26; Ill. Rev. Stat. (1845), 175–76; ibid. (1874), 392–93; N.Y. Rev. Stat., vol. 2 (1859), 879; 1880 Laws N.Y. chap. 176; Sidney L. Harring, "Class Conflict and the Suppression of Tramps in Buffalo, 1892–1894," *Law and Society Review* 11 (Summer 1977): 873–911; Paul T. Ringenbach, *Tramps and Reformers, 1873–1916: The Discovery of Unemployment in New York* (Westport, CT, 1973), 11–29; Eric Monkkonen, ed., *Walking to Work: Tramps in America, 1790–1935* (Lincoln, NE, 1984); Alexander Keyssar, *Out of Work: The First Century of Unemployment in Massachusetts* (New York, 1986), 135–38, 253–54; Michael B. Katz, *Poverty and Policy in American History* (New York, 1983), 157–237; Montgomery, *Citizen Worker*, 83–89.

15. *Portland v. Bangor*, 65 Maine 120, at 120, 121. See also "The People, ex. rel. Hattie Brown," *Chicago Legal News*, Dec. 8, 1877, p. 96. On labor reformers' opposition to the vagrancy laws, the courts' general affirmation of their constitutionality, and the incidence of convictions, see Christopher G. Tiedeman, *A Treatise on State and Federal Control of Persons and Property in the United States* (1900; repr., 2 vols., New York, 1975), 1:147; Stanley, "Beggars Can't Be Choosers," 1280–81.

16. *Portland v. Bangor*, 121. There is a rich scholarly literature on American adherence to a republican intellectual tradition that associated wage labor with dependence and unfreedom. See Sean Wilentz, *Chants Democratic: New York City and the Rise of the American Working Class* (New York, 1984); Eric Foner, *Politics and Ideology in the Age of the Civil War* (New York, 1980), 34–53; David R. Roediger, *The Wages of Whiteness: Race and the Making of the American Working Class* (London, 1991).

17. See David Brion Davis, *The Problem of Slavery in the Age of Revolution 1770–1823* (Ithaca, NY, 1975); Foner, *Reconstruction*; Thomas C. Holt, *The Problem of Freedom: Race, Labor, and Politics in Jamaica and Britain, 1832–1938* (Baltimore, 1992); Roediger, *Wages of Whiteness*; Saville, *Work of Reconstruction*; Amy Dru Stanley, "Home Life and the Morality of the Market," in *The Market Revolution in America: Social, Political, and Religious Expressions, 1800–1880*, eds. Melvyn Stokes and Stephen Conway (Charlottesville, VA, 1996), 74–96; Lawrence Glickman, "Inventing the 'American Standard of Living': Gender, Race and Working-Class Identity, 1880–1925," *Labor History* 34 (Spring-Summer, 1993): 221–35; James Livingston, *Pragmatism and the Political Economy of Cultural Revolution* (Chapel Hill, NC, 1994).

18. Berlin et al., eds., *Freedom* 3:131–32. See Stanley, "Home Life and the Morality of the Market."

19. Berlin et al., eds., *Freedom* 3:128, 150.

20. Ibid., 192, 144.

21. "Chattel Slavery and Wages Slavery," *The Liberator*, Oct. 1, 1847. On the wage slavery/chattel slavery debate see Jonathan A. Glickstein, "'Poverty Is Not Slavery': American Abolitionists and the Competitive Labor Market," in Lewis Perry and Michael Fellman, eds., *Antislavery Reconsidered: New Perspectives on the Abolitionists* (Baton Rouge, LA, 1979), 195–218; Foner, *Politics and Ideology*, 34–53. On the salience of family and gender relations in this debate, see Amy Dru Stanley, *From Bondage to Contract: Wage Labor, Marriage, and the Market in the Age of Slave Emancipation* (New York, 1998).

22. Quoted in Dorothy Sterling, ed., *We Are Your Sisters: Black Women in the Nineteenth Century* (New York, 1984), 252–53.

23. "Letters from Teachers of the Freedmen," *National Anti-Slavery Standard*, Apr. 16, 1864.

24. L. Maria Child, *The Freedmen's Book* (1865; repr. New York, 1968), 270, 271, 272.

25. Elizabeth Hyde Botume, *First Days Amongst the Contrabands* (Boston, 1893), 50, 51, 52, 51. And see Sterling, ed., *We Are Your Sisters*, 319–21. On philanthropists' home visits in the North and their preoccupation with the domesticity of the laboring poor, see Christine Stansell, *City of Women: Sex and Class in New York, 1789–1860* (New York, 1986), 193–216. On northern teachers in the postbellum South, see Jacqueline Jones, *Soldiers of Light and Love: Northern Teachers and Georgia Blacks, 1865–1873* (Chapel Hill, NC, 1980).

26. Clinton B. Fisk, *Plain Counsels for Freedmen: In Sixteen Brief Lectures* (Boston, 1866), 26, 25; J. B. Waterbury, *Friendly Counsels for Freedmen* in *Freedmen's Schools and Textbooks*, ed. Robert C. Morris (6 vols., 1864–65?; repr. New York, 1980), vol. 4:8; Botume, *First Days*, 122.

27. Both of the Charleston speeches were published in Child, *Freedmen's Book*, quotes at 260, 262. On the free labor doctrines of Republicans in Congress, see Foner, *Reconstruction*, 228–39. On the Victorian ideology of gender and separate spheres, see Nancy F. Cott, *The Bonds of Womanhood: 'Woman's Sphere' in New England, 1780–1835* (New Haven, CT, 1977); Mary P. Ryan, *Cradle of the Middle Class: The Family in Oneida County, New York, 1790–1865* (New York, 1981); Linda Kerber, "Separate Spheres, Female Worlds, Woman's Place: The Rhetoric of Women's History," *Journal of American History* 75 (1988): 9–39; Stanley, "Home Life and the Morality of the Market." On the "pastoralization" of housework in the North, see Jeanne Boydston, *Home and Work: Housework, Wages, and the Ideology of Labor in the Early Republic* (New York, 1990). On the significance of gender ideology to emancipation policy and liberal economic doctrine in the Jamaican case, see Thomas C. Holt, "Gender in the Service of Bourgeois Ideology," *International Labor and Working-Class History* 41 (Spring 1992): 29–36.

28. U.S. Congress, Senate, *Preliminary Report Touching the Condition*

and Management of Emancipated Refugees, made to the Secretary of War by the American Freedmen's Inquiry Commission, June 30, 1863, in *Report of the Secretary of War,* 38th Cong., 1st Sess., Sen. Exec. Doc. no. 53, 1864, p. 14; Botume, *First Days,* 53; Henry L. Swint, ed., *Dear Ones at Home: Letters from Contraband Camps* (Nashville, 1966), 23; Rev. I. W. Brinkerhoff, *Advice to Freedmen* in *Freedmen's Schools and Textbooks* 4:29–30. See Berlin et al., eds., *Freedom;* and Ira Berlin et al., eds., *Freedom: A Documentary History of Emancipation, 1861–1867,* ser. 1, vol. 2: *The Wartime Genesis of Free Labor: The Upper South* (New York, 1993). On the contradiction between domestic ideology and freedwomen's field work in Jamaica, see Holt, "Gender in the Service of Bourgeois Ideology," 36 n.6.

29. *U.S. Bureau of Refugees, Freedmen, and Abandoned Land. Records of the Assistant Commissioner for the State of Virginia* (Washington, DC: National Archives Microfilms Publications), Record Group 105, reel 44, p. 674; Mecklenburg County to O. Brown, Aug. 31, 1866, ibid., reel 45, p. 36. On the views of the bureau regarding work and domesticity, see Herbert G. Gutman, "Mirrors of Hard Distorted Glass: An Examination of Some Influential Assumptions about the Afro-American Family and the Shaping of Public Policies 1861–1965," in *Social History and Social Policy,* eds. David J. Rothman and Stanton Wheeler (New York, 1981), 239–73. On the complexities of northern attitudes toward housework as labor denigrated as unproductive but also associated with female virtue, see Boydston, *Home and Work.*

30. M. C. Fulton to Brig. Gen. Davis Tilson, Apr. 17, 1866, quoted in Ira Berlin et al., "Afro-American Families in the Transition from Slavery to Freedom," *Radical History Review* 42 (1988): 89–121, at 112–13. On former slaveholders' response to freedwomen's withdrawal from field work to do their own housekeeping, see Foner, *Reconstruction,* 85–86; Jones, *Labor of Love,* 59–60; Susan A. Mann, "Slavery, Sharecropping and Sexual Inequality," *Signs* 14 (Summer 1989): 774–98.

31. Fulton to Tilson, Apr. 17, 1866, quoted in Berlin et al., "Afro-American Families," 113; planter's complaint quoted in Sterling, ed., *We Are Your Sisters,* 321.

32. Quoted in Litwack, *Been in the Storm,* 245. On the significance of household relations to the terms of emancipation, see Laura F. Edwards, *Gendered Strife and Confusion: The Political Culture of Reconstruction* (Urbana, IL, 1997).

33. Quoted in Sterling, *We Are Your Sisters,* 322; Victoria Bynum, "Reshaping the Bonds of Womanhood: Divorce in Reconstruction North Carolina," in *Divided Houses: Gender and the Civil War,* ed. Catherine Clinton and Nina Silber (New York, 1992), 33.

34. Berlin et al., eds., *Freedom* 2:252, 253; "Address of the North Carolina Freedmen," repr. in *The National Freedman,* Oct. 1865. See Edwards, *Gendered Strife and Confusion.*

35. Whitelaw Reid, *After the War: A Tour of the Southern States 1865–1866,* ed. C. Vann Woodward (New York, 1965; orig. pub. 1866), 108–10,

486–87. See Elizabeth Ware Pearson, *Letters from Port Royal: Written at the Time of the Civil War* (Boston, 1906), 52. On the contrasts that abolitionists drew between northern domesticity and slave women's plight, see Gillian Brown, *Domestic Individualism: Imagining Self in Nineteenth-Century America* (Berkeley, 1990), esp. 3–38.

36. Circular No. 2, To the Freedmen of South Carolina, Georgia, and Florida, Issued by Brig. Gen. R. Saxton, Aug. 16, 1865, in *Report of the Joint Committee on Reconstruction, at the First Session Thirty-Ninth Congress* (1866; repr. New York, 1969), 231; "To the Freed People of Orangeburg District," enclosed in Charles C. Soule to O. O. Howard, June 12, 1865, quoted in Saville, *Work of Reconstruction*, 27–28.

37. Alexander Crummell, *Africa and America: Addresses and Discourses* (Springfield, MA, 1891), 67, 68, 81, 82. See Wilson Jeremiah Moses, *Alexander Crummell: A Study of Civilization and Discontent* (New York, 1989).

38. U.S. Congress, Senate, *Final Report of the American Freedmen's Inquiry Commission to the Secretary of War* in *Report of the Secretary of War*, 38th Cong., 1st Sess., Senate Exec. Doc. no. 53 (1864), p. 25.

39. See Boydston, *Home and Work*; Cott, *Bonds of Womanhood*, 63–100.

40. "A Translation of a Series of Articles by Samuel Gompers on Tenement-House Cigar Manufacture in New York City" (first pub. in *New Yorker Volkszeitung*, Oct.-Nov. 1881, partly repr. in *Cigar Makers' Official Journal*, Feb.-May 1882), in Stuart B. Kaufman, ed., *The Samuel Gompers Papers*, vol. 1: *The Making of a Union Leader, 1850–86* (Urbana, IL, 1986), 185. See Eileen Boris, "'A Man's Dwelling House Is His Castle': Tenement House Cigarmaking and the Judicial Imperative," in *Work Engendered: Toward a New History of American Labor*, ed. Ava Baron (Ithaca, NY, 1991), 114–41.

41. "Gompers on Tenement-House Cigar Manufacture," 174, 180, 176, 182, 181.

42. Ibid., 183, 185.

43. Ibid., 187.

44. *Report of the Bureau of Statistics of Labor, Embracing the Account of Its Operations and Inquiries from August 2, 1869, to March 1, 1870, Inclusive, Being the First Seven Months since Its Organization* (Boston, 1870), 158, 164. See Stansell, *City of Women*, 193–203; James Leiby, *Carroll Wright and Labor Reform: The Origin of Labor Statistics* (Cambridge, MA, 1960); Michael J. Lacey and Mary O. Furner, eds., *The State and Social Investigation in Britain and the United States* (New York, 1993), chaps. 1, 4, 5; Martin Bulmer, Kevin Bales, Kathryn Kish Sklar, *The Social Survey in Historical Perspective 1880–1940* (New York, 1991).

45. *[First Annual] Report of the Bureau of Statistics of Labor*, 25, 168, 171, 179, 35, 163, 178, 158. Probably written by McNeill, this part of the report articulated ideas that were very similar to those stated by the labor reform leader Ira Steward, who was McNeill's coadjutor. See Ira Steward, "Poverty," in *Fourth Annual Report of the Bureau of Statistics of Labor* (1873).

46. Henry Mullins, *A Voice from the Workshop* (New York, 1860), 9, 10. See Martha May, "Bread before Roses: Workingmen, Labor Unions and the Family Wage," in *Women, Work and Protest: A Century of U.S. Women's Labor History*, ed. Ruth Milkman (Boston, 1985), 1–21; Glickstein, "'Poverty Is Not Slavery'"; Foner, *Politics and Ideology*, 34–53; Stanley, "Home Life and the Morality of the Market."

47. Though the evidence cited directly above does not support his claim that labor's critique of wage slavery crystallized only after slave emancipation, see in regard to antebellum labor assertions of white supremacy, Roediger, *Wages of Whiteness*, 65–87. In *Manhattan for Rent, 1785–1850* (Ithaca, NY, 1989), 123–25, Elizabeth Blackmar writes that antebellum workingmen decried the wage work of wives and children and idealized domesticity, but seldom directly discussed the issue of housework.

48. *Second Annual Report of the Bureau of Statistics of Labor* (Boston, 1871), 476–78.

49. Testimony by a South Carolina freedman, in Berlin et al., eds., *Freedom* 2:250–51; *Second Annual Report of the Bureau of Statistics of Labor*, 435, 533; "Chattel Slavery and Wages Slavery." My interpretation differs here from that of Gordon and Fraser who suggest that postbellum labor reformers turned away from protesting against wage slavery in affirming a vision of economic independence based on a male "family wage"; see "Genealogy of *Dependency*," 315–16.

50. *Sixth Annual Report of the Bureau of Statistics of Labor* (Boston, 1875), 194, 183–84, 193, 384. See Leiby, *Carroll Wright*; Daniel Horwitz, *The Morality of Spending: Attitudes toward the Consumer Society in America, 1875–1940* (Baltimore, 1985); *Third Biennial Report of the Illinois Bureau of Labor Statistics* (1884); *Third Annual Report of the New York State Bureau of Labor Statistics* (1886).

51. See Alice Kessler-Harris, *A Woman's Wage: Historical Meanings and Social Consequences* (Lexington, KY, 1990); Susan Lehrer, *Origins of Protective Legislation for Women 1905–1925* (Albany, 1987).

52. Language from congressional debate quoted in Eric Foner, "The Meaning of Freedom in the Age of Emancipation," *Journal of American History* 81 (Sept. 1994): 435–60, at 455. See Amy Dru Stanley, "Conjugal Bonds and Wage Labor: Rights of Contract in the Age of Emancipation," *Journal of American History* 75 (Sept. 1988): 471–500, at 479–81.

CHAPTER 8

1. A. V. Dicey, *Lectures on the Relation between Law and Public Opinion in England during the Nineteenth Century*, 2d ed. (London, 1930), 468.

2. Richard B. Morris, *Government and Labor in Early America* (New York, 1946).

3. C. B. Macpherson, *The Political Theory of Possessive Individualism: Hobbes to Locke* (New York, 1964), 142.

4. Robert J. Steinfeld, *The Invention of Free Labor: The Employment*

Relation in English & American Law and Culture, 1350–1870 (Chapel Hill, NC, 1991), 80.

5. Ibid., 47–51.

6. See chap. 5 above.

7. Robert J. Goldstein, *Political Repression in 19th Century Europe* (London, 1983), 58–59.

8. Jurgen Kocka,"Problems of Working-Class Formation in Germany: The Early Years, 1800–1875," in Ira Katznelson and Aristide R. Zolberg, eds., *Working-Class Formation: Nineteenth-Century Patterns in Western Europe and the United States* (Princeton, NJ, 1986), 312–13.

9. Steinfeld, *Invention of Free Labor*, 102.

10. Ibid., 139–41.

11. Quoted in ibid., 156.

12. *Official Report of the Debates and Proceedings . . . to Revise and Amend the Constitution of the Commonwealth of Massachusetts* (Boston, 1853), 550.

13. For a stimulating exploration of the linkage between political rights and free labor, see Robert J. Steinfeld, "Property and Suffrage in the Early American Republic," *Stanford Law Review* 41 (Jan. 1989): 335–76.

14. *Official Report*, 550.

15. Ibid., 574–78.

16. Goldstein, *Political Repression*, 58 and (for a survey of European trade-union restrictions) 56, table 2.2.

17. Gary Marks, *Unions in Politics: Britain, Germany and the United States in the Nineteenth and Early Twentieth Centuries* (Princeton, NJ, 1989), 56.

18. Christopher L. Tomlins, *Law, Labor, and Ideology in the Early American Republic* (New York, 1993), 99.

19. *Commonwealth v. Pulis* (Pa. 1806), in John R. Commons et al., eds., *A Documentary History of American Industrial Society*, 10 vols. (Cleveland, OH, 1910) [hereafter, *Documentary History*], 3:59–348. Citations to the scholarly commentary on *Commonwealth v. Pulis* are to found in Tomlins, *Law, Labor and Ideology*, 107–8 n. 1.

20. Ibid., 232–33.

21. Ibid., 234.

22. I am relying here on John V. Orth, *Combination and Conspiracy: A Legal History of Trade Unionism, 1721–1906* (Oxford 1991), chap. 2.

23. *Documentary History* 3:132.

24. Orth, *Combination and Conspiracy*, 151.

25. Paul S. Reinsch, *The English Common Law in the Early American Colonies*, in Roscoe Pound and Theodore F. T. Plucknett, eds., *Readings on the History and System of the Common Law*, 3d ed. (Rochester, NY, 1927), 306–7.

26. Morris, *Government and Labor*, 205–7; and id., "Criminal Conspiracy and Early Labor Combinations in New York," *Political Science Quarterly* 52 (Mar. 1937): 51–85.

27. Tomlins, *Law, Labor and Ideology*, 134–35.

28. *Documentary History* 3:225, 231–32.

29. Tomlins, *Law, Labor and Ideology*; and also, in a more spacious way, David Montgomery, *Citizen Worker: The Experience of Workers in the United States with Democracy and the Free Market during the Nineteenth Century* (New York, 1993).

30. This is a main theme of Victoria C. Hattam, *Labor Visions and State Power: The Origins of Business Unionism in the United States* (Princeton, NJ, 1993), chaps. 4, 5.

31. *People v. Melvyn* (N.Y. 1809), *Documentary History* 3:385.

32. For a survey of these cases, see Tomlins, *Law, Labor and Ideology*, chap. 5.

33. 45 Mass. 111.

34. Ibid., 128–29.

35. Ibid., 123.

36. Nelles, "Commonwealth v. Hunt," *Columbia Law Review* 32 (Nov. 1932): 1149.

37. *Commonwealth v. Hunt*, 129.

38. Ibid., 134.

39. Ibid., 134.

40. On this point, see especially Leonard W. Levy, *The Law of the Commonwealth and Chief Justice Shaw* (Cambridge, MA, 1957), 202–6.

41. Most notably, in *Bowen v. Matheson* 14 Allen 499 (Mass. 1867), sustaining a combination of shipping masters that had boycotted and destroyed the business of a competing Boston labor supplier, discussed in Bernard D. Meltzer, ed., *Labor Law: Cases, Materials and Problems* (Boston, 1970), 18–19.

42. These details first came to light in Nelles, "Commonwealth v. Hunt," 1131–38.

43. *Commonwealth v. Hunt*, 132.

44. Ibid., 122.

45. Ibid., 130–31.

46. *Crump v. Commonwealth*, 84 Va. 927 (1888), quoted in Haggai Hurvitz, "American Labor Law and the Doctrine of Entrepreneurial Property Rights, 1886–1895," *Industrial Relations Law Journal* 8 (3) (1986): 212.

47. *State v. Stewart*, 59 Vt. 273 (1887), quoted in Hurvitz, "American Labor Law," 324–25.

48. Quoted in Hurvitz, "American Labor Law," 321, whose argument I am following here.

49. Orth, *Combination and Conspiracy*, 143–44.

50. *People v. Kostka* 4 N.Y. Crim. 403 (1886), in Hattam, *Labor Visons and State Power*, 147–48. Also, e.g., Hyman Kuritz, "Criminal Conspiracy Cases in Post-Bellum Pennsylvania," *Pennsylvania History* 17 (Oct. 1950): 298–300.

51. *State v. Stewart*, quoted in Karen Orren, *Belated Feudalism: Labor, the Law, and Liberal Development in the United States* (New York, 1991), 130.

52. In Chistopher Tomlins, *The State and the Unions: Labor Relations, Law, and the Organized Labor Movement in America, 1880–1960* (New York, 1985), 47.

53. 55 Conn. 46, in Daniel R. Ernst, *Lawyers Against Labor: From Individual Rights to Corporate Liberalism* (Champaign, IL, 1995), 73.

54. Hurvitz, "American Labor Law," 330–32.

55. *New York, Lake Erie & Western Railroad v. Wenger*, 9 Ohio Dec. repr. 815 (1887), in ibid., 341.

56. *Emack v. Kane* 34 F. 46 (Ill. 1888), in ibid., 338.

57. *Casey v. Cincinnati Typographical Union* 45 F. 135 (Ohio 1891), in ibid., 337–38.

58. Felix Frankfurter and Nathan Greene, *The Labor Injunction* (New York, 1930), 11–17, 210.

59. William Forbath, *Law and the Shaping of the American Labor Movement* (Cambridge, MA, 1991), 126.

60. Ibid., 144–45.

61. *Old Dominion Steam-Ship Co. v. McKenna* 30 F. 48 (N.Y. 1887), in Hurvitz, "American Labor Law," 329–30.

62. 52 N.Y. 33, 46 N.E. 297 (1897), in Ernst, *Lawyers Against Labor*, 93.

63. *Jacobs v. Cohen* 183 N.Y. 207 (1905), in Charles O. Gregory, *Labor and the Law* (New York, 1949), 80.

64. Quoted in Tomlins, *State and the Unions*, 47.

65. *Erdman v. Mitchell* 207 Pa. 79 (1903), in Orren, *Belated Feudalism*, 132.

66. Testimony, U.S. Industrial Commission, *Report* (1901), repr. in Sigmund Diamond, ed., *The Nation Transformed* (New York, 1963), 194.

67. *Johnston Harvester Company v. Meinhardt* 9 Abb. New Cas. (N.Y.) 393 (1880), in Orren, *Belated Feudalism*, 133.

68. *Congressional Record*, 49th Cong., 2d sess. (1887), 2375–76, cited (and partially quoted) in Melvyn Dubofsky, *The State and Labor in Modern America* (Chapel Hill, NC, 1994), 18–19.

69. *Documentary History* 3:235.

70. William E. Forbath, "The Ambiguities of Free Labor: Labor and Law in the Gilded Age," *Wisconsin Law Review*, 1985, 772–73, 781–82.

71. *Coeur d'Alene Consolidated & Mining Co. v. Miners Union* 51 F. 260 (Idaho 1892), in Hurvitz, "American Labor Law," 344.

72. Quoted in Tomlins, *State and the Unions*, 49.

73. Quotations in Ernst, *Lawyers Against Unions*, 64–65.

74. *Hunt*, 111, 128.

75. After a thorough search, Joel D. Seidman, *The Yellow-Dog Contract* (Baltimore, 1932), 37, finds no record of breach-of-contract suits against employees.

76. *Hitchman Coal & Coke Company v. Mitchell* 247 U.S. 229 (1917), repr. in Benjamin J. Taylor and Fred Witney, eds., *Cases in Labor Relations Law* (Englewood Cliffs, NJ, 1987), 12.

77. Quotations in Daniel Ernst, "The Yellow-Dog Contract and Liberal Reform, 1917–1932," *Labor History* 30 (Spring 1989): 258–59.

78. Paul C. Weiler, *Governing the Workplace: The Future of Labor and Employment Law* (Cambridge, MA, 1990), chap. 3; Sheldon Friedman et al., eds., *Restoring the Promise of American Labor Law* (Ithaca, NY, 1994), pt. 2.

79. David Brody, "On the Representation Election," *Dissent*, Summer 1997, 76.

80. For an account especially stressing this change, see James A. Gross, *Broken Promises: The Subversion of U.S. Labor Relations Policy, 1947–1994* (Philadelphia, 1995).

81. See, e.g., the statement of Walter Gordon Merritt in *Legislative History of the National Labor Relations Act, 1935*, 2 vols. (Washington, D.C., 1959), 1:1018–20.

82. 208 U.S. 161, repr. in E. Edward Herman and Gordon S. Skinner, eds., *Labor Law: Cases, Text, and Legislation* (New York, 1972), 85–89.

83. Quotations in Ernst, "Yellow-Dog Contract," 263–65; Seidman, *Yellow-Dog Contract*, 31, 33. On the AFL's thinking, see the perceptive analysis in Forbath, *Shaping of the Labor Movement*, chap. 5.

84. *Adair*, 89.

85. *NLRB v. Jones and Laughlin* (1937) 301 U.S. 1, repr. in ibid., 104.

86. *Adair*, in Herman and Skinner, *Labor Law*, 89.

87. Donald Dotson, quoted in Friedman et al., *Restoring the Promise*, 90.

88. See David Brody, "Criminalizing the Rights of Labor," *Dissent*, Summer 1995, 363–67.

CHAPTER 9

1. Frederick Jackson Turner, *The Significance of the American Frontier* (Madison, WI, 1894).

2. Robert Fogel listed denial of economic opportunity as one of his four counts in the moral indictment of slavery. See Robert W. Fogel, *Without Consent or Contract* (New York, 1989), 395.

3. For a sample of the discussion of social mobility in American history, see Stephan Thernstrom, *The Other Bostonians* (Cambridge, MA, 1973); Edward Pessen, *Riches Class and Power* (Lexington, MA, 1973); Lee Soltow, *Six Papers on the Size Distribution of Wealth and Income* (New York, 1969).

4. For a summary of American economic growth, see Robert Gallman, "Pace and Pattern of American Economic Growth," in Lance Davis et al., *American Economic Growth* (New York, 1972), chap. 4.

5. For a cross-country review of health and economic well-being see Richard H. Steckel and Roderick Floud, eds., *Health and Welfare during Industrialization* (Chicago, 1997). For a discussion of the role of health and nutrition in economic growth see Robert W. Fogel, "Economic Growth, Population Theory and Physiology: the Bearing of Long-term Processes on the Making of Economic Policy," *American Economic Review* 84 (1994): 369–95.

6. Robert W. Fogel and Stanley L. Engerman, *Time on the Cross* (Boston, 1974), chap. 2.

7. Ibid., chap. 6. For a critique of their efficiency estimate see Gavin Wright, "The Efficiency of Slavery: Another Interpretation," *American Economic Review* 69 (1979): 219–26.

8. Steckel and Floud, eds., *Health and Welfare during Industrialization*; John Komlos, *Nutrition and Economic Development in the Habsburg Monarchy* (Princeton, NJ, 1989); Robert A. Margo and Richard H. Steckel, "Heights of Native-born Whites During the Antebellum Period," *Journal of Economic History* 43 (1983): 167–74.

9. For an explanation of this point see Douglass C. North, *Growth and Welfare in the American Past* (Englewood Cliffs, NJ, 1974) 26–27. For a discussion of growth in the early period (1780–1840), see Thomas Weiss, "U.S. Labor Force Estimates and Economic Growth, 1800–1860," and Robert E. Gallman, "American Economic Growth before the Civil War: The Testimony of the Capital Stock Estimates," in Robert E. Gallman and John Joseph Wallis, eds., *American Economic Growth and Standards of Living before the Civil War* (Chicago, 1992) 19–120.

10. See Richard A. Easterlin, "Regional Income Trends, 1840–1950," in Seymour Harris, ed., *American Economic History* (New York, 1961), 525–47.

11. Roderick Floud, Kenneth Wachter, and Annabel Gregory, *Height, Health and History: Nutritional Status in the United Kingdom, 1750–1980* (Cambridge, 1990), 184. The mean height of working-class fourteen-year-olds has increased more than the mean height of working-class adults because stature in a poorly nourished population increases through late teen-age years and even into the early twenties.

12. David R. Weir, "Economic Welfare and Physical Well-Being in France, 1750–1990," in Steckel and Floud, eds., *Health and Welfare during Industrialization*, 174–77.

13. Steckel and Floud, eds., *Health and Welfare during Industrialization* reports data on Sweden, Japan, Germany, Netherlands, and Australia. Heights for Swedish males may be found on p. 129. For further discussion see John Komlos, ed., *The Biological Standard of Living on Three Continents* (Boulder, CO, 1995).

14. Robert Fogel, *Escape from Hunger and Premature Death* (forthcoming).

15. For estimates of mortality for the late eighteenth and early nineteenth centuries see Clayne L. Pope, "Adult Mortality before 1900: A View from Family Histories," in Claudia Goldin and Hugh Rockoff, eds., *Strategic Factors in Nineteenth Century American Economic History* (Chicago, 1992), 277. Modern estimates are widely available including U.S. Bureau of the Census, *Statistical Abstract of the United States* (Washington, DC).

16. U.S. Department of Commerce, *Historical Statistics of the United States, Colonial Times to 1970* (Washington DC, 1975), 57; *Statistical Abstract of the United States 1995*, 90.

17. Steckel and Floud, eds., *Health and Welfare during Industrialization*, 129 (Sweden), 116 (England), 177 (France).

18. *Historical Statistics*, 168–70. For a discussion of this issue, see Dora L. Costa, "Less of a Luxury: the Rise of Recreation since 1888," NBER Working Paper 6054. David R. Roediger and Philip S. Foner, *Our Own Time: A History of American Labor and the Working Day* (New York, 1989) recounts the fight by labor to shorten the working day.

19. Alan Blinder, "The Level and Distribution of Economic Well-being," chap. 6 in Martin Feldstein, ed., *The American Economy in Transition* (Chicago, 1980), has a useful summary on this point.

20. Useful discussion of the trend in the distribution of wealth may be found in Alice Hanson Jones, *Wealth of a Nation to Be* (New York, 1980), chap. 8; Lee Soltow, *Men and Wealth in the United States, 1850–1870* (New Haven, CT, 1975); Jeffrey Williamson and Peter Lindert, *American Inequality* (New York, 1980).

21. The estimate given here is made by combining estimates of adult mortality found in Pope, "Adult Mortality before 1900," with model life table data found in Ansley J. Coale and Paul Demeny, *Regional Model Life Tables and Stable Populations* (Princeton, NJ, 1966). The comparisons in the text use levels 14 and 24 for the point about the increased equality.

22. For example, at the turn of the century, male life expectancy at birth for African Americans and other minorities was 67 percent of that of whites. By 1994, it was 92 percent of that of whites. Similar percentages hold for females. However, male life expectancy as a percentage of female life expectancy has declined somewhat during the twentieth century. See *Historical Statistics*, 56 and Center for Disease Control, "Monthly Vital Statistics Report," Sept. 1996, 18.

23. There appears to be little trend in the distribution of wealth. See Jones, *Wealth of a Nation to Be*. There has also been little trend in the distribution of income although there is some evidence of a trend toward more inequality in the past two decades driven by an increase in the ratio of skilled to unskilled wages. See *Historical Statistics*, 301 and U.S. Census Bureau, "Historical Income Tables—Household," *Current Population Survey* (Mar. 1998).

24. Jones, *Wealth of a Nation to Be*, 260–61.

25. *Historical Statistics of the United States*, 298–302; *Statistical Abstract of the United States 1996*, 474–75.

26. J. R. Kearl and Clayne L. Pope, "Choice, Rents and Luck: Economic Mobility of Nineteenth-Century Utah Households," in Stanley L. Engerman and Robert E. Gallman, eds., *Long-Term Factors in American Economic Growth*, vol. 51 of *Studies in Income and Wealth* (Chicago, 1986), outlines this general approach to the classification of characteristics.

27. Richard J. Butler, James J. Heckman, and Brook Payner, "The Impact of the Economy and the State on the Economic Status of Blacks: a Study in South Carolina," in David Galenson, ed., *Markets in History; Economic Studies of the Past* (Cambridge, 1989) 231–346.

28. D. W. Galenson, "Economic Opportunity on the Urban Frontier: Nativity, Work and Wealth in Early Chicago," *Journal of Economic History* 51 (Sept. 1991): 581–603; Steven Herscovici, "The Distribution of Wealth in Nineteenth-Century Boston: Inequality among Natives and Immigrants, 1860," *Explorations in Economic History* 30 (1993): 321–35; D. W. Galenson and Timothy G. Conley, "Quantile Regression Analysis of Censored Wealth Data," *Historical Methods* 27 (Fall 1994): 149–65.

29. Claudia Goldin, "The Political Economy of Immigration Restriction in the United States, 1890–1921," in C. Goldin and G. D. Libecap, eds., *The Regulated Economy: A Historical Approach to Political Economy* (Chicago, 1994); T. J. Hatton and J. G. Williamson, "The Impact of Immigration on American Labor Markets Prior to Quotas," NBER Working Paper No. 5185, National Bureau of Economic Research; Joseph P. Ferrie, "The Impact of Immigration on Natives in the Antebellum U.S. Labor Market, 1850–1860," Working Paper, Department of Economics, Northwestern University, Jan. 1996.

30. See Kenneth J. Winkle, *The Politics of Community: Migration and Politics in Antebellum Ohio* (Cambridge, 1988); and David W. Galenson and Clayne L. Pope, "Precedence and Wealth: Evidence from Nineteenth Century Utah," in Goldin and Rockoff, eds., *Strategic Factors in Nineteenth Century American Economic History*, 225–42.

31. Maris Vinovskis, *Education, Society and Economic Opportunity* (New Haven, CT, 1995); David W. Galenson, "Neighborhood Effects on the School Attendance of Irish Immigrants' Sons in Boston and Chicago in 1860," *American Journal of Education* 105 (May 1997): 261–93.

32. Claudia Goldin and Lawrence F. Katz, "The Decline of Noncompeting Groups: Changes in the Premium to Education, 1890 to 1940," NBER Working Paper 5202; and id., "Why the United States Led in Education: Lessons from Secondary School Expansion, 1910 to 1940," NBER Working Paper 6144.

33. *Historical Statistics*, 370.

34. Galenson, "Neighborhood Effects on the School Attendance of Irish Immigrants' Sons."

35. *Historical Statistics*, 369–71.

36. *Statistical Abstract of the United States 1997*, 157.

37. *Historical Statistics*, 385–86; *Statistical Abstract of the United States 1997*, 191.

38. For discussion of these institutional changes, see Claudia Goldin, *Understanding the Gender Gap: An Economic History of American Women* (New York, 1990); and Robert A. Margo, *Race and Schooling in the South, 1880–1950* (Chicago, 1990).

39. *Historical Statistics*, 139–40.

40. Stephan Thernstrom, *The Other Bostonians*; id., *Poverty and Progress: Social Mobility in a Nineteenth-Century City* (Cambridge, MA, 1964); Clyde and Sally Griffen, *Natives and Newcomers* (Cambridge, MA, 1978); Peter Blau and Otis Duncan, *The American Occupational Structure* (New York, 1967).

41. Thernstrom summarizes many of the social mobility studies in *The Other Bostonians*, chap.9.

42. See ibid., 246.

43. For an example, see David F. Crew, *Town in the Ruhr: A Social History of Bochum, 1860–1914* (New York, 1979).

44. Hartmut Kaelble, *Social Mobility in the 19th and 20th Centuries: Europe and American in Comparative Perspective* (Leamington Spa, UK, 1985), 8–20.

45. Richard H. Steckel, "Poverty and Prosperity: A Longitudinal Study of Wealth Accumulation, 1850–1860," *Review of Economics and Statistics* 72 (May, 1990): 275–84.

46. Donald Schaefer, "A Model of Migration and Wealth Accumulation," *Explorations in Economic History* 24 (1987): 130–57; J. P. Ferrie, "Immigrants and Natives in the U.S.: Comparative Economic Progress in Two Centuries, 1850–1860 and 1970–1980," *Research in Labor Economics* 16 (1997): 319–41.

47. Merle Curti et al., *The Making of an American Community* (Palo Alto, CA, 1959); David Galenson and Clayne Pope, "Economic and Geographic Mobility on the Nineteenth Century, 1850–1870 Farming Frontier: Evidence from Appanoose County, Iowa," *Journal of Economic History*, Sept. 1989, 635–56; J. R. Kearl and Clayne Pope, "Wealth Mobility: The Missing Element," *Journal of Interdisciplinary History*, Winter 1983, 461–88.

48. The social mobility of Utah households is discussed in Kearl and Pope, "Wealth Mobility: the Missing Element"; id., "Mobility and Distribution," *Review of Economics and Statistics*, May, 1984, 192–99; id., "Choices, Rents and Luck."

49. Kearl and Pope, "Choices, Rents and Luck," 222.

50. For a summary of intergenerational studies of wealth mobility see Gary S. Becker and Nigel Tomes, "Human Capital and the Rise and Fall of Families," *Journal of Labor Economics* 4 (July 1986): S1–S39.

≺ ≻

Index

In this index an "f" after a number indicates a separate reference on the next page, and an "ff" indicates separate references on the next two pages. A continuous discussion over two or more pages is indicated by a span of page numbers, e.g., "57–59." *Passim* is used for a cluster of references in close but not consecutive sequence.

AABA, *see* American Anti-Boycott Association

AASS, *see* American Anti-Slavery Society

Abolition, abolitionism, 26, 44, 48f, 85–86, 169, 284n32, 286n18, 323n49; British, 8, 59–70, 76–78, 82, 290n64; and economics, 46, 56–57; and indentured labor, 72, 286–87n21; and free labor, 79–80; focus of, 171–73; and labor issues, 173–74, 176–79; and Ireland, 174–75; and women's rights, 180–85; slavery metaphor and, 185–87; and family, 196–97

Act Concerning Vagrants and Vagabonds (Mass.), 192

Adair v. U.S., 240–41

Adams, Henry Carter, 130–31

Adams, John, 117, 119

"Address of the New York State Convention to Their Colored Fellow Citizens," 171

AFL, *see* American Federation of Labor

Africa, 38, 72, 282n17; slave trade and, 3, 26, 32, 48, 54, 278n24

Africans, 2, 38, 53, 61; migration to New World, 27–32 *passim*, 51, 281n4; as slaves, 33–34, 36, 41–43

Agriculture, 248; and slavery, 54–58 *passim*, 75–76; freed labor and, 66–67, 68–69; Russian, 97–101; post-emancipation Russia, 111–12

Alabama, 189–90

Alexander II, 87, 89ff, 110

Alexandria (Va.), 197

Algeria, 76

American Anti-Boycott Association (AABA), 234–35

American Anti-Slavery Society (AASS), 172–73

American dream, 245–48, 271

American Economic Association, 130

American Federation of Labor (AFL), 130, 230–31, 240

American Fourierites, 124

American Freedmen's Inquiry Commission, 191

American Revolution, 117, 118–19

Americas, 53, 76; slavery in, 2–7 *passim*, 26–27, 35, 43, 48–55 *passim*, 81, 280n31, 299n24; migration to, 27–34; master-servant relationship in, 37–38. *See also various regions; countries*

Amerindians, 27, 32, 38, 42, 48

Angola, 44

Anthony, Susan B., 181

Anticonspiracy laws, 228

Anti-Peonage Act (1867), 151, 156

Anti-property activists, 172–73

Antislavery argument, 7, 283n27. *See also* Abolition, abolitionism

Appanoose County (Iowa), 268

Appeal in Favor of That Class of Americans Called Africans (Child), 82

Apprenticeships, 4; and British emancipation, 71–73

"Appropriate Sphere of Woman" (S.E.P.), 184

120; introduction of, 4–5, 87; ideology of, 8–11, 22–23, 218–19, 232–34, 320–21n27; in Great Britain, 59, 77–78, 80–81; in West Indies, 74–75, 84–86; abolitionists and, 79–80; in Russia, 99–100; and social mobility, 121–22, 246–47; and dependency, 123–24, 212; and slavery, 168–69; cotton cultivation, 192–93

Free markets: and breach of contract, 144–47

Freemen, 50, 66–67, 68–69

Free Soil, Free Labor movement, 122

Friendly, Judge: on involuntary servitude and peonage, 138–40, 142, 313n10

Friendly Counsels (Waterbury), 199

Frontier, 246, 261f, 268–69

Fugitive Slave Law, 182–83

Fuller, Margaret, 180

Furner, Mary, 131

Garment workers, 232

Garrison, William Lloyd, Jr., 128, 173ff, 196–97

GDP, *see* Gross domestic product

Gender roles, 34–35, 125

General Trades' Union, 124f

George, Henry: *Progress and Poverty*, 128

Georgia, 201, 299n24

Germans, 259f

Germany, 215, 220, 276n6

Gewerbefreiheit, 145

Gewerbeordung, 145

Glickstein, Jonathan A., 121

Goa, 44

Goldberg, Barry, 168

Gompers, Samuel, 130, 206, 231; "Slaves of the Tobacco Industry," 207

Goods and services, 1, 9, 254–55

Government, 14, 247; and free labor, 4–5; and emancipation, 89–90, 91–92, 108–9, 111; land redemption, 93–94; village commune, 106–7

Gramsci, Antonio, 46

Great Britain, 8, 21, 30, 47, 50, 81, 253; slave trade in, 31, 33–34; master-servant relationship in, 37–38; contract labor in, 40–41; labor in, 43, 276n4; abolitionism in, 59–70, 76–79,

82, 290n64; and American cotton, 75–76; coerced labor in, 79–80; and West Indies, 84–86; and Ireland, 174–75; poverty in, 177, 282n17; trade unionism, 220–23 *passim*, 227–28. *See also* British Empire

Great Depression, 242

Great Reforms, 113

Greece, 6f, 46f, 284–85n40

Greeley, Horace, 173, 177

Griffen, Clyde, 266

Griffen, Sally, 266

Grimké, Angelina, 180f, 323n49

Grimké, Sarah, 180f

Gross domestic product (GDP), 252, 256; in United States, 249–51

Guadeloupe, 63

Guatemalans, 135

Gunton, George: *The Economic and Social Importance of the Eight-Hour Movement*, 132

Haiti, 67–68, 70, 76, 79, 89, 102

Hamilton, Alexander, 117

Hammond, James, 178

Harbinger, The (journal), 176

Harlan, John Marshall, 152, 153–54

Hat manufacturers, 234–35

Hatter's Union, 234

Havana, 44

Haywood, Big Bill, 130, 133

Health, 252–53, 301–2n33, 335n11, 336nn21, 22

Henderson (N.C.), 135

Hersh, Blanche Glassman, 180–81

Herzen, Alexander, 110–11

Hewitt, Nancy, 182

History of the Condition of Women (Child), 182

Hitchman Coal, 166

Hitchman Coal & Coke Company, 235

Holden v. Hardy, 161f

Holmes, Oliver Wendell, 157–58, 241, 316n77

Homestead (Penn.), 135

Homestead Act, 260

Horne, Jeremiah, 225f

Households, 268; labor in, 17–18; dependent labor in, 188, 195–96; maintenance of, 203–4; New York tenement, 206–7; textile workers and, 209–10

Library of Congress Cataloging-in-Publication Data

Terms of Labor : slavery, serfdom, and free labor / edited by
 Stanley L. Engerman.
     p. cm.
 Based on a continuing series of conferences held at the Center for
the History of Freedom at Washington University in St. Louis
 Includes bibliographical references and index.
 ISBN 0-8047-3521-2 (cloth : alk. paper)
     1. Slavery—History—Congresses. 2. Labor—History—Congresses.
3. Contract labor—History—Congresses. 4. Labor movement—
History—Congresses. 5. Civil rights—History—Congresses.
6. Liberty—History—Congresses. I. Engerman, Stanley L.
HD4861.T47 1999
306.3'6'09—DC21   98-41714
                                                                CIP

This book is printed on acid-free, recycled paper.

Original printing 1999
Last figure below indicates year of this printing:
09 07 06 05 04 03 02 01 00 99